CMJ

A Cricketing Life

CHRISTOPHER
MARTIN-JENKINS

**SIMON &
SCHUSTER**

London · New York · Sydney · Toronto · New Delhi

A CBS COMPANY

First published in Great Britain by Simon & Schuster UK Ltd, 2012
This paperback edition published by Simon & Schuster UK Ltd, 2013

A CBS Company

3 5 7 9 10 8 6 4 2

Simon & Schuster UK Ltd
1st Floor
222 Gray's Inn Road
London WC1X 8HB

www.simonandschuster.co.uk

Simon & Schuster Australia,
Sydney

Simon & Schuster India,
New Delhi

All pictures supplied courtesy of the author

A CIP catalogue record for this book is available from the British Library

ISBN: 978-1-84983-268-7
ISBN: 978-0-85720-083-9 (ebook)

Typeset by Hewer Text UK Ltd, Edinburgh
Printed in the UK by CPI Group UK Ltd, Croydon CR0 4YY

To our children, James, Robin and Lucy, who have given me so much pleasure; and to their children, Molly, William, Freddie, Missy, George, and any still to come.

CONTENTS

1   Summer's Lease   1
2   Hooked   7
3   Family Matters   18
4   Eastbourne   33
5   Westborne: Life at Marlborough   45
6   Cambridge   62
7   *The Cricketer* Magazine   79
8   Off to the Beeb   95
9   Test Match Special – Commentators   116
10 From Brown to Boycott   144
11 The West Indies   156
12 A Second Family   176
13 Books and Speeches   185
14 County cricket and the *Daily Telegraph*   198
15 Australia Then and Now   212
16 India   234
17 Pakistan   252
18 New Zealand   270
19 Sri Lanka   277
20 South Africa   287

2 1 *The Times*   298
2 2 Sparkling Teams and Champagne Moments   306
2 3 Change – But Not All Decay   3 1 7
2 4 Sussex and England   3 2 5
2 5 R.M-J   3 3 0
2 6 Playing the Game   3 3 9
2 7 From Cricket to Golf   3 5 4
2 8 Faith   3 6 3
2 9 Confessions   3 6 9
3 0 Crises – and Consolations   3 7 4
3 1 Frustrations   3 8 2
3 2 Cricket's Future   3 8 6
3 3 MCC President   3 9 6
3 4 A Bend in the River   42 1

     Index   42 5
     Acknowledgements   4 3 9

I

SUMMER'S LEASE

The Kennington Oval, south London; I am watching professional cricket for only the second time. In the 1950s it is still a smutty place, brown brick abounding, a working-class playground if ever there was one, where early F.A. Cup finals were played. Cloth caps are the prevailing fashion on the wooden seats where my young brother and I sit uncomfortably, the sun like a hot blanket bearing down on us through a heavy sky the colour of pale lead, though it is August in a heat-wave. The youthful Ken Barrington, looking small in the green middle distance, albeit with the chunky build of a middleweight boxer, lifts a bat guided by white-gloved hands and brings it sharply down on a ball pitched outside his off stump. With amazing speed the hard red ball skims precisely towards us on the boundary's edge. 'All the way, all the way', says a wizened old watcher to our left, pleased to see a late cut executed with such mastery by so inexperienced a batsman. The white fence in front of us absorbs the impact and it drops to the grass, close enough to touch. I so want to pick it up and throw it back. Sore bottom or not, I am already besotted with the game.

The Oval again on 23 August 2009, sun still shining down, this time from a bluer sky on a brighter afternoon at a ground now developed for business executives; as much glass, steel and plastic as brick these days. Thousands watching in the ground but millions listening on the radio, to me for some reason! Michael Hussey, all angular style and nose-to-the-earth determination, heroic in defeat for Australia, gets an inside edge onto his pad off Graeme Swann's off-break. Alastair Cook envelops the ball at chest height at short-leg and little umpire Asad Rauf's finger is raised towards the sky. England have won the Ashes.

That does not happen very often. To be on the air to describe the moment is a special privilege and it felt almost as exciting to me in 2009 as it had thirty-two years earlier, in 1977, when Rod Marsh, like Hussey raging against the imminence of defeat during a defiant innings, skied a drive off Mike Hendrick towards Derek Randall at wide mid-off. Randall's were the surest hands (and the swiftest feet) in the England team. He circled below the descending red blur, held the ball securely in both hands, threw it high in the air and, keen schoolboy in an adult shell that he always was, turned a cartwheel that signified a nation's joy.

All this I described as best I could in the instant of its happening, before uttering (subconsciously aware, even in 1977, of the contemporary need for soundbites), the magical words: 'And England have won the Ashes.'

There is a civilised tradition that allows a home commentator to describe the moment of victory, be he English or Australian. I have given way to a few in my time, from the silver-voiced Alan McGilvray to the laconic Jim Maxwell. In 2009 Jonathan Agnew, the BBC's bright and industrious correspondent, on the air when England's eighteen-year drought ended in a welter of patriotic fervour four years previously, had left the box to be the first to interview Andrew Strauss. To my amazement he bobbed up in the middle with a microphone in hand, scarcely more than a minute after Hussey had been caught, to give listeners the first breathless reactions of the 2009 summer's ultimate hero.

Emails had poured in to *Test Match Special* from all quarters of the globe, including Mozambique, Ghana, South Georgia and the base camp at Everest. Somehow people had found ways to listen to the radio commentary. Five or six million was the estimated audience. For an objective commentator there should not even be reflected glory at moments like this but it is hard not to rejoice within. It would be boring, after all, if the same nation were always the top dog.

The pleasure has been all the greater on those even rarer occasions when England have claimed the urn in Australia itself during my forty years and more of writing and talking about cricket for a living, not least when Strauss and his team enjoyed an even greater triumph early in 2011. Three innings' wins for England on that trip lifted the spirits of millions during a cold, grey winter in Britain. There is something special about being there to record victories won in foreign lands, particularly unexpected ones. I think of Derek Underwood bowling Gary Sobers as the West Indies collapsed against spin bowling at Port of Spain in 1974; of Steve Harmison blazing his way through the West Indies at Sabina Park in 1994; the game at Karachi in 2000 when the winning runs were scored by Nasser Hussain's side in almost pitch darkness; or the time in 2001 when the Sri Lankans, so hard to beat on their own pitches, collapsed like dominoes one stifling Saturday afternoon in Colombo.

It is the Ashes that resonate loudest. Having taken over from Brian Johnston in 1973 as the third of the four cricket correspondents so far appointed by the BBC, it fell to me to describe the moments when Bob Willis bowled Australia's number eleven, Alan Hurst, at Adelaide in 1979 and, seven years later, when Merv Hughes swung a ball from Phil Edmonds into the waiting hands of Gladstone Small at deep square-leg at the Melbourne Cricket Ground. Through eighteen years of reporting for the *Daily Telegraph* and *The Times* there were no such good tidings to tell, but the 2010/11 series helped to erase from English memories at least the humiliation of losing all five Tests against Ricky Ponting's great team four years previously. The emergence of England as the strongest team in Test cricket in 2011 when I was not only commentating but also, to my agreeable surprise, acting for a year as President of MCC, prompted the thought that I might have reached the autobiographical stage of life.

Cricket has been the central theme, although not the only one, since early boyhood. I can see myself now at the age of about eleven, sitting at a brown, ink-stained desk in the fusty form-room at my prep school in Eastbourne in early May, circa 1955, as a soft hum from outside the windows betrayed the mower, pushing its way up and down the playing field outside. At such times my thoughts inevitably drifted from whatever was being taught beside the blackboard. Mowing meant cricket then and, even in what might be called mature middle age, my nose still tends to twitch, like a deer's on the wind, when it sniffs the beckoning scent of newly cut grass. In those relatively carefree days it used to lure as irresistibly as bread in the oven or the salty tang of the sea.

Fresh air and cricket always tended to take precedence over academic study, except perhaps when examinations loomed, but at least some of what I learned in other contexts has stood me in good stead during my working life. A few suns have set since I surprised Dennis Silk, later a distinguished Warden of Radley, during a lesson in A House at my senior school, Marlborough, by responding to his request for an example of alliteration with a headline from that morning's *Daily Express*:

Stupendous Statham Skittles Springboks.

Yes, he confessed: that was alliteration, if not very *literary* alliteration. Some forty years on, I found myself writing for a tabloid, too, although it was a broadsheet when I joined it, honest guv. Becoming cricket correspondent of *The Times*, having been in the same role at the *Daily Telegraph* and, for even longer, the BBC, marked the completion of an extremely fortunate hat-trick.

'Did you ever, in your wildest dreams, imagine that I would achieve all that?' I asked my wife not long ago. 'To tell the truth, darling', she replied: 'I'm not sure that you have ever appeared in my wildest dreams.'

Not my joke, unfortunately, but it is true that many have fancied making a living from talking and writing about cricket and that, alas, not many have ever had the chance. I have indeed had a fortunate innings, if not one to be especially proud about. We are all blessed, after all, with some talents, and making good use of them, especially if sometimes it can genuinely serve others as well as yourself, is what life should be about. 'You should always give more than you take', as my distant cousin Tim Rice observed in his lyrics for Sir Elton John's 'Circle of Life'.

The odd thing is, however, that there is as much satisfaction to be gained from overcoming one's disadvantages as from making the most of abilities. Every cricketer knows that bowlers are especially proud when they score a fifty, or batsmen when they surprise themselves by taking a wicket.

What has made me proud, apart from the achievements of my children, has been the occasional small victory over natural hamfistedness. Hanging pictures without knocking out the plaster from the wall, mending plugs (in the days when that was an essential household skill), growing a few vegetables in our early married days, creating a sandpit for the children years ago or laying a patio in the garden have all been little triumphs. It is true that I managed to break two toes in the latter endeavour by dropping a paving stone onto my foot shortly before my wedding, but few great victories come without cost.

The doers of society, the manufacturers and the carers, add more to the sum of human happiness than the talkers, writers and observers. Happily for me and a few like me, it takes all sorts to make a world. I was never destined to do anything very serious for a living.

Up to a point, however, I am still doing it, and I don't really want to stop – for 'summer's lease hath all too short a date'.

2

HOOKED

In some ways it has never got any better than it seemed in the first fine careless rapture of my youth. Cricket in a garden or on a beach was, for me, as good an experience of bliss as could be found. Only when it became an organised game did the harsher realities start to bite: the need for personal discipline and responsibility to the team; and sometimes the disappointments of getting out early, dropping a catch or being taken off wicketless. But that is part of the point of cricket: it teaches lessons about life, how best to succeed and how to react when you don't. Also that, having striven to do your best, contentment lies to some extent in finding your own level.

From pride and all vainglory good Lord deliver me, but the fact is that I have achieved a minor celebrity by broadcasting and writing about the game. I know that thousands – probably an understatement – would love to have done the same. Aware always of the famous C.L.R. James question 'what do they know of cricket who only cricket know', I neverthe- less make no apology for attempting to justify a whole career based on a mere game, and a life-long affair with its character and characters.

With a bat and a ball it would be no problem. The sheer pleasure of timing a stroke for the first time, the sound of that resonant click, the swift dispatch of the ball to some gratifyingly distant place, can be enough to hook a person for life. As for the bowler's joy in hitting the stumps and hearing that different, distinctive clip of parting bails, it could conjure up images and analogies more appropriate to a novel.

What sets these experiences apart from all the other games, of course, is the team context in which they occur once the garden, the street or the beach has been swapped for a field; and the childhood battles have been exchanged for real matches. Then the fielders become as important as batsmen and bowlers, able to create their own moments of ecstasy from a swift swoop, a one-handed pick-up and deadly strike on the stumps; or a dive, an outstretched arm and a magical realisation that the flying ball has been grasped inches from the ground.

Baseball alone shares with cricket (and team golf, a form of the game that too few golfers learn to appreciate) the intensity of individual duels within a team battle. No doubt it offers also these same moments of personal triumph, but without the 360-degree canvas on which a cricket match unfolds, or the same variety, strategy, or infinite capacity for sudden changes of fortune. The longer the game of cricket, the more this is true.

It is hard to convey to the uninitiated these heady moments of delight. To attempt it is the literary equivalent of trying in music to convey a trout, rose-moles all in stipple, muscling up a chattering brown river. Schubert managed it in music and I dare say that Elgar could have interpreted the ebbs and flows of cricket just as well had he watched beside the Cathedral and the water meadows at Worcester rather than drawing his inspiration from the Malvern Hills. In words, the game at its best really needs a Shakespeare to do it justice, but at least there was

Neville Cardus to embroider its characters in days before television and Raymond Robertson-Glasgow to observe 'all summer in a stroke by Woolley'.

These days there seems to be all summer in a kick by Rooney. Until soccer and its highly skilled, grossly spoiled 'superstar' professionals swamped every other game on television and in the newspapers, cricket was indeed the chief sport of every summer, so much a part of the English way of life that Siegfried Sassoon could write at the height of the First World War:

> I see them in foul dug-outs, gnawed by rats
> Dreaming of things they did with balls and bats.

W.G. Grace was famously stimulated to his greatness by a keen cricketing mother, but the seeds in me were sown by my father. I was already entranced by the time that we moved to South Holmwood, near Dorking in west Surrey, in 1951. We had a garden with what seemed to me like a long strip of grass between the vegetable and soft fruit patches. It was meant to be a pathway for wheelbarrows, conveying waste and weeds to the rubbish dump at the bottom; but it was used by my two brothers and me in summer for the much better purpose of running in to bowl, in our imaginations, like Ray Lindwall or Alec Bedser or Jim Laker, across the lawn to the waiting sibling. If I were batting I might have been Len Hutton, Denis Compton or my favourite player, Tom Graveney. When I bowled, right arm pumping after the manner of Lindwall or T.E. Bailey, a hapless Australian would be facing, perhaps Neil Harvey if the recipient were my left-handed younger brother, Timothy; or Lindsay Hassett if it were David, the elder one, also red-haired.

Across the road outside our house, there was a village green, separated from the pub, the Holly and Laurel, by an increasingly busy road, and from the church by half a mile. There, on Saturday afternoons, my father batted and bowled with the sallow-skinned Stan Pierce, who ran the garage at Mid-Holmwood, Phil Hoad, the fair-haired left-hander who delivered the coal with his father Bill, puffing Les Harris with the Bobby Charlton hair, who bowled off the wrong foot, and Syd Knight, who, with his long run-up and high, stately action, seemed to run in all afternoon from the end behind which stretched miles of bracken-covered common.

In my case at least that pleasure of a thousand fathers, watching a son carrying on the tradition, worked the other way too. I was deeply proud when, more a Pietersen than a Bell, my father launched a heave towards the cowpats beyond the boundary. Even more so, a year or two later, when he did it in the Father's Match at my prep school in Eastbourne, using only a cut down bat after he had got to twenty. When the magic fifty had been reached, he was allowed a tiny miniature. In other words it was time to get out but his big hitting was legendary in these games and my brothers and I enjoyed the reflected glory.

If I became a better cricketer than my father, imagine the pleasure when the next generation repeated the process, certainly in the case of Robin, of whom more anon. (James, like me, probably lacked the conviction and concentration to make the fullest use of his ability.) My sons used to bowl to each other for hours on end with a hard rubber ball on a tennis court that, because of the reliability of its bounce, did more for their batting than the net I had amateurishly rigged on the flattest piece of lawn I could find at our family home at Rudgwick in West Sussex. The netting was inclined to fall down in high winds and the pitch, an artificial surface first laid one Easter holiday with the help of Peter Drury, who used to advertise his Notts Non-Turf Pitches in *The Cricketer*, was not entirely reliable.

That it is better to learn on good pitches than bad ones will always be true but these days the helmets worn by all the young must take away to some extent that fear of being hit hard by a cricket ball that often holds back the talent in a player. Moreover, uneven bounce can train the eyes and sharpen reflexes: both Sunil Gavaskar and Sachin Tendulkar, two of the greatest of India's batsmen, attribute their adaptability and quickness of eye to playing on uncovered, unpredictable public pitches in Mumbai.

The greater the pity, then, that neither ever had to face a really good finger-spinner on a drying pitch in England. When they decided to cover all the pitches for first-class games in England to keep them dry (in 1981) they may have saved a good many matches from being abandoned after rain but they also took away part of the game's priceless variety and one of its greatest challenges: batting against a spinner on a drying pitch.

Pitches themselves are an endlessly fascinating element of cricket. The nature of the surface on which it is played determines the course of every game. To give an extreme example, South Africa would simply not have had a chance of chasing 435 to win a fifty-over match, as they famously did against Australia at The Wanderers in Johannesburg in 2006, if they had been playing on the same pitch as the one at Gloucester on which the home county bowled out Northamptonshire for twelve in 1907. I don't care how badly Northamptonshire batted or how well Herschelle Gibbs hit the ball!

On the other hand the attitude of players is no less interesting. Sometimes they can rise above inimical, even apparently impossible, conditions. There are plenty of examples, of which Ian Botham's counter-attack at Headingley in 1981 is one of the most famous, but one has only to look at how batsmen and bowlers meet the vastly differing challenges of Test and Twenty20 cricket to appreciate how enormous a part the mind plays in an intensely physical game.

Records and figures are another part of the game's allure. In my case, however, beguilement lay in the sheer joy of hitting and bowling balls. It happened, I think, because of that paternal encouragement, even before I started to watch great cricketers on television in 1953 and became captivated that year by a tussle for the Ashes that fired the imagination, just as future pilots drew their passion from jets scorching overhead or from reading the gripping yarns of W.E. Johns.

Soon I was either playing by myself with a hard little rubber ball from Woolworths, throwing it at a wall and defending or attacking it with a stump from close quarters, or conducting Tests in the garden with one or both of my brothers. I kept the scores and, for good measure, commentated as I went along, little knowing that thereby I was preparing the ground for a means of making a living. Indoors in the winter ping pong balls had to suffice. The bat was a toy rifle, supposedly made for a cowboy shooting at Indians.

To me, unusually I believe, acting the part of real cricketers of the time became insufficient for the imagination and I invented wholly fictional English, Australian, Indian and West Indies teams who would play out their own Test matches in summer holidays in the garden. Only recently I found the first chapter of a handwritten unfinished story (novel?) written at some point in my schooldays, which begins with the well-known (fictional) England all-rounder Robin Crale opening a letter from the chairman of the England selectors, one Geoffrey Smailes (all too often misspelt), asking him to take over the captaincy of England. Ah the romance of it all!

My younger brother and I would stage games involving these imaginary players through the day, recording the scores against the names of such as Albert de Beewee, the fearsome West Indies fast bowler, who was so strangely reminiscent of Wes Hall. The 'Albert' was correctly pronounced as by a Frenchman because he hailed from Martinique before moving to Barbados. He opened the bowling with Peardrax Marsh, a subtle swing bowler from Trinidad. These men grew in the imagination from real players I had read about, or seen on television.

I could imitate real players too, however. The way in which Tom Graveney touched his long peaked cap, slightly rounded like his shoulders, a moment before he settled again into his stance; and, I liked to think, the flowing elegance of his blade as it caressed the ball into gaps. The pumping run-up of Lindwall and the distinctive, loose-limbed delivery of Brian Statham were, in my mind's eye at least, no less at my command. They fired the mind but no one, alas, ever instilled into me the thought that actually playing the game for a living might be a possibility, with the accompanying ambition to achieve it by sweating to get fitter and stronger, then working equally hard on technique. These days every coach in every professional sport constantly emphasises these essentials.

My future career was perhaps more accurately foreshadowed by my first book, 'written' in a scrapbook that I still possess, sometime in my teenage years. It was entitled, with shameless plagiarism, 'Cricket, Lovely Cricket' and boasted a foreword by no less a star than Brigitte Bardot. That photos of the gorgeous French actress took precedence on the cover over anything reflecting cricket perhaps reflected my priorities at the time. The foreword was brief: *Mes amis, je pense que cette livre est superbe; non, merveilleux. J'adore le Cricket et j'adore cette livre. Bonne chance!*

Of course I practised as hard as anyone as a schoolboy, out of sheer amateurish enthusiasm. For years my sights were never set further, however, than on playing for my school at Lord's.

The decision to try for a place at Cambridge came late – after A levels had been taken, in fact. The wise and respected John Dancy, who had taken over from Tommy Garnett as Master of Marlborough, suggested in my final report that I should have a go, but my eyes had never been firmly set on a Blue, as I believe they would need to have been for me to get one. Once there and on the fringe of the University team it seemed a very nice idea, naturally, but defining and visualising ambition as early as possible is halfway towards achieving it. Equally significant was the fact that I did not join a cricket club until I left school. In those days there were no club or county XIs from the age of ten to seventeen as there are now.

It is just as well that I fell short of playing the game professionally, although I was paid what then seemed generous expenses to play for Surrey Club and Ground in the season after I had left school. Several years later, in 1971, when I was already embarked on another career, I made a fifty against the county's second XI that impressed Arthur McIntyre, the coach. He invited me to play for the second XI when I could but by then I was married and working flat out for the BBC, so it was necessary to take days of precious holiday to play. I played in a three-day Championship match against Warwickshire at The Oval but a match against Kent in the parallel one-day competition was rained off and to have changed horses at that stage would have been a mistake.

I did at least have one happy day at Guildford that season when I managed to reach the final of a single-wicket tournament for the whole Surrey playing staff at Guildford, beating the England batsman Graham Roope amongst others. Single-wicket, in which each man did all the batting and bowling with nine fielders and a wicket-keeper, was, of course, briefly a popular spectacle in 18th-century England when two great players would challenge each other, or a promoter would pit renowned players such as Alfred Mynn and Thomas Marsden, the respective champions of Kent and Yorkshire, against one another. At Guildford on this occasion, the stars were on a hiding to nothing. Geoff Arnold was beaten by my fellow Marlburian, the Guildford captain Charles Woodhouse, and John Edrich also fell at an early hurdle, his bowling being as weak as his batting was strong.

McIntyre, always a man of few words, saw the exercise as a test of character for his established players and looked mildly amused that the closely-fought final was played between an amateur and the rising second XI batsman Roy Lewis, who, if I remember the details correctly, passed my total of about thirty with a ball or two of his permitted four overs still in hand, much to the relief of Surrey players who were strongly supporting one of their own professionals. Lewis was a fine player but never quite established himself when his chances came in the Championship side. Instead he was prolific in club cricket, one of countless thousands who have proved that the key to enjoying cricket, sport, even life itself is to find a level at which you can excel; or, at least, one where you may feel that you are swimming in your depth.

I was a stronger player all-round now than I had been as a student. Still, I cannot claim that it was much better than a long-hop that dismissed Alvin Kallicharran in that match against Warwickshire at The Oval. He pulled it to mid-wicket, surprised, I like to think, by the deadly extra bounce. The same Kallicharran had run me out with a brilliant throw from the distant extra-cover boundary in the first innings as I foolishly attempted a third run, but at least I made sure that Surrey did not lose the three-day game, on a typically true Oval pitch, by batting out time for eighteen not out in the second innings.

McIntyre probably disapproved of the stroke with which I hit a Peter Lewington off-break into the empty seats at mid-wicket, although it pleased me. I *was* an amateur, after all.

It was too late now to change career and my talent was almost certainly insufficient, not to mention my temperament too lacking in patience and confidence for a game that requires both and plays such havoc with hopes and emotions. I might have ended up hating cricket, as have some who embraced it as a profession in high expectation, almost like marriage, but ended disillusioned. Instead I remain fascinated by its subtle evolution and infinitely unpredictable charm.

It is certainly easier to talk and write about cricket than to play the game professionally, especially in hot and heathen lands afar, but that is not to say that I would not have jumped at the chance of doing so if it had come early enough.

I dare say that every generation feels that cricket is not so enjoyable as it once was but in all its various guises and tempos it remains, for the most part, a joyous, captivating, beautiful game. The great thing is to keep passing on the torch to the next generation. That can give pleasure in itself, as Edmund Blunden expressed so simply but graphically in his little poem 'Forefathers':

> On the green they watched their sons
> Playing till too dark to see,
> As their fathers watched them once,
> As my father once watched me;
> While the bat and beetle flew
> On the warm air webbed with dew.

There have been moments of even greater pleasure away from cricket fields, naturally, notably the first heart-popping sighting of my wife Judy across a crowded Hall in Cambridge in 1966, seeing her give birth to our first child in 1973, and hearing late on the evening of Boxing Day in 2009 that our third grandchild had arrived after some tough years of waiting for her parents. Such blessings put obsessions like mine for cricket into proper perspective.

The infatuation remains, however. In a way, perhaps, I have never grown up, which is why I have managed to extend into adult life roughly what I was doing as a young schoolboy: watching cricket, playing when I could, writing about matches in old exercise books and amusing my mates by commentating in the dormitory on imaginary games. The luckiest people may be those who can make a living out of childhood fantasies.

3

FAMILY MATTERS

The earliest memory is of a small trauma: a military plane flying low over my pram in Scotland, frighteningly noisy. It cannot, for me, have been any legacy from the war, but there were others, such as my mother cutting up a Mars bar into twelve slim pieces. One slice a day was all that Government rationing and her own frugality would allow a young child. It did not prevent my having poor teeth, as much, I think, from deprivations during my mother's pregnancy as from too much sugar. A few years later, I startled a dentist in Cheshire, as he was about to use his drill for the second time, with an abominable barrage of the worst language I knew. 'You biggees man, you weewees man', I yelled at him.

I was born in Peterborough in the last year of the war (a fact I frequently mentioned to my growing children when putting tiny portions of uneaten food back into the fridge) to Rosemary and Dennis Martin-Jenkins. My father was still doing his bit for King, country and the Royal Artillery, having joined the Territorial Army some time before Neville Chamberlain gave his sombre broadcast in 1939. He was lucky to avoid any serious conflict overseas until joining the mopping-up operations in

Germany in 1945, by which time he had reached the lofty rank of Lieutenant Colonel and received the Territorial Decoration, which, much to the admiration of his sons, he wore on his chest on Remembrance Day as chairman of his local British Legion.

Daddy was a friendly, highly-strung character with great energy, charm and good looks, despite being on the way to near total baldness by the time that he married in 1937. These days it would have been fashionable. Kind, with his emotions never far below the surface, he was a good father and husband who loved to please people, although he was prone to mood swings from great merriment to what for a time became a life-threatening depression. It was his gregariousness as much as anything that enabled him to rise to the top of what was for many years one of Britain's biggest private companies, the shipping-based group Ellerman Lines.

He first worked for them just before the war and rose rapidly afterwards to become first a director, then eventually both chairman and managing director. He was, by the account of several witnesses, fun to work with and an excellent, inclusive chairman. He became president of the UK Chamber of Shipping, chairman of the International Chamber of Shipping and Prime Warden of the Shipwrights.

In all these roles he was widely popular but for all his success he was curiously insecure, tending both to solipsism and paranoia. There is nothing unusual about that sort of paradox. In my father's case I think that from time to time he simply felt out of his depth at a period when the British shipping industry was sinking below the waves of subsidised foreign competition. It was, too, a time of rapid technological change in the shipping industry. Staff changes had to be made and even relatively large companies were vulnerable as containers became the new and more efficient means of storing cargo.

He was devoted to his job but the more demanding it got the more it weighed him down. I learned many years after that he had taken an overdose in 1967, when he was fifty-six. I was on the point of taking my final exams at Cambridge and my mother, typically, told me nothing of the crisis to avoid troubling me. Even after his mind had been calmed by pills my memory of him, when for a time I shared his London flat in Hallam Street, was of evenings that he spent tied to a paper-strewn desk, sighing frequently and looking as crushed in spirit as an abandoned dog.

In those days he relaxed only on the golf course or on holiday. Like me, I fear, a sense of duty meant that he sometimes got less fun out of life than he should have done. It was a joy, occasionally, to see him totally relaxed, not least when roaring with laughter at a comedian such as Tommy Cooper or Norman Wisdom.

When he finally retired there was a party on board HMS *Belfast* to 'celebrate' his retirement. I fear the word might have been chosen mischievously by the new group managing director, Jim Stewart, with whom he had fallen out. My father missed the company of his working companions but now he was able to spend more time watching the sport he had always loved. A move to Thurlestone in Devon had the attraction of a scenic golf course for him and lovely walks for my mother but they felt too cut off from their family and came back to Cranleigh in Surrey before, when he was nearly eighty-one, prostate cancer ended his life in 1991. Only the previous year the same disease had accounted for his younger brother, Alan.

Dennis could not have had more moral support than he did from my mother, Rosemary Clare Walker LRCP, MRCS (physician and surgeon), who had studied medicine at the Royal Free Hospital after her schooldays at Benenden, where she was unhappy, and Penrhos, where she worked hard enough to follow her father and earlier generations of Walkers into medicine. She was a locum during the war in the Gorbals in Glasgow while my father was involved in firing back at marauding German aircraft. She spoke with immense admiration afterwards of the courage and uncomplaining graft of the Glaswegians, doing their best to bring up their families in tough conditions and keeping their slum houses, she said, spotlessly clean.

If that conjures up a picture of a tough, pragmatic woman in a white coat it is a false one. My mother was tender as a petal, a gentle dreamer, warm and sympathetic. She thought and cared deeply about many things but kept her own counsel and, quite unlike her husband, usually managed to hide her emotions. Her profound intelligence was hidden beneath a very large bushel and it took alcohol (which, unlike her Scotch-loving husband she never drank to excess) to loosen her tongue. Oddly for a doctor, she hated anything raw or rough – including, like Doc Martin, the sight of blood.

She suffered her own occasional physical afflictions with silent stoicism, unlike the male members of her family, but she avoided hard work if she could, especially once her family had flown the nest. She was probably more affected than she ever said by the experience of giving birth to a still-born daughter, Diana, between my elder brother, David, and me. To her dying day at the age of eighty-nine she breathed not a word about that trauma to any of her children and to my children she was a strangely hands-off grandmother, albeit a very affectionate one. Scottish blood she may have carried but she was, I suppose, a perfect example of English reserve. She cared deeply about many things, not least her family, or right and wrong; but hers were still waters.

Sadly, vascular dementia restricted my mother to an undigni-fied last few years at a nursing home near Guildford. At least she was always able to recognise her family and to appreciate the visits that my brothers and I made on a rota basis until she died, in 2000, nine years after Dennis.

Rosemary had three sisters, May, Beryl and Anne, and a brother, Bob, who became a film cameraman, never happier than when he worked with Harry Belafonte and Joan Collins in Barbados on *Island in the Sun*. Bob, who had two wives and three children, was a laid-back, gentle, vague character with a wonderful twinkle in his eyes. His charm exceeded his ambition by about ninety-nine to one. He died young of a brain tumour.

Anne, the youngest daughter, lost two fiancés at the beginning and end of the war, the second indeed after official hostilities had ceased. Mercifully she married at last after the conflict. She shared her sisters' softness and romanticism but the various experiences of them all demanded a certain toughness too. My mother had shown it by driving herself to success in her medical exams at a time when women doctors were a rarity.

May, the eldest, was a merry soul who never stopped talking and seldom stopped laughing. She was the ideal extrovert wife for her gentle, deep, shy husband, John Neale, who had been profoundly affected by his experience as a prisoner of the Japanese during the war.

The longest lived of the family was Beryl, known to them all as Bix. In the end she had by far the toughest life but never gave in and she touched everyone by her warmth and vigour. She and my mother were closest in age and temperament. They were introduced to a love of the countryside and all that went with it by their surroundings in what was then a rural Northamptonshire. There were trips to Lincolnshire and coastal Norfolk, and family holidays amongst Perthshire hills and Lake District mountains. They all wanted to climb every peak they could see, and often did. Bix would remember the birds and the flowers she had seen and record them in her diary, which she kept daily for perhaps eighty-five years. One of my grandfather's patients was the novelist L.P. Hartley and there was something of the dreamy life of *The Go-Between*, or *The Shrimp and the Anemone* about the upbringing of the Walker sisters.

Reality had to intrude, however. In tune with the times, they were all sent away to boarding schools, in Bix's case to Queen Anne's, Caversham. Later she trained as a nursery teacher at the Froebel Institute and applied her techniques at Westwood House High School until, shortly before the war, she married a dashing young officer, Captain Burls Lynn Allen. Their very big and happy wedding in Peterborough, in July 1939, gave way to the dreadful consequences of Hitler's egomanic ambition and to Germany's hypnotised compliance. Burls was murdered within a year in heroic circumstances in a small village called Wormhoudt, on the road from Cassel to Dunkirk.

He and what remained of his troop, the 2nd Battalion of the Royal Warwickshire Regiment, had been herded with a remnant of the Cheshire Regiment into a hot and stinking cowshed after fighting overwhelming numbers of German forces for five hours. The orders to Burls two days before, 26 May 1940, had been as clear as a bell on the breeze: 'Tell your men, with our backs to the wall, the division stands and fights.' That they and others did so enabled thousands of British troops to be evacuated from Dunkirk in the shadow of the encircling German troops.

Captured at last by the SS Liebstandarte Adolf Hitler regiment, the Führer's personal bodyguards, Burls must have known his fate when, according to the surviving soldier that he was shortly to save, he banged on the door of a shed packed with about 100 soldiers, all weary and many wounded, and shouted: 'For the love of God, there is no room in here.' A voice from outside responded chillingly: 'Where you are going there will be a lot of room.'

Bert Evans, then just nineteen and the sole survivor of the massacre that followed, told a *Sunday Telegraph* journalist when the barn was restored in 2010 how, after a final cigarette had been negotiated by their Captain, grenades were thrown into the barn and everyone inside was raked by machine guns. The door was then hauled open and any survivors were individually shot in the back of the head. Evans had his right arm almost blown off by the blast but Burls, who was miraculously unscathed and could have run for his life alone, grabbed the wounded private soldier and dragged him away at the double. Chased by an SS officer they plunged into a pond. Burls was shot at close range through the forehead and Evans in the neck. They sank below the surface, apparently dead, but the private lived to recall: 'That's how my captain died; saving my life.'

Burls and Beryl had been due to take a posting in India, a country where her mother's forebears had served for generations. In time Bix met and fell for a charming Czech soldier, billeted with his Free Army, and they were married in far less grand circumstances in January 1944. When Karel Matyasek stepped on a mine sixteen months later she found herself widowed for a second time at the age of thirty-one but she wrote to her parents 'although I have been unlucky like so many others I have twice for a time been wonderfully happy'.

The consolation for her second shattering blow was the birth of Karel's son, Jiri, in March 1945. He became the racing journalist James Lambie, author of *The Story of Your Life*, an outstanding recent history of the newspaper that employed him for most of his career, *Sporting Life*.

Beryl's compassion must have had something to do with her genes. My maternal grandfather, Alec Russell Walker, MB, BC,

BA, FRCS, was, like his own father and uncle and several of his brothers, a doctor, in his case a surgeon with a great reputation amongst his patients. According to the family tree he was descended from both Robert the Bruce and John Knox and came from Leslie in Fife. In the Victorian era the Walkers practically were medicine in Peterborough, it seems. A photograph taken on my great-grandfather's eightieth birthday, celebrated during the First World War, shows a sturdy middle-class professional family, each doing his or her bit for the national effort. Of the eight men in the group young enough to serve directly, four are in the army, two in the navy. Charles, whose son became an Admiral, is described as a civil engineer from Sheffield; my grandfather was surgeon to the Peterborough Recruiting Station.

Alec's family adored him. Sadly, I only remember him swallowing a fish bone that got stuck in his throat when we were having dinner at the Old Manse in Tyndrum, his retirement home in Perthshire. I remember my grandmother Ettie better, if only from visits to her bedside at Achdalieu. She was a Goadby, another large middle-class family. Of her several sisters the one I knew best was Aunt Edith, who supplied me with most of my early religious counsel. She had been a missionary in Egypt and lived to 105, latterly at a nursing home in Tunbridge Wells. I still have the pocket version of St. John's Gospel that she sent me one Christmas and I remember also the howler I committed when writing my bread and butter thank-you letter for another present. 'As I write this letter', I penned in an attempt to spin it out until it at least got over the first page, 'I am listening on the gramophone to a new record by the singer Michael Holliday, which was also amongst my favourite presents.' No doubt my missive had my usual spelling mistakes because she replied by return, abjuring me never to try to do two things at once.

Another sister, Hilda, was also a favourite of my mother's. So much so that when she was shopping one day in Knightsbridge she suddenly heard Hilda's voice saying, softly, 'Goodbye, Rosemary'. She turned to look for her, in vain. As soon as she got home she heard that her aunt had died that afternoon.

I know less about my paternal family, at least on the Martin-Jenkins side, although the games-playing gene was obviously there because my grandfather was captain of Woodcote Park Golf Club in Surrey in 1916/17. The only story that I can remember my father telling of him is when he caused a rumpus in a tube station by retaliating when a man going up an escalator accidentally jabbed him with his umbrella. There, no doubt, is the seed of my own impetuosity.

Frederick Jenkins, as he apparently was until adding a second barrel, probably to appease his parents-in-law when he got married, seems to have made up in personality anything that he lacked in 'background'.

I remember my paternal grandmother – Auntie Pat to the rest of the family – with affection. Tall and boney, she had been very beautiful in her youth in a Keira Knightly sort of way. She was artistic – a talented sculptress – excitable, kind, opinion-ated and very amusing.

She was Roman Catholic and remained faithfully so to her dying day at Mount Alvernia Nursing Home in Bramshott, where the nursing nun who saw her out of the world, Sister Gemma, a lovely Irish lady, was also the one who, a few years later, was on hand to help the doctor to deliver James, our eldest child, at Mount Alvernia Hospital in Guildford. There was a wonderful sense of continuity about that.

I have no memories of my paternal granny until our move south but vague ones of my mother's parents, 'Grandpa and Nanny', from visits to their home in Peterborough, Foxwall, where the garden with its long herbaceous border had an instant attraction for me, my brothers and cousins on summer holiday visits. There was a Wolseley, driven by a chauffeur called Crowson, whom I called Crocus and muddled with the gardener. Most of my first two years were spent in Scotland, first at Fairlie in Ayrshire, in accommodation rented from an upmarket landlady named Lady Boyle, then in the same area at Skelmorlie, where the prevailing smell emanated from the next door gasworks. I vaguely remember that heavy odour, especially when, once or twice since, I have encountered it again, notably in the Athlone area of Cape Town where the late Basil D'Oliveira was brought up.

While brother David went to his first school at Miss Johnson's Academy in Skelmorlie Castle, I was being watched to make sure that, once toddling, I did not disappear through the back gate into the Clyde. The great river wound below a steep bank immediately beyond the gate, within sight and sometimes sound of the shipbuilders' 'measured mile'.

As a result of this Scottish start my brother has supported their various lost causes – trying to beat England at various sports for instance – ever since. I give them my loyal encouragement whenever they play any country other than England, but in the cruelly cold winter of 1947 we moved south to Birkenhead as my father's work for Ellermans took him from Glasgow to Liverpool.

My younger brother, Tim, was well on the way by the time that we had completed our move over two snowy February days. He was wise enough to wait until towards the end of May to make his first appearance in a warmer world. Home for the now complete family was a white-stuccoed semi-detached house, 26, Elm Road North, Prenton. I have only vague images of that period, amongst them a sloping street, friendly neighbours, an evening paper salesman yelling repetitively into misty darkness half lit by yellow street lamps and a shamelessly ostentatious rendering by myself of 'Away in a Manger' at someone's Christmas party. Something deep inside rather liked the feel of an admiring audience.

Certainly I recall that experience more clearly than anything about my first school, Pershore House. David's education continued first at Prenton prep, then, as a boarder, at Kingsmead. Elder siblings play a large part in a younger child's upbringing and I dare say that I was shaped to an extent by his enthusiasms. He loved all sport and still does, although never blessed with more than an average eye for a ball, and I liked nothing better than to play football with his friends, sometimes on the basis of that typically British method of team selection: two older boys as captains choose one player each in turn until the duffers are left to make up the numbers. It was during an impromptu game that David broke two front teeth when they collided with my head. The cut bled profusely. It turned out to be negligible but I got all the sympathy at first.

Amongst our neighbours in Liverpool were the Wales rugby international Raymond Bark-Jones, and Tranmere Rovers footballer Peter Bell, a neat, smart and dignified figure.

We had two more years in the north, moving to leafier surroundings at Higher Bebington on the Wirral peninsula. It was a yellow-painted, four-bedroom house, bought from friends of my parents, Don and Kay Smith, who were killed together in the Manchester air crash several years later, leaving four young children.

In 1951 my father was promoted to a directorship in the London office and he and my mother ended a swift search near their first marital home at Ockley by buying the Dutch House at South Holmwood from Sir H.P. Hamilton for £7500. It was a big enough house to have been commandeered during the war as a billet for the Canadian Army, who had dug up what had once been a beautifully manicured tennis lawn in order to grow potatoes.

At no stage of our stewardship did the Dutch House have central heating, which, in addition to its too close proximity to the Dorking to Horsham road, no doubt explained why it failed initially to attract its asking price of £10,000 when my father put it on the market in 1964, but it was attractive for all that. White with blue windows on the outside, it was given its character by its curved front aspect, with an inverted centre in the Cape Dutch style. It was approached through a gate marked on each side by two beautiful cherry trees, followed by a short gravel drive. The front door was guarded by a porch with twin pillars and immediately inside the hall there was a Latin inscription carved into the plaster of a horizontal beam, placed there to celebrate the return from prison of one of the earlier occupiers, the famous (some thought notorious) suffragette, Mrs. Emmeline Pethick-Lawrence. As a member of the Women's Social and Political Union she had been imprisoned for nine months in 1912. She later edited the journal *Votes for Women* and continued to fight the socialist cause long after that fight had been won.

I can remember virtually every inch of what, by some standards, was no more than a medium-sized family home, with four main bedrooms, two very small ones and a single bathroom. But there were also a number of smaller rooms whose nomenclature was redolent of a more leisured era. There was, for example, a pantry, a larder, a scullery, a boot-room, a sewing-room and, if you please, a 'maid's sitting-room' leading down from the kitchen. The only thing it lacked was a maid.

In her place there was room for a tiny billiard table. For some reason I seldom used it and remain one of the worst players ever to have attempted to pot a black. Table tennis in the playroom was more fun for me. It was a very large room with a leaky glass roof, linked to the main house by a cold corridor which, for the purposes of at least a couple of dances in the Christmas holidays when we three boys were teenagers, we restored to its original status as a 'ballroom'. It had its own chimney and is now a separate house. It was an exciting day when we lit a fire there for the first time for one of these dances, before spreading French chalk on the wooden floor to aid the quick-stepping, fox-trotting debs and debs' delights of west Surrey.

Like his father, David never lost his enthusiasm for mickey-taking of one kind or another. He became a chartered accountant, for a time the group financial director of Ellerman Lines and for many years a trustee of the huge charitable trust left by the second Sir John. Ever a supporter of the underdog, a natural British trait, he had also been involved for thirty years with the Chichester Liberal Democrats, but his real love in life has been nature generally and mountains in particular. Since the age of sixty, and in short bursts over a period of only nine years, he has climbed over half the 283 Munros, the hills over 3000 feet in Britain. He scaled the 21,200-foot peak of Mera in Nepal in his forties and then, at the age of fifty-two, the still more demanding 22,835 feet of Aconcagua in Argentina, the highest mountain in the world outside the Himalayas. Four years later he climbed another Andean peak, Pisco, in Peru, a mere 18,867 feet.

I admire but do not envy him. In 2009 I had planned to walk the 100-odd miles of the South Downs Way with David, only to have to withdraw when I got hepatitis. Determined to make amends the following September, I had to set out from Eastbourne to Winchester with a septic toe, which made the exercise painful from the outset. No doubt unbalanced in my walking as a result, I strained a hamstring muscle severely enough during the first few gorgeously scenic miles above the chalk cliffs beyond Beachy Head for my walk to have become an increasingly pathetic shuffle by the following morning, despite a comfortable bed, two pints of Harvey's and a good pub meal at Alfriston. Two days later I abandoned the unequal struggle after fifty-nine miles, leaving my brother, also hobbling from dreadful blisters, to plough on alone. I completed my own missing section of the journey the following spring.

My younger brother, Tim, played what many men might consider to be a blinder by keeping a succession of girlfriends at arm's length until he was past fifty, then marrying a sparky and good-looking French-speaking Algerian, Nadjoua (now shortened to Najwa to assist the English!). She is young enough to be his daughter. Even this and the further distraction of having to control two young children when some of us were becoming grandfathers did not seem greatly to alter his lifestyle, certainly not when it came to golf.

Tim missed a golf Blue at Cambridge but got better and better with age and determined application so that, in his sixties, he considers it unexceptional to nip round the Royal and Ancient at St. Andrews in the seventies, not to mention others in the large handful of clubs to which he belongs. Winning the foursomes with him at West Sussex Golf Club was one of the happiest of my recent memories and we almost achieved a reprise the following year only to chuck away the final after leading all the way to the 17th. If I could meld his consistency to the flair of my son James (who *did* get a Blue and still plays off four despite being a dedicated father and breadwinner) I should be a decent player. I love the game almost as much as I do cricket but so far I appear to have fooled myself that semi-retirement would bring an instant plummet in my handicap.

Tim followed me to an MA at Cambridge and progressed to an MBA at Harvard. The latter has always seemed to me to be a licence to print money and he duly made plenty, relatively speaking at least, not to mention making a multitude of friends and contacts during his years as a shrewd, industrious business-man, based in Hong Kong. His last great task was to manage the creation of a new town on the Gold Coast of Queensland, the centre-piece of which, to no one's surprise, was a smart golf course, Robina Woods. He has used his rewards with immense generosity, not least when, summer after summer, he rented a house at Thurlestone in the South Hams of Devon, and played host to family and friends.

I have been as happy playing the magical first six holes of Thurlestone golf course on a summer's evening as anywhere else at any time of my life. Aiming a three iron at the flag into a stiff breeze blowing straight off a glistening sea, knowing that an over-hit would send the ball straight over the grassy, flower-encrusted cliff top behind, was an invigorating, irresistible challenge. Invariably my shot would drift short into a bunker. Once in a silvery moon it would hover above the pin and drop to within a foot before being tapped, in a re-enactment of John Betjeman at St. Enedoc, 'oh most securely in'.

Anyone who has played links golf will understand the joy our late Poet Laureate felt after that 'quite unprecedented three' one glorious evening at his home course in Cornwall:

> Ah seaweed smells from sunny cliffs
> And thyme and mist in whiffs
> Incoming tide, Atlantic waves,
> Slapping the sunny cliffs.
> Lark song and sea sounds in the air
> And splendour, splendour everywhere.

4

EASTBOURNE

The main school building, ivy clad with mock Tudor timbers on white
stuccoed walls, is so tall that it sways as I lie awake in one of the
top-floor dormitories, with a particularly high wind howling in off
the English Channel. It is set high on the western tip of Eastbourne,
at the very foot of the Downs, looking out on one side through a gap
at the end of the playing field beyond which the sea is almost always
visible, either a grey blur or a shimmering blue.

Life in a boarding school in the 1950s meant being isolated from
one's parents for large chunks of the year. Until the age of about
fifteen I could never leave home and face the prospect of school
food, Maths prep and all the other rigours of boarding school
life without crying inconsolably on the last day of every holiday.
Yet from my very first day at St. Bede's School, still going strong
as a prep school and now the junior partner to an extremely
successful senior school on the Sussex Downs, I always forgot
my misery the moment that a term started and I was with my
friends again.

Nothing much has changed here since I first played cricket
and football on the playing field that separates the imposing

school building from the sea. To my adult eyes it is a pocket handkerchief but on my first day, as a nervous eight-year-old in the April of 1953, it seemed vast. My brother David introduced me to his cricketing friends on the first warm evening after our arrival and my morale got an immediate boost when I impressed them with what I could do with bat and ball. A few words of praise sent me to bed happy. Twenty-four hours earlier I had been blubbing like a baby.

We were sufficiently elevated to see the dirty British coasters butting through the Channel in the mad March days and close enough to walk to the pebbly beach on summer days and to take gingerly steps into the ice cold, crystal clear water in air pungent with ozone. I loved ships and there was seldom a shortage of them, heaving east or west through the waves, smoke emerging from their chimneys in a black curl, as if in a child's drawing. When it was foggy, as in the memory it often seemed to be, you heard rather than saw the vessels, their fog-horns blasting into the thick atmosphere like cows in labour.

The old and generally elegant holiday town stretched down the hill to the east. It was, proclaimed the posters on the walls of the station to which I would travel every term from Victoria on the special school train, the *Sun Trap of the South*. Perhaps so, but it was viciously cold in winter when snow had stopped games and restricted the afternoon's compulsory exercise to a walk along the sea-front, crocodile, the boys paired two by two, dressed in shorts, with a single grey pullover, long socks, thin black shoes and a navy blue macintosh as the only bulwarks against the biting sea wind. I can feel now the agonising tingle of chilblained fingers and feet, exposed to hot water or a radiator after one of those freezing winter walks.

The school was named after the venerable monk whose monastery at Jarrow was rather closer to Lancashire than

Sussex, but his eighth-century 'Eccelesiastical History of the English People' was written at a time when some of the familiar features of the Sussex landscape were being formed. Windmills and coastal defences like the Martello towers and Second World War 'pill boxes' came later; so, even, did the village churches; but, long before Bede, Celtic farmers were forming here the first genuine village communities in England.

The rare visits by my parents to take me 'out' consisted usually of picnics on the Downs in the summer and in winter visits to one of the piers at Eastbourne or, better still, Brighton. The old Palace pier there used to have little cars that one could drive round a circuit, like dodgems without the collisions, and they gave me such a thrill that it is a little surprising that I did not develop into a Lewis Hamilton. Not that I would have had the required daring: I just liked driving, and to some extent still do, be it a car or a ride-on mower.

We were a close family but in the 1950s home was home and school was school. When David and I were at prep school, he was M-JI and I was M-JII. Tim was briefly M-JIII before David moved on to Marlborough and I was elevated to M-JI.

Looking back it was quite a tough place for little boys to learn the disciplines of life. The food, on the whole, was basic. The best meal of the week was toad-in-the-hole and boiled vegetables, followed by 'squashed flies' – currant tart – and custard. The rest of the menu was littered with dishes that I loathed, amongst them horse-meat, tinned spaghetti (the dreaded, slimy 'worms'), tinned sardines, boiled eggs that often seemed to be bad, rice pudding and, equal first with the worms as the most inedible of them all, tapioca.

I forget which of these it was that I was unable to start, let alone finish, when one of the three joint headmasters, Rex Lord, seized my shoulders and ordered me with risen voice to finish it up immediately. 'Good Lord, boy', he added, 'soldiers in the war had to live on GRASS.'

I was probably a terrible weed when it came to eating things that I did not like and I dare say that I lacked resolution generally. Academic work to me was more or less an unequal struggle until it came to History and English. Maths remained a foreign country for most of my academic years; I struggled with Latin; and Science was not even taught at prep schools then. Yet I opened a new Science wing at the flourishing modern St. Bede's not long ago. It enabled me to risk a public airing of the definition of a metallurgist as a man who, looking into the eyes of a platinum blonde, can tell at once whether she is virgin metal or just a common ore, but I have to admit to shameful ignorance whenever a question on the sciences is fired by Jeremy Paxman on *University Challenge*.

That is more my fault than that of any of the teachers. In any case huge dollops of consolation for the more trying aspects of life in Eastbourne came on the playing field. There was cricket in the summer, soccer in the Michaelmas term, rugger played on a hollow in the Downs until half-term after Christmas, then hockey at All Saints in the second half.

That Lent term was almost the best time of the year for me. Cricket beckoned, the weather was getting less freezing, Easter and the joys of spring were round the corner. I could kick a rugger ball further than most and was just about elusive enough to keep out of the reach of heavier youths, so I played at fly-half. Later on my extreme reluctance to tackle anyone who was not much smaller than me found me out but at prep school I got away with it, especially given a scrum-half, David Englefield, who was both quicker and braver. Hockey was even more fun. Passing and running into space seemed to come fairly naturally.

All first-team games, and all teaching of History and Latin, were the preserve of the Old Marlburian Mr. Lord, who was an exemplary schoolmaster, with a smile that creased his face like ripples in the sand. His dark hair was neat even in a wind and except on Sundays when a dark suit was *de rigueur*, he dressed always in a tie and a navy blue blazer, usually flecked with blackboard chalk-dust. The kind of irritation displayed at my reluctance to eat perfectly good food was rare but when his equable temperament was seriously disturbed it made his very occasional bursts of anger all the more chilling. There was a particularly naughty Anglo-Greek boy called Christopher Hourmouzious – alias 'Mouzie' – who was always getting into trouble and I can still hear the rising volume of Rex's voice as it rang out one afternoon in the school gym: 'Mouzie, Mouzie, DON'T DO THAT.' Instantly the mischief ceased.

It was Rex who took me and other keen young cricketers to see our first county cricket at The Saffrons. Jim Parks and Robin Marlar, both future presidents of Sussex (and in Marlar's case of MCC too) made an immediate impression, as did two from the opposing team, big Jim Stewart of Warwickshire and Peter Richardson of Worcestershire, whose white batting gloves I coveted and who smiled at us as we sat on the grass by the boundary rope.

Rex Lord's apparently effortless authority and the respect he commanded were not, alas, shared by the more prominent of his partners, Jack Keeling, who instilled little else but fear in all the boys under his command. Bespectacled, chain-smoking and volatile, the sight of his slightly dishevelled figure in the day, or by night the smell and simultaneous red glow of his cigarette, were enough to terrify me, and most of my friends, especially if we were guilty of the heinous crime of speaking after lights had been turned off in the dormitory.

Jack's weapon of vengeance was the slipper or, just

occasionally and considerably more painfully, the cane. Because I was frightened of him his attempts to teach me the rudiments of Maths were largely in vain and in an effort to avoid punishment for bad marks I would often resort to charming brighter arithmetical brains to do all or most of my sums for me. That, of course, is fatal because no one will ever make progress until he understands the problem or how to solve it. One day I was caught by Jack colluding in a Maths class with an amiable boy called David Boumphrey. Both of us were told to 'get down to the lower changing-room' which always meant that you were to be 'whacked' with the slipper. There was no time for the insertion of blotting paper into the pants to soften the dreaded blows but on this occasion Boumphrey's punishment, whilst I waited outside the changing-room with cold insects apparently creeping across my stomach, seemed to go on much longer than usual, most unjustly since he had only been trying to help me. The reason became apparent when Jack's harsh voice roared through the closed changing-room door: 'WILL YOU KEEP YOUR BOTTOM STILL, BOUMPHREY!'

Once upstairs the question always asked by other boys was 'four or six?'. In poor Boumphrey's case it had been at least twelve.

I was probably beaten half a dozen times in all during my five years at the school, never savagely and always when I deserved it. The only occasions that Jack used the cane on me, however, were both for imitating members of staff and making fools of them for the amusement of other boys. There was a harmless but rather unpredictable old buffer called Mr. Wells who looked like Mr. Pastry, and an eccentric old lady called Miss Hobjoy who used to supervise bath nights. Clearly Mr. Keeling felt that he should defend the dignity of his staff but in the case of Mr. Wells there was, for once, a nod and a wink that suggested that he rather agreed that my victim was a figure of fun and the cane was wielded less vigorously than sometimes. That is not to say that it did not sting, but there was no mutual grudge between Mr. Wells and me afterwards and I was delighted for him when he surprised everyone by playing a mighty innings in the staff match, getting so excited in the process of becoming suddenly a hero that I feared he might have a heart attack. I believe that he did, eventually.

Miss Hobjoy, all rosy cheeks and bony elbows, soon forgave me too, but I was less fortunate with the other matrons. A certain Mrs Ashton took a profound dislike to me – I never discovered why, but perhaps because I talked too much – and victimised me to the extent that she is the only person in my life whom I think I have truly hated. I may not have been alone because she was not at the school for more than a year or two. The senior matron, Mrs. Walford, was efficient, consistent in temperament and usually caring. The unfortunate exception came when, half-way through one Michaelmas term at the age of ten, the sharp tummy pains that I had occasionally been suffering in uncharacteristic silence (I can remember pressing the end of a compass into the right hand side of my stomach during lessons to ease the pain), suddenly became vicious. I was sick several times during the night but Mrs. Walford, having to clear up my first unpleasant expulsion, had no sympathy. She was convinced that I had had too much of someone's pink birthday cake for tea the evening before, and said so several times. It was therefore a small triumph for me when the following morning the school's visiting medic, Dr. Wilson-Hall, diagnosed acute appendicitis. I was taken out on a stretcher before a contrite Mrs. Walford and a silent cast of boys, thence by ambulance for an emergency operation at Princess Alexandra's hospital.

There were exceptions to these female harridans. Miss

Collard was another matron, very young and very beautiful. Alas, she soon got married. Gladys Candlin, wife of the senior headmaster, Hugh – whom I hardly knew as a teacher because his main interests were playing the organ in chapel and teaching Greek to the sixth form – was very sweet. Her fame lay in having taught ballet in Shanghai to the future prima ballerina, Margot Fonteyn, although where and for how long I never learned. Occasionally one was asked to sit beside her at breakfast before Chapel on Sunday morning, while Hugh, a large man with a fringe moustache and a certain similarity to Oliver Hardy, warmed up for choir practice by consuming at least eight pieces of toast. I disgraced myself once by having a nervous twitch (of the sort to which I have always been prone when on edge, not least on the putting green) and knocking a jug of milk all over the table-cloth and into Mrs Candlin's lap.

Rex Lord's wife was, like some in BBC soaps, never seen, although he was happily married with a daughter and a son who, like his father, was a fine cricketer. David Lord bowled me first ball in the old boys' match, a potential disaster for the school team since I was supposed to be its star, but Rex was equal to the situation, uttering a stentorian 'No Ball' the instant after my stumps had been shattered.

The third spouse, Valerie Keeling, would do her best to smooth out her husband's rough edges whenever she, too, invited one to sit at her table. Her staple question was always: 'Are your people coming down this weekend?' When they did it made Saturday even more emphatically the best day of the week. An outing with the parents or not, Saturday meant a free afternoon and evening and a strictly rationed hand-out of sweets after morning lessons. Even now the first day of the weekend seems special to me.

Halfway through my five years a Miss McLean arrived from

Scotland to teach Maths. Her stock expression when trying to drum something into me was 'Has the penny dropped?'. Foolishly I always said yes to please her, but it seldom had. Exam results told the truth: Maths hopeless, Languages mediocre, History and English good. How early the die is cast!

Perhaps the most important source of a basic education was my first female teacher at St. Bede's, the delightful round-figured Miss Barnard, who had also taught my father. A motherly but firm old dear who used to take the first form, she had a face like an owl's and taught me many things by heart that have proved useful since, such as French pronunciation, tables up to twelve, major dates of British history and the invaluable *thirty days hath September, April, June and November; all the rest have 31 except for February alone, which has but 28 days clear and 29 in each leap year*.

As at all independent schools in those days, religion played a big part in the daily curriculum, let alone on Sundays. St. Bede's had a small, simple and very intimate chapel with an organ and a stained-glass east window, extending from the main form room. We had a short service every morning, with hymns. I was soon in the choir, able to sing in tune if never very beautifully. 'Away in a Manger' remained my only solo performance, other than in many a bath and shower, but carol services at the nearby All Saints Church were an annual highlight.

Boarders were never bored. Keeling supervised an elaborate Hornby model railway to the delight of many of the boys and painted exceptional scenery himself for the annual school play, always a highlight of the Michaelmas term. Music teaching was available at extra cost, which may be why I never had any, but I learned to shoot a rifle – not a skill I maintained – to jump a wooden horse, to climb a rope in the gym and to box. The mentor there was Ken de Torre, a former sergeant-major who taught PE, gymnastics and the art of self-defence with just the right mixture of humour and enthusiasm. For some reason I was quite good at boxing, winning little silver cups at more weights than one in the annual competitions which would be judged by an outsider, a Captain Stansfield, whose qualifications for the task were unclear. Presumably he was simply military and lived conveniently close.

One year he ruled that I and my opponent, a tough but slight little boy called Denison, were inseparable after three rounds so we fought a fourth which was deemed to be an epic. Eventually I triumphed but when I came to apply the skills taught me by de Torre in my one and only boxing tournament at my next school, Marlborough, my experience was very different. I was matched on that occasion against a tough little nut called James Tweedie who was stronger but shorter. He was wary of my reach and I of his aggression. After a couple of minutes the judge, Ivo Payne, whose squashed nose advertised his own qualifications, rang the bell and pronounced that, much as he admired our mutual elusiveness, it was high time for one of us to throw a punch.

I subsequently made Tweedie's nose bleed, but he was adjudged the winner and I retired from the ring. I was not so clever or devious as the now successful literary agent John Rush, my contemporary at Fitzwilliam College, Cambridge, who worked out an ingenious way to get a Blue. Word had got round Cambridge that Oxford's heavyweight representative in that year's University boxing match was John Coker, a massive African who had already made a name for himself as a powerful wing three-quarters for Oxford and the Harlequins. He had knocked out his light blue opponent the previous year and such was his formidable reputation in the ring that Rush was the only entry for the 1964 Cambridge team at heavyweight.

I was amongst several of his friends to go to the Corn

Exchange in the middle of the City to support him, all of us aware that he was almost certainly about to be mangled. When the bell went, however, Rush was true to his name. He dashed straight at his magnificently muscled opponent with his bearded head down, aiming straight for his private parts. Immediately the bell sounded and the referee warned the Cambridge man that if he did that again he would be disqualified. He did and he was. Thus he won a Blue without throwing or, more importantly, receiving, a single punch.

If boxing was a passing success for me, acting in the various plays brought out a more genuine minor talent. I apparently brought the house down as the King of Hearts in *Alice in Wonderland* with the line 'If he's got a head of course you can cut it off!' The school Chronicle used such words as 'authority' and 'mastery' about my performance, undoubtedly from a generous reviewer, but there was a serious actor in the making (not to mention a keen little wicket-keeper) in Nicky Henson, son of the music hall star Leslie Henson. He had been brilliant in a production of the Brothers Grimm's *Rumpelstiltskin* and sparkled as the Mad Hatter. He duly became a professional, although I have only occasionally seen him performing since he reduced a slightly inebriated Sybil to loud laughter with his 'Pretentious, moi?' story in the wedding episode of the immortal series *Fawlty Towers*.

Henson was not the only thespian produced by St. Bede's. Peter Cook had gone before him and Eddie Izzard arrived later. As for cricketers, the best days may lie in the future. Recent products have included the Sussex players James Pyemont, Ollie Rayner and Luke Wells, son of Alan, the former county captain who now coaches at the senior school. Pyemont, son of one St. Bede's headmaster and nephew of another, captained Cambridge but I doubt that he had the tactical acumen of my own contemporary Nicholas De Jong, who captained the prep school in my penultimate year. We had been bowled out cheaply by Ascham, the Eastbourne College preparatory school, a fine example of one of those catastrophes that abound in Under-13 cricket. Our captain was not fazed. He instructed me to loosen my bootlaces and to bend to do them up frequently on my way back to my bowling mark. What is more, I was told to double the length of my run up and not to hurry back after each ball. If memory does not play tricks, we came very close to drawing the game.

These days I might have written a pompous article about such shameless delaying tactics but at the time I think the adults rather admired De Jong's brazen tactics and ingenuity. Cricket played by boys of that age remains wonderfully zealous, innocent and error-strewn. I thoroughly enjoyed watching my own sons when work allowed but I feel for the schoolmasters and their club counterparts, running junior teams, because results are so unpredictable. I have never been able to verify one story in all particulars but believe it to be true. Richard Parsons, who became a wine merchant, was, during his brief time as a schoolmaster, put in charge of the Under-11 team of the Wellington College prep school, Eagle House. To his immense embarrassment they were all out for one. Apologising profusely to his opposite number, he suggested that it was a little early for tea. So the opposing school batted instead. Fifteen minutes later they, too, were all out: for nought.

5

WESTBORNE: LIFE AT MARLBOROUGH

A large Georgian house, but not too large, its two wings in perfect symmetry, joined by a pillared porch and approached through an avenue between a double row of lime trees. This is the old Castle Inn, the heart and birthplace of Marlborough College, solid below the Wiltshire Downs.

I was a borderline entrant to Marlborough. My Common Entrance exam was a curate's egg, the bad outweighing the good I suspect, and the school's austere-seeming Master, Tommy Garnett, summoned me to be assessed by various 'beaks' (teachers) in subjects in which I had failed to reach a pass mark. Having produced such an uneven performance in my written exams I apparently rose to the occasion in the oral ones and was accepted in Shell C, the lowest form, in May 1958.

Garnett had forgotten about my inauspicious start when I sat next to him years later at a dinner in Melbourne after his retirement as headmaster of Geelong, but at the time my cricketing reputation no doubt helped because he himself had been an outstanding schoolboy batsman at Charterhouse. Unlike Charterhouse, Marlborough was a genuine country school with a wide intake of boys whose parents needed to make sacrifices to afford the fees. I was lucky to be there.

In his *Rural Rides* Cobbett somehow managed to observe that Marlborough was an 'ill-looking place' in 1821 but his was a singular view. If there is such a thing as a quintessential English market town, Marlborough might be it, with its long, very wide high street, St Peter's Church at one end, St. Mary's at the other, the river Kennet meandering through and the Downs beyond. It is ancient, with a borough charter first granted in 1204, and almost literally magical. Right behind my first dormitory at the school was a small prehistoric hill known as 'the Mound' with legendary association to Merlin. A few miles away along the road to Bath lies Avebury, with its circle of sarsen stones, not so huge as the ones at Stonehenge but just as mysterious in origin; and the much larger 'mound' of Silbury Hill.

My teenage mind, alas, was not exactly bursting with curiosity about these things – the Mound was strictly out of bounds for a start – but I could and did appreciate the timeless beauty of the general environment of a school created by a few public-spirited philanthropists in 1843 for the education mainly of the sons of Anglican clergy. Its original centre was the large country house built for the Seymour family (Jane Seymour, Henry VIII and all that) between 1702 and 1715. In 1751 the Duke of Northumberland leased it to an entrepreneur called George Smith, who had previously managed the most famous of the early cricket grounds of London, the one still staging cricket matches for members of the Honourable Artillery Company almost 300 years later.

Under Smith's management it became the Castle Inn, the most famous stopping point for well-to-do passengers travelling by coach and horses from London to Bath. It was, in fact, one of the largest inns in England, with its twelve 'parlours', each with two beds, situated on each wing of the hall, a spacious ballroom and outside attractions that included the Mound, a wilderness, pleasant gardens, stables and, as the *Bath Journal* reported in August 1751, 'a dog kennel with all conveniences'. When the swiftly burgeoning railways began to put the coach owners out of business less than a century later, an even better use was found for this classical example of Georgian elegance. In my day it was divided into C1 and C3. With typical public school perversity, C2 was in a completely different building on the other side of the Bath Road at the base of the playing fields. For the last four of my five years at the school I lived in the other half of Field House, known by the same lack of logic as B3.

As the school grew, however, it began to take in smaller 'outhouses', some of which, like Elmshurst, Littlefield and Preshute, were allowed to keep their original names. They were less specifically functional, more homely and a bit more expensive for the fee-paying parents. We in-College boys looked on the out-College types as northerners do southerners. They had to be softer.

All bravado, of course. Not that I was not a fairly soft little boy at thirteen, enough to be deeply distressed in my first few weeks at the school when a letter from my mother told me that our much adored Staffordshire bull terrier, Garry, had been put down. I can remember crying bitterly during a service in Chapel but there was so much going on all day that there was little time to wallow in homesickness. Marlborough, albeit much reformed since Victorian times, still had a reputation as a tough school but I had a caring first housemaster in Ian Beer and the sensible system of placing boys in 'junior' houses for a year eased the transition for those coming from smaller prep schools or, in a few cases, boys boarding for the first time. By the end of my time Garnett's successor, John Dancy, was preparing the way for sixth form girls and, eventually, full co-education.

Had they been there in my time I would undoubtedly have been less shy with the opposite sex than I was until life became more normal at University but apart from one swiftly passing attraction my experiences of the well-known danger of being incarcerated in an all male adolescent community were limited. Totally unaware that rugger practice with a plastic ball in a class room was an arousing experience for a friend in my house I was very surprised one afternoon when he suddenly began rubbing himself against my leg like a randy dog. I laughed it off and he remained at a respectful distance thereafter before going on to a distinguished army career. On another occasion I found myself involved equally unexpectedly in an attempt at mutual masturbation with two or three older boys after an invitation to 'tea' in a study shared by two of them. A joss stick had been lit to add atmosphere but, happily, I found it embarrassing rather than exciting.

There were better things to do with spare time. Town, Downs and the majestic Savernake Forest were all easily accessible by foot or bicycle and although one might constantly have been, as John Betjeman famously put it, 'summoned by bells' for various activities at all hours of the day, there was just the right amount of freedom. Being able simply to wander in the town after lunch gave a sense of release, even if my £10 pocket money a term seldom allowed any actual purchases from the shops. Most of it went at Bernard's, the tuck shop. Little corn flake cakes encrusted with chocolate were the favourite treats, at threepence a time. Over the road stood Crosby and Lawrence, the sports outfitters, where I was able to sign for longed-for equipment, such as my first squash racket and fives gloves.

Starting with the Sun Inn at the College end of the town, the high street was littered with pubs and small hotels. The Ailsbury

Arms and the Castle and Ball were the two best hotels but for those with less to spend there were plenty of alternatives. A year after leaving the school my brother David planned a return with one of his old mates and asked me to book him a shared room at the Green Dragon to save money. Much too innocent to enter pubs by myself normally, I duly stepped sheepishly into the dusty hostelry after lunch one day and, peering up to the man behind the bar, asked rather nervously for a double room. Whether it was my halting tongue, in my embarrassment at being in a pub, or the rather elderly landlord's hardness of hearing, I don't know but, after a quizzical look, he placed a glass to the base of a bottle above the bar and poured me out a double rum. I wish that I could claim that I was bold enough to drink it.

The school itself was going through an enlightened era under Garnett's guidance. His great belief, like St. Paul's, was that everyone has a talent and at Marlborough he made it his business to develop each boy's gift. There was a beagle pack, a pottery school, a printing house, fishing and climbing expeditions for the country types, an extra music hall built by the boys at his instigation, a farmhouse bought with a legacy to be restored by other boys wanting to learn the arts of building, and other additions to the traditional curriculum of academic subjects, sport, art, religion, the Corps, music and theatre.

Marlborough has produced more than its fair share of poets, notably the contemporaries Betjeman and Louis MacNeice and three at the school just before the Great War, Siegfried Sassoon, Charles Sorley and Frank Lewis, but of my contemporaries the stars came mainly from other fields. Looking, for an aide-memoire, at the December 1962 issue of the *Marlburian*, the school magazine produced once a term entirely by the boys, I am amazed by its sophistication and lack of pretence, except, perhaps, in a poem written by myself and published by the editor, Angus Dunn, with whom I had shared a study for a term or two. He lived then in a village quaintly named Christmas Pie. A tall, academic, serious chap as a schoolboy, he became first a diplomat, then a successful banker.

My less than immortal lines, entitled 'The Bitter Rose', apparently reflected an unrequited love affair that I no longer recall, unless I was imagining the grief of the delightful girl from St. Mary's, Wantage, one of the local schools 'against' whom we had occasional social fixtures. I spent a romantic evening with her during a school dance, only to ditch her, callously, when it became apparent that she was looking for a serious relationship.

My efforts as a poet – I am surprised to find that others found their way into the magazine at different times, including an anonymous one under the initials C.A.D, were colourful but superficial. By lack of pretence, however, I mean the matter of fact way in which it was mentioned that Peter Medawar, at Marlborough from 1928 to 1932, had just won the Nobel Prize for his work on skin tissue grafting, which paved the way for medical transplants; and that 'F.C. Chichester', an older Marlburian, had 'successfully completed the double crossing of the Atlantic in *Gypsy Moth III,* outward passage 33 days, homeward 26'. Good British understatement. Sir Francis Chichester and his little boat had not, of course, finished their liaison.

Naturally, for every outstanding boy there were scores of ordinary ones, almost certainly no less worthy contributors to society in their later lives. Contemporaries of mine who made a larger than normal impact in the early sixties included the shy, precociously gifted Mike Griffith, who later won Blues for cricket, hockey and rackets, captained Sussex and played hockey for Great Britain; and Jonathan Harvey, a fair-haired giant who won Blues as both flannelled fool and muddied oaf, the first as a fast outswing bowler, the second as a strong second row forward who could also kick like a prototype Jonny Wilkinson. 'Jack' Hopper was a natural at all games who briefly became a golf professional and remained a very good amateur, and Bill Hadman, an Oxford scholar who must have played rugby for England but for injury. He was made, apparently, of solid teak and I can still feel the force of his customary greeting, a 'genial' punch on the shoulder.

The sheer diversity of types and talents at that time reflects well on Garnett's philosophy, not to mention his staff. Amongst my other contemporaries, Iain MacDonald-Smith, slim, frail and freckled in his youth, partnered Rodney Patterson to an Olympic sailing gold medal; the 400-metre runner Martin Winbolt-Lewis, another British Olympian, could have done many things well but was content as a prison and hospital chaplain; Ian Balding, trainer of Mill Reef, and Peter Makin both became successful racehorse trainers; Ben Pimlott was a renowned left-wing historian; and Alastair Goodlad, who won a school election as a flamboyant Conservative candidate, became Tory Chief Whip then Tony Blair's surprise choice as 'Our Man' in Australia, where he served a second term because he was so popular. In his schooldays Goodlad's main fame came from being a mazy wing three-quarters, although he was not so fast or powerful as two of his successors in my time, the brothers Louis and Charles Mbanefo, sons of a Nigerian judge at the time of the tragic Biafran War.

Amongst the more artistic types, Christopher Lloyd, engaging but wonderfully pompous even as a mere A level history student like me, went on to become Surveyor of the Queen's Pictures, in the footsteps of the more notorious Marlburian Sir Anthony Blunt. Robin Janvrin is now ennobled, having served with the utmost distinction and discretion as the Queen's private secretary. Crispian Steele-Perkins, a mischievous boy with a twinkle in his eye, was clearly destined to make a name as a trumpeter and duly did. Nick Drake, the singer, guitarist and songwriter, was part of a talented little school band group that I believe briefly included one Christopher Davison, alias Chris de Burgh, the hugely successful singer. He has made a fortune and maintained his dignity far better than most pop stars. Drake by contrast was little known in his time and was brought to an early death by drugs and depression, but he is revered by the cognoscenti as a highly influential musician, whose songs had a pained originality.

Unlike similar schools Marlborough's theatre, the Memorial Hall, was hardly state of the art, but I briefly trod its boards from time to time with the character actors Paul Brooke and Michael Elwyn (real name Michael Emrys-Jones and, like so many actors, the keenest of cricketers) and the versatile Shakespearean Michael Pennington, whose brilliant perform-ance as Prospero in the school production of *The Tempest* was undoubtedly enhanced by my memorable appearance as a sprite. What I remember most about Pennington was his voice. It had an Olivierian timbre and clarity at the age of eighteen and still does, on stage, screen and radio.

I never wanted, nor had the talent, to become an actor but I did take the lead role, that of a character called Dobelle, in an Irish play called *The Moon in the Yellow River*, written by Denis Johnston in 1931; and also in a house production of John Osborne's *Luther*. Both received a reasonable local press but what I most remember about *Luther* is the hours of repeti-tive memorising of the lines that took up most of my time in the previous holiday. I can see myself now on the floor of the study at the Dutch House with my hand over the page repeating speech after speech until each was drummed into the conscious-ness like a cork being squeezed back into a bottle-neck. It was enough to dissuade anyone from the stage.

Much more fun were the end of term concerts in which, towards the end of my schooldays, I used to take a leading part as a mimic, often in cahoots with Humphrey Carpenter. Son of the Bishop of Oxford, Humphrey was another brilliant musician who was equally adept on the tuba, the piano, the bass saxophone and the double bass. He was a natural broadcaster and a prodigious author whose biographies included works on W.H. Auden, Benjamin Britten, Ezra Pound and J.R.R. Tolkein. Both as boy and man, Humphrey, occasionally spotted again at Broadcasting House, always looked dishevelled and, with his long nose and sticking-out ears, a bit like a baby elephant. He was genial, dishevelled and unassuming, although he could bash out fierce critiques on a typewriter.

There was, I suppose, the odd rather dull schoolmaster in my five years at the College, but generally they were a sparkling bunch of characters, not least the ones handpicked by Garnett. They included the two in-College junior housemasters, Dennis Silk and Ian Beer, later headmasters respectively of Radley and Harrow. Garnett had gone to Cambridge to appoint them when they were still undergraduates, one the captain of cricket, the other of rugby.

A house had been designed by a prison architect with stone steps and iron railings around a central well and my father reported that nothing had changed it since his spell at the school in the 1920s. The two dynamic young housemasters counterbalanced the spartan building in which they lived. Both believed that to encourage uncertain adolescents was far more productive than scolding them. Ian was a good-looking fellow with what seemed a permanent half-smile on his face, although his predominant feature was a pair of cauliflower ears, in those days a badge of honour for self-respecting rugby forwards.

Dennis looked and behaved like a great, amiable bear. He had a huge, open, welcoming face with a chin like Desperate Dan's and lively dark eyes. His voice, always beautifully modulated, was distinctively soft: every sentence he uttered seemed to have been carefully considered first, such was the deliberate manner of its deliverance. His first words to me were instantly captivating: 'Well *done,* M-J: you played a blinder.' He was referring to my effort on the left wing for the A2 hockey team, who had defeated his own A1 earlier in the afternoon. Later it was my good fortune to find myself in his fifth form after my O levels. He encouraged me to read far more widely than ever I had before, including works that I would otherwise have avoided, like *Boswell's Life of Johnson* and the poems of A.E. Housman, or others that I might never have considered, such as Robert Graves's *Goodbye To All That*, Sassoon's *Memoirs of a Fox-Hunting Man*, and Elspeth Huxley's *The Flame Trees of Thika*. One way or another Silk remained the biggest influence on my schoolboy progress, bringing the same mighty enthusiasm, sensitivity and bonhomie to his running of the Colts cricket team and, although I did not experience it personally, the always competitive first XV.

In the previous academic year I had begun, at last, to broaden my academic horizons a little under the lead of another outstanding teacher, Arnold Ronald Donald Wright, soon to become headmaster of Shrewsbury. An imposing figure, very tall with a slight stoop, he had a loud voice and was never either dull or predictable. On one occasion he threw a book at a boy called Horsey who had offended him in some way. On another, if the memory does not deceive, he threw a whole desk at someone as well. It was, I think, the tragic Michael Maxwell, one of seven children of the mighty but notorious Robert. A clever, very reserved boy, Michael was involved in a car accident from which he emerged with irreparable brain damage. He remained in a coma for years before dying in 1968.

Wright's philosophy was that his charges should not wait to be taught something. We had to go out and get it. Once our O levels had been taken he allowed us all to do a project of some kind. My friend Timothy Osborn-Jones and I decided that we would write a joint report on the youth of Swindon, which involved cycling to the nearest big town and more or less doing as we pleased. It included going to see *Frankenstein's Monster* at the cinema, with a careful eye on other attendant youths, naturally. The document that I subsequently produced, undoubtedly a fascinating contribution to Sociology in Mid 20th Century Britain, was never read by A.R.D. Wright, because it was lost in a major fire at his house, Littlefield.

That I got sufficient A level grades in History and English to be offered a university place owed much also to the learned Peter Carter, an expert on monasticism, whose handwriting was so minuscule that he could have written the whole of Bede's 'Ecclesiastical History of the English People' on a few pages of foolscap. I caught some of his enthusiasm for monks but not, perhaps, to the same extent as more intelligent and academically minded form-mates, such as Lloyd.

The more down-to-earth Bill Spray, another future headmaster, guided me academically through my last year. He, too, set a fine example as a human being.

My housemaster, Percy Chapman, was an austere clergyman whom few if any of us got to know, but his successor Jake Seamer was a Marlborough 'character' of real character. He remained in the town into his nineties, serving it as Mayor after his retirement from the staff of his old school. He had returned there after colonial service in Sudan, where, in the broiling heat, he claimed a very unusual variation on the rare feat of scoring a hundred before lunch. Jake scored one before breakfast.

With his straight back, craggy jaw, prominent proboscis and spectacles he had a formidable presence and personality and with a bat in his hands you could somehow sense that this was a man of backbone who would neither countenance anything underhand, nor give his wicket away lightly. There was, however, a notable exception, the occasion on which he played for Somerset against Hampshire the morning after a Commem Ball at Oxford. He had not gone to bed, so he was dropped down the order to allow him to get some lost sleep on the physiotherapist's couch.

Alas, Somerset collapsed, an experience not wholly without precedent in those days. Jake was summoned from deep slumber, hastily got his pads and gloves on to go out at the almost instantaneous fall of the next wicket and arrived at the crease in a daze, with a headache, to face Alex Kennedy. Remembering his education at Marlborough – if in doubt, push out – he took a large forward stride to the first ball and heard an ear splitting appeal as the ball thudded into his pad. To his disappointment it was given not out but the second ball struck his front leg again. This time there was no reprieve. Out he walked, aching head down, his emotions a mixture of relief, dejection and embarrassment. When he saw the white of a picket fence ahead of him he was aware of laughter from the crowd. 'Sorry, mate', said Lofty Herman of Hampshire, pointing in the opposite direction. 'The pavilion's that way.'

That story told against himself masked a sporting career of solid achievement. At school he had been a star cricket, rugby and hockey player and at Oxford in the mid 1930s he got both cricket and hockey Blues. His courage and powerful frame must have made him a formidable rugger player too, not least as a hefty, accurate place kicker who would summon a fag from the touchline to hand him his glasses when there was a penalty or a conversion to be taken. Having booted the ball between the posts he would hand the boy his glasses again.

In 1948, a season when Somerset had five different captains, he was one of the three official ones, with his distinguished Oxford and Sudan contemporary 'Mandy' Mitchell-Innes and his fellow Marlburian George Woodhouse. Jake was by now thirty-five, playing on leave from Sudan and although Somerset did not have a great season his personal record of 223 runs in ten games, not out five times batting at number eight, was creditable.

Jake was an obvious candidate to be master in charge of cricket but he preferred to take the second XI while keeping a benign eye on events elsewhere. Mike Griffith recalls his advice that if you were going to play a long innings it wasn't necessary to take a quick single off *every* ball.

John Thompson, known to all as 'JRT', was no less wise an observer of schoolboy cricketers. One of the greatest of all rackets players, he had been a batsman of high class for Cambridge and Warwickshire and he ran the first XI with skill and quiet authority until handing over to David Green, another former county cricketer, in 1964.

JRT too, lived to a great age, ninety-two. He was a wise counsellor, never inclined to exaggerate the importance of cricket in the general scheme of life. Speaking softly, with the words coming slightly from one side of his mouth, he commanded respect and I would hang on every word all the more because there were so few of them. He organised all the practices with quiet efficiency but left much of the coaching to his professional, the jockey-sized all-rounder David Essenhigh, who spoke with a lovely Wiltshire burr and was utterly devoted to the players in his care. JRT seldom intervened. He preached accuracy to his bowlers and, working on the old saw that the best professional bowlers could 'pitch it on a sixpence', he placed a sheet of paper on a length on the off-stump one day and ran a competition to see who hit it most often. To my delight I was comfortably the most consistent of the first XI bowlers and a few days later received a specially produced certificate from JRT pronouncing me officially 'the World's Most Accurate Bowler'. It rammed home the message and made me feel better than I was.

The motto was 'style ahead of strength' when it came to batting, which, sadly, may not fit the bill for the age of the Twenty20 cricketer, even at school. 'The best kind of four is the one that makes the fielder chase the ball all the way to the boundary before it crosses the line ahead of him' he would say. 'You don't need to smite the ball, just to stroke it.' His own batting, still gracing the Wiltshire side in the sixties, demonstrated his message perfectly. His rackets partner was another Marlborough 'beak', David Milford, a shy man with a genius for games and revered as one of England's greatest hockey players.

Hockey was Marlborough's great sport. The main pitch, Level Broadleaze, was always one of the best in the land until artificial surfaces took over. There were at least three future internationals in the school in my time – Griffith, David MacAdam and Rupert McGuigan – and there were always at least a couple of internationals on the staff. Graeme Walker, later headmaster of Harberdashers' Aske's School in New Cross, was the one I remember best, both for his nimbleness and his sense of humour.

School life got better and better for me. Captaining the cricket XI at Lord's and in the weeks leading up to that match against Rugby in 1963 was, despite the distraction of A levels, the focal point. The big disappointment in that last year was that the hockey term was wiped out by the coldest winter since 1947, eliminating any chance I might have had of making the XI. But I left in a mood that mixed elation, nostalgia and optimism, after one last end-of-term concert and a final, hearty rendition of the two school songs that always sent everyone to bed happy on the last night of term. One, to a rollicking tune by Sir George Dyson, had been sung by leavers since the Christmas Concert of 1912, with rousing lines by J. Bain that included 'we all must go in time my lads'; and the heartfelt chorus: 'We're all going home in the morning'!

'The Old Bath Road', the other hardy perennial, also had a memorable tune by Dr. J. W. Ivimey and lyrics by C. L. F. Boughey that started: Strong and true on its western stages/Girt by downland and tree-clad hill/Strong and true as in bygone ages/the Old Bath Road fares onward still/And strong and true the young with the older/Stands the school, our youth's abode/Side by side and shoulder to shoulder/Guarding the flanks of the Old Bath Road.

There had been 800 boys at Marlborough at any time in my five years so it is not surprising that a week seldom goes by without my bumping into one of my contemporaries. Sadly, that is not true of any of my closest friends at the school. Richard Allen, whose sense of humour was absolutely the same as mine, went to Canada and died of cancer in his thirties. Two others, A.J. (Adrian) Coote, a brilliant games player, and Robert Tiarchs (son of the Archdeacon of the Isle of Wight, rather a fine title I always thought), who was a good companion in Bill Spray's History Upper Vth class, went to University in Canada and remained there; and Nick Parkinson, whose pink podginess belied his great natural ability as a games player, especially as a left-arm swing bowler who had defeated Winchester almost by himself in 1963, followed the melancholy example of his father, a doctor from the Fens, by taking his own life.

I did not really begin to understand the dreadful spectre of depression until years later when an even more gifted and far more extrovert friend, Robin Skinner, a respected solicitor loved by everyone and the successful head of a thriving family, left his office in Sussex one afternoon and walked in front of a train. In Robin's case the tragedy might to an extent have been caused by a prescription for the wrong pills and I have since witnessed how a change of medicine brought about the sudden revival of a famous cricketer, Hubert Doggart, following years of depression.

There were no such shadows over my own outlook at the age of eighteen. Immediately ahead lay Lord's, a family holiday in Portugal and a gap year that gradually took shape after John Dancy, a classical scholar of high intellect, had suggested in his final report that this workaday academic might develop further at a University. Once the future had been planned I used the rest of that precious year enjoyably, if less altruistically than so many of those leaving sixth forms at both state and independent schools these days. I worked a passage on a ship to and from South Africa; taught a summer term at a prep school in the Surrey hills (where the irascible and cricket-ignorant headmaster wanted to beat an unfortunate boy called Morton-Clarke for practising the shot he had just played after being dismissed); and wrote a naïve novel about a cricket commentator in love with a Scots lassie who had accidentally killed an intruder at her cottage in the Highlands.

Neither this nor a subsequent attempt at acquiring literary fame through a thriller, written in a summer vacation, about an England cricketer kidnapped by a terrorist during a tour of the West Indies, deserved to see the light of day. I had kept quiet about these absorbing but misguided hours of toil, until admitting them to, of all people, Jeffrey Archer. I felt unable to fib when, sitting beside him one day at a lunch or dinner, he asked me directly if I had ever tried writing a novel. Persuasive as he was, at least before his unfortunate fall from grace, I found myself digging the second manuscript out of a drawer and sending it to him. I had to press hard for its return many months later. That he felt unable to recommend a publisher and that not a hint of plagiarism has been evident in any of his best sellers since is, I think, a fair enough indication that I was never cut out to be a serious writer.

Many journalists are to be admired, certainly, but not so much as good novelists. The cross that each of the successful ones must bear, of course, is that, like professional sportsmen, they are seldom able to reach the heights time and again.

6

CAMBRIDGE

October 1964. A huge sky, coloured pale blue like sunlit Arctic ice from horizon to horizon. I am riding a battered old bicycle at pace, biting wind smarting the ears and making the nose run despite a striped and voluminous woollen scarf wrapped round my neck and jammed below the collar of my duffel coat as I speed down the hill into the majestic centre of the second oldest University city in England. The journey continues beside the river for a time, then out towards one of those tree-lined, flat, quiet streets towards the comfortable but characterless suburban house where the lofty, red-nosed Mr Hide is waiting to start my first supervision in Economic History. At University you go looking for knowledge.

At school I had been a boy. At Cambridge I was suddenly, officially at least, a man. A gentleman indeed. Letters from Fitzwilliam College in advance of my arrival addressed me as 'Mr.' and any written regulations always referred to gentlemen, a quaint throwback to the days of the fictional Sebastian Flyte and earlier, when you had to have money, if not necessarily manners, to go to Oxbridge. Fitzwilliam, sometime 'House, sometime 'Hall', had actually been founded by 19th century philanthropists wanting to offer a Cambridge education to those who could not afford to pay for it. My poor father, having sacrificed a lot in order to educate three sons at Marlborough, willingly forked out a bit more to keep me fed, watered and brain-trained for three more years, and glorious years they were.

There were virtually no rules and everyone was entirely responsible for himself. Nobody told you what to do. You found everything out from notice-boards and the grape vine. This was a first taste of real freedom and arguably the last because once marriage, mortgages and children come along, most of us are tied to our responsibilities like string to a balloon.

No wonder I, like so many, remember my University years as the happiest of my life. Once the complete strangeness of it all had passed it was like walking out of a dark room onto a high and windblown downland path. Life, suddenly, was what you made it, not what someone made for you.

Other than a reputation for being a useful all-rounder I did not really have much to offer Cambridge but if I were being kind to myself I would say that someone had spotted unrealised potential when they offered me a place to study the Modern History tripos. Then, as now, there were advantages for some in failing to get to University and sometimes thereby stealing a march in the workplace on those who spent three years or more as a student, but in my case three years at Cambridge were the making of the rest of my life. There I met and fell in love with Judy Hayman, my future wife, although not until my final days in residence, which enabled me to plough my own cheerful furrow while I continued the process of growing, as it were, to my full height.

In the three years leading to my last minute invitation to Judy to come with me to the May Ball at her father's old college, St. John's, in June 1967 (life at Cambridge sometimes seemed like a fantasy so May week was, as Clive James has observed, naturally, in June) I learned to discipline my writing. Infinitely more than that, I broadened my knowledge of much more than Modern History, the subject in which I somehow emerged with a 2.1 and an MA.

All things are relative but the many bright and industrious school leavers who do not get even a sniff of Oxford or Cambridge these days would, quite rightly, feel infuriated that I should have been offered a place at both the great universities of England on the basis of two A levels, neither of them in the top grade. Both offers were conditional on my passing Elementary Maths O level, which I had failed twice.

I managed it with ease after leaving school, thanks largely to a retired colonial servant called Laurence Edwards, who lived at Dorking and made it all seem very simple. He encouraged me to write my own handwritten book of geometrical theorems, entitled something like 'The Golden Treasury of Knowledge'. It said little for my previous Maths teachers and even less for myself that I had believed it all to be so difficult. Yet I can understand how some people can actually find beauty in Maths because I still remember my delight when one of my St. Bede's Maths teachers (Mr. Hilary-Smith, whose other main attribute was having a beautiful daughter named Magnolia) taught me algebraic equations that I actually understood and found easy. Edwards told me that detectives are taught algebra and geometry to help their brains take logical steps from one point to another. Suddenly I came to see the purpose of it all, but I still envy those who find Maths easy. Even supposedly great economists do not always do so. A journalist acquaintance of mine happened to share a train carriage with Lord (Nigel) Lawson, the distinguished former Chancellor of the Exchequer, who, so he claimed at least, spent the whole of a longish journey wrestling with the easiest Su Doko puzzle in his newspaper.

I would have been quite pleased with a second class second and not surprised if it had been a third. The higher grading had not the slightest effect on my subsequent career, but it had two advantages. I could pretend, fooling nobody and strictly in jest, that I had narrowly missed a first; and I could claim parity with the tubby little bespectacled fellow from Kendal in Cumbria who had sat the tripos with me amongst a small group of historians accepted by Fitzwilliam College in 1964. He was quite obviously cleverer than any of us.

David Starkey went on to become the nation's best known and best paid television historian. Perhaps the examiners thought that he needed taking down a peg or two but he soon became more famous than any of them, even the mighty Geoffrey Elton, uncle of Ben, whose lively lectures had been the greatest attraction for history students in my time and whose books on and around the Tudor Constitution had changed previous opinions of the likes of Henry VIII, Thomas Wolsey and Thomas Cromwell. It was only when he and I accepted an invitation, from one of the many university societies, to return to Cambridge to discuss current affairs questions from an intellectual audience that I appreciated why he had pursued his calling with such relish despite somehow having failed to get the first in his final year that everyone had expected of him. It did not seem to knock even a puff out of his sails, let alone the wind. He had got firsts in parts one and two and had always spoken as a student as if he were already a don. Tested by a live audience, the adult Starkey, exuding confidence like Toad in his motor car, was sharp, witty and opinionated on any subject raised, while I floundered in the shallow end but raised a few laughs.

Of all the brilliant intellects with whom I have briefly worked in some capacity or other only Clive James or Stephen Fry would have shone with even greater brilliance in the same circumstances. Starkey incidentally is openly homosexual, but at Cambridge in the 1960s his inclination had never crossed my mind. Those with similar genes no doubt recognised each other but I don't think that the rest of us even noticed.

It would not be true to say that I was as unaware of social class as I was of sexual orientation, because I always had a keen ear for regional accents, but where a person had been to school really did not matter. Public school 'types' were in a smallish minority at Fitzbilly anyway – it had been founded originally for those who could not afford to pay the fees – but I'm sure I would have been as much at home in the broad social mix had I accepted an offer from University College at Oxford to read English Literature. That had appealed to me just as much, if not more, than a History course but I had got on well with the Fitzwilliam Tutor for Admissions, Norman Walters, known to the undergraduates as 'Ron', when I went to see him as I weighed up my two offers. I did not enjoy the prospect of having to learn Anglo-Saxon, then a compulsory discipline for anyone reading English at Oxford, and I liked the way that the genial Walters stressed the corporate spirit of Fitzwilliam House. Kicking against the increasing trend towards taking in undergraduates solely on their academic ability, Walters, who died much too young a few years later, believed in a broad, eclectic mix and it worked wonderfully well. The Fitzwilliam of my time held a respectable place in academic tables but also won more than its fair share of sporting trophies and produced plays and revues of a relatively high standard from a small and up-to-date theatre. I had fun taking part in two of the revues, entitled, as I recall, *If It Fitz* and *Fitz The Bill*.

Fitzwilliam was about to receive full collegiate status and had just moved into new buildings on the Huntingdon Road. To my eye the architect, Denys Lasdun, had created a design of little beauty: low, flat-roofed buildings in a particularly unattractive mud-brown brick encircling what were then immature lawns. But the glass and concrete Hall, especially its striking roof, was light and interesting, foreshadowing his more famous National Theatre. Moreover, like the NT, the buildings worked in practice. Now that new courts have been added and the gardens have grown and matured, 'Fitz', as the students call it today, or 'Billy', as it was known in my time, is a pleasing place to live and work.

In my first year I regretted only the fact that, with limited accommodation for its expanded intake, the freshmen were posted to digs some way from the college. Mine were at Chesterton Road, which meant endless bicycle rides up the hill to get to meals, playing fields, the library, the chapel (in those days not purpose built) and all other college activities. Lectures on the other hand were more easily accessible, over Magdalene Bridge and down King's Parade towards the Backs. That was the heart of Cambridge and getting there was a good reason to go to lectures, but I soon learned, alas, that the weekly essays, written for various supervisors in different aspects of the syllabus, were best written with the help of books rather than lecture notes.

My digs overlooked the Cam and what in summer were majestic weeping willows. It was a large and draughty house, however, and my landlady would have given the unreformed Scrooge more than a run for his money. She stuck the plug of the electric fire to the wall with sellotape to discourage unnecessary use of such a luxury as heat. Baths, in a freezing garret like the one in which Mimi expired with consumption in *La Bohème*, had to be applied for in advance. The water was hot but the air around it so cold in winter that one felt for the soap (one's own, naturally) through a thick fog of steam. Within minutes, moreover, the water in the bath would be lukewarm and any attempt to refill was likely to create a thump on the door and an enraged entreaty not to use up all the hot water.

I made the first of several good Cambridge friends at Chesterton Road: David Martin the future MP for Portsmouth South, and uncle of the Coldplay lead singer Chris, alias Mr. Gwyneth Paltrow. The fact that we were Martin and Martin-Jenkins suggested that the allocation of digs by the College was strictly alphabetical so it was fortunate that we got on so well. We had spacious individual rooms, more expensive than most because of their size and the view. David, reading Law, had right wing views quite out of tune with the swinging sixties but inherited from his father, a staunch rural Conservative who had made his own money running a caravan business near Exeter. He was less energetic than I, although a hard-hitting left-handed fives player who got into the Cambridge team in his last year to claim, with some espousal from me, his coveted membership of the Hawks' Club. That entitled him to the tie, a status symbol at Westminster if ever there was one. I owe him most for my proper introduction to classical music. The surging climax of Elgar's Nimrod was my easy way in.

We shared digs in our second year, too, much nearer Fitzwilliam at 14, Priory Street, where our landlady, Mrs. Robinson, was much more hospitable, although not to the extent of her namesake in *The Graduate*. She cooked her tenants breakfast every day and had a heart of gold rather than cold like her predecessor. Her husband, a retired policeman, kept himself to himself and was more in evidence at night when his snores would resonate through the little house. In a cartoon the walls would have bulged and contracted with every breath.

Priory Street was only a short bicycle ride away from the College's playing fields at Oxford Road, where excellent cricket, rugby and hockey pitches, not to mention grass tennis courts, were tended by 'Sarge' Bemmant, who had a house next door to the pavilion. Cambridge's flat playing fields were generally marvellous surfaces on which to play any sport and Sarge's acres were no exception, although, like most groundsmen, he would have been happier if no one had actually played on them at all, especially after rain.

I failed to get a cricket Blue despite playing in three final trials on freezing April days at Fenner's and I have sometimes wondered if a different selection system in Oxford cricket might have worked better for me than the one then prevailing at Cambridge, whose captain had supreme power of selection but who tended to rely on the necessarily hasty opinions of George Cox during the April nets. George, whom I later got to know a little when we were speaking together at cricket dinners (he was brilliant in that role), only looked closely at my batting once in the April nets in my first year, when I was in one of those apprehensive moods that I often used to have in the nets rather than in the middle. It was cold, someone was bowling quickly at me and I was reluctant to get fully behind the line. Had helmets been around then I suppose I would have shown my capabilities better but I was not surprised that he wrote me off.

The Cambridge captain in my year as a freshman, Raymond White, seemed more interested in my potential. Apart from a one-day game for Cambridge against a Dutch university, in which my rival for an all-rounder's place, captain for the day, seemed to me to make sure that I batted low in the order and got no chance to bowl, a single three-day game for the Quidnuncs against the University was the only real opportunity to come my way. Fate decreed that I did not take the opportunity. I held a swirling skier but failed to take a wicket in a brief spell of bowling while Cambridge built a total well in excess of 300 on a sunny Saturday. The game resumed on a misty morning on the

Monday when the ball swung like a swallow and the Quidnuncs collapsed rapidly. I managed to make batting look impossible as my former school captain, Jonathan Harvey, curved the ball late past my groping edge two or three times before hitting my off stump.

White, who had made his mark indelibly with a century against the 1964 Australians, became one of the more liberal figures amongst white cricket administrators in his native South Africa. Years later he told me that he regretted having not given me a run in the University side. There were a lot of small politics involved in selection and I was not good at selling myself by drinking with the right people. You have to look after yourself in this world to get on, a lesson I learned in those days and perhaps applied to an extent when I got to the BBC. At least I captained Fitzwilliam to its first ever win in Cuppers, the inter-collegiate tournament, got two half-Blues at Rugby fives, made several life-long friends and revelled in the sheer fun of University life.

Several sporting contemporaries were already familiar to readers of newspaper back pages. Mark Cox was Britain's best tennis player; Mike Gibson was one of the great Rugby Union all-round three-quarters and Deryck Murray, captain of the University in my second year, was already established in the West Indies Test team, a diminutive hero from Port of Spain with a high-pitched voice.

I liked Deryck both then and in occasional meetings in future years but unfortunately for me he refused to change his team during my second year, when belatedly I showed some form for the college and the Crusaders (University second XI). Perhaps he gave cricket too much attention, however, because when it came to the History exams I was, since our names both began with the same letter, seated close enough to him to witness his putting his name at the top of the paper before sighing deeply several times. He wrote nothing further about questions that were clearly on subjects that to him were a total blank. He was duly sent down but he took his studies more seriously at Nottingham and whenever I have seen him since he has been doing something important, such as representing Trinidad and Tobago at the United Nations.

Winning Cuppers in my third season was easily the highlight of my cricket at Cambridge. There was a wonderful spirit in the Billy side that I led, especially in the field. We had several talented players but only one Blue, my friend Vijaya Malalasekera, who has ever afterwards called me 'Skip'. He played one brilliant innings in the semi-final against St. Catherine's that helped him to get back into the University team, but we won the final without him, thanks to some steady new ball bowling in particular by Peter Hickson, a great trier who went on to become a captain of industry with such companies as Powergen, Anglia Water and Scottish Power.

I also played hockey for the Billy XI and a final game of rugby for one of the less exalted College teams one afternoon when they were short. I scored a try after a long run when all I had to do was catch the ball and run with it, virtually unopposed. It seemed the right moment to announce my retirement.

It was Rugby fives, however, that took most of my sporting time in the winter months. For me, although I played some squash for the College too, it was more fun than the more commonly played of the small court games, mainly because so much of it was doubles, played by pairs, rather than in singles. Whacking the little white ball round the court with gloved hands was tremendous fun, demanded quick reactions, fitness, good hand-to-eye co-ordination and a rapport with one's partner. If it was a left-hand/right-hand combination it helped, of course, but both my partners for Cambridge in the University match were, like me, right handers. Chris Bascombe went on to be an actuary, Chris Hirst to become the very successful headmaster first of Kelly College, then of Sedbergh.

Fives and schoolmasters seemed to go together, not least because the president of Cambridge Fives, the remarkable Jock Burnet, founder of the Jesters Club and bursar of Magdalene, played a part in encouraging potential teachers amongst the many undergraduates he befriended. Peter Commings, my first captain, was one of them. Jock was a smallish, sturdy, very quietly spoken man with an owlish look and a quick, dry wit. He had an extraordinary influence without ever pushing anyone into anything against their will. He would get up at five o'clock every morning to write copious letters in a neat hand. Having dealt with the College's finances and staff matters, he pursued his other interests as a governor of several schools, an expert on Church history and books generally, and mentor to many undergraduates. The sherry parties given every Sunday by Jock and his faithful wife, Pauline, at their house, 28, Selwyn Gardens, were legendary. He was driven by the sort of Christian faith described by Edward Lyttelton as 'the quiet resolve to believe what you hope may be true before you know that it is'.

My own journey during my Cambridge days to a faith much like that expressed by Lyttelton, as opposed to any evangelical certainty, was encouraged instead by Peter Nott, the chaplain at Fitzwilliam, an excellent preacher who seldom gave a sermon without raising a laugh. I have often used a story he told during one evening service about Field Marshal Montgomery, who allegedly interrupted the lesson that he was reading at a service in St Paul's Cathedral when he got to the point where the disciples asked Jesus who was the greatest in the Kingdom of Heaven. 'Jesus said', intoned the great soldier in a voice echoing down off the dome, 'and I must say that I am inclined to agree with him.'

As Bishop of Norwich, the one referred to by Princess Diana in a letter as 'that bloody Bishop' after a Christmas at Sandringham, Peter Nott's most valuable contribution may have been to insist that the reforming Church did not try to modernise the Lord's Prayer as it had so much of the Church's liturgy. Thanks to his wisdom 'deliver us from evil' did not, in most churches, become 'do not bring us to the time of trial'. Nor were any of the other familiar words altered, as many phrases from Thomas Cranmer's Book of Common Prayer have been, to no great purpose and often at the expense of the lovely rhythm of the old language.

Peter told me two stories about one of his earliest services in the Cathedral, held at eight am on a freezing winter's morning. Blue with cold the new Bishop remarked to one of his oldest choristers that it was not very warm in the vestry. 'You should feel what it's like when the central heating isn't on' was the veteran's response. It may or may not have been the same stalwart of whom Peter inquired, at their first meeting, whether he had lived in Norwich all his life? The answer, in broad Norfolk dialect, was precise: 'not yet'.

Dialects, once heard, came naturally to me, and I put that small talent to good use when I plucked up the necessary courage to perform an act based on impersonations at one of the 'smoking concerts' by which one gained entry to that famous reservoir of British comedy, the Footlights. The smoke, trapped like thick fog inside a fusty upper room, was positively disgusting, but from time to time I made further appearances in these concerts and I was always generously received, as performers invariably were.

My brother Tim, who followed me to Fitzwilliam along with several other Marlburians in the next few years, joined me in what was probably the best of these acts, in my last year. It was a simple parody on Kipling's poem 'If', in which both of us recited the lines in front of a mirror with appropriate variations, he as Harold Wilson, myself as Edward Heath.

For a time we appeared as a double act, 'Brothers In Cabaret', entertaining during parties at Cambridge, auditioning at Quaglino's and the Blue Angel in London, and getting a shortlived professional contract at the Burford Bridge hotel in Dorking, until, following two more or less triumphant half hour cabarets, we caused offence to our third audience when I impersonated the Queen's Christmas message. I had done this many times before without annoying anyone but it is extraordinary how differently audiences will react. The manager, a European with the unusual name of Otensooser, decided that he could not risk further complaints from customers offended by such irreverence. My career as a professional comedian was abruptly terminated.

At that time the Footlights always performed a concert at the Edinburgh Festival. I went to a final selection audition for this, performing before Clive James, the President, the equally forceful Germaine Greer and Eric Idle, who was the outstanding comic genius in Cambridge at the time and who succeeded James as President the following year. Musical talent was also required to get into the Edinburgh cast, however, and my rendition of Cole Porter's 'Night and Day' was almost certainly excruciating. (Try singing it: it is not easy, unless you are related to Frank Sinatra.) In any case my ambitions were certainly not fixed on anything thespian. I had gone to the trouble of learning the song with some reluctance, knowing that if I were to be invited to join the Edinburgh cast it would mean missing the two-day match between the respective cricket second XIs, the Cambridge Crusaders and the Oxford Authentics. I was therefore relieved not to be invited, but I fell firmly between two stools because I had an undistinguished match against the Authentics, making a particularly bad duck in the first innings after overindulging, uncharacteristically, the night before.

There were other, more 'serious', comic talents up at Cambridge at that time. One of the most brilliant was a medic named David Lund, a pianist and gifted comedy writer, but Clive and Germaine, both graduates from Australia destined to spend much of their life in Cambridge, and Idle, soon to make his name, and fortune, as the zaniest and most original writing contributor to *Monty Python's Flying Circus*, were the brightest stars. Eric was the funniest, Germaine the one who wrote the most influential book; but as a writer, poet, essayist and broadcaster, Clive James would get my vote as victor ludorum.

He would do more justice than I can to the greatest experience in anyone's life, falling in love. There are many ways to do it and there is a great paradox to mine, because my relationship with Judy was at once love at first sight and a slowly developing realisation that she was the one.

Attraction at first sight would therefore be the truer description of the night in the dining hall at Fitzwilliam that I spotted her several tables away: a dark-haired, slim, tallish girl with hazel eyes and a wide smile. She was the guest of someone else for dinner that night and even if she had shared my attraction we would both have been far too polite to approach one another. We had not, after all, been introduced. This was only 1967, neither of us had been brought up in London, she had been to a sheltered girls' school in Oxford, Greycotes, I to one at Marlborough which had not yet taken the bold step towards co-education.

It was later in that same term, I think, that Fitzwilliam staged a winter ball. Convention required my attendance. Tina Tipper, a sweet girl from Shalford, closely guarded by her father, a retired Major, and a welcoming mother who seemed less suspicious than her spouse of this young man's intentions towards their very pretty daughter, had been my companion at one or two social occasions at Cambridge in the previous year but for some reason – perhaps that she had already sensed that she was more a useful adornment at parties than a girlfriend to whom I was seriously committed – she was not available for the Billy March Ball. So I plucked up courage and asked a luscious girl from the neighbouring female college, New Hall. Susanna Duncan was buxom and something of a Cambridge Zuleika Dobson. I dare say there was even some envy that she had accepted the rare pleasure of acting as my partner for the occasion. But the moments in the evening that lingered in my memory were those when Judy, her beauty less confidently advertised, came to my little study/bedroom at Fitzwilliam to leave her coat on my bed.

She was partnering David Martin that evening and I was the slowest of suitors. The looming reality of exams took precedence in my life, with fives, cricket and evenings with the lads at pubs like the Castle and the Cricketers. Only in the last few weeks of the summer term of 1967, with exams at last over, did I think properly again about Judy. I needed a pretext and in those last few days of a total freedom such as none but post examination students ever experience, I was given two. With five friends I hosted a drinks party on one of the College lawns. A few days later Judy accepted the invitation to the St. John's May Ball that I had driven over to Homerton in the Morris Minor to deliver.

Nothing else in my Cambridge life had been redolent of *Brideshead Revisited* but this long evening was, starting with a candlelit dinner in the St. John's hall that included, like some Tudor banquet, roasted swan. We danced all night, literally, whenever we were not attending various cabarets by various well known artists at the time. The singer Long John Baldry stays in the memory as one of them. By the time that we were having coffee by the river some time after dawn (I am afraid that I did not risk trying to punt along the Cam in my state of at least semi-inebriation) I knew that I was not going to let Judy go if I could help it.

Despite that it was some time before I stirred myself to ask her out in London. It should really have been something more highbrow – Judy knows her Shakespeare well for a start – but I plumped for the extremely undemanding *Way Out In Piccadilly*. Frankie Howerd was the star. Brilliant with a live audience, he had everyone helpless with laughter simply with 'Ooh, yes, no, listen' etc., accompanied by a familiar range of facial expressions and the occasional anxious look over his shoulder, indicating that we alone were party to his revelations. His co-star, Anita Harris, sang 'I could spend my life just loving you, if you would only learn to love me too' which summed up my feelings rather well.

I haunted Cambridge periodically for the rest of Judy's time at Homerton and when she began teaching at Abingdon we would meet halfway at Henley every week and spend weekends as often as possible at one or other of our parental homes. My parents soon adored her and I greatly liked her mother, a modest but tireless bastion of local good causes at Brackley in Northamptonshire, where she had lived since marrying the widely revered headmaster of Winchester House School, C.H. Telford Hayman. Sadly, he had died when Judy was only two.

We knew that we would get married long before I finally got round to a formal proposal in my car on the edge of the Thames at Henley in May 1970, following an especially good dinner. By then my future at the BBC was looking reasonably assured. I had a regular salary and, by staying at my father's business flat in

Hallam Street during the week rather than taking up what would have been, no doubt, a more enjoyable option to join two cricketing friends, Richard Johnson and Graham Prain, at their flat in Chelsea, I was able to save enough money to get a mortgage the following spring. We were married at St. Peter's Church in Brackley on 17 April 1971 and ever since I have been thankful for my good luck. Everyone who knows Judy will know why.

7

THE CRICKETER MAGAZINE

A few short hours after breakfast and the bright June dawn that ended a blissful first evening with Judy at the St. John's May Ball, we have gone our separate ways on urgent business. Typically dutiful, she is off to a lecture after two May Balls in a row — I was not her only suitor. I, bleary-eyed, am on my way to The Oval to make my first acquaintance with the legendary Daily Telegraph *cricket writer and BBC pundit E. W. Swanton. He has chosen the Surrey/Kent match to meet me in The Oval pavilion's version of the Long Room, interviewing me informally for the post as assistant to the deputy editor of* The Cricketer. *He looks a little too big for the high chair on which he sits, making occasional notes, and sometimes humming. 'This is my man' he says, smiling paternally as the youthful Alan Knott comes out to bat.*

I was by no means the only one on the shortlist for the vacancy at *The Cricketer* and it took some time for an offer to come my way: £700 a year, I think it was. Slave labour it was to be, too, but I was on my way and Ernest William or 'Jim' Swanton, known and respected, if not universally loved, by everyone in cricket, was as good and influential a mentor as an aspiring cricket journalist could wish to have.

Unless you were training for a rigorous mountain climb you ascended to the single office of The Cricketer Ltd in the autumn of 1967 by means of one of those old lifts typical of London clubs and small hotels, with two gates, the first one made of iron that needed to be clanged shut by hand before you pressed a button for the relevant floor and waited for the second door to labour by electric power to a closed position. Then, after a dignified pause, like an old person catching breath, the cage began to lift slowly and with almost human creaks and groans to the main floor of the Hutchinson Publishing group. Jim, persuasive as ever, had urged two cricketing and golfing friends to become the proprietors of a magazine that had been living from hand to mouth since its foundation by Pelham Warner in 1921.

Down the corridor from the spacious offices of the chairman and vice-chairman, the charming Bimby Holt and bluntly-spoken Noel Holland, Old Harrovians both and in their different ways not unaware of the grandeur of their status, stood an office occasionally visited by an even more important and much more famous representative of the Kent establishment, Swanton himself, no less.

Being editorial director of *The Cricketer*, to whose future well being he was devoted, gave Jim a convenient London base, more private than the Bath Club, his other haunt in town. His role was to write magisterial editorials each fortnight, to plan the magazine's editorial strategy and to use his huge circle of world-wide cricketing contacts to order articles for future issues. No one in my memory ever refused him, despite a miserly payment of one guinea per 100 words, 'for all our contributors great and small', as Jim's standard letter, typed for him by a lean and beautiful blonde secretary named Julie Firmin, always made clear. J.J. Warr once responded: 'Dear Jim, delighted to write the 500 word piece on Cambridge's prospects for the season as you request, at your usual rate of a guinea a word.'

In spite of his reputation for pomposity Jim was quite capable of seeing the funny side of that but he never pretended to be a hands-on editor. The nuts and bolts of getting the magazine edited, designed and printed he left to others, very *few* others indeed as I was rapidly to discover.

If John Warr's letter hinted to me that it was possible to get beneath the haughty carapace of Jim's character to the more considerate heart of the man, it was not until he asked me to play for his Arabs team on a short tour of Kent that I began to relax in his company. Colin Ingleby-Mackenzie was a fellow guest for supper at Delf House, Jim and Ann Swanton's elegant house in one of the narrow medieval streets of Sandwich. Throughout the meal he pulled the great man's leg so frequently and to such hilarious effect that I never again took him quite so seriously.

Despite that I remained to some extent as a pupil to a schoolmaster in relation to Jim during my first stint at *The Cricketer*. I remember his ringing me on the Sunday morning in August 1968 after Basil D'Oliveira had been left out of the MCC touring party to South Africa that winter despite his commanding innings of 158 against Australia in the Oval Test match the previous week. 'Morning, Christopher', he began. 'You've read the *Sunday Times* I suppose?' Alas, I had not.

'Yes', of course, I lied hesitantly, terrified of not being on the ball on so important an issue.

'What do you think?'

I felt like a child caught cheating. No doubt it was obvious from my subsequent blustering prevarication that I was unaware of the precise nature of allegations of a cover-up by the establishment and of political collusion with the hated, and soon to be assassinated, John Vorster. There had been at least a nod and a wink that the controversial 'Cape Coloured', as South Africans knew him, would be left out of the team to avoid controversy wherever he played in his native land.

Jim was no establishment man himself when it came to race issues but he subsequently disapproved of the uncompromising cover that I had chosen for the September issue of the magazine two days before, with the single word REJECTED screaming from a picture of D'Oliveira driving during his great innings. Like most people I was incensed that he had been left out and smelt a rat, almost certainly wrongly.

Unless Jim was paying one of his occasional visits to the office my only confidant and sounding post, even that early in my time on the magazine, was a hard-bitten, experienced and likeable *Daily Mail* journalist, George Rutherford, who helped me with the layout. One of his sub-editors, Ken Willson, would come down with me to the printers, Taylor, Garnett, Evans, to 'put the paper to bed' in Watford every fortnight. That was a tedious business because the compositors were so incredibly bound by Trade Union rule and custom, apparently to make every job as time consuming and long-drawn out as possible. I would play jocular verbal games with Stan Taylor, a world-weary old boy in a cloth cap and long brown overalls, who was father of the chapel and would call a meeting (virtually) every time that I wanted to change a word on the stone.

'TGE' was a modern lithographic printer but this was still the days of hot metal and every alteration had to be paid for. Thus, like every editor, I was caught between my desire to produce as accurate, readable and attractive a magazine as possible and the wish of the proprietors, in this case Hutchinson, to keep down costs. I had been thrust into the editorial deep end because within a month of my arrival at Great Portland

Street the official deputy editor, the unique, eccentric Irving Rosenwater, had resigned on some matter of principle that he never explained to me.

Irving had originally made himself more than useful to Swanton as a sort of Man Friday and he continued to read his copy to the *Telegraph*, saving the great man from the considerable chore of getting his pieces across at matches, making sure on his behalf that every comma was in the right place and no doubt prompting him on such matters as dates and records. Despite his humble background, Irving spoke, like his master, in a clear, well modulated voice, so there was little room for doubt from the copy-taker on the other end of the line.

Even in our short time together Irving taught me quite a bit about the nuts and bolts of producing a fortnightly, particularly how to prepare 'copy' (usually typewritten, sometimes handwritten) for the printers, who had to be told what typeface and what sized type were wanted; and how to make corrections on the side of galleys (proofs) which would come back from the printers each day on a van, full of errors. He pointed out to me how dangerous a little knowledge could be. For example the printers' reader would invariably change M.J. Smith of Middlesex to M.J.K. Smith (of Warwickshire) because he had heard of the latter but not the former.

Irving was by then in his forties and the ideal workhorse so far as Jim was concerned. He was the most precise, punctilious cricketing scholar I ever met, far more stubborn than any mule who has ever dug his toes into the sliding grit of a mountain pass. Born and bred in Stepney, presumably of pre-war Jewish immigrants, he lived until his death in 33, Diggon Street, surrounded and eventually virtually buried by paper, because he hoarded everything like a squirrel in autumn. He would even go fossicking into waste-paper baskets at Lord's in case any letter that might be of historical interest had been discarded.

I believed he thought of nothing else until years later when, as a television scorer, he was accused of groping a young secretary and lost his job with Channel Nine.

When I started pressing, in due course, for some supplementary income and experience, both badly needed, Jim typically did his best for me, writing to Roger Fowler-Wright, sports editor of the *Sunday Telegraph*. It led to some free-lance soccer reporting in the winter months, which I greatly enjoyed, although Jim would not let me write under my own name. Instead my pieces appeared, not very subtly, under the by-line 'Christopher Martin'.

Producing reports of the right length at speed to meet the various Sunday paper deadlines (often before the match had finished, indeed) required careful wording and certain foresight, although the matches that I attended were relatively lowly and I knew little about any of the players. Before the first match, at Vicarage Road, Watford, I did my best subtly to pick the brains of the local fans with whom I was travelling by public transport. As we got to the entrance to the ground the man to whom I had been talking (who had assumed that I was a fellow fan) said: 'Still, I expect it'll be a different game when we read about it in the morning.'

I was on safer ground writing about cricket, but it was only a matter of days after Irving's abrupt departure, which he assured me had nothing to do with my arrival, that someone rang up and asked a question about 'Kortright'. 'Do you mean Cartwright, Tom Cartwright of Warwickshire and England?' I replied. 'No', he said with irritation. 'Kortright. Haven't you heard of Kortright?'

To my shame and embarrassment I had indeed not heard of Charles Kortright, the fastest amateur bowler of his (and W.G.'s) day. I resolved at once to read, mark, learn and try inwardly to digest my cricket history. I loved the game but knew insufficient about its legacy to be in the lucky position that I now found myself. Far too many pundits since have been ignorant of the past. Without a knowledge of those who went before your own era you cannot put modern players and events into perspective.

By reading and subbing the pieces of such gifted writers as the elegant and imaginative Neville Cardus – whose copy was always handwritten and by no means easy to discern in places – or the lighter but always readable and often amusing Ian Peebles, I learned quickly about former events and players, not to mention the art of writing.

Jim gradually trusted me to do some writing of my own, having covered his tracks by disassociating the magazine from some of my views in my first 'feature' piece for the magazine which, being entitled 'In Defence of Professionalism', was not entirely in accord with his own philosophy. Most of my early pieces were anonymous, under the title of 'Cricketer's Notes' which allowed me to convey small items of news, mainly from the game's lower reaches. Club cricket also came within my compass – all grist to the mill – although I did find myself having to produce something nearer the front of the magazine, in a hurry, very early in my editorial role.

At Jim's insistence we had trumpeted the fact that in the 1968 Spring Annual Richie Benaud, revered Australian captain turned sharply observant journalist, would be assessing the newly selected Australia team to England. When the deadline for the piece came there was no sign of any copy from Richie and all my attempts to contact him failed. Jim must have been abroad or also out of reach for some other reason, so there was nothing for it but to delay publication, which would have been ruinously expensive, or to ghost a piece myself on Richie's behalf. With what now seems to me like brazen presumption I duly did so, affecting a certain racy Aussie style and affecting also to give my opinion on players such as Doug Walters and Paul Sheahan, who were about to visit England for the first time and whom I had never seen play.

When the piece appeared Jim said nothing and apparently approved of what I had concocted. I felt obliged to own up. Richie never complained either, although whether he got paid and what had happened to delay his material I do not remember. I am sure that he would never knowingly have missed a deadline. As a broadcaster, of course, he became a legend, still going strong in Australia as I write, making his shrewd, wry comments on Channel Nine with measured poise and jutting lower lip, at the age of eighty. 'Good bit of bowling that by Graeme Swann, that was the top spinner', he would say, and, though Richie spotted more top spinners than most, invariably the observation would be sagacious. Unlike almost all the other TV commentators, Richie understands the value of silence; of letting pictures speak for themselves.

It was, I believe, Tony Greig, guaranteed a job for life by Kerry Packer, who prompted the changed methods of those who followed. For a time Channel Nine toyed also with a challenge to the ABC on radio and, no doubt as a consequence, I remember him saying to me with typical candour: 'We TV blokes have got to be more like you guys on radio.' The Greig/ Bill Lawry banter on Channel Nine, so brilliantly, albeit crudely, played up by the Australian comedian Roy Birmingham, can certainly be fun sometimes and 'Greigy' was probably correct in the implication that all Benaud and no Greig would make for dull listening.

On the other hand over-indulgence was one of the reasons, no doubt, why so many in the days before satellite transmission used to say that they watched the television but listened to *Test Match Special*. To his credit Greig himself has never lost his enthusiasm but he became, and remains, overinclined to hyperbole as a commentator. When every 'game on our hands' is 'marvellous', every ball 'a gem', every shot a 'real beauty', every dropped catch 'atrocious' and every situation 'absolutely sensational', there is not much room for anything prosaic. This is the voice of the salesman, not of the expert. It is better to be honest.

My radio career, however, was still no more than a bright ambition as I found my feet at *The Cricketer*. The trick with producing a topical cricket magazine of record was to try to provide something for different sorts of readers. Some were interested only in a bit more depth on contemporary events than the daily newspapers had space to provide, but real students of the game needed sufficient historical fare to please them. There are and always have been any number of amateur cricket historians, many of them excellent, who would ply the office with articles sent in on spec.

Finding the right balance was not easy, especially when the only rival magazine in the late 1960s, *Playfair Cricket Monthly*, concentrated only on first-class cricket and ignored the recreational game that was always part of *The Cricketer*'s remit. Later the challenge became more serious when one of my successors as editor, David Frith, broke away to set up his own rival magazine, *Wisden Cricket Monthly*.

An Anglo-Australian who became probably the best cricket historian of recent times, Frith shared some of Irving's faults and qualities. He, too, was stubborn and punctilious, a perfectionist, inclined to be free with his criticism of others, especially if they had anything to do with *The Cricketer*. Unlike Irving he was a useful club cricketer himself, taking the game extremely seriously. For a time, until taking umbrage over selection and coaching issues, he was president of Guildford CC. He has always been prickly but he has a real feel for the game and for the characters who play it, especially the English and Australian ones whom he had hero-worshipped from an early age. I was the first to publish his work, I believe, making room for one or two characteristically poignant articles on the gravestones of famous past players. He still writes sharp, affectionate pieces about the cricketers he has known personally during his durable and single-minded career.

The ownership of the magazine for which I slaved all day and most evenings for more than two years changed hands after Hutchinson had sold it to an American magazine group called Mercury Press. One of the directors was the former Somerset cricketer and captain Ben Brocklehurst, whom I had first met when he played for R.J.O. Meyer's XI against Marlborough. He had already had a part in my destiny by missing one of his tremendous drives against my bowling and being stumped by Mike Griffith, the first, as it turned out, of three wickets for me in four balls that turned that match early in the summer term of 1962 and more or less guaranteed my place in the team.

Brocklehurst was appalled that Mercury's chairman, after a brief look at the profit and loss account of a magazine that had been running since Pelham Warner had founded it in 1921, was proposing to close *The Cricketer*. Taking a brave gamble, encouraged by his loyal, attractive and forceful second wife, Belinda, Ben bought the magazine himself and ran it successfully as a business for most of the rest of his life. He was a big red-faced, jovial, occasionally cantankerous man who had a gift for bringing people into a business with a family feel to it. He and Belinda ran it from their home on the Kent/Sussex border, with the considerable help of loyal lieutenants from the same area. They expanded by starting Cricketer Holidays, based originally on cricket visits to Corfu. They found a niche, selling holidays to middle- and upper-middle-class folk of a certain age: typically they were *Daily Telegraph* readers of the old school.

I had just started to get used to Ben, and had moved office at his behest from Hutchinson's base in Great Portland Street to Argyle Street in the shadow of the London Palladium, when my opportunity came to join the BBC in 1970; but he was fully established as the life and soul of his little empire when I rejoined the magazine.

I returned to *The Cricketer* as full-time editor in 1981, the year that made an immortal hero of Ian Botham. There was an overriding reason for leaving the intense but privileged life of cricket, travel and hotels that I had enjoyed since succeeding Brian Johnston as BBC cricket correspondent seven years before. The family and my life with Judy had to come first.

The balance between work and family life is one of the hardest for anyone to strike correctly but there was no doubt now that the time had come to be at home more regularly for the children. When I took my place behind one of three desks in the cosy but cramped little editorial office that Brocklehurst had rented from the printers in Redhill, James was seven and about to start as a day boy (until he was eleven) at Cranleigh prep school, Robin was five and learning his Ps and Qs amongst a small class of local boys starting out under a retired schoolmistress named Mrs. Pakeman and Lucy was, at eighteen months, already a bundle of laughs and smiles.

For all the pleasures of touring, I was really looking forward to a winter at home in Sussex. I had taken a big drop in salary by rejoining *The Cricketer*, one that I was tempted to supplement when Bill Gray, who had become the owner of *Wisden* after the bat-making side of the business had been swallowed by Grays of Cambridge, offered me the job as editor of the *Almanack*. I have kept the offer a secret until now. Already I knew that the BBC were keen to retain my services as a commentator for home Tests – needless to say the feeling was mutual – and it was not long before a sudden illness suffered by Jim Laker led to an offer from BBC television to commentate on Sunday League games and any Tests for which *Test Match Special* did not need me.

It was tempting to be invited to edit *Wisden*, flattering too, but I knew it would be no sinecure, even before meeting Graeme Wright, who assisted John Woodcock before becoming editor himself in 1987, at the London home of my first book publisher, Richard Johnson. He was by now an editor at Macdonald, the publishers of *Wisden*. Planning and producing a monthly magazine was a full-time job in itself without all this extra-curricular activity and it would have been madness to pursue the idea, besides which Gray quite rightly had suspicions that Brocklehurst would like to use my association to buy and bury *The Cricketer*'s fledgling rival, *Wisden Cricket Monthly*. In any case Woodcock, Alan Gibson's wise and lucid 'Sage of Longparish', was worthier than I. *The Cricketer* was not a bad forum from which to pontificate on the game, although I little knew then that in time I would be granted two even better ones.

Brocklehurst had faced a crisis when his editor, the studious and fastidious Frith, suddenly announced that, tired of being dictated to by his boss and those who helped to keep such a tight rein on his expenditure, he was intending to start up *Wisden Cricket Monthly*. Reg Hayter, the highly regarded manager of a press agency that serviced newspapers all round the country, filled the gap until I arrived to become the Editor and, for what it was worth, a member of the Board. I was allowed a free editorial hand and did my best both to widen its influence and sharpen its topicality.

Swanton maintained his interest, writing for the magazine throughout his eighties, and Woodcock, now retired from *The Times*, could occasionally be prevailed upon to write too, although it was like trying to squeeze juice from a dry lemon to persuade him sometimes that people wanted to read him as much as ever. The genial, and quietly shrewd Vic Marks, whom I had encouraged to write for us on his tour of Australia in 1982/3, later joined the board and Colin Cowdrey had been a member too for some time, as had John Haslewood, a long-time friend of Jim's who had been a director of Watney-Mann. Once a year we met at the In and Out Club in Piccadilly for a two hour meeting under Ben's chairmanship, followed by a three hour lunch. Wine flowed freely and the company could not have been more convivial. No one remembered in detail what had been discussed at the formal Board meeting: Ben continued to run the company's financial affairs precisely as he pleased.

I had a good and loyal editorial 'team'. It consisted at first of Mandy Ripley, a plump warm-hearted girl for whom nothing was ever too much trouble and who, like us all, worked until the job was done; and Andrew Longmore, recently down from Oxford, a fine schoolboy wicket-keeper/batsman for Winchester and in Sussex club cricket for Chichester. He was determined, a fast learner who became one of the best of Sunday sports feature writers. Andrew and I made our mistakes when it came to the presentation of the magazine, with which Ben was seldom satisfied, but I think we produced an interesting monthly, more varied in its approach than *WCM*, if, for a long time, less colourful.

Our expenditure – the amount of pages, the extent of colour pictures, fees to contributors, charges for printer's corrections and the like – was always very closely monitored. It meant that we made a profit while *WCM*, soon to be underwritten by an even bigger sugar daddy when Paul Getty bought *Wisden*, never did.

When Andrew got his deserved chance to spread his wings, Ben introduced Peter Perchard, a skilful production man who loved cricket, quickly learned the other elements of editing and, like Mandy, worked his socks off . That little office in Redhill was a hive of industry from soon after dawn until long after dusk. When I resumed my duties as BBC cricket correspondent in 1984 I was able to give less of my own time – sometimes it seemed like blood – to the cause of *The Cricketer* but I remained as a less hands-on editor until moving to the *Daily Telegraph* in 1991. I made sure that Peter got a pay rise but Ben was keen to have a 'name' on the masthead and it was on my suggestion that the title of editor went then to Ben's son-in-law, Richard Hutton, the dry, acerbic and highly capable former Cambridge, Yorkshire and England all-rounder. I thought he wrote rather well, especially about the finances of the game, and I personally found him amusing company, but his bluntness and slightly cynical approach to life was not always appreciated by those around him. Moreover, he had a paymaster of equally strong will in his father-in-law. Despite the natural sweetness and diplomacy of his wife, Charmaine, he and Ben eventually fell out, leaving Peter to assume the editorial seat that he deserved.

There were plenty of frustrations as editor of the magazine, especially those that related to keeping to the budget set by the proprietor. In both my stints editorial costs were watched by Ben's cost-cutting Rottweiler, Harry Constantine, a portly fellow who was likeable but always knew better than anyone else. He would have been just the man to enforce George Osborne's spending cuts. When colour pages became a possibility they had to be justified by securing coloured advertisements and the size of the magazine was rigidly dependent, at most times of the year, on the amount of business that could be drummed up by our advertising manager. Originally this was the genial and experienced Colin Pegley of Jackson Rudd & Associates. He was soon succeeded by an amiable bumbler named Christopher Bazalgette, a tubby red-haired Ronald Fraser lookalike who was employed by Ben to work solely for *The Cricketer*. That gave him every incentive to sell as much space as possible.

Christopher was known to everyone in club cricket in Hampshire as a shrewd trundler of slow-medium 'nothings'. They lured a quite extraordinary number of batsmen to destruction over more than forty years of playing mainly for the Hampshire Hogs on their gorgeous ground at Warnford in the Meon Valley. Nothing came ahead of Hogs cricket for 'Baz', but his need to make ends meet made him an assiduous gatherer of cricket-based ads, gleaned mainly from his many friends and contacts in the game, not least the equipment manufacturers. Each year, to keep his contacts 'sweet', we would be obliged to produce an 'Equipment Supplement' which the editorial staff would try to sell to the reader as an additional bonus. Chris, the most well-meaning of souls, cannot have passed many English exams and was, I have always assumed, dyslexic. Translating into English the endless reams of semi-literate copy that he produced for this supplement was an annual chore, but Christopher was, no doubt, well aware of his shortcomings. Despite them he produced several books, usually co-written with somebody else. Nothing ever seemed to dim his enthusiasm.

As long as Ben remained strong enough the magazine itself remained robust, never rising above the circulation of around 45,000 reached in the early eighties, but always cutting its coat according to its cloth. Having swallowed its first competitor, *Playfair Cricket Monthly*, in 1973, and having thereby increased the circulation substantially overnight, Ben's dream had always been to do the same to *WCM*, which might never have been viable but for Frith's masterstroke in acquiring the name Wisden in return for a royalty.

Ben's only mistake was not to put away sufficient into his own pension. The need to draw more cash from the businesses led, quite quickly, to an amalgamation between *The Cricketer* and *WCM* in which the latter, despite its smaller circulation, came out effectively as the winner, certainly so far as editorial personnel were concerned. Under the able, sharp editorial direction of John Stern, *The Wisden Cricketer* has continued to provide a thorough coverage of the whole game. It has a considerably bigger staff than I was allowed under Ben's parsimonious control, but I would say that it is in every way superior to *The Cricketer* under my direction. It may have more of the look of *WCM* in terms of design, but it is more comprehensive and imaginative than the latter was under Frith and it has continued to serve the game as a journal of record and an independent voice, the two objectives that I always tried to keep in mind for *The Cricketer* itself. The wheel came full circle for me in 2011 when *The Wisden Cricketer* was acquired from its previous owners by a consortium that had for some time run the website Test Match Extra.com. If only for old time's sake, I took a small stake.

8

OFF TO THE BEEB

*Saturday afternoon at Broadcasting House in London in the early
1970s. There is nothing in all the realm of human labour quite so
intense as a room full of journalists close to a deadline.*

In the case of the BBC Radio Sports Room it was deadline time
on Saturdays from a little before noon until seven pm, each man
and woman absorbed utterly in the immediacy of the task in
hand. Desks were strewn with papers at one end of the long,
bright room on the sixth floor of BH. At the other end the tele-
printer machines kept up a constant chatter. They spewed out
news of goals, runs, wickets and the one, two, three from the
latest races, with the urgency of a dawn chorus. In the little
studio, partitioned and sound-proofed behind the teleprinters,
the red light would be almost permanently at the ready for live
broadcasting, the room beyond peopled by three or four studio
managers, urgently spinning or editing tapes. Down below in
studio B9, the hub of the operation to bring news of the afternoon's sporting events to the nation was no less hectic.

I must have got some things right during those ten years at BH
but I certainly got a few things wrong too. On my first frenetic

95

Saturday I was given charge of compiling highlights from the third and fourth division football. This involved ripping off sheets of paper from the teleprinters and sorting out who had scored for which team where. Come the *moment critique* I got hold of the lip microphone the wrong way round (I had used only open mikes for my *Sports Session* reports) and my immortal words were lost until Bob Burrows seized the mike and turned it round the other way.

As I learned the ropes I would sometimes be charged with giving running news from the teleprinters as the final whistles sounded at football matches round the country at 4.40 pm, which meant having a good working knowledge of all the clubs and players. In those days I was interested and I did. I certainly do not now: overkill has dulled my interest. Even then I was accused of overdoing the mentions of Jim Cumbes, Ted Hemsley and Phil Neale, who all combined league football with county cricket.

Saturday was the focal point of the sporting week for the Sports News department of the BBC, whose ranks I joined on the first day of March 1970. It was also the first day for Desmond Lynam, who became famous.

Desmond was marked for stardom from the moment he arrived, having made a small name for himself already at Radio Brighton. Angus Mackay, founder of *Sports Report*, had already spotted his potential as a successor to two more obviously Irish presenters, Eamonn Andrews and Liam Nolan. Peter Jones, another natural broadcaster, a romantic about sport and life who was blessed with immense self-confidence and, Welsh though he was, more blarney than most Irishmen, did the same job equally well. Curly-haired, blue-eyed and attractive to the girls, he had left his former job as a teacher at Bradfield after an affair with one of the matrons. An ebullient, personable extrovert, he continued to burn the candle at both ends, which no doubt contributed to a sadly early end to his life when he suffered a fatal stroke midway through his commentary on the Boat Race.

One Saturday afternoon in the Sports Room I passed on some information to Peter about who had scored against whom in the afternoon matches in the first division. It was his job that day to summarise the main matches and events. 'Aren't you going to write them down', I asked him. 'No', he said, tapping his head: 'They're in here.'

Even had they not been, he would have bluffed his way through once he was on the air. Unlike Desmond, who could be nervous, Peter had supreme confidence. He developed a style of delivering news, not entirely naturally, that other reporters used to follow, ending the last word in each sentence on a slightly upward inflexion. I found it irritating and much preferred Desmond's more intimate delivery methods, seldom followed, alas, by today's bombastic presenters.

Peter was, however, a gifted performer with a touch of the poetic in his descriptions. He enjoyed football commentary more than anything so he was seldom in the studio. Desmond, smoothly at home in front of a microphone before he ever faced a television camera, took every challenge in his unhurried stride, blessed as he was with a good voice, a quick wit and a sense of humour. Working with Mackay, he needed it.

The boss of the Sports Room was a formidable, bespectacled, red-faced, chain-smoking, whisky-loving Scotsman with a biting tongue. He was seen in the BBC as an innovator because of the success of *Sports Report* in summarising the main events of the afternoon in his quick-moving programme every Saturday between five and six o'clock. By the time that I joined his staff, having been told to apply for a job after doing some free-lance broadcasts – and duly being chosen by the BBC 'board' that interviewed candidates for every job – the redoubtable Angus ruled his Sports News department with a rod of iron and, to my mind, absurd inflexibility. At home he was apparently a mild family man, but he could be ruthless at work. Amongst his regular pundits was the well known and opinionated J.L. Manning of the *Daily Mail*, who, towards the end of his life, suffered from the ill health that affects too many workaholic journalists. One early Saturday afternoon his wife rang Angus to say that he would not be appearing on *Sports Report* that evening because he had just been taken to hospital after a heart attack. Soothing remarks were heard from Angus's end of the line: 'That's terrible news. Don't you worry a bit. You give Jim our very best wishes . . .' Immediately he had put the phone down he yelled to his assistant, Bob Burrows: 'Bob, come into my office *now*. Bloody Manning's let us down again.'

I eventually rebelled against the bullying nature of his leadership, which did me no good, but I survived my first test of character in his presence. 'We're calling you Chris Jenkins, is that all right?' he demanded with an icy stare on my first Saturday morning in studio B9 at Broadcasting House as he pored over the script for that morning's *Sports Parade*. 'I'd prefer my full name if you don't mind, Sir', I replied. He cursed, took a drag on his cigarette, rubbed out the shorter name and inserted the additional letters that would take up a few more split-seconds in his tightly-timed schedule.

Angus had passed his peak by the time that I joined the staff. What had once been an innovative collection of sports programmes, including regular bulletins throughout the day during the week, had become, perhaps, a little staid. He taught me two things at least which I have never forgotten, however: it is *less* coal, but *fewer* sacks; and you should say Notts County but never Notts Forest – always Nottingham Forest.

The latter might not be considered a matter of crucial inter-national importance, unless you are from Nottingham, but I like to think that in those mainly scripted programmes there were far fewer solecisms than one hears on the air every day now. Sports broadcasters in these laissez-faire days of Five Live are natural and confident but I wish most of them had had a few more lessons in English grammar. Presenters are forever 'sat' here' or 'stood' there.

It would not have been tolerated by Angus Mackay, who could call upon virtually anyone he chose to appear on his programmes. Amongst my early reporting colleagues were W. Barrington Dalby, who used to do inter-round summaries when Eamonn Andrews commentated on big fights in boxing; the gregarious Geoffrey Green, football correspondent of *The Times*, who had a twinkle in his eye and a wonderfully bibulous voice, and Harold Abrahams, the sprinting hero of the Olympics no less, now an athletics expert who would sometimes also turn his hand to humble football reporting. All of them fastidiously spoke the Queen's English.

The reputation of *Sports Report*, and the large circle of contacts built up by Angus by the early seventies, certainly attracted some of the biggest names. Fred Perry, three times Wimbledon cham-pion, made regular appearances when the Grand Slam tourna-ments were nigh, always looking sun-tanned whatever the time of year. His moustache was perfectly trimmed and his accent transatlantic. His wife, by then his fourth – and, obviously the right one because they looked devoted and the marriage lasted forty years – would accompany him, looking very expensive in a white fur coat if the weather was cold. The young Tony Jacklin also used to come in with his wife, the beautiful green-eyed, Vivien, who died young, a tragedy that no doubt curtailed his brief reign as the world's best golfer.

The most regular visitors, however, were Henry Cooper and his fat, cigar-smoking manager, Jim Wicks. I got quite good at imitating 'Our Enery's modest cockney voice, complete with occasional spoonerisms, and the quiet London-Jewish drawl of Wicks. Indeed they were amongst the well-known characters whom I used to take off to entertain colleagues in spoof broadcasts at the end of the year, long forgotten about now. I mixed them with the broad northern tones of 'Mr. Rugby League' Eddie Waring – 'Sullivan 'as the ball, woofs it upfield to Murphy. Neil Fox is underneath it – 'ello there's a bit of hokey-pokey going on' – and the sharply contrasting showjumping commentator Dorian Williams: 'One more double-barred gate and it'll be a clear round for Anneli Drummond-Hay. Come on Anneli . . . Oh, my word, she came a cropper there . . . She literally took orff . . . we can see it again, I think . . . Poor Anneli, she literally took orff.'

Light-hearted days, some of them! I used this limited ability as an impressionist whenever Robin Marlar, another of *Sports Report*'s favourite polemicists, was performing. I would read his various quotations from the week's news in the appropriate accent (or try to do so: I never quite mastered Scouse). Robin, always entertaining and often impetuous, once used a longish paragraph on some sporting issue of the moment from a letter to *The Times* by Air Vice Marshal Sir Dermot Boyle. When I had read it Robin added with feeling: 'Wise words. Well said Mr. Boyle of Maidenhead.'

Angus had three main assistants: Bob Burrows, Vincent Duggleby and Godfrey Dixey. Vincent was bright, genial but occasionally volatile; an outstanding broadcaster in his own right who can still be heard introducing the money programmes on radio that became his forte. Burrows was well named. He busied himself like a ferret at his duties, always careful to keep his boss on his side and leaving no stone unturned to get the programmes as sharp and accurate as possible. Often I would be longing to get home on a Saturday evening only for Bob, with characteristic blinks of his eyes, to suggest a phone-call to someone to set up a new angle on some story for the following Monday.

His eventual reward was a well-paid job in charge of ITV sport but I had foolishly crossed swords with Bob on a man-management issue when, goaded into action by a disgruntled colleague, I passed on some general discontent with his leadership to the boss of BBC Radio, Aubrey Singer, whom I had recently met. Quite rightly Singer supported his manager. I should have tackled Bob directly but that approach had not worked when, some years before, I had walked through what Angus claimed to be an 'always open door' in order to make a criticism about something to do with one of our programmes.

I had badly misjudged the moment and the issue. Incredibly, Angus, prickly as holly, never spoke directly to me again. He would say to another man in the Sports Room: 'John, tell Mr. Martin-Jenkins that there'll be an interview with Sir Matt Busby for him to edit.' On one occasion soon after my misguided attempt to make some constructive suggestions, he ordered Desmond not to buy me a beer in his presence during the 'quick drink after the show' that was expected to be attended each Saturday night by all concerned. To his great credit Desmond replied that he had ordered a pint for me and another for himself and that we were jolly well going to drink them.

Godfrey Dixey could not have been more different from all these forceful characters. He was intelligent, nervous and a loyal, slightly frightened assistant producer, very competent but terrified of getting things wrong. He was a bachelor, good company off duty, a dapper, round-faced little fellow who wore gold-rimmed spectacles on the end of his nose that made him look like a Victorian clerk. He liked his pint and a good chat about cricket. His main responsibilities on a Saturday were a regional sports programme called *Sports Session* and the digested version of *Sports Report* that went out on the BBC's World Service later in the evening. I would sometimes present both these programmes and on one occasion took a leading part in a somewhat catastrophic broadcast that almost caused Godfrey to self-combust.

First he (and I) discovered, on the air, that my friend Jeremy Allerton, to whom he had entrusted a report on the after-noon's rugby matches, was a stutterer. A charming fellow who has been extremely unlucky in life, his consolation came from being very attractive to women. His former house now belongs to David Gower.

It was only under the intense pressure of broadcasting live that Jeremy's stutter returned to haunt him, much as it must have done the future King George VI in the 1930s. It was, of course, excruciating for him and deeply embarrassing for me. I had no option other than to put an end to his agony and move on to the next item. Then, however, I contributed further to Godfrey's visible chagrin. All these programmes, whatever their overall length, had to be timed to the second, to ensure that the next one would itself start bang on time. Every contributor carried a stopwatch – BBC issue to staff – and Angus drummed it into each of us that a minute report meant 60 seconds, not 59 or 61, although any over-run was the cardinal sin. Producers had to be good at maths, forever calculating how long they had in hand to the end and if some-thing unexpected happened, such as Jeremy's misfortune, adjustments had to be made on the hoof. Godfrey, like Angus, always used the racing results as a buffer at the end of the programme. It meant that the reader, in this case myself as presenter, could read them slowly or quickly to order.

For some reason on the evening in question I had misread the clock and was starting my closing words – a quick trail of the following week's sport – with about ten seconds to go to what I thought was the optimum second to say goodbye or good night. Suddenly I was aware of a desperate Godfrey beside me. He could have used the talkback to warn me through my earphones but in his panic did not. Instead, unable to speak because of the open microphone, he was alternately pointing at his stopwatch, which showed just over a minute to the hour, and waving his arm from his shoulder to his backside in a very good imitation of Lester Piggott riding a close finish at Epsom. Just in time I got the message that I had failed to read the last set of results. 'So that's next week', I blarneyed, 'but for those of you waiting for the results from Towcester, here they are.' I sped through the first three placed horses and their starting prices in the six races with as much dignity as possible and got off the air in the nick of time.

I was amused in the bar afterwards by a story from John Webster, an amiable newsreader who for many years read both the football and racing results for *Sports Report*. He had, he said, put on his best Italian accent to read the winner of the 4.20 at Uttoxeter, 'Thinice'. An apologetic typist told him afterwards that he had failed to put a gap between 'Thin' and 'Ice'.

The typist in question was no doubt an eccentric fellow called Bill Ross, a fierce and often angry bearded man with brown horn-rimmed glasses, who dressed a bit like a tramp and occupied a large desk nearest to the teleprinters. He had the quickest of brains, always zipping through the *Times* crossword in under half an hour during his lunch hour. He hated fools and foolishness and since he was always confronted by one or the other he was usually in a lather about something. He was, however, extremely good at his job, which was to collate results at speed. He also kept large exercise books inside blue hard-backed covers – everyone knew them as Bill Ross's blue books – which recorded every detail of each football season under club headings. Any member of the Sports Room was allowed to consult the blue books for such details as who had scored the fourth goal for Huddersfield Town against Plymouth Argyle on 23 September. Ask any stupid question of Bill, however, and your head was almost literally bitten off, especially as it was obvious to him that a University education had been utterly wasted on you.

Another singular character was an Oxford graduate of high intelligence with a Walter Mitty streak, named Roger Macdonald. He had a high-pitched voice and made himself an expert on European football. He claimed to know everyone and said to me once as I left for a reception: 'If Sean Connery's there, give him my regards.' Roger sped up the inside of the BBC as a producer, but his imagination eventually got the better of him and he was dismissed.

I did most things during my time based in the Sports Room, including reading the football results occasionally after the manner prescribed by Webster, which allowed the listener to tell from the inflexion of the voice as the first team was named whether it was going to be a home win, a draw or a home defeat. A bright, positive pronunciation of 'Tottenham Hotspur 1' told the knowing listener at once that it would be followed by 'Chelsea nil'. A downbeat 'Tottenham Hotspur 1' would mean that Chelsea had won. An even voice, the verbal equivalent of a perfectly balanced see-saw, denoted a draw. I rather enjoyed the challenge but it was not exactly the limit of my ambitions. James Alexander Gordon, nevertheless, became quite famous in later years as radio's football results man with the mild Scots accent.

I suppose that I had made a reasonable reputation as a broadcaster before crossing swords with Angus but I dare say that he could have finished me had he wanted to pursue the vendetta. The BBC had a system of annual reports on every member of staff, written by the head of department, who would read the assessment to him and invite any reaction before it was passed higher up the hierarchy. 'Christopher is a hard-working and talented broadcaster but very naïve' was the gist of my report that year. On the last score Angus was no doubt spot on.

I had probably incurred his wrath for more than this one failure to realise that 'if you ever want to talk to me about anything, whatever it is, don't hesitate' actually meant 'don't you dare criticise my way of doing things, however old-fashioned you may think it is'. I had also become, quite early in my career at Portland Place, a small pawn in an internal battle between Mackay's Sports News department and the longer established Outside Broadcasts department which had responsibility for all the live commentaries.

Eventually the two empires were amalgamated under the benign, wise and unselfish leadership of Robert Hudson, later succeeded by the brilliant and mercurial Cliff Morgan, supreme fly-half turned passionate broadcaster. Such internal politics were never far below the surface at the BBC, however, and eventually they drove me off the staff in frustration after ten mainly happy years.

Fortunately, I have never stopped working as a freelance broadcaster for the BBC, nor have I broadcast for any rival organisation, despite one characteristically blunt telephoned offer from Kelvin Mackenzie when his talkSPORT was starting to win some of the radio cricket commentary contracts. 'Come on' he said: 'You take your bat where the bowling is, don't you?' Fortunately the bowling did not stay at his end for long. I would probably have been better off now had I stayed on the staff and held on for a BBC pension because the final salary scheme was still going strong when I reached the age of sixty, but for all sorts of other reasons I was pleased to be free when I went back to *The Cricketer* early in 1981. Above all, as I have said, it gave me much more time at home with Judy and our three children.

The producers and administrators I left behind could sometimes be small-minded. Angus's chief antagonist was the courteous but dour South African Jacob De Vries, who saw me as someone more suited to the tradition of Brian Johnston, Raymond Baxter and the rest of the early denizens of sports broadcasting. When Angus was on his summer holiday and De Vries took over temporary responsibility for the Saturday sports output I was asked to present both the live coverage during the afternoon and *Sports Report* itself. Looking back, that was quite an honour but I did so only in the short gaps between football seasons.

Bryon Butler, with his honeyed voice, and the earnest and conscientious John Motson were other highly professional performers, as were Derek Thompson and Gerald Williams, passionate respectively about racing and tennis; and the engaging Scotsman Bill Hamilton, who somehow kept going one sunny summer afternoon even as all the lunchtime cricket scoreboard scripts were being blown round the studio after a sudden gust of wind through the open window.

A pair of Scottish rugger internationals, Chris Rea and Ian Robertson, also joined the Sports Room not long after me. At one stage of their careers they were fortunate enough to find a wealthy Roman businessman who had become enthusiastic about his rugby. They would take a flight to Rome every Saturday night to play for his club there the following day, for rather better recompense than their BBC employment offered them.

Both were excellent broadcasters and fun to be with. Like me, both also enjoyed a game of golf on days off. Chris, always inclined to be irascible, became frustrated by his bosses and has had various jobs in rugby since, not to mention one as a slightly unlikely Press Relations chief for MCC, helped by his acquaintanceship with the then secretary, Roger Knight. Their respective wives were old friends.

Ian is a funny man either in conversation or on his feet after dinner. His gravelly commentaries still make Rugby Union come alive on radio and he remains a passionate follower of racing. He persuaded me to take a twelfth share of a syndicate that bought a quarter share in a horse trained and co-owned by the royal trainer Ian Balding. The former rugby international Ben Michaelson had another quarter share. Most of the members of the group of twelve persuaded by 'Robbo' to part with rather less of their money were also rugger players, so the horse was named Twickenham.

We were told by Robbo, a most conscientious syndicate secretary who would write us all witty summaries of the horse's progress from time to time, that, even if our handsome but modestly bred chestnut was no good, the great advantage was that we would get inside tips from the stable every week that would make us all a small fortune. Most of them, of course, were hopeless – none worse than those from the trainer himself who, masterly as he was with his most famous horse, Mill Reef, predicted the result of races involving his own stables about as accurately as Michael Fish did hurricanes. On the other hand Twickenham turned out to be a willing stayer and when he was released (gelded by then, unfortunately) to peaceful retirement in California, he had won eleven races over five years, despite a blank year as a three-year-old when he got a virus and had to be nursed back to fitness by Terry Biddlecombe. He made us all, after all the regular expenses, a profit of exactly ten shillings, which is ten shillings more than most of those who invest in racehorses. It was great fun to go into the paddock with an owner's badge on but it was my luck that on the few occasions I was able to see him run Twickenham never finished better than fourth.

Nigel Starmer-Smith, the former Oxford and England scrum-half, was a third ex-international in the Sports Room at the time. A charming man, later to suffer tragedy with his lovely wife, Ros, when two of their three children died in their teens from the same rare disease, he could also be a nervous broadcaster, especially when not in his own area of expertise. 'Comfort zone' is the apt sporting cliché. Asked to round up one half of the day's highlights in county cricket on the evening sports programme one day (I was doing the other one) Nigel was so uptight that he started on the second page of his script, beginning in the middle of a sentence and therefore responding to his introduction with something like 'taking six for 74 to bowl Derbyshire out for 198'. A little non-plussed, like everyone, by this surprising beginning to his report Nigel became the only man in my experience actually to utter the words: 'I'm sorry, I'll read that again.'

Years later Nigel was the chief commentator while I was happily watching a rugby international from Twickenham on the sofa at home, with a log fire adding to my feeling of well being. To my momentary horror I heard Steve Ryder, the link-man, saying to the millions of other viewers at the end of half-time: 'Let's get back to the action now. Your commentator for the start of the second half is Christopher Martin-Jenkins.'

The most famous rugby player on the staff, however, and

presumably the man who encouraged the employment of all these estimable men, was Cliff Morgan. Alas, I never saw him play fly-half for Wales or the British Lions, except on black and white film clips. But I knew him as a lyrical commentator on the game who had recovered from a serious stroke in his forties to continue his regular contributions to radio sports programmes. He was also a deeply knowledgeable rugby TV commentator before Robert Hudson encouraged his appointment as his own successor as head of Radio Sport. Cliff thus became my boss, not long after I had been made cricket correspondent.

He was different from the restrained and dignified Hudson. Cliff acted by instinct in life, with fire in his belly and passion in his heart. He would have phrased that differently: 'You've got to speak from the balls, boy' he would say. He was probably happier broadcasting than managing, but that was the way of the BBC. The best paid jobs were 'inside' and no doubt he needed the money. I was grateful when he backed me following a complaint from the Director General of the ABC about something that I had written as a guest writer in a newspaper column during a tour of Australia. I was very worried at the time by the possible repercussions but, having established the facts, Cliff simply said: 'pompous ass. Remember, boy, you can get away with anything if you've got class.' He did not mean class in the social sense, so, given the source, it was one of the best compliments I have ever had.

He had a good sense of humour, too. Norman Cuddeford, a regular free-lance athletics commentator who also loved his cricket, had made an embarrassing but very funny faux pas during the sports slot on the *Today* programme when, thinking he was just doing a microphone test rather than actually live on the air, he responded by replying to Chris Rea's question

'Can you bring us up to date with the latest score, Norman?' by replying: 'No, I'm awfully sorry, I can't.'

The incident occurred in 1975 shortly before the Montreal Olympics. Naturally it brought an abject apology from Norman, who added: 'I hope this won't affect my chances of going to Montreal.' Cliff feigned fury: 'Montreal?' he said. 'You'll be lucky if you go to the bloody Albert Hall!'

Wise as he was, Cliff knew that no one makes mistakes on the air on purpose, and also that, nine times out of ten, they bring unexpected joy to listeners or viewers.

I spent far less time in the Sports Room once I had broken through as cricket correspondent but life was generally fun there and has been ever since, I think, for the long succession of reporters who have followed, many from local radio and these days servicing listeners to Radio Five Live. They are heavily biased towards football, which the likes of Mike Ingham, Alan Green, and the charming north-easterner John Murray, who once bobbed up on a cricket tour in Sri Lanka, cover very well indeed, although Green, like anyone who proclaims his opinions loudly, is not everyone's cup of tea. Would that more of them were interested in cricket but football, especially since the arrival of the pernicious Premier League, tends to swallow all in its over-hyped wake. Arlo White, a confident, professional and personable all-round broadcaster, managed to straddle both sports for a time before going free-lance. The amiable Johnny Saunders and the capable Mark Saggers, both knowledgeable cricket-lovers, have moved away from the game for the time being because of a lack of opportunity and poor Kevin Howell and Alison Mitchell, who handle such coverage of county cricket as there is on Five Live, get all too little air-time.

That is a case of *plus ça change*. In my time on the staff live coverage of county cricket on Saturdays became limited to frustratingly inadequate one minute or thirty second reports. The failure of producers to realise that a vast silent corps of interested cricketers yearned for more was one of the things that drove me back to *The Cricketer* in 1981, but as I shall explain later that was an argument that I never won.

Desmond and I had been taken on originally to share presentation duties for the new sports slot on the *Today* programme, then introduced each morning, to a devoted audience, by Jack de Manio and John Timpson. De Manio, more popular in his day than John Humphrys and James Naughtie combined, was urbane, avuncular and apparently a bumbling amateur, but that was a part of his charm. He was famous for getting the time wrong. I liked him immensely and he seemed also to favour me as someone who spoke the Queen's English, had a proper respect for his elders and provided five minutes of light variation from the heavier political stories at twenty-five minutes past six, seven and eight each weekday morning. The formula has stood the test of time.

When, shortly before my marriage in 1971, I broke two toes in my right foot by dropping a paving stone onto them, De Manio found humour in my discomfort. Seeing me enter the studio with crutches during the first edition he somehow armed himself with a brick before my second appearance and dropped it with a sickening thud in front of my microphone by way of explanation.

I liked John Timpson too. He was sharp, acerbic and professional but had little interest in sport. Nor, come to think of it, did most of their successors in the high-profile roles of *Today* presenters. In my time I worked also with the delightful and admirably competent Sue MacGregor; the splendidly pontifical Robert Robinson, who always seemed to be operating on a plane far above the trivial world of sport; the forthright, politically-minded Brian Redhead, who died sadly young, and Libby Purves, yet another outstanding talent. Few *Times* columnists write more sensibly and lucidly than she. The high standards have been kept up to this day, most notably by Naughtie and John Humphrys, who is not everyone's favourite but with whom I invariably seem to see eye to eye. He is a wonderful communicator and, despite roughing up politicians as they have seldom been since the days of the inquisitorial Sir Robin Day (once, as I shall relate, my guest on *Test Match Special*) he strikes me as being both fair and humane.

Although I miss Ed Stourton, the current team maintains the high standard. I took part in a fund-raising dinner for the Lord Mayor's charities at Guildhall in the City in 2010 with 'one of the newer fellahs', Justin Webb. He is exemplary in that he does not impose his personality unnecessarily and proves, as the best of his predecessors did, that it is possible to be firm with political interviewees without being rude to them. He has lost no dignity since revealing himself to be the 'love-child' of the normally professional Peter Woods, who became even more famous for appearing in a tired and emotional state to read a late evening news bulletin on BBC2, before Robin Day, with a wry smile, announced that '*Newsnight* is starting rather earlier than usual'. Woods had been cut off for slurring his words and telling us that the balance of payments situation was . . . (after several unavailing attempts to get out the word on his autocue) . . . 'awfully bad'. His problem was ascribed to a reaction to taking medicine for sinus problems. Like Lt. Commander Tommy Woodrooffe when the fleet was lit up at the 1937 Spithead Review it was bad for his career but certainly not for his popularity.

Curiously, I can remember only two instances of an inebriated broadcaster being obviously unable to give of his best. One was a radio newsreader, quite unable to read his bulletin during one of those countless sports programmes – it was hilarious to me, and, happily, I think he was forgiven on the promise of no repeat performance. The other was the multi-talented Alan Gibson, for whom, as I shall explain later, the consequences were, unfortunately, immediate.

Being part of the *Today* programme involved night shifts, which, for my constitution anyway, was wearying. I would leave Judy at home at Pilgrim's Cottage in Albury and travel to London in her little green Hillman Imp (I had never owned a car, having previously driven my father's black Morris Minor – numberplate 7381 U). The Imp being even more liable to break down, I went more often by the Tillingbourne Valley bus to Guildford, then by train, tube and foot to Broadcasting House.

Once there one would prepare first for a 'sports desk' in the middle of an evening programme on Radio Two called *Late Night Extra*, which ran for many years introduced by a number of presenters including the charming and intelligent John Dunn (a giant of a man physically); the super smooth music specialists David Jacobs and Brian Matthew; Bob Holness, who became better known on television; and 'Diddy' David Hamilton, a jaunty little chap with a twinkle in his eye. To a man they were highly polished performers.

By the time this job had been done, at 10.30 or thereabouts, the Sports Room was like an abandoned ship, brightly lit (as Commander Woodrooffe would have confirmed) but empty of all life. Isolated in the large, garishly-lit room, and keeping an eye out for late evening news chattering through on the teleprinters, I would slave for several hours in an attempt to make the most of my three sports slots the following morning, editing tapes with razor blades and yellow chinagraph pencils.

Precious time could always be saved from any interview or report by taking out ums, urs, repetitions and even breaths. It was a skill at which I became quite adept, despite my natural hamfistedness, but there was always the dangerous possibility that the white tape, sticky on one side, that joined the two pieces of tape together at the various edits, might come apart when the tape passed through the machines as the programmes went out live.

When everything had been sorted out and my script had been typed on one of the enormous typewriters that sat on top of most of the desks (always allowing room for ad libs when it came to broadcasting live) I would go over the road to the BBC Club at Langham Place and sign in to a stuffy, harshly-lit room for what was never more than a few hours of fitful sleep. An alarm would go at about 5.30. After a quick shave (a discipline to which I always adhere no matter where I am) it was back to BH for a quick bulletin after the Six, followed by the main appearances at 7.25 and 8.25.

The great advantage of being assigned to *Today*, apart from the fact that there was a large, influential and intelligent audience, was that one enjoyed editorial control over what was included. When I was on duty those interested in cricket – and to a lesser extent rugby and golf – probably had more than their fair share. They get less than they should nowadays, unless the balanced Rob Bonnet is on duty. The popular Gary Richardson enjoys a good cricket controversy and, like all who are not really interested in cricket, he has registered that any Ashes series is 'big', so has to be given the full treatment. He is certainly not alone in underselling other series and the game at below international level and I do not blame Gary personally. I greatly like his sense of humour, but rather deplore his down-market idea of what a Radio Four audience wants.

In summer especially it was also nice to get back home for a late breakfast and have the rest of the day to oneself. I would go to bed during the day only if I had another duty that evening, but doing three days a week of night shifts was like living with permanent mild jet-lag.

9

TEST MATCH SPECIAL
– COMMENTATORS

I am in my last year at school, hoping for guidance along the path to the fulfilment of a youthful ambition. I have written to Brian Johnston asking him how I might possibly become a cricket commentator. He has invited me to Broadcasting House at Portland Place, up the road from Oxford Circus. Nervously I have found my way through the maze of corridors (they took years to get to know) to the office in the OB department that he shares with Raymond Baxter. The walls are lined with 'naughty' seaside postcards, most of them, I suppose, by Donald McGill, which give an immediate indication of how seriously he takes life. Being Brian, he relaxes me at once. It is my first encounter with the bubbly charm, rosy cheeks and famously large nose that will lift my spirits every time I am in his company in the years ahead.

Raymond, with his crinkly hair, equally prominent nose and distinctive, authoritative voice, is no less familiar a face to me. He, too, gives me a jovial welcome before Brian guides me over the road to the BBC Club for a convivial sandwich lunch, I drinking a beer, Brian his favourite glass of Muscadet-sur-Lie. He simply tells me to practise commentating by myself with a tape recorder and to play

and watch as much as possible, advice I have handed on since to
many an aspiring youngster including Mark Pougatch, who has
made better use of it than most.

The BBC in the 1970s, and I dare say as much so now, was a vast bureaucracy. My file from those days contained any number of administrative memoranda, many about what was and what was not allowed to be spent when away from Broadcasting House on duty. £18.82 for an overnight hotel stay and 14.4 pence per gallon of petrol seem a little out of date now. Amongst these dusty archives, however, are one or two letters and memos that remind me how vigorously I pursued my ambition to become a cricket commentator.

The internal political divide between OBs and 'Sports News' made it harder for me to get a foot into the door of the coveted Test match commentary box but I pressed with as much tact as I could for a commentary test and was given one at The Oval in August 1970. I had already been to a few county matches that season to report for the various Saturday programmes, starting with one for the World Service at the Surrey/Yorkshire match in May when Chris Old dismissed Stuart Storey early on the Saturday morning. I duly concluded my first dispatch with the words 'it's been a good morning so far for young Old', to which Paddy Feeny, the long-serving presenter of World Service sport, responded: 'Oh, really; I used to know his father, Old Young.'

Later that day came my first commentary audition. After plenty of practice on a tape recorder, and years of 'pretend' commentaries as a child, it seemed quite natural to me. Rex Alston, Brian's predecessor as cricket correspondent, supervised the audition, which simply meant guiding me to the microphone, withdrawing tactfully and leaving me to it for the next twenty minutes.

Rex was a dear, benign fellow, an athletics Blue who captained Bedfordshire at cricket and who, with his spectacles, trim figure and sharp features, looked every inch the schoolmaster he had been at Bedford before and during the war, prior to making his name after it as a cricket, rugby and athletics commentator. He lived into his nineties, having taken a cold bath every morning until late in a life that was accidentally 'ended' prematurely by *The Times*. In 1986 they published his obituary by mistake after John Woodcock, prompted by the news that Rex had been taken to hospital – as it turned out with mere food poisoning – phoned the paper to make a small correction to the obit that had been filed for future use. It makes a pleasing story that Rex, waking the following morning in hospital, feeling much better, discovered his decease whilst reading *The Times* as he munched his toast and marmalade. As soon as he could he rang the paper and asked to be put through to the obituaries' editor. 'This is Rex Alston speaking' he said. 'Would you kindly explain why you have published my obituary this morning, albeit a very generous one?' To which the dumbfounded editor, confident of his newspaper's infallibility, replied: 'Where are you speaking from?'

Robert Hudson, never a man to over-egg any pudding, wrote to me after the audition to say that 'we felt you made a very good first attempt'. Coming from him, I believe that was quite high praise. I was given another trial run the following year but wheels turned slowly and it was not until the first one-day international to be played in England, at Old Trafford in 1972, that I was let loose on an unwary public. Bob Burrows had by then taken over from Angus Mackay and had to give written permission for me to be released for the day so long as I returned to London 'fairly smartly, to prepare for *Sports Report* and *Sport on Two* the following Saturday'.

I had been reporting Test matches for Sports News programmes all that season so the established pillars of the commentary box, Brian, John Arlott and the young scorer, Bill Frindall – and their friendly but world-weary producer, Michael Tuke-Hastings – were all familiar to me. Nevertheless it was a tremendous thrill to dine with Brian, John Woodock, Michael Melford and Jack Fingleton at the Swan Inn at Bucklow Hill the night before the match. 'Fingo' got into a furious lather over what he believed to be England's deliberate preparation of a spinner's pitch for the Headingley Test and it was evident from an article in *The Australian* newspaper as the Australia v. England series began to generate extra heat in 2011 that many of his compatriots still believe that the fuserium disease that afflicted the Headingley square in 1972 was a foul Pommie conspiracy to allow Derek Underwood to bowl them out. But 'Fingo' was in a relaxed mood the following day and I thoroughly enjoyed taking part in the commentary on what, fortunately, was a memorable game played on a lovely sunny day. Dennis Amiss made the first hundred in a one-day international in England and ever since these games have been used to blood both cricketers and commentators.

My performance at Old Trafford apparently met with general satisfaction. To my great good fortune I have been part of the commentary team in every season since. The pleasures are twofold: the actual business of cricket commentary, a delight in itself; and the interaction with those who listen. They include some very interesting and important people, as guests on our Saturday lunchtime programme, *Beyond the Boundary*, regularly prove. But it was still a pleasant surprise when, as *TMS* producer and cricket correspondent Peter Baxter and I were summoned to lunch at Westminster a few years ago.

Sir John Major was 'only' the First Secretary to the Treasury then but, like many MPs, he was concerned about a threat to the future of *TMS*. Cricket commentaries had not until then struck me as being the sort of issue that might be debated in the House of Commons. Bodyline, the 1970 South Africa tour, and more recently cricketing relations with Zimbabwe, have all been legitimate political issues, but was the question of whether or not cricket commentaries might be interrupted by football really a matter of national importance?

. To the future Prime Minister there was no question that it was. Over a convivial lunch round the corner from Parliament, the amiable future president of Surrey and MCC committee member, and his Lancastrian political ally Robert Atkins, also now knighted, left us in no doubt about how strongly they felt the need to preserve the programme's individual identity.

The interplay between commentators and listeners both then and now suggests that he was right. People of all ages and types love the combination of cricketing know-how and friendly chat in an atmosphere of relaxed enjoyment. The threat that was worrying followers of *TMS* then was that ball-by-ball commentary on Radio Three was destined to take its chance with other sport on a wavelength carrying a burgeoning news and sports service called Radio Five Live. The Government had decreed that in 1990 the BBC would lose two of its eight wavelengths and the plan was for Radio Five to take the Test match commentaries under its wing the following year, or as soon as the old Radio Three medium wave disappeared.

In 1989 no fewer than 140 MPs signed a motion deploring the proposed changes. Gillian Reynolds supported them in the *Daily Telegraph*, calling *TMS* 'a piece of radio which is very British yet which transcends class, age and gender'. *The Times* reported a spectator at Headingley, Denis Read from Ramsbottom in Lancashire, as saying of *Test Match Special*: 'It's cricket and it's

England and it's marvellous. It wouldn't be the same without it. It just makes me feel good and it always has done.'

Happily, and thanks largely to the public outcry, a solution was found, namely to reposition *TMS* on Radio Four long wave. Now we also transmit to a growing audience on Radio Five Live Sports Extra, in the crystal clear digital quality of DAB.

From Howard Marshall through John Arlott and Brian Johnston to Jonathan Agnew and Henry Blofeld; from Norman Yardley and Freddie Brown through Trevor Bailey and Fred Trueman to Mike Selvey, Vic Marks, Geoffrey Boycott and a wide choice of overseas summarisers, the programme has carefully mixed its characters, never ignoring the cake and champagne but, touch wood, never taking its eye off the ball. All of us are forever reliant on the wonderful variety and unpredictability of cricket to keep a devoted audience interested; sometimes even enthralled.

It may seem just the same as it was in the Arlott/Johnston era, when 'Blowers' and myself were cutting our teeth and Frindall was already established as the statistical pillar of the programme. In truth, however, the approach has gently and subtly changed, maintaining its light-hearted, civilised, authoritative approach to a day's cricket, with no holds barred on any topic thrown up by events in the middle and on the fringes, but gradually developing a sharper journalistic edge without ever abandoning its core role: to tell the listener what is happening in the match and why.

Listeners to *Test Match Special* of a certain age – and there are many still about – look back with nostalgia to the days of the 1960s and 1970s when Johnston, the jester, and Arlott, the poet, jointly built the programme's reputation. John became a treasured companion in the commentary box and Brian a personal friend, despite our difference in age.

A mix of voices and personalities has always been part of the attraction of *TMS*. The two most famous and fondly remembered commentators proved it. In voice and character alike they were poles apart; but as a professional act (although in both cases they were natural broadcasters who never needed to act) they were as complementary as cornflakes and milk.

They were linked by their talent, their love of cricket, the freedom offered them by the burgeoning OB department in the years after the war and the affection and admiration in which they were held by grateful listeners.

They were separated by much more. Where Arlott was often sombre and serious, Johnston was skittish and comical; where Arlott paced himself like an Oriental spinner, Johnston rushed in like an Aussie fast bowler; where Arlott treasured words like the poet he was and mulled them over as if he were testing the nose of a vintage Château Lafite, Johnston used them with gay abandon, without art or pretension. One was the student of the game who became a professor; the other the eternal schoolboy who believed that every day's cricket might, at its dawn, become the greatest and most exciting he had ever witnessed. One was sometimes maudlin, heavy as a brooding cloud, the other invariably light as a soufflé. One carried and dwelt upon the burdens of life; the other cast them aside as quickly as he could.

Both were original, completely true to themselves. If Arlott was more troubled by self-doubt and insecurity, deep down he knew that he was a man worthy of his calling. Johnston never doubted it: he could not believe his good fortune at finding a medium that suited him so well. If Arlott's performances as a cricket commentator were less even than Johnston's he was capable of truly virtuoso performances of inspired description. The occasion I remember best was the one when the BBC's managing director, Ian Trethowan, came into the box during the World Cup final in 1975. Clive Lloyd was batting majestically and John knew that there was an influential audience. Besides that, like all of us at Lord's on that glorious day, he was enjoying himself.

'The stroke of a man knocking a thistle top off with a walking stick' was his description of one majestic Lloyd pull to the Grandstand. Equally graphic was his portrayal of little white-capped Dickie Bird, with his hunched back, catching the excitement like everyone. 'And Umpire Bird is having a wonderful time, signalling everything insight, including stop to traffic coming on from behind.'

Brian was not capable of such imagery but in their contrasting way both were consummate broadcasting professionals. To listen to them was a delight and to work with them an extraordinary privilege for me, in John's case from 1972 until he retired to a quieter, contemplative life on Alderney in 1980, and in Brian's until he had a fatal heart attack while still working hard at the age of eighty-one in 1993.

It was not possible to be their colleague for so long without becoming immensely fond of them both. I knew Brian longer and better; often during Lord's Test matches staying with him and Pauline, his pretty, forceful, sometimes impetuous but always staunchly supportive wife. Exactly ten years younger than her beloved spouse, she still lives in the house at Boundary Road in St. John's Wood that succeeded the family home a few hundred yards away, at Hamilton Terrace, one of the most elegant streets in London.

'B.J.' was wonderful company, as funny in private conversation as he was on his feet after dinner on a public occasion. He loved to pun, and gossip, not least, of course, about people in cricket. All his huge fund of stories became familiar in time but it was his flair for entertainment, both in private and in public, that made them genuinely funny every time. Barry Johnston, his eldest son, recalled in his biography of his father how, sometimes, his reaction to something that had amused him on television – a bad piece of acting, perhaps or the way that someone had said something, would start Brian giggling and soon have the whole family overcome by tears of laughter too, sometimes without even knowing what had started it.

The famous 'leg-over' incident with Jonathan Agnew, a classic example of why live broadcasting is so often more interesting or amusing than recorded, was a case in point. What created the uncontrollable mirth, of course, was the very professionalism of them both: the desperate attempt to keep going. Aggers soon became speechless but the old trouper did his best to carry on.

Everyone listening loved it and of course the giggles were utterly infectious. I wish there had also been a recording of the day that Brian and I simultaneously collapsed into similarly uncontrollable laughter during a meaningless World Cup match between England and Canada to which practically no one can have been listening. On that occasion there was simply a long silence as Brian, unable to believe the name of the Canadian player that I had just identified for him, Showkhat Bash, retreated from the microphone to try to regain his power of speech. The hiatus seemed to us interminable. In the studio in London the engineers thought the line must have gone down. I have got the giggles on air only once since, in 2008 when, commentating as Stuart Broad bowled to New Zealand's captain, Daniel Vettori, I said:

'Broad runs in, he bowls, and this time Vettori lets it go outside the off stump. It was a good length, inviting him to fish, but Vettori, so to speak, stayed on the bank and kept his rod up.'

Jeremy Coney, my summariser, offered no assistance as I realised the *double entendre*. According to a report in the *Evening Standard*, 'seconds later listeners could hear the veteran commentator . . . struggling to keep his composure. His voice got steadily higher as he said: "I don't know if he's a fisherman, is he?"'

It's as well Brian was not there. It did not matter what age you were with him. He simply loved company although on the rare occasions when he allowed himself a holiday he was no less happy relaxing in a deck-chair with a book. Pauline was a professional photographer and one of her most memorable images of her husband was taken in just such a pose on the Greek island of Lefkas, with a floppy sun-hat on his head, the prominent nose and ears in profile and the sea lapping at the frame of the chair.

As a young and impecunious married man I found dining with John, as I sometimes did at hotels during Test matches, at once stimulating and somewhat daunting. Not because one knew one was out of one's depth as far as knowledge and experience were concerned but because John, the gourmet and wine expert, would choose what he fancied and say to the head waiter – 'split the bill between all of us if you will'. It was worth it for the conversation, which might range anywhere, always with the great man directing it. Hotels were one thing, however; an invitation to lunch at his wonderfully spacious house in Alresford – Hampshire, of course – quite something else. You could forget plans to do anything else for the rest of the day.

When his second wife, Valerie, was alive, a woman as intelligent and bibulous as himself, they were as hospitable as each other and I cringe still at my state of inebriation when I left their company at about five o' clock one late autumn afternoon, having stayed 'for a spot of lunch'. I had already been several times to the loo but the first thing I did after turning my car in the direction of Sussex was to find the nearest hedge in a country lane for further relief.

By then John was wearing a black tie every day – as he did for the rest of his life when a tie was necessary dress – as penance for the decision to give his beloved eldest son, James, a sports car which, tragically, he drove beneath a lorry having fallen asleep at the wheel after a new year's party. No one who loses a child can ever be the same and John could not, even for a day, forget the loss.

Brian had known tragedy too. He was only ten and in his second year at prep school in Eastbourne when his father was drowned in rough sea off Bude in Cornwall, the traditional venue for Johnston family holidays. In the space of three months, indeed, Brian lost his father and his shattered grandfather, Reginald, who had been Governor of the Bank of England. As a consequence both the home where he had been brought up and much of the family's financial security were lost too.

Not, however, young B.J.'s inclination to go through life as the joker. The truth, I think, is that he was one of those rare human beings (my daughter, happily, is another) who simply have a God-given gift for sharing their pleasure in life. How misguided was the retort of his subsequent housemaster at Eton, A.C. Huson: 'You won't get anywhere in life because you talk too much.' But there was a much more perceptive verdict from the same source in a report later in his school career, when he had become captain of games. 'He has been if anything more conscientious. I cannot recall one single instance of his not being present to encourage, and instruct, any one of his teams, when it was even remotely possible for him to be there. It is a great gift this of Bri's, being able to keep up his enthusiasms . . . he has a very great power over his fellow creatures.'

These gifts were wasted to a large extent in his brief period in the coffee business before the war but as a Guards officer who gained a Military Cross for his 'dynamic personality, coupled with his untiring determination and cheerfulness under fire' they were very much to the fore and they came across throughout his BBC career.

Born two years later, in 1914, John had a very different upbringing. Having left Queen Mary's Grammar School at his home town of Basingstoke after a dispute with his headmaster, he worked for a time at the local town planning office and then as a diet clerk, calculating food allocations, at a mental hospital. In 1934 he joined Southampton police force and remained with them for the next eleven years, starting on the beat. When the war came he worked for Special Branch, screening aliens. His first marriage, in 1940, was to Dawn, a cheery looking hospital nurse who bore him two sons, James and Timothy. John himself was a good-looking fellow in his youth, solidly built and naturally strong. He kept his hair, and a pair of prominent eyebrows that added to his aura of wisdom, into old age.

Encouraged by John Betjeman and Andrew Young, he began to write his own poems, many of which have found their deserved way into anthologies, not least – but by no means only – cricketing ones. His lines on Jack Hobbs, the master, were themselves masterful. His own gravestone on Alderney contains lines from his poem to Andrew Young that neatly encapsulate his own sharp eye for the human drama of cricket, so evident in his commentaries:

> So clear you see these timeless things
> That, like a bird, the vision sings.

Arlott wore his deep literary knowledge lightly, in fact, during his commentaries – and in his cricket writing for the *Guardian* too – but he was familiar with and to many of his contemporary writers, poets and artists—Betjeman, Edmund Blunden, Cyril Connolly, T.S. Eliot, Osbert Lancaster, John Piper and Vita Sackville-West amongst them. He became a collector not just of books and, subsequently, of wine but also of aquatint engravings – he was an expert on these too – and of other objects as diverse as Sunderland glass and herbs from the Himalayas. It was his poetry that led him to Geoffrey Grigson, a BBC West of England producer, who gave him his first chance to broadcast. He was told that he had 'a vulgar voice but an interesting mind'. It was true, yet the voice became one of the most imitated there has ever been outside politics, not least in my schooldays by myself.

Towards the end of the war he began to feature on various talk radio programmes until, in the summer of 1945, he was appointed literary programme producer in the BBC's overseas service, a position formerly occupied by no less a literary talent than George Orwell. Rather like Brian, but in quite a different way, the war proved to be a watershed in his life, but perhaps there was hardly anyone of a similar age for whom that was not so. He remained on the BBC staff until 1953, for the last two years as an instructor in the staff training unit, but he operated as a free-lance for the broadcasting, cricket commentating and writing that increasingly occupied his time. Although for the rest of his life he was busy and in demand – even in retirement on Alderney – he never quite lost the feeling of insecurity common to most people who work only for themselves and their families.

His first opportunity to commentate on cricket (as opposed to contributing talks on the subject) came when the Indians toured in 1946. No one could fail to notice his flair for words or the distinctive slow pace with which they were used and the deliberate, rough voice, always glibly described as a Hampshire burr but actually unique. From 1947, when he commentated again on the South Africa tour and on county cricket, he became an established part of the BBC commentary team. It missed the point that John's accent was so different from the more stereotypical BBC voices around him, notably those of Swanton and Alston. It was talent, his unhurried, measured style of delivery and his breadth of general knowledge, not the Hampshire accent, that made him so famous so quickly and for so long.

He had played just enough cricket to be able to interpret what was going on with insight and he knew enough of the players to be able to add an extra ingredient to his natural – indeed police-trained – eye for detail. He superimposed knowledge of the history of the game and of the character of those he was describing to a grateful unseen audience. He loved the players and they loved him to the extent of making him President of the Cricketers' Association. His innate liberalism – and actual support for a Liberal party for whom he stood as candidate for Epping in both the 1955 and 1959 General Elections – gave him an awareness of public affairs, and a knowledge about the procedure of institutions and committees.

He was therefore especially useful to the Association when debates raged over the two great issues of his later years as a journalist and commentator, and of my early years. These were, of course, cricketing relations with South Africa and the schism in world cricket over television coverage of the game in Australia. Professionals were pushed into one of two camps by Kerry Packer's two-year programme of international matches, using players whose services he had bought for salaries vastly greater than those they had previously been earning.

If John was broadly neutral in the battle between Packer and the establishment he was emphatically and implacably opposed to the South African Government and its pernicious apartheid policy. He had seen and abhorred it at first hand on the England tour of 1948/9. If his commentary role did not allow him to express much personal comment on that subject, other than when it was raining, his better-paid role as cricket correspondent of the *Guardian* enabled him to enlighten readers of a like mind.

He kept up a prodigious work rate in and out of the cricket season. He produced numerous character sketches for various publications and his books included a wonderfully astute study of Fred Trueman, with whom he worked happily in the *TMS* box for his last seven years. Later he also wrote for the *Guardian* on wine which had the added advantage, no doubt, of adding some free bottles to the major collection he had in the cellars of the Old Sun, only some of which was shipped across to Alderney, although there was never a danger of his falling short of supplies there.

Policeman he may have been but I never heard him say that he never drunk on duty, unlike Jonathan Agnew, who quite rightly spotted the signs of a little too much levity, leading to a lack of professionalism, on the part of some. Arlott, however, could take it and I never saw the extremely large glass of red that he liked to have late in the morning affect his performance, with one notable exception, or near exception, in his final year, 1980, when he had announced his retirement in advance and was feted at every ground he attended. During the interval of the Test at Nottingham that year I remember the sales manager of Ansells, the brewery that owned the Trent Bridge Inn, getting up to say what a great privilege it had been to have John at their lunches for so many years. In truth he had not needed much condescension, and nor did I, to eat their best beef and drink their finest claret!

In the Lord's Test of that summer he gave his usual immaculate description of the play in the last twenty minutes before lunch — if, perhaps, a little more ponderous in pace and tone

TEST MATCH SPECIAL – COMMENTATORS

than he had been in his prime. The moment, however, that he said his last words – 'And for his summary of the morning's play it will be Fred Trueman' – he slumped forward on the desk in front of him and went instantly to sleep. This was a matter first of concern, then of amusement to the rest of us in the box, but Fred, eyes fastened on the players coming off the field in front of him, was blissfully unaware until some two minutes later he completed his not uncritical comments on the England fast bowling with the words 'That's my opinion, anyway. I don't know what you think, John?'

He turned to see Arlott's heavy form slumped unconscious across the desk beside him and with wonderful presence of mind – despite a look of some horror on his face – he added: 'Well, John is nodding his head vigorously, and with that, back to t'studio.' Some weeks later, at the Test at Lord's to celebrate the centenary of Australia's first official Test in England, John, famously, refused to make any dramatic farewell and simply handed over to the next man (who happened to be me) as the final act of his career as a Test commentator. He was not unaware, however, that it was a moment of national importance and when the public address announcer, Alan Curtis, said at the end of the over that John Arlott had just finished his last stint as a Test commentator the great man himself was visible, making his way out of the box at the top of the pavilion. The players turned towards him and joined a standing crowd in a generous ovation.

It was a moving tribute and one that Brian would certainly have received too had he chosen his moment to go. It was his natural friendliness, after all, and the atmosphere of gaiety and fun that he brought to his radio commentaries when television was unwise enough to say that it no longer wanted him in 1970, that expanded the range and, definitely, the popularity of the programme. Hudson, the wise head of OBs at the time,

snapped him up by simply creating space for four commentators instead of three at each match. By then he was fifty-eight,
only two years away from his official retirement with the BBC.
Already he had been working for them for twenty-six years, the
result of his yearning to be an entertainer – originally, he hoped,
on the stage – and a chance meeting with two OB stalwarts,
Wynford Vaughan-Thomas and Stewart MacPherson, when they
were reporting on the Allied advance towards the end of the war.

Invited for a voice test by the respected head of outside broadcasts, his fellow Etonian Seymour de Lotbinière, alias Lobby,
Brian impressed him when, instead of going to Piccadilly Circus
to produce a five-minute written report on what he had seen,
he recorded one instead by going into a record shop and using
the 'record your own message' service. His second test was to
interview passers-by, in Oxford Street, under the supervision of
Vaughan-Thomas. The result, by Vaughan-Thomas's reckoning,
was 'gloriously uninhibited'.

He soon made his mark in a pioneering department of the
Corporation. His love of musicals and the music hall gave him
the pleasant job of sifting plays and comedy material for broadcasts, then introducing and linking excerpts from West End
shows. It brought him into contact with comedians he revered
such as Arthur Askey and Bud Flanagan, whose 'Underneath
the Arches' Brian later performed with the great man and
with anyone else who would sing with him in years ahead. He
carried in his head a tremendous stock of material from those
days, especially of the music hall double-act variety. Example:
'Excuse me, do you know you've got a banana in your ear?'

'I'm sorry?'

'I said did you know you've got a banana in your ear?'

'I'm sorry, I can't hear a word you're saying: I've got a banana
in my ear.'

He was as likely to come out with something like this on the air at appropriate moments as he was in private. He had already made his mark on listeners by the time that he was invited to revive a feature called 'Let's Go Somewhere', started by John Snagge before the war, as part of the Saturday night Home Service programme *In Town Tonight*. Starting with a visit to the Chamber of Horrors after dark at Madame Tussauds he made a tremendous success of an enormous variety of features, from serving in a fish and chip shop or broadcasting from the driver's cab in a tube train, to quite dangerous stunts such as being shot sixty feet in the air up a vertical tunnel by a pilot's ejector seat (microphone attached), riding bareback on a circus horse or feigning a robbery and being attacked on a padded arm by a police Alsatian.

It was his old friend Ian Orr-Ewing who, as head of outside broadcasts in the BBC's fledgling television service, first recruited him for cricket commentary. Working with Jim Swanton, Robert Hudson and, a little later, Peter West, on home Tests, he, and from 1964 Richie Benaud, paved the way for the former Test cricketers who now have almost a monopoly as television commentators. As ever Brian was sunny of voice and mien, a pleasure to listen to and charming company whenever his face appeared at intervals in the match. Gradually too, he began reporting on tours overseas, both for radio and television and in 1963, to his great pride, he was appointed the BBC's second cricket correspondent.

Such was his energy that in 1993, still loving his work and claiming that his five children and, by now, several grandchildren, needed his financial support, he undertook a series of one-man autobiographical shows at provincial theatres (thirty-two in all, over nine months) that must have been both mentally and physically demanding. Invariably *An Evening with Johnners* played to full houses, and always to delighted ones. He loved cricket, he loved life and he himself was greatly loved both by everyone he knew and a huge array of listeners whom he never met. The cakes sent to him in the commentary box to keep him – and us – going were but one symbol of that affection.

Brian's death in London on 5 January 1994, a few weeks after a severe heart attack that had affected his brain but, even then, not his spirit, was the signal for widespread expressions of affection and tribute. His status was such that a few days later Raymond Gubbay organised a tribute at the Royal Albert Hall, which I presented at short notice before a large audience. There was an incredible feeling of warmth and affection towards him that Sunday afternoon as there was at the service of thanksgiving in Westminster Abbey, five months after his death.

As Arlott and Johnston were paired in the memory, so up to a point, I suppose, have been myself and Henry Blofeld. We got to cricket commentary at almost the same time (I in 1972, 'Blowers' a season later although he was well established as a cricket reporter by then) and before long we were joined by a more experienced broadcaster at the time than either of us, Don Mosey, who flew the northern flag with resolution. I had always imagined that I got on well with Don, who was a highly professional wordsmith inclined to be a little slow on the ball when things that he was describing happened quickly, but we all have strengths and weaknesses. It transpired when he wrote his autobiography that he harboured various grudges, including one against myself for, in a nutshell, becoming cricket corre-spondent before him despite being younger. Don got his chance when I resigned the job in 1980.

At least Don was content with a single book about his career. Henry, by contrast, is well ahead of most in the autobiography stakes, having reeled off a series of books with the apparent ease of a conjuror pulling rabbits from a hat. Recently too he has emulated Brian by travelling to theatres all round the country, talking about his life. He even hired the Albert Hall to celebrate his seventieth birthday in 2009.

He has had several different agents, a policy that has worked well for him, and has dashed off columns for many different newspapers. In his time he has been 'big' on radio in the West Indies and Australia, where they were intrigued at first by what might be called his 'broad Etonian', and very big in the smaller pool of New Zealand, where for a time he was also the host of a television chat show. Unlike Chris Cowdrey, whose quick wit was missed on *TMS* when he switched to talkSPORT, Blowers was forgiven for leaving *Test Match Special* for a time to do television commentary for Sky, who offered better rewards, in monetary terms at least. It was in that role during an England tour of India that he informed newly joining viewers that during the tea interval there had been a minute's silence to 'celebrate' the assassination of Mrs Gandhi.

We have all had moments of embarrassment like that and in his life generally Henry has had his ups and downs, including the argument with a bus towards the end of his time at Eton that set back an extremely promising career as a cricketer. As a schoolboy wicket-keeper and batsman he had scored a hundred at Lord's against the Combined Services in 1956 that promised fame as a player. He still played for Cambridge (averaging a very respectable twenty-four in first-class matches, including a hundred against MCC at Lord's) and time and again in his life he has shown the same remarkable resilience.

If the gift of the gab is the first essential for a broadcaster, Blowers has never been found wanting. His other great gift was his voice which seems to make women of all ages melt down the airwaves, especially if they come from the same social background as himself. He has never made any secret of his high society origins in Norfolk, nor the education at Eton and Cambridge that separates him from the great majority of his listeners. Most of them rather like his plummy accent, although for this and other reasons he probably divides opinion more than most.

No one would accuse Henry of overdoing his research but he has always used his experience cleverly, not least when it comes to the identification of one Sri Lankan cricketer from another. It was a standing in-joke that when the relatively easily pronounced John and de Silva were playing for Sri Lanka they seemed to do all the fielding between them while Blowers was at the microphone.

In fact he has an excellent memory for anything other than names and will turn his hand to talking or writing about most things, especially if someone will pay him for it. While most of his *TMS* colleagues settle for a break at lunchtime, Blowers will often dash round to someone's box to sip a glass or two and chat to the clients.

He never fails to amuse me when he recounts, at great length, the occasion when he mistook the entrance door of a hotel room for the bathroom door as he went to answer a call of nature in the night. Thus it was that he found himself in the nude in the middle of a corridor with the door locked behind him and no key. The consequences were the hilarious stuff of an Ealing comedy. Unlike Brian, however, he is not always as amusing an entertainer of a live audience as they expect him to be. Despite that, his roadshow continues to be in demand because he is a genuine eccentric and has a fund of anecdotes. He also has extraordinary energy. I asked him once whether he really needed to work as hard as he does. In a rare moment of revelation about his real — as opposed to public — personality he replied: 'If I didn't I know I would simply stay at home and drink myself to death.' It is a wise man who knows himself.

If his voice and its effect on women have been the chief secrets of Henry's success, members of the fairer sex have also caused him plenty of problems over the years. He got out of the habit of marrying after three attempts but for years whenever one saw him at the start of a new season, he would declare that he had fallen in love again, usually, so it seemed, with a wealthy widow who had one comfortable house in somewhere like Gloucestershire, another in Chelsea and a third in a desirable place in the sun. Recently he has found genuine happiness with an Italian widow and his commentaries seem to have revived as a direct result.

For most of our time together in the commentary box Henry and I were shrewdly guided by Peter Baxter, producer of *TMS* for thirty-four years. Peter is a gentle soul although the sometimes impossible demands of his job would occasionally drive him into foot-stamping rage. His general approach was to allow the programme to evolve naturally but that is not to say that he was afraid of change. It was in his time, for example, that the idea of the commentators chatting through the rain became a habit, one that was greatly appreciated by our listeners. The tradition started by accident when the lightest possible rain began falling on the Saturday of the England v. West Indies Test at Lord's in 1976, but seemed unlikely to hold up play for long. Until then it had been the custom to go back to the studio for some Bach, Berlioz or Beethoven when there was no play – this being in the days when ball-by-ball commentary was transmitted, somewhat incongruously, on Radio Three.

On that occasion there was never a time that the prospects of play were hopeless so the chat carried on all day. Many a listener has written in since to say that the commentary is all well and good but it is when it is raining that it really becomes entertaining. True or not, Baxter had the sense to realise that to the millions who love the game almost any cricket talk is better than none.

I first met this affable, conscientious fellow, with a retentive memory for many things other than cricket, at Stamford Bridge, in the days when Bobby Tambling was on the wing and Peter Bonetti was leaping between the goalposts. I was reporting a Chelsea match; Peter was sent along to guide me, if I remember correctly, on the art of using a COOBE, shorthand for 'commentator operated outside broadcasting equipment'. He retained a quick sense of humour in the years that followed despite the Corporation's complex internal politics and his occasional volcanic eruptions when the line suddenly went dead in some hot and dusty commentary point thousands of miles from Broadcasting House.

On the air his was a voice of pleasing calm, often heard in the intervals or filling in with capable commentary off a television screen when he was in London in the early hours of the morning. He would love to have commentated more regularly but behind the scenes he was invaluable. He would arrive at his post earlier than anyone except the groundsman (or perhaps Dickie Bird) to make sure that the indispensable engineers had everything in order, and leave it at the end of the day, often in darkness, only when the last interviews had been dispatched.

I worked closely with Peter during my two stints as the BBC cricket correspondent. He was shrewd enough to spot the outstanding Jonathan Agnew as my successor, for which listeners have been heartily thankful ever since! 'Aggers' has been kind enough to say that he had admired my 'gravitas' in that role, to which I would reply that I greatly admire his own lightness of touch. In no way does that imply that he is a lightweight: far from it. He has gone out of his way to build the profile of *TMS* still further and has deliberately assumed the role of leader of the band by linking his own personality and experiences to the commentary, building shrewdly on the Johnston persona. He is highly influential in cricket, having bowled with great distinction for Leicestershire, played for England and then buckled down to a career as a journalist with real determination. His reputation leapt as a result of the 'leg-over' giggles with B.J. in 1991, his first season on *TMS*. Regularly played back on the air ever since, it never ceases to make people laugh. I shall probably take it on my desert island.

Affable and amusing, Jonathan nevertheless gets to the heart of important issues, interviewing people with just the right mixture of respect and, when necessary, hardness. Had he been politically inclined he would have been brilliant as a presenter of the *Today* programme. He manages to make all his subjects feel relaxed, in the true spirit of *TMS*, but he, like Peter Baxter's conscientious successor, Adam Mountford, have sharpened the programme's news sense, particularly when probing topical matters in the lunch and tea intervals. In this both Peter and Adam have been greatly helped by their ubiquitous assistant Shilpa Patel, who is much more than *Test Match Special*'s equivalent of Samantha, the imaginary helper to Humphrey Lyttelton and Jack Dee in *I'm Sorry I Haven't a Clue*.

Tiny, attractive, beguiling and determined, Shilpa has been able to persuade almost anyone – be they prime ministers like Sir John Major, pop singers like Lily Allen, actors like Daniel Radcliffe, or unknown enthusiasts going off to play cricket for charity in the Himalayas – to come up to the box to talk during the course of a Test match. She is especially predatory during the Lord's Tests, keeping an eagle eye (actually, usually my binoculars) on the President's box and seizing upon any celebrities there.

The early BBC managers believed that cricket was far too slow for commentary. In fact, of course, its ebbs and flows allow all sorts of diversions, as long as the cricket, the *raison d'être* after all, comes first. Interviews such as these, whether they occur during commentary or in the intervals, add much to the scope and appeal of a programme that might otherwise be too recondite.

Peter Baxter made a regular feature of the Saturday lunchtime interviews with celebrities from fields other than cricket. A genuine interest in the game was supposed to be the common denominator. Over the years I have greatly enjoyed talking at leisured length to such different enthusiasts as the warm and greatly respected Lancastrian footballer Jimmy Armfield, the widely experienced politician Peter Brooke, alias Lord Brooke of Sutton Mandeville, the playwright Nick Warburton, actors like the engaging Charles Collingwood, and the unruly Sir Robin Day, who was definitely a better interviewer than interviewee. He came to the box determined to say his prepared piece about Wally Hammond, whatever I asked him!

These days 'Aggers' likes to do all these celebrity interviews and I don't blame him because they are great fun, but he met his severest challenge when the distinguished actor Edward Fox for some reason answered virtually all his questions with extremely brief answers. He was thoroughly chastened by that experience, but, being a child of the Twitter age, he was like the cat with the cream when Shilpa acquired interviews with Lily Allen and Daniel Radcliffe.

Assiduous homework on the subject can be important on these occasions even if, for someone so busy as Agnew, research has to be done by others. The salutary story is told of Sir Thomas Beecham, the great conductor, arriving very tired at Sydney airport one day and being pushed by a brash young radio reporter to appear on his evening magazine show a few hours later. 'We'll only need you to talk for twenty minutes, Sir Thomas', the reporter assured him. 'Delighted', said Beecham, taking an instant dislike to the cocky familiarity displayed by the persistent young Aussie. 'Just send a car to my hotel half an hour before the programme and ask me if I've had an interesting life. I'll talk for as long as you want.'

Thus encouraged the youngster enjoyed a longer lunch than usual. Come the programme he introduced Sir Thomas as 'the great British composer', turned to him and said: 'Sir Thomas, you must have had a long and interesting career?' 'Long, yes', replied the maestro, 'but interesting, no, not particularly.' And that was all that he had to say, leaving his over-confident inquisitor to flounder.

It is largely due to Baxter that *TMS* is now as much a winter programme as a summer one. He loved travelling, although his devotion to the job cost him the second of his three marriages. He had responsibility for all aspects of broadcasting cricket on radio, including the design of commentary positions as grounds began to develop their facilities. With a lot of encouragement from me he managed to persuade the architect of the *avant-garde* media centre at Lord's, and MCC's charming 'chairman of Estates', Maurice de Rohan, to have a window in the commentary box that opened.

Down below, the writers have had to make do with a huge glass window that seals out the natural air and, with it, the 'feel' for whichever cricket match is being played far below them. To my mind that close affinity with events in the middle is essential to a full understanding of what is happening. These days at Lord's, and in too many other modern press boxes, one might just as well be watching the game on television.

As for *TMS*, touch wood it will continue to please. Adam and Jonathan have been good at embracing old-fashioned technologies such as emails and brand new ones like Facebook and Twitter (will it all get more instant and more trivial?) while this old fogey tries to keep up. It is, I must admit, remarkable that people can react instantly to something that has been said. Contributions are often either pertinent or funny. We have to keep moving with the times, as long as we do not forget that the whole purpose is to describe the cricket match itself.

It took one of the newer commentators, Simon Hughes, a talented writer with an inquiring mind and a thick enough skin to ask anyone anything, some time to realise that commentary is not a matter of debating cricketing issues, however interesting they may be, with the game as a background: it is exactly the opposite. He established a reputation on television but, with that lesson now learned, he could also become a popular radio performer. Simon Mann deserves to be that already. As a professional broadcaster he, like Mark Pougatch and Arlo White, two more recent commentators who did not always hit the right notes, Simon is a professional broadcaster who understands the necessary disciplines. When I am listening he tells me what I want to know, not always the case with others.

That essential job is quite simple, really. Listener first, commentator second. The commentator's essential responsibility is to tell the listener what he or she wants to know: the score, the context of the match, who is bowling to whom, what an unfamiliar player looks like, where the ball has pitched (both its length and its line), what shot the batsman has played or attempted and what is happening in the instant of his playing the ball. After every ball the field is free for wider observations: for humour, colour, history, statistics and anything else that may interest or engage the listener; but only until the bowler runs in again.

The sheer volume of international cricket guarantees that there will be plenty of opportunity for new voices. The chosen few will be inheriting a great tradition.

I have been portrayed as the sober presence in the box who keeps both eyes on the cricket but I like to think that those who listen properly and regularly to the programme appreciate that there is some wit and wider wisdom occasionally imparted along with (as often as possible) the score. Only once, however, have I departed on a flight of fancy that might have got out of control. That was the result not of alcohol but a sudden burst of Christmas spirit. The occasion was a phone-in during a Test in Australia when I was the ABC's guest commentator. Rain had stopped play for a while. Someone rang the programme to ask if anyone knew the origin of the name 'Dodemaide', Tony Dodemaide having just made the national side as an all-rounder. Norman O'Neill fielded the question but said he had no idea of the answer.

For some reason I decided to have some fun and said that I did. The name was derived, I said, from an old custom in the Caribbean at Christmas-time in the days when wealthy land-owners had lots of servants. I set the scene of a husband and wife discussing in their drawing-room who would give Christmas parcels to which servants. 'I'll tell you what' said the wife at last. 'You do de butler and I'll do de maid'. It was the sort of pun that Frank Muir and Denis Norden used to produce in the old radio programme *My Word* and, to my relief, it was deemed to be hilarious, not least by Norman, who mentioned it every time I saw him in later years.

He was a convivial companion as a summariser on the tours when the BBC would simply transmit ABC commentaries, and there have been many others.

FROM BROWN TO BOYCOTT

'He's a good bowler. Good bowlers take wickets, good batsmen score
runs. It's quite simple.'
  'I am very, very sorry but will someone please tell me what's going
off out there? I have never seen anything like it in my en-tire life.'
  'My Granny could have caught that.'

Bailey, Trueman and Boycott. You recognised them, no doubt.
More and more of the occupants of both press and commentary
boxes these days are ex-Test players but for a long time the *TMS*
summarisers were, first and foremost, radio specialists.

In my early BBC days I worked briefly with Norman Yardley,
who was charming, Freddie Brown, a bon viveur who could
not have been more friendly, and Jack Fingleton, who could
be mischievous, although not so much as Lindsay Hassett, the
Australian Broadcasting Commission's main 'expert voice' for
many years. Lindsay, his pixy eyes twinkling as once his feet
had done when he batted against the spinners, encouraged me
to drink plenty of the excellent white wine that was on offer
at lunchtime one day at the MCG and during the commentary
later he frequently remarked that I seemed to be unusually

prone to giggling. Alas, I was, although I doubt whether any of the listeners worried about it.

There were two or three other occasions over the years when I probably drank a glass or two more than I should have done before commentating although I would never have let it affect me to the extent that it did the accomplished Alan Gibson, who was banned from ball-by-ball for ever by Cliff Morgan after a day at Headingley when his state of inebriation was all too obvious. In recent years I have generally followed Agnew's example and kept off all alcohol until the day's work has been done.

There have occasionally been modest exceptions at Lord's when Judy and I have been guests in the President's box, where the company is always stimulating and the effect of the slope on that Grandstand side of the ground allows both a commanding and an intimate view of the cricket. I have also broken the rule to allow myself a glass of wine at lunchtime at Leeds, where Carol Rymer, Yorkshire's first female committee member, has for many years included me in one of her picnics, held on the edge of the rugby football ground. I have never tasted better sandwiches than hers.

Adam Mountford has added a number of new voices in recent times, most of them lively enthusiasts in touch with the modern game, although one or two of them have been inclined to talk so much that they allow no time for the natural rhythm of a commentary and that vital moment of suspense, just before each ball is bowled, that ought always to be the preserve of the designated commentator.

Phil Tufnell and Michael Vaughan are two of the lively new recruits to *TMS*. One brings a mischievous sense of fun and wide experience of life, the other up-to-date knowledge of the England camp. 'Tuffers' is an extraordinary chap with a real flair for entertaining people. His past is chequered, especially off the field, but, having now found the right wife and the right agent, he is making a small fortune from his various media outlets, to the extent that we are lucky to have him with us as often as we do. He has a lively mind, a good memory and, if not as on the ball as Michael when it comes to knowledge of the players, he is much cleverer than he likes to disclose. I find him good company on and off the air.

Working with Michael is like sitting next to an electric fence. Neither his mind nor any of his senses seem to be still for a second. His iPad and Twitter messages are never far away. He has quickly built a large following although he has had to learn (like many before him) that the commentator needs time to set the scene, to give the score and to recap on events earlier in the day. There is nothing worse than listening for ages until he does. But, like all ex-Test captains, England's general in the marvellous 2005 campaign against Australia has much to offer in interpreting the tactics and thought processes of the players

Two of his England predecessors were amongst the best 'summarisers' I have worked with, both, alas, all too briefly. Ray Illingworth should have been snapped up by radio and given a long-term contract when he stopped playing in the mid-1970s but BBC hands were no doubt tied both by his budget and by the commitment to the established double act of Fred Trueman and Trevor Bailey. Loyalty is important on these occasions: listeners feel that familiar voices are their friends. All the same, Illy read a game so well on his infrequent radio appearances that he would have been worth filtering into the mix. The same would have applied to Mike Atherton, with whom I briefly worked in the Caribbean. He had everything: humour, quick powers of observation and the all-important sense of rhythm and timing that most other former professional players acquire only with difficulty.

Illingworth and Atherton were both quickly signed instead by television. So was David Lloyd, alias 'Bumble', whose sense of humour was ideal for *TMS*. Our loss has been Sky's gain, radio budgets being more limited, unfortunately, especially for cricket. But summarisers do not have to have been outstanding Test players to be worth hearing. I am glad that I have never had to take decisions about which of all the many possible ex-international cricketers should be employed.

Trevor and Fred were a nicely complementary pair. Fred was full of bombast, suspicious of the establishment, not always without foundation because he had played in an era when snobbery was all around him and there was a class structure, like it or not. In particular, he never trusted Gubby Allen, the *éminence grise* at Lord's when he was in his prime. He was inclined to be repetitive and over critical of the contemporary scene, especially when he was discussing fast bowlers, but his views were invariably just and always to be respected. Like his fellow Yorkshireman Geoffrey Boycott, he could labour a point, but when it started raining he was a peerless raconteur with an amazing memory for matches he had played and characters with whom he had locked horns or shared a dressing-room. Trevor, by contrast, was quite vague and imprecise when it came to the past but as an assessor of current events he was sharp, pithy and an excellent judge of any player. He could always see the wood for the trees.

Like the redoubtable 'F.S.', T.E. Bailey was rightly and widely adulated. He had been in his prime as an England all-rounder in the middle 1950s, when England were for four or five years the best team in the world, blessed with a variety of bowling resources that has not been equalled before or since. At home in 1953 and 1956, and in Australia in 1954/5 he was at the core of the teams that won series against Australia.

His famous rearguard with Willie Watson at Lord's in 1953 was one of the great events of the momentous Coronation year. It happened just as television was burgeoning, so this and the subsequent regaining of the Ashes were on a par in national consciousness with such achievements as the first ascent of Everest.

In short he was a national hero, much as Ian Botham and Andrew Flintoff were to become in other stirring series for the Ashes since. Only Botham, and arguably also Tony Greig, have exceeded him as an England all-rounder since the war. As the figures illustrate, he was wonderfully consistent, the sort of cricketer who seldom let a match go, either for Essex or for his country, without contributing something valuable to the team cause.

His greatest strength as a cricketer, unshakeable belief in himself, applied also to his magisterial comments from commentary boxes. He was both a likeable companion away from the microphone and a most sympathetic working colleague who fully understood that the relationship with a commentator needed to be a partnership. His timing was perfect, except just occasionally when it was raining. Then, Trueman's capacity to ramble reminiscently was more useful than Trevor's penchant for the succinct comment.

Both tended to be sharper in the mornings than they were after a good lunch but Trevor was brilliant when it came to shrewdly observed summaries of a day's play or of a player's performance. I always enjoyed our double acts when, with the clock ticking towards the end of *Test Match Special* for another day, I would read out each bowler's analysis and he would give his characteristic assessment of their performance in the manner of Mr Jingle in *The Pickwick Papers*. 'Very good bowler; bad day.' Or 'Good county bowler, struggling at this level'. Or

'Distinctly promising'. I once called him the greatest distiller since Johnny Walker.

He absolutely loved to make predictions, always with breezy confidence. Sticking his neck out was part of the fun. Comfortably seated in the corner of the box, and always giving the appearance of enjoying himself thoroughly, he would give his opinion on the likely course of the day as early as possible. 'Sunny day; no clouds to worry about; very good pitch; one good New Zealand bowler – Hadlee, he's *high* class; the rest honest trundlers; no decent spinner; England . . . what shall we say . . . 308 for three at the close.' When, very occasionally, such prophecy went spectacularly wrong, he took the leg-pulling with chuckling good humour.

He was impatient of committees but a generous, kindly soul, who, though he relished a challenge on the sporting field – the bigger the better, in fact – was by nature a peacemaker off it. As such in commentary boxes not short of contributors with sizeable egos, he was a precious team member. He was, too, a curious mixture of sharp perceptiveness and woolly vagueness, not least with names.

The story most characteristic of Trevor is the one that he often told himself of his first Test match at Headingley when he decided to take his wife, Greta, to the seaside on the Sunday, always, in those civilised days, a rest day in the five-day game. Never thinking of consulting a map, and vaguely under the impression that Harrogate was a well-known resort, he drove her to that elegant spa town, searching all afternoon in vain for the sea-front.

Trevor always thoroughly approved of Shilpa Patel's habit of opening one of our generously donated bottles of champagne shortly before the close of a day's play. 'Ah, the medicine', he would exclaim, without need for further explanation, if he was on the air when the cork was popped. Life was as much fun for him, it seemed, as it had been in his playing days. On trips abroad he would take cine-films that graphically illustrated the pleasure that he was having off the field with companions such as Denis Compton, Godfrey Evans, Frank Tyson, Jim Laker and Brian Statham. (His captains, Len Hutton and Peter May, were usually a step away from any high-spirited frolics.)

I last saw Trevor in 2009 when I was helping the film-maker Michael Burns with *Cape Summer*, a DVD produced by MCC and based on Trevor's films of the 1956/7 tour of South Africa. Sadly, he could remember nothing of that trip but his amiable willingness to please had not changed.

Fred was a brilliant entertainer when telling stories at cricket dinners, especially on the subject of his second tour of the West Indies in 1959/60 when 'all them Cambridge undergraduates kept dropping catches off my bowling'. The Cambridge men who appeared in that series – Peter May, Ted Dexter and Raman Subba Row – actually only just outnumbered the Oxford ones, Colin Cowdrey and Mike Smith, but anyone with a light or a dark blue cap anywhere in his bag was viewed by Fred as part of the establishment whom he darkly accused of making life difficult for him. The future Bishop of Liverpool, David Sheppard (Cambridge and Sussex), came in for some especially ribald comment whenever the great fast bowler recalled the 1962/3 tour of Australia and David's (quite untypical) spate of missed chances. 'Let's face it', Fred would say, 'when the Reverend puts 'is 'ands together he ought to 'ave more chance than you and me, not less.'

The nearest equivalent to Trueman and Bailey in the latter days of Baxter's control of *TMS* was the pairing of Vic Marks and Mike Selvey. Both are nearer my own vintage and have long been good friends. Vic, with his famous chuckle, like an old engine starting up on the third or fourth turnover on a cold morning, is deservedly popular with everyone; listeners and colleagues alike. He is a most sympathetic colleague, invariably with something interesting to say and a shrewd sense of when best to say it.

Mike may not have the same warmth in his voice, but he knows all there is to know about the art of swing and seam bowling and his was a subtle humour ideally suited to Radio Four, unlike the sledge-hammer variety preferred by some more famous. That both these two are still regularly in the press-box means that they are au fait with all that is going on in dressing-rooms. On tour this has often given radio the edge over Sky television, whose commentators, with the notable exception of the concientious 'Bumble', truly a national treasure, often missed matches between the international games to play some golf. I never blamed them (often envied them in fact!) but sometimes a fringe player would force his way into the England as a consequence of taking his chance in a three-day game and one or two of the pundits would express surprise. Perhaps those who suddenly decided to sever their links with Mike Selvey, after twenty-four years of contributing to *TMS* at home and abroad, will think again. While recognising the need occasionally for a new voice and a 'big' name, there are plenty of relatively low-key series overseas, not to mention World Cups, when they should be glad to call on his experience and know-how.

Inevitably a few who might have been talented summarisers have never made it to the microphone for one reason or another. Peter Richardson of Worcestershire, Kent and England was one such. After his playing days he was too busy running a farm in Kent, but with his sense of humour he would have been an asset. I enjoyed our occasional meetings, not least in a taxi on the way to a cricketing lunch one day when he was musing on the logic of one of his teenage children. 'You don't hold your knife like that' he had instructed his son at breakfast that morning, to which the unanswerable reply was, 'Why?'

The same son, a fine games-player like all his family, later ran the Emirates Golf Club in Dubai and allowed me and other cricket journalists to play there without paying a green fee. His generosity was put to the test when John Etheridge of the *Sun* accidentally allowed his motorised buggy to slide down a bank into a lake, complete with his set of hired golf clubs.

Richardson senior was one of those involved when in 2006 I was asked by the former Surrey president Brian Downing to interview some of the survivors from both England and Australia at a dinner at The Savoy to commemorate Jim Laker's nineteen wickets against Australia, fifty years before. That momentous day at Old Trafford, watched by me on television at home in South Holmwood, was one of the most revelatory days of my life, so, naturally, I was delighted to do so.

There was some film shown to the audience of Peter reaching his maiden Test hundred in the same match. Having pushed a ball into the covers and run his single he briefly raised his bat and accepted a congratulatory handshake, before everyone got on with the next ball. Referring to that, knowing his famous sense of humour and trying to raise a laugh, I said to him: 'I noticed that you didn't run round the pitch with your arms in the air; in fact you didn't even kiss the badge on your cap.' To which, to my disappointment, he replied: 'Well, after winning the toss it was important that we got away to a decent start . . .' I was not aware until that moment that Peter had become almost totally deaf!

Commentators and summarisers have come and gone but for more than forty years Bill Frindall was indispensable to *TMS* as a scorer and statistician. By making an art of scoring Test matches on radio Bill had become something of a legend, the man on whom we commentators on BBC Radio relied. Sometimes he was the willing butt of our humour, especially when there was a possibility that some very obscure record might just have been broken, but at all times he was also the consummate professional to whom we looked for facts and figures. Coming from Bill they had an imprimatur which no one ever seriously questioned.

He died soon after getting home from Dubai on the annual fund-raising trip for the Lord's Taverners. It was sheer malign fate that he – and he alone of those who supported that trip – should have contracted legionnaires' disease. It cut him down at a time when, though he was about to turn seventy, he was still fit enough to be playing a few games of cricket each season with the boundless enthusiasm he had always shown since captaining the colts at Banstead, presumably without a beard. For the touring team that he founded, the Malta Maniacs, he took lots of wickets, each of them precisely recorded in his personal records. He ran in with energy to bowl as fast as he could, his hostility enhanced by a beard which turned from jet black to grey like W.G.'s.

Professionally he was an essential element in the eclectic mixture of personalities in *Test Match Special*. From the moment that he joined the programme in 1966 soon after leaving the RAF he was commercially savvy, being known to George Rutherford as 'Bill Swindall' but he was certainly not alone in making the *TMS* brand name work for him, reasonably so indeed considering how modest the pay has always been!

Bill conducted a complicated private life with a number of women posted in various parts of the world, and had two unsuccessful marriages before finally settling down in Wiltshire with Debbie, a bright and attractive primary school head teacher. He gave of his spare time generously to cricketing charities, a factor, no doubt, in his being honoured with an MBE in 2004. He was also the scorer at Wormsley for Paul Getty's XI, keeping meticulous records, naturally.

He had a quick wit and the sharpest of brains. He was often way ahead of other commentators in spotting things, be they records or the well-endowed lady in the fourth row of the Tavern Stand. Sometimes events can unfold with dramatic suddenness on a cricket field and there is much to be recorded, both on paper and, more recently, online too, but Bill, though he could sometimes be testy like most of us, would practically never be flustered into an error. His many books of records, and an entertaining autobiography, are his legacy.

Unlike their radio counterparts, television scorers are neither seen nor heard. It does not make some of them any the less eccentric. The one whom I remember best was Michael Fordham who got so excited on BBC television during the Headingley Test of 1981 that I had to stand in for him for an over while he dashed to the Gents.

Malcolm Ashton has taken over as the *TMS* scorer at home. Another intelligent and able man, with a great sense of humour (especially for a professional tax expert) he has a broader range of contacts than his famous predecessor. He also has less of an ego! Overseas, South Africa has produced the most remarkable of all the members of this singular breed. Listeners to radio during the 2010/11 Ashes series will have heard Andrew Sampson, another literally bearded wonder. He is a masterly user of all the information available online and misses no milestone, however obscure.

Imagine my astonishment when, after a passing reference to Don Bradman's highest first-class score of 452 when England reached that total as a team during one of the Tests in Australia in 2010/11, Andrew piped up seconds later in his clipped, slightly high-pitched South African voice: 'And Bradman scored those runs off 465 balls in 415 minutes with 49 fours.' I know that sites such as Cricket Archive make such information available but it is the industry and curiosity that ferrets it out so quickly that is so extraordinary.

11

THE WEST INDIES

This is the life! No need here for a vest or pullover, nor a blanket at night, especially in Trinidad's clammy climate which, in the early months of 1974, gave me my first experience of tropical warmth. It was an open-necked shirt by day and a fresh one after the evening shower, ready for rum punches in the brief twilight with fans whirling like dervishes from high ceilings to cool the laden air and blow the mosquitoes back towards the wide Savannah across the road.

Touring in the winter months started for me fortuitously young. There was no better place to begin than the Caribbean. I had only just had my twenty-ninth birthday when I set off for Port of Spain at the end of January 1974, excited but apprehensive as a child on his first day at a new school.

Heart-wrenching as it was to leave Judy and James behind, I had been given a tremendous opportunity to advance my career when I was told that I would be the BBC's only reporter in the West Indies. Fail and I would not have been cricket correspondent for long. But this was to be the first of a long succession of tours, none more enjoyable than those in the Caribbean.

There is little to match the excitement of a maiden trip to a strange land. While a part of me pined for home and those left behind, I also felt suddenly and gloriously free from the rotas of the BBC Sports Room. For the first time I was their man in the field, free, as far as programme schedules permitted, to do the job my own way, reporting every day on a cricket tour that everyone of my acquaintance wanted to hear about.

Home at the start of that first tour of the West Indies was the Queens Park hotel, a large, white-painted plantation-style building constructed entirely of wood, elderly but stately, not yet eclipsed in reputation by the more modern Holiday Inn by the docks or the avant-garde Hilton, newly arrived half-way up a hill on the other side of the Savannah. But the Queens Park's slow decline was already underway, despite its relative closeness to the Queens Park Oval itself. You could walk to the ground in fifteen minutes from the established hotel, but when the team returned to Trinidad later in the tour they persuaded their travel agent to switch their patronage to the flashier and more expensive option of the Hilton, a striking piece of architecture with the public rooms on top of the bedrooms and a striking foyer with vases full of magnificent lilies and a vast expanse of highly polished wood.

The journalists, trying to turn a blind eye to the occasional cockroach, stayed where they were. It saved time and avoided the expense of a ride in one of the huge, swaying Lincolns, Pontiacs and Buicks that queued up the drive to the Hilton. Their Indian drivers spent their days waiting for guests, then ferrying them round the Savannah in their long, swaying vehicles, or up the narrow road to Santa Cruz where the island's interior is fleshy with riotous verdant growth but scarred at the edges by ugly concrete buildings and vulgar advertising hoardings. Man's inhumanity to nature.

Some people hate touring. It has its disadvantages, of course, but I enjoyed, above all, the independence that it allowed. Working far from home enables the traveller to give absolute attention to the job in hand. Alan Bennett expressed it well (naturally) in his *Writing Home*:

Being on location with a [film] unit, like being on tour with a play, concentrates the experience; one is beleaguered, often enjoyably so and for a short while the film becomes the framework of one's life. I am more gregarious than I like to think and to be working on a film with congenial people in an unfamiliar place seems to me the best sort of holiday.

I felt exactly like that about touring overseas. From the moment that I left home, always an agonising wrench from Judy and worse as our family grew, the truth is that, with a few exceptions when life got tough or wearisome, I was totally absorbed in the small, yet at the time apparently all-important, ups and downs of a cricket tour. The everyday telephone calls, the social obligations of home, the bills that had to be paid, the letters to be answered or fuses to be mended were all left behind as soon as the plane landed at a distant airport overseas.

The camaraderie of life on tour was enjoyable. So, for a time, was life in hotels; and in press and commentary boxes with witty and, on the whole, like-minded journalists. On that first trip the press and radio boxes included only one journalist of my own age, Jon Henderson of Reuters, but the remainder were mainly very good company too: there was John Woodcock, who had seen it all but loved his job and did it with consummate authority; Swanton himself, nearing the end of his road as a full-time correspondent; the mustachioed old smoothie Crawford White of the *Express*; the experienced, rather world-weary Alex Bannister of the *Mail* (who nevertheless lived to a great age); the amiable and highly capable *Sun* correspondent Clive Taylor, destined to die tragically young from septicemia contracted in India; and the cheeky chappie Peter Laker who, apart from writing for the *Mirror*, spent his days planning practical jokes, spinning a little rubber ball and working imaginatively on his expenses. He and his wife, Connie, who looked a little like Barbara Windsor, usually managed to move to a smarter house after each tour.

Another who became a friend on that trip, John Thicknesse of the *Evening Standard*, had been advised by a senior colleague, the boxing writer George Whiting, to 'thieve a little, leave a little' when it came to filing expenses on trips away from home. Thickers was a card: independent, immensely conscientious and caring to the point of obsession about his job, but a great companion at any time other than when a deadline was looming. Impetuous and often infuriatingly stubborn, he could also be kind. He was very intelligent, a shrewd judge of character, irreverent of authority, a fund of stories and an unshakeable opponent of anything he felt was wrong. He would gamble on almost anything, but only when he had calculated the odds.

He always said that his job as the *Standard*'s cricket correspondent from 1967 to 1996 was the best in the business. He was invariably an informative, opinionated, interesting read. Before he got onto cricket full time his first assignment for the paper had been to cover Donald Campbell's attempt on the world water speed record on Coniston Water. With his capacity to make immediate friendships he played cards with Campbell on the night before the fatal drive and reputedly dealt him the same 'unlucky' hand that Wild Bill Hickock received before getting shot.

He was commended by the editor, Charles Wintour, for his report of Campbell's noble failure and continued to give his employers dedicated service, not least when reappearing on the front page after Mrs Gandhi's assassination at the start of

England's tour of India in 1992/3. It apparently amused the editor that John gave equal prominence to the murder of the leader of the world's largest democracy and the fact that, despite it, the England tour would proceed.

Plenty of good companions there undoubtedly were on that and subsequent trips, but I missed my wife and family. In the age of air travel one was never so remote that a return home was not possible in a crisis, but a chasm, in those days filled more by letters than by expensive phone-calls, parted Judy and me until, on this first tour, she joined me for a blissful fortnight in Barbados.

Meanwhile she had been left with all the problems of running a home while I took the kudos for reporting daily to the high-profile *Today* programme and the various sports news bulletins throughout the day. I did many more of these than Brian Johnston had been accustomed to on previous tours, simply because I had worked for the Sports News department for the previous three years and was used to the hourly service that is now staple fare on Radio Five Live. In those days, mind you, cricket took its proper place in the order of things. When I left the BBC staff several years later it was already beginning to come a poor second to what we then sometimes still referred to as Association Football.

During Test matches on that first tour of the West Indies I also voiced reports for national news bulletins, including, very occasionally when a story was big enough, the nine o' clock television news. Just such a story came along in the first major match of the tour, on the second day of the first Test. It was the famous running out of Alvin Kallicharran after the last ball of the day had been bowled.

Everyone on the ground knew, because of the time, that it *was* the last ball. Derek Underwood, with his customary pin-point accuracy, had bowled six 'dot' balls to Bernard Julien while Kallicharran, the hero of the day, relaxed at the other end, 142 not out. As Julien pushed the last ball just past the right hand of Tony Greig, fielding close at silly point, his partner continued walking towards the pavilion opposite him and Alan Knott pulled up the stumps before making his way back to the dressing-room. Greig, meanwhile, picked the ball up, took a few paces towards the unprotected stumps at the non-striker's end and threw them down from close range. The respected little Jamaican umpire Douglas Sang Hue raised a a finger, slowly and sadly, in answer to Greig's jubilant appeal.

Greig clapped his hands and walked briskly off but he was quickly made aware that what might have passed as a fair piece of gamesmanship in his native South Africa was considered beyond the pale in both England and the West Indies. The great batting hero of the day, a young and dazzling left-hander from a few miles across the water in Guyana, was out through no fault of his own other than failing to wait for an official call of 'time' from the umpire. The confusion of the other England players was matched by that of the crowd's. There was indignant booing as the wickets on the big scoreboard were changed from six to seven.

Up in the commentary box at the Northern End, with the Maraval Hills behind me, I was quickly given a hospital pass by the local commentator, Raffie Knowles, a charming old boy who knew his football better than he did his cricket. 'There's pandemonium at the Queens Park Oval' he said in a shaking voice: 'And to explain what's happened, over to Chris Jenkins'.

I had a wiser and more experienced observer next to me on the other side, Gerry Gomez, who supported my view that it was morally if not technically wrong for England to take a wicket in these circumstances. I mentioned that I had seen Mike

Denness, the England captain, in earnest conversation with Mr. Sang Hue as they walked off the field and speculated that he would be asking for the appeal to be withdrawn and for the decision to be rescinded. Thereupon the scoreboard operators, listening, like many in the crowd, on their transistor radios, put the wickets on the board back to six. It may not be too much of an exaggeration to suggest that thereby a riot was averted.

Other than another umpire-related incident in the series in England the previous summer, when Arthur Fagg temporarily refused to go on umpiring because of the hostile reaction of Rohan Kanhai after Geoffrey Boycott had been given not out, this was, I think, the first of many cricket stories in my time as a commentator and reporter that made national rather than sporting news. I must say that I always got a special kick from the suppressed excitement and apparent importance of these events, storms in tea-cups though most of them were. I suppose it is a legacy of Empire, and cricket's perceived role as an acceptable symbol of British patronage, that gives these scandals such resonance whenever they involve an England team. This one really got the adrenalin flowing, with several of my press colleagues suggesting that the tour might be called off. It was only at eight that evening in Port of Spain, after a tense meeting between the MCC team manager, Donald Carr, and Jeff Stollmeyer, the relaxed and urbane Anglophile Trinidadian who was, fortunately, chairman of the West Indies Cricket board, that the crisis was dispelled. It had been agreed that Kallicharran would be allowed to continue batting the following morning.

'Greigy' remained the central character of that tour and indeed of English cricket in the three hectic years that followed it. He was a genuinely charismatic character with a charm to match his overbearing presence. From the start I liked his friendliness, marked by a winning smile and an engaging chuckle.

He made no secret of his self-confidence, nor of his ambition. Shakespeare, the great reader of human character, would have called it 'o'erweening'; but he was no mere solipsist: he was interested in other people and his nature remains a generous one. I first met him when I played against him on a Cambridge College tour when he was nineteen and in England playing some games for Sussex second XI in 1967. He was obviously a prodigious talent, even though he holed out to my modest off-spin for eighty or ninety during a hectic run chase by the club for whom he was playing at the behest of the bibulous chairman of Sussex's cricket committee, Tony Crole-Rees.

Greig became, rapidly, a superb and aggressive all-round cricketer who immediately made his mark for Sussex with his 156 in his very first innings for the county's Championship team the following summer. Eventually, judged against other great all-rounders, his Test averages as a batsman (40) and bowler (32) suggested that he was an even better player than he was but he was the original fighting cricketer and no one in my experience ever made more of his natural ability. As the Kallicharran incident had demonstrated, he was an opportunist as well as a pragmatist. He had already been on tour with great success in India and Pakistan under Tony Lewis the previous winter and he was vice-captain to Denness in the West Indies, to the displeasure of Boycott, who felt he should have been captain on that tour.

I got to know and like Denness himself in later years. As captain he had what might have been a typical Scottish reserve, despite his ready smile. To some extent I think he felt that the leadership had been thrust upon him. It was not done so against his will but despite his successful command of the talented Kent side of the time, he might have been happier as one of the ranks. The press relations side of his job did not come naturally but it was not his fault that he should have run into the fabled combination of Dennis Lillee and Jeff Thomson in Australia the following winter. He took it on his dimpled chin and finally enjoyed some sweet personal success at the end of that tour, albeit only after the main prize had been lost.

The relatively venerable Boycott and the youthful Frank Hayes apart, other members of the team on my first tour were all more or less my contemporaries. I did not spend much time on the tour with them – even then, players and journalists mainly kept apart except when they were travelling – but it was my job to put a microphone before them on rest days or the occasions when they had done well and I got on well with all of them: Dennis Amiss, who had a prolific tour, scoring 1120 runs in sixteen innings, and who has become a good friend; the Kentish trio of Alan Knott, Derek Underwood, and Bob Woolmer; the salty-witted Jack Birkenshaw and two gentle northern fast bowlers, Mike Hendrick and Chris Old; the highly individual Bob Willis; the other Surrey bowlers, the chirpy and friendly Pat Pocock and his equally likeable but much more moody mate Geoff (G.G.) Arnold, known to all as 'Orse; the bluff and amiable John Jameson and, the best tourist of the lot, Bob Taylor. Forever smiling and revealing a gold tooth in the process – wicket-keeping repairs I assume– Bob's nickname was 'Chat'. He would talk to anyone about anything and no team ever had a better natural diplomat.

It was a good side, not a great one and they were outplayed by a West Indies team whose batting was of significantly higher class. The top six of Roy Fredericks, Lawrence Rowe, Kallicharran, Clive Lloyd, Gary Sobers and Rohan Kanhai was as powerful as any that has ever represented the West Indies. Yet England contrived to draw the series when on the second visit to Trinidad Boycott belatedly found his best form, scoring 99 out of 267 and 112 out of 263, and Greig produced

from almost nowhere the most sensational bowling performance of his frequently dramatic career. He switched from his
usual bouncy fast-medium to bowl off-cutters at slow medium
pace, often with the sort of dip achieved by another who could
switch paces in the same way, Bob Appleyard, who had been Len
Hutton's Yorkshire trump-card in Australia in 1954/5. Now,
Greig enabled Denness to come home at the head of a side that
had somehow shared the spoils, taking thirteen wickets for 156
on a dry, turning pitch.

I was an excited witness to it all. More than that, on the last
day of the match I was the first to commentate ball-by-ball on
radio on a BBC-produced programme overseas, when Bob
Burrows managed to persuade Radio Three that the game was
building to a climax that deserved a big audience.

Gradually we did more and more commentary on tour in
future years although in Australia we continued, as of old, to
take the ABC's coverage. Representing the BBC as the guest
commentator in local transmissions in Australia, the West Indies
and New Zealand was a huge privilege and one of the reasons
that I enjoyed touring so much, especially as I never established
the right to commentate on every Test at home, even when I was
officially the BBC cricket correspondent.

Even in the Caribbean, life on tour could drag and home
seem a long way away. In Barbados, of course, there were
always the beaches on occasional free days, not to mention
beach parties of the kind that Tony Cozier, the king of the
Caribbean media and one of the shrewdest and best commentators there has ever been, threw at his little holiday house on
the Atlantic coast.

Smaller islands visited, usually in the early weeks of a tour or
at the end for rather more demanding one-day internationals,
were a joy, amongst them St. Kitts, St. Lucia, St. Vincent and, in

1974, Antigua, before it became a part of the cricketing main-stream thanks to Viv Richards and Andy Roberts.

When I turned to writing rather than broadcasting for my main living, the tour of the West Indies every four years or so was the one I most enjoyed, as much as anything because the time differ-ence allowed one to write pieces for three or four editions during a day's cricket, each one of them urgent and up to the moment, before relaxing completely in the evenings in the knowledge that nothing that happened in the hours of darkness could reach news-papers that had been put to bed almost as soon as the last ball of the day had been bowled. But these tours were not all about swimming before breakfast in a shimmering light blue sea or drinking those inimitable rum punches as the sun set at the end of a day's enjoyable work. Large chunks of each tour were spent far from any beach, often in hotels whose rooms were old-fashioned and whose food brought back memories of school meals. As tour-ism developed, so life on tour became more comfortable but it was always, essentially, a job of work not a holiday.

In Port of Spain there was no beach near the city and the same was true of Kingston, so a lot of time on all my tours would be spent in two vibrant, potentially dangerous cities where sensi-ble folk watched their step when they left the safety of their hotel. In Kingston I once tried to find some white leather shoes of the kind that look and feel right for evening wear, without socks, in tropical climes at night. I had not gone far into New Kingston, the safer part of Jamaica's rough capital city, when I was approached by a youngish man, built to my height but several stone heavier and stronger, who asked if he could be of assistance. 'I'm just looking for some shoes', I said. 'Follow me, man', he replied, in a friendly enough way but also in a manner that suggested that I would be better not to argue.

I sensed, without any negotiations being required, that he would assure me of a safe escort so long as he was properly paid. Two or three shops did not have either the type or the size of shoe that I was looking for and on a hot afternoon we went further and further into the meaner streets of a Kingston Town somewhat different from the one envisaged by anyone listening to that sweet song about the girl left behind 'down the way where the nights are gay and the sun shines daily on the mountain top'. My anxiety had grown to apprehension when he finally guided me into a shop that had a pair of hand-made leather shoes that cost very little, fitted my aching feet to perfection and which I still wear on hot evenings overseas. Without any need to annunciate our understanding, he led me back to within sight of my hotel and I handed over a tidy sum of US dollars.

I once woke in the middle of the night at the Pegasus hotel in Kingston, where poor Bob Woolmer ended his days at the start of the 2007 World Cup, to hear in the middle distance the despairing cries of a girl or woman whose pleading screams sounded horribly as though she was being raped. The city has a reputation for murder and brutality linked to drugs but the Jamaicans I have known have always been delightful.

At Cambridge a larger than life (albeit slimly built) chap called Alva Anderson had arrived from Jamaica in my second year with a reputation as an outstanding cricketer and footballer. It proved very exaggerated unfortunately but Alva, a happy-go-lucky fellow with a touch of the Walter Mitty about him, did not seem to mind and he has done well in life since. By contrast the first really well-known Jamaican cricket commentator, Roy Lawrence, was a modest fellow who had settled in Leeds by the time that I knew him, disenchanted with his own island. Roy was known for his occasional faux pas during his running commentaries, including: 'Trevor Bailey has been batting for just over an hour and he gets a single off Valentine which takes him to ten, nine of them in singles'. He was also happy to confess to: 'It's another beautiful day at Sabina Park. The sun is blowing and the breeze is shining all over the ground'.

Allan Rae, one of the heroes of the 1950 West Indies tour of England, was very kind to the young English commentator who arrived wet behind the ears in Jamaica for the first time in 1974. He was happy to watch Test matches from the little pavilion of the Kingston Cricket Club at Sabina Park, where he was the president, a modest man for all his status. A capable barrister who shouldered most of the administration of West Indies cricket in the 1950s with his former opening partner, the charming Trinidadian Jeff Stollmeyer, he asked me to dinner at his house in Kingston to meet the great Clyde Walcott. Rae, whose piercing green eyes were his most striking characteristic, and Walcott, a commanding figure with a voice as deep as Paul Robeson's, were fascinating to hear both on their experiences in England and on the inter-island rivalries in the Caribbean.

Clyde, later knighted, went on to become an influential administrator in the affairs of world cricket, succeeding Colin Cowdrey as chairman of the ICC. He was always a dignified figure who more or less held the balance of power between the old governers of the game from England and Australia and the pushy rising forces of the Orient. I never knew the most revered of the three Ws, Sir Frank Worrell, merely admired his cricket from afar on the 1957 and 1963 tours; but, like all who knew him, I warmed immediately to (Sir) Everton De Courcy Weekes when I worked with him in commentary boxes in the Caribbean. Whereas one always felt that Walcott, like Viv Richards, was aware of his colour in the presence of people who had not yet come to terms with genuine racial equality, Everton has always seemed absolutely at ease in his own skin and situation, both a happy and a wise man. He was, too, the old Bajan aficionados will tell you, Cozier amongst them, the greatest of three immortal cricketers.

Guyana, on the South American mainland, was the place that everyone seemed to dread, simply because it rained so much there at the time of year when cricket took place. Georgetown, the capital, is a singular place, laid out by the Dutch below sea level with a system of dykes and locks. Its wooden buildings, painted white and green, have great charm, none more so than the beautiful old wooden Cathedral, outside which I should have been more generous one Good Friday to a terribly crippled man whose constant pain and terrible poverty were obvious. I did not have much more than the taxi fare for the journey back to the hotel after the service, so gave him only what remained. The look of disappointment on his face when I handed over what would have been the driver's tip has lived with me. This from a Christian on Good Friday of all days. 'I was hungry and you did not feed me; I was naked and you did not clothe me.' I could so easily have walked back to the hotel – it was not much more than a mile, although very hot – but he, with his crutches, could not have gone half as far as he limped off to continue his suffering. Too often in my life have I regretted momentary decisions that quickly become irrevocable, especially those when a generous impulse has been overruled by the voice of 'reason'. O bring back yesterday, bid time recall.

Most of Georgetown's spacious wooden houses are painted white under green roofs. The old ground at Bourda has a pavilion as redolent of cricket history as any outside Lord's, its bar well frequented by local members and its walls covered by black and white photographs of past players and teams. For the 2007 World Cup foreign investment made possible the building of a large but soulless modern ground, built amongst cane fields and marshland out of the city centre. It had none of the character of Bourda, but it drained immeasurably better after rain. Sadly, most of the Bourda Tests I saw there were spoilt by the ground's inability to absorb heavy downpours. I took a pair of galoshes with me in 1990 especially for Guyana but one would have needed wellies on the morning that the whole field was ankle deep in water. Shoals of small fish were swimming about on the edge of the outfield, surely a phenomenon unique to Bourda. In half a dozen visits to Georgetown the abiding memories, unfortunately, are of rain falling from a slate grey sky into a sea the colour of porridge.

Even when the sun shines the sluggish water beside the sea wall looks the same uniform grey because of the mud from the Demerara river. Litter often floats about a little off shore and I have never known a coastline anywhere that screams *Schwimmen Verboten* quite so loudly. At least there is an inviting pool at the Pegasus, the circular hotel on the edge of this forlorn stretch of the Atlantic. It has changed owners, and its name, at different times but it remains the best place to stay for visitors. When I first encountered it in 1974 it was a third world building doing its best to seem more like a hotel than a prison. Its rooms were spartan and its food basic, although during one of my stays they tried to make the dining more sophisticated by employing a pianist whose favourite tune was 'Tea For Two', thumped out slowly on an instrument that was clearly in need of tuning and no doubt suffering from the damp. He sounded like a schoolboy who had just learned to play.

Perhaps because of its isolation from the main tourist routes and the economic deprivations that became worse during the dictatorship of Forbes Burnham, experiences in Guyana are actually more memorable than those that linger from more comfortable places. I recall exciting boat trips up the river, a snake hanging down from a mangrove tree, exotic birds from circling eagles to minute humming-birds, monkeys cavorting in the thick jungle, a swim amongst rocks in swirling brown water near a waterfall, another pool where jaguars still drink, and the breath-taking noise and splendour of the Kaieteur Falls. The 822-foot drop is one of the longest in the world and the sheer volume of water plunging down a sheer cliff, with trees thick on either bank, is spectacular.

The people made Guyana different too. As in Trinidad theirs was, and is, a real melting pot of races – Amerindian, Indian, African (the former slaves of the sugar plantations) and whites of European origin. I was rung up one day during one of my earlier tours by a young fisherman, the youngest son of a proud Hindu family, who called himself, simply, 'Junior'. He asked me twice on subsequent visits to dine with his family in their large house and once took me to the market in the early morning to witness the morning's catch from the ocean. Junior knew everything about contemporary West Indian cricket and had strong views, like all proper Caribbean enthusiasts for the game. Alas, his sister, a doctor, emailed me in 2009 to say that he had died suddenly in his thirties.

That Mike Atherton has become an even better journalist than he was cricketer (which is saying a great deal) perhaps owes something to the fact that he married a Guyanese girl whom he met on tour, Izzy, the bright and attractive granddaughter of the Test player F.C. De Caires, and daughter of the editor of the only independent local newspaper, the *Starboek News*. During the ill-fated World Cup in 2007 I played golf with Mike's mother-in-law, also a stalwart of the newspaper, the feisty Dorothy De Caires. The Georgetown Golf Club, laid out on flat ground amongst the sugar-cane fields, was never destined to be numbered amongst the great courses, but it was thriving again. A decade or so before it had been neglected, with cows wandering everywhere to keep the grass down, puddles abounding and a darts board in the shack which called itself the clubhouse that sent out a cloud of dust when one of our four (Martin Johnson, Mike Selvey, Peter Hayter and I) threw what was probably the first arrow to have struck its surface for twenty years.

Barbados was always the most popular place for English visitors on a tour of the West Indies. It is an over populated island in the south and west, but the sunshine, the bustle, the expensive restaurants and the daytime glimpses, every few hundred yards, of an eau-de-nile sea, are captivating. Inland and on the northern and eastern parts you can drive along deserted roads and, in my case, usually get lost. The island has a unique charm, reflected in the Bajans themselves, a fact that made their sudden hostility to me during England's tour of 1989/90 all the more shocking.

It became for me an unexpected personal crisis. It stemmed from a report delivered at the close of the fourth day's play of the fourth Test for the *Today* programme. Late on the day in question the Northamptonshire and England batsman Rob Bailey was given out caught down the leg-side, after a long delay, by the umpire at the bowler's end, the tubby, bespectacled Bajan Lloyd Barker. To me and all other reporters on the ground, especially those of us behind the batsman who could see clearly enough that the ball had brushed only Bailey's thigh pad, it appeared that Mr. Barker had initially said 'not out', indicated that it was 'over' and made his way towards square-leg. Then, seeing Viv Richards bearing down upon him in a prolonged appeal, he belatedly lifted his finger. Judging these leg-side catches, and whether they have come off bat, thigh-pad or glove, is notoriously difficult for all umpires, a fact that I should have made clearer at the time.

The cricketing background was that the West Indies were one down in the series, had been lucky to escape with a draw at Port of Spain when Richards was absent, and in another close match were desperate to win, something to which they had become accustomed. The social context was that some West Indians had been offended by criticism of their team on Sky television, which was transmitting the matches to the Caribbean (and to the UK) for the first time that winter. At Bridgetown, several members of the local press were offended, naturally enough, to be placed in an overspill press box, pushed out of their normal positions by the sheer volume of visiting British journalists.

These factors no doubt contributed to the hysterical reaction when my report, which had been re-transmitted to the Caribbean on the BBC World Service, was picked up by a local producer with a 'chip' who quickly spread the word that I had called the umpire a 'cheat'. This was anything but the truth. I had been critical throughout the tour of the over rates (saying in this report that both sides were cheating each other by slowing down over rates deliberately) and I deplored the growing tendency of players *on both sides* to put pressure on inexperienced umpires by appealing en masse, sometimes when they knew a batsman was not out. Bailey had been, I suggested (in common with most of those reporting to newspapers), an unfortunate victim of this practice. I was specifically critical of Viv, whose exaggerated appeal seemed to have persuaded the umpire (whom I had not named) to 'change his mind'.

For the next two days I was the object of mass criticism on local phone-in programmes and the main item in national news bulletins throughout the Caribbean. It was suggested that I should be deported, shot, or introduced to a bull-pizzle. I was served with a writ for defamation of the umpire in the final Test in Antigua the following week, for which I had been taken off the local airways and allowed to commentate only for the BBC.

It was extremely unpleasant for a time, and alarming for Judy and the children, who had been with me in Barbados and feared for my safety in Antigua. It all blew over, of course. Mr Barker made a small amount – $100 I think – when the subsequent case was settled out of court by the BBC lawyers. But I knew for certain that I had been forgiven in Barbados when my son Robin toured there with his school the following winter. Handing over his passport at the immigration desk he was asked if he was any relation of Christopher Martin-Jenkins and for a moment he feared the worst. Instead, when he had answered in the affirmative, he was greeted with a beaming smile and the comment: 'I just love that man's commentaries.' The Lloyd Barker incident apart, my most unusual experience on Barbados occurred during England's 'sex, drugs and rock and roll' period in the mid 1980s. On the rest day of the Test match I interviewed Ian Botham in the room he was sharing with Les Taylor at the Rockley Beach resort, at a pre-arranged time in the afternoon. He introduced me first to a strikingly attractive green-eyed girl who turned out to be Lindy Field, the former Miss Barbados whose subsequent Sunday newspaper revelations made her some money and caused the great all-rounder much embarassment. Later on that tour Paul Downton's wife had arrived in Antigua and was swimming in the sea when a Sunday 'news' man, sent out to dig for dirt and mistaking her for a young lady in search of fun, finished their brief conversation with: 'You'll get some luck soon, darlin', the England cricket team are flying in tomorrow.'

Cricket writers, thank goodness, can concentrate on the game and mind their own business otherwise. In any case, cricket always came first in Barbados. Years before, on my first tour, shortly before Judy's arrival, I had been to a police station to get on her behalf the necessary local driving permit which all visitors require before being allowed to drive on the island. She was bringing her British driving licence with her and at first I was firmly told that there could be no permit without the physical evidence of a licence. Then, the local sergeant on duty noticed my name. 'You de fellah who talk on the radio 'bout cricket'? he inquired. 'Yes I am indeed', I said, hope rising that the red tape might be circumvented. Then a second question: 'What you think of Collis King and Nolan Clarke?'

That was easy. Both had made centuries that day against MCC. I described at some length what terrific batsmen I thought they were before adding, 'Well, I must be getting back to my hotel now'.

'What d'you mean', he said. 'You haven't got your wife's permit.' He handed it over with a broad grin on his face.

I wonder, sadly, if cricket would mean so much to every young Barbadian policeman these days.

12

A SECOND FAMILY

It is the curse of the free-lancer to feel a permanent sense of insecurity. One imagines that if one offer is turned down, similar opportunities will dry up. With apologies to Oscar Hammerstein for a minor bowdlerisation, I'm just a guy who can't say no. I claim a noble motive, however. Although it must from time to time have seemed not to be the case to my wife and children, all my work over the years — writing, broadcasting and making speeches — has been done primarily for my family.

For Judy and me there was never much of a surplus in the bank but until the housing market turned sour on us we were extremely fortunate with our choice of homes. Pilgrim's Cottage at Albury was the most exciting, simply because it was the first. Anyone who has had the experience of actually owning one's own home knows the feeling. It was a romantic place to start married life and we spent our second night there, before a honeymoon on Corfu at a hotel that seemed glamorous at the time but seriously down market when we revisited it many years later.

Our first night, after the wedding in Brackley, was supposed to have been spent at a hotel specially chosen by me on the banks

of the Thames in Oxfordshire. But we had had a long engagement and I had made the booking so long before that the hotel
had lost it when we arrived in the early evening, full of expectation. Fortunately I had been efficient for once and had their
letter of confirmation in my pocket. Much embarrassed they
booked the best room in the George Hotel at Dorchester-on-
Thames instead so after a short journey we were welcomed to
a large room with a four-poster bed and a free bottle of champagne waiting on ice for us, courtesy of the originally chosen
hotel. Judy already knew from my accident with the paving
stone and consequent broken toes that life with me would never
be entirely straightforward, and this was confirmation.

Pilgrim's Cottage stood (and still stands) in the centre of
Albury, a pretty little village, with a 100 foot garden (well,
strip of grass) at the back leading to the Tillingbourne stream.
Mallard frequently waddled up our lawn, herons sat like statues
on the bank waiting for their breakfasts and very occasionally a
kingfisher flashed downstream in a little streak of shimmering
blue.

In our first three years of marriage there was at least a pattern
to my working and family life. Once the touring started that was
less the case and the decision to turn free-lance in 1980 pushed
me closer to becoming a workaholic.

The worst example of mistaken priorities, however, had
nothing to do with over-work. When our elder son James was
called to the bar in 1997 I was playing golf in Norfolk at the
annual meeting of the Gibbons, a collection of cricket writers
who let their hair down every October after the rigours of the
cricket season.

We play in an arduous competition – thirty-six holes a day in
all weathers – each of us in the hope of winning but primarily
to have fun on two beautiful links courses at Hunstanton and

Brancaster. I was relatively new to this convivial little society and felt that it would be bad form to leave them in the middle of the week. I thought that James, as a golfer himself, would understand. He has never said that he did not, but I deeply regret having missed the chance to see him enjoying one of the great achievements of his life. It was quite the wrong decision.

When such things as school fees – once one has decided to go down the route of independent schooling – or keeping up a reasonable standard of living at home are taken into account, accepting a fee for travelling on a Friday evening to some welcoming but obscure cricket club in, say, Nottinghamshire, becomes, perhaps, more understandable. Increasingly Judy has taken to seizing my diary and entering family or local social engagements in the space for the relevant day in large letters so that I do not double book. But she understands financial imperatives and she has been remarkably tolerant about my disappearances from home to pay for the bread and butter.

James was born at Mount Alvernia Hospital in Guildford on 12 June, little more than six months before my first winter tour for the BBC. His arrival was the happiest experience of my life bar none, even though Judy had bombarded me with pillows, flannels and anything close to hand as I tried to be a solicitous husband in her moments of worst agony. I had dashed down the motorway on the fourth evening of the Trent Bridge Test when our doctor, the genial Tony Davies, decided that it was time to give nature a push. I would have been on hand already had not Bev Congdon and Vic Pollard delayed England's apparently inevitable victory with a heroic stand for New Zealand.

James himself was in no hurry. Even when he was finally delivered it took some gentle bottom slapping and quiet verbal urging from Dr. Davies before we heard the first sounds emerging from a voice-box that was far less reluctant to make itself heard ever after. James Telford Alexander M-J was fortunate enough to inherit his mother's quick brain. He spoke intelligibly at about eighteen months and amazed us by waking from a deep sleep at the back of the car soon afterwards to announce that he was feeling 'a bit tired'.

I had never gone to bed in a happier state than I did in the wee small hours of that June morning. Judy's mother, Muriel, had heard my return as she tried in vain to sleep in the spare room at Pilgrim's Cottage. 'Well done', she said with heartfelt joy when I told her that we had produced a son. She would prove to be a marvellously devoted grandmother and it was desperately sad for her and for Judy that she should have suffered a heart attack only six months after the birth of our second son, Robin, in October 1975. I shall never rid myself of the image of Judy, sitting wretchedly in the 'drawing-room' of our second home, Old Harry's Cottage at East Clandon, when she received the call from the hospital in Banbury that her beloved mother was not going to recover. She died at only seventy after years of selfless service to her local community at Brackley.

Of Robin, the calmest of babies who could always be diverted from almost anything else as a toddler when a ball was produced, I shall write more later but James was also lucky enough to be a useful sportsman. At Oxford he missed the first in Theology for which he had hoped but won the British Universities Rugby fives doubles with his partner, Matt Cavenagh, and won Blues for golf and fives. He might well have added one for cricket had he not concentrated more on golf. At least his batting and off-breaks helped the Authentics to defeat the Crusaders in the Parks.

In the next few years he worked even more assiduously on his law than his putting, met his future wife, Nicola, while at Law School, and overcame fierce competition to get his pupilage before being taken on by a well-regarded Chambers, 2, Harcourt Buildings. He is now a devoted father of three, putting his experience in the law to good effect for Hakluyt, the Corporate Intelligence experts, while Nicola concentrates on being a good wife and mother to Molly, William and Freddie.

Lucy, born like her brothers at Mount Alvernia in Guildford, was a character from the moment that she appeared in July 1979. A beaming smile came readily from the start, she overcame mild dyslexia by sheer conscientiousness and all her life she has not only adored children but been adored by them. Mothers lucky enough to employ her as a Norland-trained nanny have begged her to stay when the time has come to move on. She never shone on the sports field but always loved the outdoors so she has cycled and walked every inch of West Sussex. She hurtled like a hare up and down the 100 miles of the South Downs Way and when she ran in the London Marathon to raise money for research into muscular dystrophy she finished in the same time as Sir Steve Redgrave, still smiling broadly despite shin splints.

Like her father's, her life has been full of little dramas, invariably shared mainly with her patient mother until, at last, she met a worthy suitor, Henry Forbes, in 2010. She had been determined to wait for the right man so her happiness when she did so was palpable and thoroughly deserved.

We had all too few holidays while the family was growing up, although this was to some extent compensated for by trips abroad when I was away on tour. The home-based breaks were special, notably to Thurlestone in Devon, where the first six holes of the golf course, known as the 'boozers' loop', are a constantly fascinating challenge with a glorious seascape all around, and the local beaches, especially at Bantham, are perfect for children. Once we ventured to North Cyprus, once to Tenerife but schools and houses always consumed most of the hard-earned gains including those made by Judy in her role as a primary school teacher and later as specially trained tutor to children with special learning difficulties.

Most parents are proud of their offspring but we have certainly been lucky with ours. I have naturally revelled quietly in my sons' sporting achievements and had hours of enjoyment encouraging them to bowl, throw and hit balls when they were young. They both had a natural eye but I like to think that I at least imparted first principles, such as the importance of bowling a length and trying to hit a moving ball in the direction from which it has come – as opposed, usually, to mid-wicket.

It is probably our property owning democracy and the evolved system of independent schools that accounts for the lingering of a class structure in Britain but there is undoubtedly some virtue in the fact that so many aspire both to the best education and to owning their own home, not to mention keeping it in good repair if they reach their goal.

We have moved four times in forty years, the first three very successfully. After three years at Albury, surrounded by lovely walks and within an easy walk also of church, pub, garage, baker and post office, we went a little further north to an even greater gem of a village, East Clandon. It remains to this day one of the very few unspoilt Surrey villages and although it has now lost its post office it still has the other essentials, church and pub. Our half of an Elizabethan cottage, known as 'Old Harry's', had a bigger garden and sufficient oak beams to start a Tudor warship.

As soon as I decided that I would risk leaving the security of the BBC staff and that I would therefore no longer have to make the regular return journey to London, we moved further south in 1978 into Sussex. We have been in the county ever since. Little Swains, our first home there, tucked away at Tismans Common in the sprawling old parish of Rudgwick, was another old cottage, this time big enough to accommodate our third child and still to have a spare room for the visitors whom Judy always encouraged. For more than twenty-five years she insisted on being the host to various relatives at Christmas, starting her preparations weeks before the gathering of the clan and working ceaselessly to make everything perfect.

Naldrett House, our family home from 1983 to 2005, was ideal for a big family gathering, whether at Christmas or on the glorious summer's day on which we celebrated my parents' golden wedding. Built in 1790 for one of the Naldrett family who had been registered at Rudgwick since the Domesday Book, the house was surrounded by fields and had at one stage had direct access to the river Arun. There was a large pond (the estate agents called it a lake), a tennis court, a fairly ancient swimming pool that we could never afford to heat but that caught the sun all day, and plenty of fine trees including what the agents referred to in their particulars as a 'laburnum walk'.

The rooms were large rather than plentiful – five bedrooms and a large study for my work seemed ideal – and the Georgian frontage at the end of a short drive flanked by lime trees made it all look, especially when I had just mown the lawn, statelier than it actually was. But we were very happy there and the day that we acquired Naldrett House in the first place was one of the most exciting in my life.

The original farm was being sold off in lots when we walked past with our first dog, Sandy, one Sunday afternoon and gawped at a property that seemed well out of our range. It had even been advertised in *Country Life* for heaven's sake! I used my cricketing connection with Nat West Bank to discover the maximum amount that they would lend me against a salary that by then was coming in from a hectic mixture of writing and broadcasting adornments to my main job as editor of *The Cricketer*.

It was one of those gambles in life which felt right if we could pull it off. I had to make a sealed bid without a guide price and we went as high as we realistically could. After the phone-call to tell us that we had got the house, I drove into the village to tell Judy quietly while she was helping to run one of the stalls at an early Christmas sale for Save the Children. It really felt like divine providence.

We moved in just before Christmas and never regretted it although, apart from acquiring two of the original farm fields, during our twenty-two years at Naldrett House we could seldom afford to spend much on the house itself. But for a time I was able to spend a more stable home life.

Between 1974 and 1980 I had been away for long periods four times, to the West Indies, India and twice to Australia, so it was time for a rest from winter tours. On my way to Blackpool by train to make a speech one day while England were playing overseas, I recorded some lines to convince myself that I was in the right place:

> Lovely winter country pastures,
> Sheep and puddles in cropped green fields,
> Crows heavy on straggling thorn trees
> Lanes a-glisten under watery blue.
> 'Missing Australia, are you then?
> All that lovely winter sun?'
> Give me messy, squelchy England,
> Grey stone walls and a northern sky.

A full winter at home, the lot for most of us, has the added virtue of heightening both the anticipation and the eventual pleasures of spring. As for May, the month of months, it has moved me since to further wonder:

What a pity Eve succumbed;
On a May morning, perhaps, much like this;
When trees are bursting with green promise,
Like sails in the wind, or proud expectant mothers waiting
   the day;
When hawthorn and cow parsley abound,
Daubed with blossom like Jersey cream;
When you must walk through the shady coolness of a wood
To escape the glare from the pale blue heights,
And breathe the earthy richness of the leaf-moulded floor,
The nectary remnants of the bluebells.
Perhaps – that word again, if only we knew for sure –
Heaven will be like this: Eden regained; England in May.

But I discovered that, if I was honest, I did miss Australia and the other winter haunts a little. More than that, I felt that if I were to remain at the top of my chosen profession I had to start touring again. The game was moving on fast as usual and it was necessary to remain in the thick of it, or lose authority as a commentator and writer. The offer from the BBC to return as cricket correspondent while remaining editor of *The Cricketer* solved that problem and also made it easier to pay all those bills. Life was a constant juggle, with several balls aloft at any one time, and I could not have managed it without Judy's calm support.

13

BOOKS AND SPEECHES

My return to The Cricketer *in time to prepare for the magazine's diamond jubilee issue in 1981 meant accepting a much smaller salary and leaving the shelter of Auntie BBC, with the generous pension that would have come my way at sixty if I had been able to stomach the Corporation's frustrating internal politics and archaic wage structure. There were no Jonathan 'Woss' style deals on offer in those days, certainly not to radio cricket commentators.*

Settling to a different style of office life at Redhill, but with school fees already biting in earnest, I supplemented my income by taking on books, regular freelance articles for the *Scotsman* newspaper and after-dinner speeches all over the country.

Over the next ten years balancing the need for money with family life was always a challenge but on the whole the two dovetailed fairly well. After a three-year break I was again taken on as BBC cricket correspondent, this time on a contract, so renewed travelling in the winters required careful organisation. It meant also, of course, that life was never dull.

In the first ten days after my return from Pakistan and India in November 1987, for example, my diary tells me that I arrived home from Delhi on a Wednesday, oversaw press day at *The Cricketer* on Thursday, spoke at a black-tie dinner at the Plaisterers' Hall that evening, went to Lucy's school on Friday, followed by a supper party at home, then to the fortieth birthday party of a friend of Judy's on the Saturday. The next week included lunch and dinner speeches, my weekly piece for the *Scotsman*, a school match, a school play and a memorial service for Judy's favourite uncle. Variety is the spice.

I usually had a book project on the go during these years but making speeches was less time consuming and, gradually, more lucrative. For years I had spoken at cricket dinners without reward but Brian Johnston told me one day while we were discussing the art of after-dinner speaking, curiously enough at a café in Dubrovnik during a 'working holiday' cruise on the P&O ship *Canberra*, that I was mad not to get an agent. He recommended me to his own man, another irrepressibly cheerful fellow called Tony 'Dabber' Davies, and henceforward I joined the list of paid speakers for many of my appearances.

The *Canberra* cruise was one of three that Judy and I made when cricket seasons had ended in the early 1980s. I had been approached by P&O to organise a small band of cricketing celebrities to help them to sell Mediterranean cruises at that time of the year by using cricket as one of the themes. Apart from Brian I invited, at different times, Tom Graveney and Chris Cowdrey, both wonderful mixers, Dennis Amiss, Ray Illingworth, Richard Hutton, E.W. Swanton (who pleased some and offended others) and the lovable Colin Milburn, who almost drank the ship dry, moving down to join the crew when he had finished with the passengers!

It was my job to provide some cricketing 'entertainment' for the cricket devotees on board, most of them very experienced pensioners. We had talks and question and answer sessions in the evenings and enjoyable games of cricket on deck, designed partly to enable me to select some teams for matches that I had organised in advance of each cruise at some of our ports of call. We had some successful fixtures, especially on Gibraltar where, according to Amiss, Swanton politely refused my invitation to do some umpiring until he heard that the Governer was going to be present.

We played a match at Malaga in southern Spain, where cricket has taken quite a hold since. At that stage it was a novelty. The majority of the spectators were dripping with gold chains and watches, a fair few of them almost certainly on the run from Scotland Yard, enjoying their good life in an extradition-free area.

The problem fixture was always at Corfu where I always had letters of confirmation from the Anglo-Corfiot Cricket Society that the local team would honour our agreed fixture at such and such a time on the concrete pitch in the middle of the famous square at the heart of Corfu Town. They never actually produced an XI, put off, it seems, by the famous names I had mentioned in letters, thinking that they were going to be confronted by a formidable old England team rather than a very motley bunch of old men from amongst the passengers. Each year I had to think on my feet at the last moment, not helped one time when 'Illy' did a bunk when he sussed that things were not going to go according to plan, choosing to go shopping with his beloved Shirley instead. Usually, however, my celebrity 'team' rallied round and we had some amusing games between quickly assembled teams from the ship, cheered on by local spectators. One or two Greeks did play, too, so I was able to witness at first hand how they always pinched a quick single in the first over when one opener would shout a loud 'Ne' to the other. All fielders in the area of the pitch would immediately relax, unaware that 'Ne' meant 'Yes' and that 'No' would have been 'Ochi'.

Sometimes I adapted for the *Canberra* passengers the sort of after-dinner speech that I was by now being regularly called in various directions to make. An ability to master regional accents, if not always to impersonate people with the accuracy of a Mike Yarwood or the truly remarkable Rory Bremner helped me to gain a bit of a reputation as someone who could make people laugh, although, inevitably, some evenings went better than others. I soon learned that no two audiences were the same, each occasion requiring subtly different approaches, and that, occasionally, the circumstances were beyond your control.

Two in South Africa come to mind. Indeed I shall never forget the centenary banquet of the Orange Free State Cricket Union when, incidentally, the dignified parents of the soon to be disgraced Hansie Cronje were amongst an audience of 750 people scattered on tables over the large stage of a theatre in Bloemfontein.

The organiser of the evening had had the apparently bright idea of lowering me from the ceiling by steel wire, like Peter Pan in a Christmas production, but instead of flying I was standing inside an open-fronted 'commentary box' which was lowered as I was introduced and then suspended above the audience. Delivering my speech as the box swayed some ten feet above an auditorium full of tables I must have made an extraordinary, and distracting, sight.

Moreover, the acoustics were poor. There is nothing worse than a bad microphone for any speaker and, for one of only two occasions in my career, a section of the guests, inebriated no doubt, began to talk loudly amongst themselves as I tried to amuse those who were listening or, more to the point, those who could actually hear me. In vain I borrowed Peter Parfitt's story of the speaker who asked if people could hear him at the back. 'Yes', came the reply, 'but I'll gladly swap places with someone who can't.'

An attempt by one of the organisers to quieten the offending minority almost resulted in a punch-up. It was a disaster such as I had only experienced previously when my agent arranged for me to talk, mainly about cricket, to a convention of power-boat enthusiasts.

Later on that evening in Bloemfontein the amusing and attractive Diane Chandler, a north country girl who had made a reputation in Johannesburg, failed even more comprehensively to capture the attention of the unruly element during a double act with the ubiquitous Franklyn Stephenson, the globe-trotting Barbadian cricketer who also played professional golf. This strange and painful experience (because I had been well paid to appear) proved to me that bad acoustics are more often the cause of failed speeches than poor material or delivery.

I have made a few speeches in South Africa over the years, as I have almost wherever I have travelled, usually with a better reaction, although few occasions there seemed to go quite as planned. On another evening I got an immediate laugh from a large gathering of diners celebrating the centenary of the first Test match in Port Elizabeth when I started with the words 'Good morning, Ladies and Gentlemen'. There had been several speeches already and I had finally got to my feet on the stroke of midnight.

It is the impromptu things that come to mind when an event takes shape that often give the most satisfaction, although there is always an element of risk. That same evening, since there were Australians present in an international audience, I hazarded re-telling a story about the Afrikaans gentleman who had made an inquiry in Sydney about the little black things bobbing about in the water just off Bondi Beach.

189

'Those little black things?' replied a local Aussie. 'Oh they're just bouys to keep the shark nets in place.' There was a pause before the visitor replied: 'Black boys? For 'eaven's sake, we'd never get away with that in South Africa.'

A fellow journalist told me that there was a mixed reaction. One can never tell for sure how well any joke will go down. Speaking at the request of a former Cambridge University contemporary who had become an executive in the food business I failed to sense the presence of a strong feminist feeling amongst some of the guests. Not long after I had sat down, aware that things had not gone quite as swimmingly as usual, the microphone was seized by a lady who said in a loud voice, 'I'd just like to say that I thought that speech was chauvinist, sexist and racist.'

That was putting it rather strongly but the fact is that most humour is at somebody's expense and has the capacity to offend. In this case I had started with a jest about the long admitted sexual orientation of a famous and much admired lady tennis player. (It's a funny world; we can get a man on the moon, but we still can't get one on Martina Navratilova.) I like to think that she would have laughed. It had certainly gone down rather well elsewhere, but you win some and lose others.

I had a delicate balance to strike in Kingston in 2004 when asked by Pat Rousseau, president of the Jamaica Cricket Association, to speak at a special anniversary dinner at the Pegasus hotel. This was a great honour and my only disappointment, on the eve of the first Test, was that the England team, having enjoyed their dinner, did not stay to listen to me, leaving myself and my fellow journalist, Pat Gibson, as the only English folk in a room full of distinguished Jamaicans and senior cricketing folk from elsewhere in the Caribbean including the great Bajans Sir Everton Weekes and Sir Garfield Sobers.

I still have the notes of what I said that evening because it happens that I made a remarkable prophesy, largely to soften the blow of expressing to a partisan audience my firm view that England would win the forthcoming series quite easily. Sure enough, the reaction was mixed, but I quickly added: 'But. Don't worry; there will be consolation for Brian Lara. He will regain his individual Test batting record by scoring 400 in the fourth Test in Antigua.' It was uncanny that this is precisely what happened after England had won the first three Tests, Lara having recently lost his record, also set against England in Antigua, when Matt Hayden thrashed 380 against Zimbabwe in Perth. I wished that I had acted on my intuition by putting some money on it. The odds against would have been enormous.

Other than at University sports dinners my first public speech was made in my early days at *The Cricketer* in the late 1960s when, like almost anyone who wrote anything professionally about cricket, I was summoned by Jack Sokell, the industrious secretary of the Wombwell Cricket Lovers, to speak to the Society. They used to meet in a pub on the outskirts of Barnsley and they had a charming custom of introducing the visitor by presenting him with a glass mug on which a local artist had engraved a likeness of his face.

Thinking on my feet as I began speaking after this surprise gift, I said: 'I think I can say that this is the ugliest mug I have ever seen'. I looked down the ranks of the locals, all of whom seemed to me to be rather ancient men in cloth caps, each clutching his pint, and saw not a flicker of amusement. Fortunately someone eventually got my meaning and the rest of my debut performance was generously received. Like most north country folk they were warm-hearted and, of course, they loved their cricket.

The faux pas is familiar to most who listen to a lot of speeches. Quite often they pass over the heads of inattentive audiences. I seemed, for example, to be the only one who noticed a familiar Grace being muddled by a nervous club chairman as follows: 'For what we are about to receive may the Lord be truly thankful.' But I was certainly not the only one to gain innocent joy from a solecism by Col. John Stephenson, the greatly liked and respected secretary of MCC, when we spoke together at a fund-raising dinner for a cricket tour to be made by his old school, Christ's Hospital, the great Bluecoats School at Horsham. Reminiscing as he looked down the imposing dining hall John declared in his stentorian, army-trained voice: 'When I was a boy at this school we had capital punishment and I can honestly say that it never did any of us any harm.'

Thanks to 'Colemanballs' in *Private Eye* many of the faux pas made on the air are recorded: such gems as Murray Walker's 'Every colour of the rainbow – black, white and brown' or 'Did my eyes deceive me or is Senna's Lotus sounding a bit rough?'. Like Brian Johnston, Walker has been in demand as an after-dinner speaker partly because of this propensity.

It would be a dull world without human frailty or humour and happily most people, certainly most who follow cricket, seem to be more or less on the same wave length, whether they are in Canberra, Cape Town, Carlisle or Calcutta. It is always a relief when, having worked hard to try to get a speech right for the occasion, it goes well. I suppose that my biggest triumph, if that is the word, was at a Lord's Taverners' Christmas lunch at the Grosvenor House in Park Lane, with about 1000 happy revellers present. I was nervous because the star speaker was the late Mike Yarwood, then at the height of his fame as a television impersonator. I went on before him, with the witty actor and comedian Peter Jones (he of the *Rag Trade*, *The Hitchhiker's Guide to the Galaxy* and many other TV and radio shows) as the meat in the sandwich.

Opening the batting, I decided to risk a few amateur impersonations of my own, tailored to the occasion. As the *Telegraph*'s Peterborough column reported the next day they brought the house down, and I got a standing ovation. Peter Jones, beginning by joking that he did not wish to be competitive, was witty, brief and very well received before leaving the floor for the other professional comedian. Alas, Yarwood went down like a lead balloon. He simply attempted to do part of his television act, not very well, and it was highly embarrassing when he lost an audience who had started very much on his side.

He had probably had a little too much to drink which cannot have helped. I have always acted on the principle that a glass or two of wine (or perhaps a beer beforehand and a glass with the meal) has the effect of dulling the critical side of the brain without destroying the creative side. Besides, dinners can be long affairs and food needs wine as an accompaniment. I am usually driving home anyway so there is always the need for moderation.

It was not alcohol, but a developing brain tumour about which no one knew, that made a famous England batsman's last appearance at a cricket dinner a sad embarrassment. There was some amusement at first when, soon after his initial reminiscent story, he began to tell it again. When he repeated it a third time no one knew what to think or do.

More often, alcohol is the villain. An inordinately lengthy retirement speech was given by a distinguished former cricket writer in London a few years ago. He is still going strong years later so I shall not mention his name, respected as he is, but nerves and booze had got the better of him. He began with a brilliant story about Walter Hammond but ended an hour later by asking if he should sit down and being affectionately told by everyone in the room that he should do so. They had started to laugh at him as well as with him, which was a shame.

You should try to leave them wanting more and as a matter of fact people are usually quite happy to talk to each other at dinners so don't mind if the speeches are short. Vivian Jenkins, the former Welsh full-back, Glamorgan cricketer and rugby writer for the *Sunday Times*, was once rather too well entertained by the local president as he sat on the top table in the hot and stuffy room at a club dinner. Rising to his feet to propose a toast to the club, he swayed slightly and uttered the words 'Wally Hammond was a bloody good player' before slowly subsiding into his chair for a long sleep. No knowledgeable person in the room could possibly argue.

More than once I have not even got that far, albeit through no fault of my own. Once I had just been announced, at the Grand Hotel in Eastbourne, when an elderly person on one of the tables collapsed to the floor, apparently having had a heart attack. The subsequent delay while a doctor was summoned and an ambulance ordered was not much of an aid to the atmosphere. On another occasion, at Reigate Priory Cricket Club, I was about to say my first words in the club pavilion at the end of the meal when all the lights – which were on a time meter – went out and the room was plunged into pitch darkness. Actually that helped the feeling of general merriment, but twice since members of my audience have fainted, to the natural consternation of all those in the room, who usually assume the worst. On the last such occasion, at the Haslemere Harvest Supper, I took it as my cue to sit down.

I had by then said enough, unlike the Earl of Onslow, with whom I was speaking at a charitable function at his elegant home, Clandon Park, one evening in the 1980s. Oddly enough for the descendant of the British Parliament's most legendary Speaker, he was reluctant to speak in public. Interrupted by someone with a mild comment from the back of the hall as he made his introductory remarks, he stunned everyone by responding: 'I don't particularly want to make this speech and it is clear to me from your interruption that you don't want to hear me, so I shall sit down.' Whereupon, he did so. As someone who has always cared rather too much about what people think of me, I admired his courage.

Most speakers, certainly not excluding myself, are guilty of plagiarism, and even 'new' jokes are invariably variations of old ones. I admire those who keep coming up with their own original stories, often with the help of professional comedy writers, like the always funny favourite of many a Lord's Taverner occasion, Bob Bevan. For years he has traded on being goalkeeper for the Old Wilsonian third XI (or lower). His gravelly voice and cockney accent help, but so does his topicality. He started telling stories weaved round Bobby Moore; now it is John Terry, Kevin Pietersen or whoever is in the news.

It is one thing to borrow a story, as I occasionally have from Bob, another to take credit for an entire speech. Many years ago now I heard an absolutely shameless exhibition of a kind of plagiarism that would better be described as robbery. The perpetrator was a circuit judge and, as a knight of the realm, presumably one of high reputation. He had memorised the famous recorded speech given by the barrister Humphrey Tilling at a Forty Club dinner. At a Round Table dinner (and no doubt at many others) he reproduced it virtually word for word without once acknowledging the source of the wit for which he received his standing ovation.

It was bad luck for Tilling to have his speech recorded and circulated, although Brian Johnston had most of his best stories recorded too. Incredibly, they continue to sell twenty years after his death. It never bothered him to give more or less the same speech over and over again. Geoff Miller, the genial Derbyshire and England all-rounder who has been the National Selector in recent years, is another who does the same. It is, undoubtedly, the way you tell 'em that counts.

It is often the time spent thinking about and composing the speech, not to mention travelling to make it, that really earns the fee, although most of my speeches over the years have been unpaid anyway. Those that were professional engagements certainly rewarded me better, hour for hour, than writing books but the eventual satisfaction was greater when books finally appeared. In any case I simply enjoyed writing them.

I cut my teeth on the accounts I wrote of my first five overseas tours as a means of paying for Judy, and, quite soon, Judy and the children, to join me for a time overseas. In India in 1976/7 I was already onto my third book, enabling her to come for several weeks with James and Robin, who were then only four and two. The books were far from classics but for me they were a good substitute for newspaper reporting and they at least left a fullish record of events for future cricket historians.

In 1978 I was approached out of the blue by Steve Adamson of Orbis Publishing, asking if I might produce a 'large-scale, illustrated reference book on cricket to the model of Leslie Halliwell's *Filmgoer's Companion*. I replied that there was already a superb encyclopedia on the game in the form of *The World of Cricket* which, under Jim Swanton's formidable editorial direction, was soon due to be updated.

Instead, I proposed that I should write the first book ever to publish a biography (some, obviously, very short), of every Test cricketer. This would, I wrote to Adamson, mean 1560 different biographies as opposed to 350 in *The World of Cricket*. The deal was done and I was soon embarked on feverish work on the project, helped not a little by assiduous research, in the cases of many of the players that I had never seen, by a retired civil servant from Woking, Jim Coldham. *The Complete Who's Who of Test Cricketers* appeared in the early summer of 1980. I produced two more editions but eventually I could no longer spare the candle-grease or stand the grind. Years later the book was updated and expanded in a new form by the Oxford University Press under the title *World Cricketers* but since then the rapid advance of the internet has made online sites the obvious sources of history and statistics for most of what publishers used to call 'students of the game'. Everyone can be an expert nowadays.

I burnt midnight oil over several books in the years before turning to daily journalism. *Bedside Cricket*, produced by the enterprising Adrian Stephenson, was more pleasurable to write than most of the others and I greatly enjoyed writing short profiles of some of the more colourful contemporary cricketers in another of Adrian's projects, the simply entitled *Cricket Characters* for which the caricaturist John Ireland produced some brilliant drawings.

I have written one or two books since, including one on the 2002/3 tour of Australia, co-written with Charles de Lisle. He put his heart into it and wrote exceptionally well, but it was an unhappy tour for England and Charles, brother of the talented sometime *Wisden* editor, Tim, was unfortunately having serious health problems at the time, which complicated matters. More enjoyably, and for obvious reasons less demandingly, I produced a personal anthology entitled *The Spirit of Cricket* which truly was a labour of love.

After ten years as a hungry free-lance, however, fate, chance, inclination and, perhaps, divine will, were pushing me towards a new challenge.

14

COUNTY CRICKET AND
THE *DAILY TELEGRAPH*

*A county cricket ground on a May morning in the 1980s. It might
be any number of pleasant places but let us say that it is Hove. In the
slight haze of a rapidly warming day, loyal followers of the staple
English game are happily ensconced in sagging blue and white
coloured deckchairs. Most are men but there are women too, usually
in charge of a picnic bag. Already the thermos has been opened for
a first cup of coffee. On their menfolk, panamas outnumber floppy
white sun-hats. Everyone has a newspaper. For the great majority of
them it is the* Daily Telegraph. *Each of them is cheerfully scrutinis-
ing one of the cricket pages.*

When Jim Swanton left the *Daily Telegraph* in 1975 he had a
ready-made successor in his long-time stablemate, the *Sunday
Telegraph* correspondent Michael Melford. Michael told me that
when Jim had come to the party at which he and his future wife,
Lorna, were celebrating their engagement, Jim slipped him a
wrapped package as he left, muttering as he did so: 'I thought
you would like this.' It turned out to be a signed photograph of
the great man.

With his softly spoken, dry and wry wit, Michael (whose post-humously published, limited edition memoir, *A Bowl of Cherries,* is a tiny classic) was a great companion on tour, and an inseparable friend of John Woodcock's, with whom he saw eye to eye on all matters of social propriety. A sound, experienced writer with a nice light touch, he was a shrewd observer of the game, loyal to the establishment, who kept the standards high. But the authority that 'EWS' had established as correspondent for so long slipped once 'Mellers', his near contemporary, had retired.

The no less witty Michael Carey soon resigned after disagreeing with his Sports editor, Ted Barrett, who had ordered him to report a 'racialist' incident involving Imran Khan at Worcester that to Michael's mind had nothing to do with the cricket match he was supposed to be reporting. Michael Austin and the genial, competent Peter West temporarily covered tours (Peter, famous as a versatile television performer, went to Australia in 1986/7 when he relished every moment and did his best to reduce the nation's stock of Chardonnay) before Barrett settled on a 'news man' more in tune with the approach that he required. Peter Deeley, an experienced news reporter with no deep passion for cricket, took over.

Deeley, too, was nothing if not competent but he would never have pretended to be a true 'authority' on the game. Unlike pretentious old CMJ, who at that sort of time was regularly sounding off on the air and in editorials in *The Cricketer,* his coverage lacked conviction or strong opinion. He reported who did what and when with faultless accuracy but did not much care 'how'. That, alas, is the way most reports are done these days, liberally laced with meaningless quotes. It is opinion, perspective and insight that make a good read.

Peter's relatively bland approach was soon noticed by both readers and senior men at the *Telegraph.* Soon after the tour of the West Indies in the early months of 1990 I was approached by the paper's managing editor, Jeremy Deedes, the genial son of the legendary Bill, and asked if I would like to become cricket correspondent. I had got an inkling of what he had in mind when, at his invitation, I dined with Jeremy and his wife, Anna, at the Coral Reef hotel in Barbados. Jim and Ann Swanton were also there. The naturally irascible Peter Deeley had just caused something of a stir by making a fuss after a party given by the British High Commissioner to Barbados, when taxis had not appeared as expected.

I was therefore not surprised when the offer came to become correspondent of a newspaper read at that time by the majority of serious followers of cricket. Once Jeremy and I had settled the details, I did not hesitate to take it.

Peter stayed on as a cricket reporter and I can hear him now, sitting next to me in the press box, saying 'What a terrible shot' whenever anyone was bowled. It might have been an unplayable nip-backer or a superb deception in flight but in Peter's book it was usually the batsman's fault! But he was a supportive companion who never bore me any grudge and was, I think, heartily relieved to be free of the extra responsibility. So far as I know, he has not been seen on a cricket ground since he retired.

The salary that I was offered was considerably greater than the one I was receiving at the BBC and a bit more than I had been getting for combining that job with the editorial directorship of the *The Cricketer*. Beside that, however, I had been increasingly frustrated by the attitude of those involved with the fledgling Radio Five, for whom – in a clear portent of the way that all sports reporting would go – soccer seemed really to be the only show in town.

In particular I was furious with the way that Radio Five was neglecting proper coverage of county cricket and sending me to matches on Saturdays without ever asking for more than hurried updates. I protested to Larry Hodgson, the genial former tennis correspondent who had inherited the typically grand BBC title of Head of Sport and Outside Broadcasts, Radio and, at his request, I explained my objections in writing:

'The Radio Five producers', I wrote,

simply do not understand a game that, by its very nature, is slow, drawn-out, cerebral, contemplative. It tends to meander gently and burst into sudden life. No one can predict when it will. In the hands of a competent commentator, especially if he has a second voice next to him for variety's sake, it should never be dull, however 'slow' the play itself may be. Yet Saturday after Saturday goes by with no commentary whatsoever. Even the scores are given far too seldom and twice this season I have had to blow a gasket – with no apology from the producer – when scores have been given that are three-quarters of an hour out of date because no one has even bothered to ask me at the OB for the latest score.

Nor will I hear any nonsense about the lack of interest in county cricket. If that is so why is there so much newspaper coverage devoted to it? Why are several different companies currently making money out of conveying scores *and commentaries* down telephone lines? Local radio covers cricket far more comprehensively than we do.

All that, alas, remains true today, the only difference being that newspapers no longer report the county game so thoroughly. Larry was sympathetic but nothing much changed so, relieved that he was still keen to include me as a regular *TMS* commentator and boosted by an extraordinarily generous letter accepting my resignation, I began the 1991 season as the *Telegraph*'s new correspondent under the command of Max Hastings, a brilliant editor with very little interest in cricket, and David Welch, as supportive a sports editor as one could wish for.

I certainly did not approach it in a mood of superiority or without a certain trepidation. No doubt the same was true for Jonathan Agnew, taking over my long-time role at the BBC. He soon showed himself to be completely at ease in the job and I quickly felt the same, although I had no prior knowledge of the routines of daily newspaper reporting.

I knew that I would enjoy the challenge, not least of the slower pace and gentle pleasures of the county game, which still had a certain rhythm over the course of a season in the days before Twenty20. Here, I knew, were to be found what Thomas Gray called 'homely joys', albeit with the destiny of at least some of the players obscure. It was not life or death cricket, but for the players, each one of them ambitious for himself and his team, it was important, and so it was for all who followed them and enjoyed reading about the matches. Sometimes they were slow and dull, more often full of character, the class players standing out but the journeymen doing their bit and having their days. Keenly fought and in a pastoral setting County Championship cricket comes second only to a Test match.

Before the big matches began I might start my season at Lord's: on an early April morning, especially if the weather was kind, it was a little world in itself, isolated from London traffic by high walls and trees just coming into leaf. Then I might move a week later to Hove, where the pink cherry blossom would already be leaning away from the breeze but not yet ripped apart by wind or burnt brown by summer; the sea, just down the hill, more scented and imagined than seen; homely chatter from the blue and white deckchairs: 'Another fifty off from these two and we could win this yet, you know.'

So it would go through the season. Trent Bridge, perhaps, in June: an international ground, yet still a cricket ground, local, friendly, quietly proud of a long heritage; well developed but dominated still by the greensward itself, with its rich turf and broad dark and light stripes. Or the small-ground intimacy of Basingstoke to follow in August; white tents crammed close to the boundary, flint and stone walls marking one inviting boundary; an ancient church beyond; players and their watchers close enough to touch; the big match come to town, as once it came to the villages in days when players were much smaller but no less heroic. Then they wore top hats, but it is helmets now.

All too soon, it would be Lord's again, in September: old players run-stealing in the hope of new contracts; young ones striving to make their mark; leaves beginning to stain the ground and long winter months ahead.

In the best county clubs, especially those based away from big cities, the first team is merely the focal point of a unified whole. At Sussex, especially during their run of success from 2000 or so onwards, there was a genuine feeling that everyone was part of the family: the ground staff, the stewards, the scorecard lady, even the loyal band of regular spectators. County Championship cricket in particular remains a game played for the most part away from the glare of television cameras; earnest and passionate but companionable too; not, utterly, money obsessed.

No television meant that newspaper reports in the three main broadsheet newspapers of the time were a special privilege to write and usually a pleasure to read. A band of agency reporters round the country specialised in the facts while the tabloid writers, gifted wordsmiths though they may have been, had to look for a personality or a news story. The lucky few, however, had the space to interpret, analyse, observe and speculate. In BBC days my county cricket reporting and commentating had been mainly confined to Saturdays. Now, before, after and sometimes during an international programme that was less heavy than today, there was time to see matches from start to finish and in between to have a beer and dinner with friends or even in the precious company of a good book.

For some time all the talk in official cricket circles has been of cutting down the amount of County Championship cricket. The executives and board of the ECB, for ever putting marketing and money-making before the production of the best possible England-qualified cricketers, refuse to listen properly to the views of players and coaches, frequently wasting their money instead on professional research, most of it loaded to favour the views of those fair-weather followers of cricket who seldom actually watch the game. Another such exercise was expected to recommend a smaller first division and fewer first-class matches overall from 2013. To my mind that would be a mistake, for a number of reasons that include the uncertainty of the weather and the danger that festival cricket, the very essence of the county game, will become even rarer than it already is.

Oh, my Harrogate and my Buxton long ago! There was a time, and still is in the more enlightened counties, when the county coming to town was a big event, anticipated long in advance, relished while the cricket was in progress and reviewed with pleasure months later. Sometimes such games are never forgotten, such as the one started and finished after a thunderstorm on the extraordinary opening day of the Tunbridge Wells Week in 1960.

Kent and Worcester began battle at 11.30 am, Kent reaching 80 for four by lunch before being bowled out for 187 at 3.40. The left-handed Peter Jones made 73, very nearly as many as Worcestershire managed in their two innings of 25 and 61. Witnesses reported small craters appearing when the ball pitched, much to the liking of Dave Halfyard and Alan Brown, who took nine cheap wickets each. By 7.15 it was all over.

Every now and then freak events occur and pitches are not what they should be for top-class cricketers. They are the exceptions to the general rule that county cricket is better tuned to small, intimate grounds than it is to echoing caverns like The Oval or Edgbaston, places that come alive on the big international occasion but that too often seem glum and empty when they play host to the homespun atmosphere of the County Championship game.

County cricket flourishes, absorbs and excites in places such as Arundel and Abergavenny, Bath and Burton-on-Trent, Colchester and Colwyn Bay, Dover and Dudley, Eastbourne and Ebbw Vale. I shall not try to get to the end of the alphabet but there would not be many letters missing if I did. Many of the places that no longer get the chance to stage county cricket have quite beautiful grounds and those that remain generally do so still.

The cricket is characterised by a strong local spirit and players and spectators are brought close together to the benefit of both. The surroundings, seldom far from a church or pub or both, are invariably adorned by old and beautiful trees that help the ball to swing, not to mention shortish boundaries that encourage bats to do the same. Good weather usually guarantees good sized crowds and a precious amalgam of tension and relaxation.

The reason for the decrease in the number of festival games is simple. All counties have more or less developed their main grounds, at an accelerated rate in recent years. Some of them have got into serious financial difficulties as a result. Once there has been investment at a county's headquarters it makes sense to use that ground as often as the number of pitches will sensibly allow. Overheads are less expensive that way.

The strong counter arguments are that festival matches spread the gospel around the county, encourage local cricketers and cricket-watchers, make everyone feel part of the family of the game and give a focal point to the season for those clubs on whose grounds the county team comes to play. I know from the experience of my local club, Horsham, how much that means to the members, many of whom get involved year after year in the nitty-gritty of preparing the pitches, making the teas, watering the flower-baskets, erecting the tents that go up round the ground and making arrangements for dealing with an invasion of cars and spectators.

More than this, matches on out-grounds can still be great events for the town in question. I suppose I have been to one of these games without seeing the local Mayor in attendance on one or other of the days but if so I cannot remember it. There always seems to be a large black car with a pennant billowing out from the bonnet parked in a position of prominence with a driver at the ready (albeit with an eye and a half on the cricket) to whisk the VIP back to the town hall after a good lunch.

At one match in Wales, in the glorious parkland setting of Pontypridd one wet day after play had been called off for the day and everyone had gone home, I witnessed a strange example of civic pride. The Mayor solemnly went ahead with his prepared lunchtime speech from the balcony, like Hitler at the Nuremberg rally, even though the field in front of him was empty and the handful of people who could actually hear him were all standing behind him, most of them invited journalists anxious not to waste the chance of a drink and some free sandwiches. By the same token the Mayor was not going to miss the opportunity to make a speech. 'I've prepared it boy, so I'm damned well going to give it' was the unspoken message.

It was, I believe, at another mining town, Ebbw Vale, that Emrys Davies called his partner Gilbert Parkhouse across at the end of the over to tell him that he had just tapped down the pitch with his bat on a length and had a nasty surprise. 'I could have sworn I heard someone answering back below' he said.

The fact is that if towns, cricket clubs and county executives all co-operate and appreciate the possibilities of festival games, they will benefit everyone concerned. The local economy gets a boost from an influx of visitors, helping shops, pubs, hotels and garages amongst others; the county gets a guaranteed profit if its officials have negotiated sensibly; and the home club itself gets plenty back in bar takings and prestige.

For me the likes of Aigburth and Basingstoke, not to mention more established favourites such as Cheltenham and Scarborough, are quintessential settings for the county game. Like the Championship itself they are a small but precious part of the English way of life.

If this more regular reporting of county cricket was the most enjoyable aspect of my new role, it was only a small part of it. E.W. Swanton had been very much the kingpin of the whole *Telegraph* cricket operation. Others since had no doubt done less, but at the time that I joined I felt that the cricket coverage had become ordinary and that it was in need of an injection of cricketing know-how when it came to the list of county reporters. That meant less work for some, and after a fair trial, the dropping of one or two. Mistakenly I replaced them for a time with two dilletantes, neither of whom knew the nuts and bolts of journalism. What were needed, of course, were 'proper' writers who also understood the game's nuances.

I certainly caused offence, which I deeply regretted, by demoting one of the established free-lances, Doug Ibbotson, who was a fine wordsmith but more concerned with offering a pretty piece or a clever line than genuinely reporting the cricket and offering any insight into what had happened. You had to be an Alan Gibson or perhaps a Neville Cardus to get away with that and he was not in their exalted class. He burnt his boats finally when, reporting from Fenner's, he gave several mentions to the talented Cambridge captain, Anurag Singh (captain of British Universities too and already a marked man as far as the England selectors were concerned), as 'Khan'. It was careless on his part and no less on that of the sub-editors.

As I soon learned to my irritation, these no doubt worthy night-shift workers had become accustomed to making casual changes to carefully thought out copy, in the form either of cuts or superfluous additions. Sometimes they were under pressure to get an edition out in time, sometimes doing things by the book to conform to house style, but too often they would spoil the rhythm of sentences or miss cricketing points and even introduce grammatical errors.

Thus, in my early days at the *Telegraph* at least, I might send over something like this: 'Alec Bedser, sagely watching for a time yesterday, would have been proud of the verve and stamina displayed by Martin Bicknell during the five-wicket spell that enabled Surrey to take control on the first day of their game against Yorkshire.'

And read instead the next morning something more like this: 'Alec Bedser, the former Surrey and England fast-medium bowler, who was watching for a time, would have been proud of the verve and stamina displayed by the Surrey fast bowler Martin Bicknell as he took five for 46 against title-chasing Yorkshire at the Foster's Oval yesterday.'

There were several other times, of course, when I was grateful to the subs for spotting my occasional lapses of memory. It was a team game but I had early battles to try to establish that whenever anyone wanted to change something that I had written they should consult me first.

In those days the system was to handwrite or type one's copy and then to dictate it but soon the Tandy, the neat little laptop, enabled more direct transmission, so long as the communication worked, which it by no means always did. One had to put headphones over the speaker and earpiece of a telephone, attach it to the computer and type in the requisite code. If the line was bad chunks of copy could be lost or garbled. You had to love what you were doing, because they were long days, requiring you to get to the ground at around half past ten (I was not always there quite by then!) and seldom to get away before half past seven or later.

The great thing about being in any cricket press box, be it at a relatively sparsely attended county match or one of England's games, was the company. Every county had its invaluable 'local man', prepared to pass on all but the most confidential information to help those like me who drifted into and out of the county circuit to keep more or less on the ball. Players, too, were always friendly, glad to see me at a match if only because they knew that it would be given a decent 'show' in the paper the following day.

There were some notable characters amongst the regulars on the circuit. In the west country the former Somerset batsman Eric Hill would sit on a raised chair in the corner of his uncomfortable box, peering over his reading glasses at the match and never missing a ball. The official scorers sat next door, separated only by a wooden partition. At Derby it was Gerald Mortimer, round but not so portly as his famous brother's character Rumpole of the Bailey, always polite, sometimes cynical about his county's prospects but secretly urging them on to success. At Northampton it was the assiduous Andrew Radd, at Sussex the sunny-tempered Jack Arlidge, at Canterbury the Londoner Dudley Moore, never happier than when dictating down the phone line that Kent's opponents were in trouble at 'firty free for free'. And so on. Gradually these men became familiar faces until, suddenly it seemed, someone younger had taken over from them, reporters who would themselves become part of the local furniture as the years passed.

At Leeds it needed several sages to service all the local papers, amongst them the lugubrious John Callaghan, the scholarly Robert 'Freddie' Mills, the irrepressible optimist David 'Plum' Warner and, the rising star, David Hopps, whose always thoughtful and shrewd writing has for years helped to lift cricket writing in the *Guardian* far above the prosaic. Each of these, indeed, was following a tradition set by the most acclaimed cricket writer of them all, Sir Neville Cardus, who would invent a story to illustrate a cricketer's character to add colour to his piece and for whom 'flights of fancy' were what his art was all about.

The regular free-lances were another group who became welcome companions. The *Telegraph* had some of the best. Amongst them were Mike Beddow, always on top of anything that happened at Worcester or Edgbaston; the Anglicised Parsee, 'Dicky' Rutnagur, who adored the game and kept on reporting it into a frail old age; and David Green, the former Oxford, Lancashire and Gloucestershire batsman. He never stopped telling stories from his career, kept the press box in a state of constant merriment but never veered from a straight report of the match. His dispatches had plenty of cricketing insight but showed little evidence, unfortunately, of his considerable imagination. David Llewellyn, one of the most assiduous journalists I have known, was a similar curiosity. He kept immaculate records, had a vast fund of general knowledge, was for ever helping anyone who needed assistance of any kind and had the mental capacity to be a novelist of note. He was also a quite brilliant mimic; but his work in the paper was disappointingly tied by the basic rules drummed into professional journalists: who, what, when and how, with too little emphasis on the 'how' to make his writing as lively as one felt it should have been.

One free-lance, the long-time *Guardian* writer David Foot, sailed on as a reporter past his eightieth birthday, benignly watching and talking all day before dictating a measured, elegant summary of events after tea. He used to report football in the west country too and told me a remarkable story of a narrow escape from a group of the worst sort of fans in Bristol in the days when 'hooliganism' was common. Leaving a floodlit evening match, fortunately with a small black briefcase in hand, he found himself surrounded by hostile fans after taking a short-cut towards the railway station down a dark path between some houses. He knew that he was about to be mugged and thought quickly. 'Please let me get through', he said: 'I'm a doctor and a patient needs my help urgently.' Villainy was averted by ingenuity.

The stress of having to keep on top of the ceaseless round of 'England stories' and various press releases emanating from the old Test and County Cricket Board and its succssor, the England and Wales Cricket Board, increased with the years. Most of the senior cricket correspondents gradually abandoned covering county cricket but I was loath to follow them and never did. My workload was correspondingly much greater, but I also felt that I was much better informed, especially when some young player arrived on the international scene. Quite simply, I enjoyed the county circuit. We had far more fun, jousting verbally through a day's play and discussing the latest gossip, than is possible now that all concerned are permanently online, unable fully to appreciate the cricket or anyone else's company.

I5

AUSTRALIA THEN AND NOW

Cloud laid out below like a great white duvet; above a deep blue void; the brain lulled and dulled by the soft zzum of the engines and modest sippings of beer or wine. 'We have a Shiraz from the Clare Valley for you today, Mr. Jenkins. I'm told it's very nice. Is that OK for you?' If I am being critical the stewardess seems a little, shall we say, motherly, but, yes I assure her, it is quite OK.

Once all the Qantas stewardesses seemed fresh, bronzed and young but perhaps that was before I had the privilege, sometimes, of going business class and once, through a fortuitous meeting with a cricket-loving executive, first-class. There are worse ways to while away a few hours than this, especially when the clouds part above Australia to remind you what a huge and barren country it is.

Air journeys are part of Australian life, for many of its citizens no more unusual than for people travelling by train or car elsewhere. When I first went there in 1974, magically swapping winter for summer in twenty-four hours, Ansett Airways and Trans Australia Airways (TAA) competed for the business of whisking citizens from city to city; now Qantas, always the international carrier, seem to have something close to a monopoly. The airlines have been a commercial battlefield in Australia second only to the media, and, these days, the mines in the mineral-rich west. Minerals have made multi-millionaires of a lucky few and have simultaneously immunised the whole country from the worst effects of the recession that threatened the world economy in the second half of the noughties.

For cricketers in Australia nothing but the best will ever do. From my first visit there to the shocking humiliation suffered by Andrew Flintoff's team thirty-two years later, visiting teams, English or otherwise, usually finished second. Only those mighty West Indies sides of the 1980s flew there expecting to win.

Almost invariably English ones have travelled to the wide brown land with greater hope than expectation. The triumphs of Andrew Strauss's side in 2010/11 are likely to be the last games that I shall witness in Australia at first hand. If so I can count myself especially lucky to have seen them in a dual capacity as BBC commentator and MCC President. Combining those two roles in Melbourne was both enjoyable and demanding during the match in which England secured the Ashes by means of bowling Australia out for a wretched total of ninety-eight in the first innings.

Judy and I were wonderfully well entertained by senior members of the other MCC in their spacious, comfortable committee room which, like all the expensively refurbished members' area, combines impressive modern facilities with clever use of old photographs and pictures to remind everyone of the long sporting legacy of the 'paddock that grew'. The cricket and sports museums below are models, imaginatively displaying the visual memories of cricket matches going back before the first Test in 1877, not to mention the 1956 Olympics and the internecine contests of what was once just the Victorian

Football League but is now the AFL, incorporating Rules Football clubs from every state.

The fact that the MCG, like several of the other major cricket grounds in Australia, is now staging sport all the year round, makes the financing of these sorts of facilities so much easier than it is at Lord's. The MCG museum was given a small matter of $25 million of public money, enabling it to celebrate not just cricket and football but all the other sports at which Australia has excelled over the years: tennis, both codes of rugby, athletics and many more. There is a special area dedicated to racing, with the actual skeleton of the famed hose Carbine at its centre, and a model of Phar Lap's heart, which was weighed after the great horse's death at 6.3 kilograms. Outside the massive Coliseum are superb statues of some of the great champions of the past, including one of Dennis Lillee in the final leap of his bowling action. These life-size bronzes confront the masses who walk along the Yarra river to the 'G' on big match days, across a purpose-built bridge that takes them past rowing boathouses, the Rod Laver Tennis Arena and yet another new stadium with a futuristic roof like a bubble-cover that caters for soccer and Rugby League. There is in Melbourne all that sporting life affords.

Melbourne without its sport, indeed, would be like a river without water and much the same goes for the whole country, but they do not all play. One still sees examples of those who have missed the boat: the occasional miserable looking 'Abbo' in some cities and one or two pony-tailed inebriates on the streets of all of them, but the 'good life' – something of a misnomer in some ways – has expanded to most, or so it appears. Prosperity is evident both from the burgeoning spread of skyscrapers in all the major cities and in the vastly increased volume and sophistication of the wine industry.

Wine vies these days with sportsmen and women, Rolf Harris, Clive James and a clutch of brilliant actors as the first thing an Englishman thinks of in connection with Australia. I remember John Arlott bringing his own supply of vintage Bordeaux to the Centenary Test in 1977 and challenging an Australian with whom we were sharing a pre-dinner drink in his hotel room to taste the difference between it and the local red that had been proudly produced but reasonably politely rebuffed. According to Frank Tyson, Arlott had, on his only previous visit, asked for the claret he had ordered to be poured as his second course approached. 'Don't worry, Mr Arlott', he was assured. 'We've kept it nice and cool for you in the freezer.'

It took me some time to be convinced that New World wines could be the equal of their French, Spanish or Italian rivals and I remain a dilettante in these matters but it seems to me that cross fertilisation of Europeans and dedicated winemakers in Australia, New Zealand and South Africa in particular has actually resulted in far less plonk everywhere. All the Europeans have had to look to their laurels, as English cricketers once did, pushed into higher standards by those who gradually discovered the right grapes for their region and worked assiduously to produce wine of the highest quality.

Australia has any number of wonderful wines these days, helped in the case of white grapes by the screwcap taking over from the cork. Once it seemed that Aussie Chardonnays, heavily influenced by the oak in which they were matured, tasted much of a muchness. Now there are any number of superbly produced local wines subtly peculiar to their terroir, like Barossa Valley Shiraz, Coonawarra Cabernet Sauvignon, Clare Valley Riesling and Hunter Valley Semillon.

The only problem is they cost so much. Australia's dollar had risen on the back of the mining boom by 2010/11, even as the pound had fallen after the international banking crisis. I was glad that I personally was not paying the expenses on my four-teenth visit to Australia in all. It was a shock for British visitors to be asked to pay £5 for a bottle of beer but almost as much of a surprise to discover how well the England team had prepared for success and learned from past mistakes.

So telescoped have modern Test series become that the most recent series for the Ashes was all over in seven weeks. My first three tours between 1974 and 1980 were each of three months duration. In all, I must have spent nearly three years of my life in this land of wide open spaces where the topography is generally reflected in the bold, brash, open-hearted attitude of its citizens, no matter the fact that the vast majority of them live in cities.

Australians are not used to losing at sport because they are so very good at it. The Federal and State governments all spend far more on sporting facilities than in Britain, where public money cannot by law be given to private clubs. The media give it a higher priority than almost anything else and everywhere you go in the cities you see fit young people running or cycling. Curiously, you also see more fat slobs wobbling ponderously along pave-ments than you would in the average English city. Obesity has become as much a problem as it is in the USA or Britain. Get behind one of the walking tombstones on a crowded pavement and you can be as surely restricted in your progress as if you were in a car in a traffic-jam.

More than most it is a country of contradictions. There is the obvious contrast between the vast, weather-beaten natu-ral interior and the gleaming modern coastal cities, with their skyscrapers dwarfing those that remain of the old, dignified stone civic buildings from the 19th century. But, hidden in the suburbs, road after road is full of architecturally unappealing bungalows. The same discrepancies apply in Australian society,

The Walker family in wartime. My maternal grandfather, renowned as a surgeon in Peterborough, is far right on the front row.

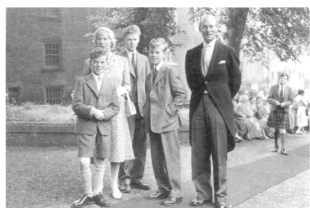

Aged 13 at a family wedding with my parents and brothers, Timothy, front left, and David, centre.

The three musketeers: David, Timothy and Christopher, on a family holiday in Scotland in 1959.

Leg stump half-volleys: meat and drink even to non-class batsmen! A boundary en route to my first 50 at Lord's in 1962.

At the *Cricketer* magazine in 1969 with Micky Stewart (Surrey and England) before drawing the winners in a magazine competition.

The formal verdict on one of my first trials as a possible BBC cricket commentator. Robert Hudson was never a man to shower loose praise. My first commentary opportunity came at Old Trafford in a one-day international a year later.

The Editor of *The Cricketer*, circa 1980.
(Photo by Adrian Murrell)

Media and team always used to get on well together on tours of the sub-continent before the days of televised coverage and specialist press officers: MCC and assorted correspondents at the Taj Mahal hotel, 1976/77: Back Row, l to r: Derek Randall, Keith Fletcher, Dennis Amiss, Bob Woolmer, Geoff Miller, Chris Old, Bob Willis, Mike Selvey, J.K.Lever, Geoff Cope, Roger Tolchard, Graham Barlow, Alan Knott, Bernie Thomas (physio and fixer). Front Row: CMJ (BBC), Clive Taylor (*Sun*), Mike Brearley (vice capt.), Alex Bannister (*Mail*), Tony Greig (captain), Peter Laker (*Mirror*), Ken Barrington (Manager), Pat Gibson (*Express*), Derek Underwood.

The media at play in an Anglo/Australia challenge match in Sydney, 1978/9, each team augmented by a Test cricketer: Players, back row, l to r: Mike Coward, Peter Meares, Brian Mossop, Jim Tucker, Jim Woodward, Dick Tucker, Ken Piesse, Steve Whiting, Peter Lush, CMJ. Front row, l to r:Paul Fitzpatrick, David Frith, Norman Tasker, Bobby Simpson, Rod Nicholson,Peter Laker, Peter McFarlane, Brian Williams, Ken Barrington, Scyld Berry, Derek Hodgson. On the ground: Henry Blofeld, politely toasting the photographer.

A gathering at The Cricketers Club in London of most of those working at the microphone for BBC radio on the 1983 World Cup. Back Row, l to r: Ian Davis, Neil Durden-Smith, John Snow, CMJ, Peter Walker, Peter Richardson, Peter Parfitt, Fred Titmus, Brian Johnston. Middle row: Fred Trueman, Colin Milburn, Bob Nixon, Rachael Heyhoe-Flint,

Don Mosey, Alan Richards, Lucien Wijesinghe, Jim Maxwell, Norman Cuddeford. Front Row: Ralph Dellor, Michael Carey, Tony Cozier, Farokh Engineer, Trevor Bailey, Mushtaq Mohammad, Mike Denness.

No jackets and ties needed on radio sometimes. Interviewing Allan Lamb before a Test match in India.

Family portrait: Robin, Judy, Lucy, self, James and Sandy, our first dog, at Naldrett House, September 1984.

With Judy and Ted Dexter at one of hundreds of sporting charity dinners.

Brian Johnston and the bronze bust by Neil Andrew that now resides in state outside the Brian Johnston Media Centre at The Oval.

I am not renowned for my mastery of computer technology. Happy to receive a little assistance in the press tent during an England match at the three W's Oval in Barbados.

With Bob 'The Cat' Bevan, entertaining players at a Lord's Taverners golf day.

Far from perfection, alas, but golf has been a great substitute for cricket and I still convince myself I am improving.

James (right), Robin and Lucy at a party to celebrate Robin's 21st and Lucy's 18th birthdays.

Something has amused Henry Blofeld and Bill Frindall – My Dear Old Thing and the Bearded Wonder – at an Oval Test match.

Leisure time on tour. With Mike Selvey of the *Guardian*, about to board a small flying boat in northern Queensland before inspecting the pitch on the barrier reef.

Test Match Special. Rain delays play at The Oval in an England v. India but the show must go on as usual. Back row, l to r: Jonathan Agnew, Vic Marks, CMJ, Peter Baxter, Henry Blofeld, Bill Frindall. Front row: Harsha Bhogle, Sunil Gavaskar, Shilpa Patel, Eleanor Oldroyd.

Proud parents with Robin, newly capped by Sussex at Horsham in 2000.

M-Js all: Robin, Flora, Anthea, David, James, Nicola, self, Lily, Tim, Najwa, Judy and Lucy at the wedding of James and Nicola in Provence, October 2002.

Photographed by Patrick Eagar in the week that I became President of MCC.

Sussex are County Champions for the first time, 2003. Carl Hopkinson (top), R.M-J and Mushtaq Ahmed, the genius who made it possible, share the joy.

which is outwardly casual but actually authoritarian. You *will* be photographed you are told by a clear notice in every taxi. You may not eat, drink or abuse the driver. This is merely a statement of what anyone would consider to be civilised behaviour but an Australian 'cabby' is not be confused with his counterpart in London, especially if, as is often the case, he is newly arrived from Ukraine, Vietnam, Eritrea or the Punjab and has not the faintest idea of the whereabouts of your destination in Warabarree Road.

The curious accents that emerge from such as these, as they strain for strine, can be hilarious. There are those who can even spot a trace of lingering Welsh in Julia Gillard, the lady who, in true New World fashion, rose from nowhere to become prime minister in 2010, demoting the first of what will probably in time be several prime ministerial Kevins. Certainly her cabinet must have been the first to have a Kevin as Foreign Secretary and a Wayne in charge of the economy. The naming of children is, I suppose, an outward sign of a nation that now does things its own way, not in the way of its fathers and mothers, but it is unfortunate that parents who were christened Robert or Catherine (or Ranjiv or Boris for that matter) after relatives of previous generations of their family, should feel the need to call their fair dinkum daughters Rayanne, Brunella – or some such invented first name beloved of Australians. English parents have unfortunately followed the trend since Jason and Kylie hit British television screens.

Like Britain, Australia has become increasingly multi-coloured and multi-cultural and, despite the problems that has brought for the poor and poorly educated of the big cities, both nations are the better for it. There is no end yet to the mad waste of wars in the world, but, gradually the wolf is learning to live with the lamb, the leopard to lie down with the kid.

I read those words from Isaiah on my last visit to Australia at the request of John Shepherd, Dean of Perth Cathedral, who has asked me to read a lesson at either the Advent or Christmas Carol Service whenever I have been in his home city. It is always a pleasure because not only does the building become more beautiful each time I see it but so also does the music, nurtured lovingly by John and his wife, Joy, the head of a renowned Perth girls' school. The present musical director, the organ recital-ist Joseph Nolan, has raised standards to exquisite levels and made it more easily possible for the fortunate congregations in a faraway city to experience that sense of the infinite that is the essence of faith.

Australia is a melting pot but her citizens tend to speak with one voice when the Poms are in town, as I was reminded when I walked out of the Brisbane Cricket Ground, the famous Gabba (actually Woolloongabba), after Australia had had much the better of the first day of the 2010/11 series against England. Reacting perhaps to the sometimes insulting, sometimes witty goadings of England's self-regarding Barmy Army, masses of chunky male Queenslanders were talking to themselves or their mobiles in voices of loud triumph, like crows over a corpse. Fuelled by their gassy and expensive local beer, their favoured adjective, often repeated, began with 'f'. But, typical of Australian discipline, they were happy to wait for minutes at a time at road junctions while equally chunky female police officers in their blue and grey uniforms controlled the moment that they could flow across the road, like collies with a huge flock of sheep. My own instinct was to use my initiative about when and where to cross. It was, however, this Australian discipline, respect for authority and the general willingness of ordinary folk to help their neigh-bours that made the dreadful floods of 2011 far less damaging in terms of human life than they would have been in almost any other country.

Over the years Australian discipline and *esprit de corps* have generally proved superior to English individuality on the cricket field. Strangely their biennial contests (now becoming dangerously more frequent because of short-sighted administrators who have made themselves dependent on the television income and believe, mistakenly, that they cannot do without it) were once seen as battles between dyed-in-the-wool English professionalism and free-spirited Aussie initiative.

In recent times both countries have come to the conclusion that the key to winning is to apply preconceived plans based on thorough analysis of the strengths and weaknesses of the opposition. England have successfully followed the Australian formula and, at the present time, are doing it better with a superior group of players, but fortunes will ebb and flow as they always have, which is why series for the Ashes fascinate so many.

From the first series that I reported England teams always set out more or less believing that they possessed the players to buck a trend that had been so evident since the end of the First World War. Even without Geoffrey Boycott and John Snow, the leading performers in Ray Illingworth's victorious team four years earlier, Mike Denness's 1974/5 side apparently had a sufficient number of world-class players – Edrich, Amiss, Greig, Knott, Underwood, Willis (and later Cowdrey) – to have at least a decent chance of retaining the Ashes that had been defended, albeit narrowly, in 1972. But two nasty surprises lay round the corner. Dennis Lillee recovered from his apparently career-threatening back injury and Jeff Thomson appeared like a bull from the bush. Australia won 4-1.

Without their best batsman, but most divisive character, Geoffrey Boycott, they had little answer to Lillee and the hitherto virtually unknown Thomson, the twin forces that hit them like one of Queensland's occasional whirlwinds at Brisbane, battering down the front of their house from one end and lifting the garage from its foundations at the other. Nor was it just 'Lilian Thomson'. Several other exceptional players, in particular the Chappell brothers, Doug Walters, Rodney Marsh, Max Walker and Ashley Mallett, made this a formidable team.

Tony Greig's century at Brisbane lives in the memory for its audacity and bravado; John Edrich showed limitless depths of courage and doggedness when he led the team in Denness's place at Sydney, making fifty and thirty-three not out with broken ribs; and Denness, Keith Fletcher and Peter Lever in particular enjoyed sweet revenge in the final match at Melbourne when Thomson was unfit and Lillee injured himself. But most of the series was dominated by Australia.

The excitement of seeing for the first time the grounds of which I had read and heard so much was great and I learned from commentating for ABC Radio with the wise, balanced, if occasionally temperamental Alan McGilvray. He got into a savage temper one day when I had asked the producer, the benign, efficient and understanding Alan Marks, to change the rota to enable me to fit commentaries round my many short reports for the BBC. To my surprise he suggested that it was an Englishman ordering mere colonials around, which revealed the chip that in those days still sat only a little below the surface of even the best bred Aussies.

I had the privilege of meeting Harold Larwood in retirement when I made a pilgrimage to his modest bungalow in the Sydney suburbs during that tour, accompanied by the future *Telegraph* cricket correspondent Mike Carey, a Derbyshire man but one who understood the traditions of the neighbouring county. We found the chief hero of the Bodyline tour – the great Nottinghamshire fast bowler who had humbled Bradman and made Douglas Jardine's ruthless strategy successful – living more like a pauper than a prince. North Sydney is very hot in summer and the street that became home for the last forty-five years of his life was a long way from the glamour of Sydney Harbour; more like one in the mining village in Nottinghamshire where he had started. In old age the wiry, muscular little terror of the 1930s looked shrunk and bony, like an old bird. But he was happy to talk and obviously very content with his wife Lois and their daughters. He allowed me to interview him for radio and we saw on the mantelpiece the famous ashtray inscribed *To Harold from a grateful Skipper*.

It is to me an alarming thought that almost as many years have passed between my first and most recent visits to Australia as had between Larwood's triumphs in 1932/3 and my meeting with him forty-two years later.

No city has changed more in Australia since the 1970s than Brisbane. Then it was a country town, with very few restaurants, no coloured immigrants and no night life. Now there are skyscrapers, a superbly developed waterfront, Indian taxi-drivers and a fast growing population of Chinese. In 1974 I stayed at the featureless, bare and basic Travel Lodge at Kangaroo Point. On recent tours I have stayed beside the river at the graceful Stamford Plaza hotel, travelling to 'work' each day of matches as often as not by ferry. The service runs like clockwork from point to point on either side of the river, much more cheaply than taxis and much more pleasurably for passengers, despite the sweaty uphill walk that awaits the Gabba-bound spectator when he or she alights beyond the sheer limestone cliffs.

The Gabba, once a quirky cricket ground with its own distinct flavour, is now a modern, functional but characterless stadium, efficiently catering for 40,000 spectators. The notorious sticky wickets of the days of uncovered pitches no longer make batting a lottery but because of its sub-tropical climate there have been low scoring Tests at the Gabba decided by as little as a couple of slip catches caught or dropped. 1990/91 comes to mind. Graham Gooch, England's captain then, specialist batting coach now, suffered a poisoned finger and missed the game. Allan Lamb took over and attracted criticism for being lured to an out of town casino by Kerry Packer when he was not out overnight. Australia won by ten wickets in three days but batting was so difficult, even for those who went to bed early, that none of the first three totals in the match reached even 100.

Tropical storms can still dictate the character of the cricket. In 1974/5, just as Dennis Lillee and Jeff Thomson were about to begin their fearsome alliance, a typical Brisbane storm caught the part-time curator with his covers off and his metaphorical trousers down. He was no less a local figure than Alderman Clem Jones, Lord Mayor of the city, who could be seen with his wellies on rolling the consequent quagmire of a pitch only a couple of days before the sun came partially to his rescue. But not, of course, to England's.

Three years later I was back in Australia after the long tour of India. It was a brief but immensely enjoyable visit, not least because everything seemed so modern and comfortable after the relative hardships and subtler attractions of the subcontinent. The reason for the visit was the staging of a Centenary Test in Melbourne to celebrate the anniversary of the first official Australia v. England Test, at Melbourne in March 1877.

This time Greig and his team arrived for a 'warm-up' game in Perth after the team triumph in India, designed to get them used to the utterly different cricketing conditions of Australia. I saw the start of the game but then went off by myself to Canberra where the Queen was to open the Australian Parliament. Wholly unaccustomed though I was to such events, Bob Hudson had sufficient faith in me to suggest that I should cover the event for BBC World Service.

I was invited to a reception in Canberra on the evening before the State Opening where I had the great thrill of talking to the Monarch for a minute or so. Beautifully dressed in blue, she was, I thought, dazzlingly pretty and much younger looking than her photographs. Of course, too, she was disarmingly at ease and perfectly briefed about why I was there, so we talked of England's success in India and the game in Melbourne the following week. I had been made to feel at home already by one of her ladies-in-waiting, the charming Susan Hussey, whose husband, 'Duke', became chairman of the BBC Governors and would make occasional 'royal' visits of his own to the commentary box in later years.

All I had to do in Canberra was to record a 'package' rather than to describe events 'live' but the best way of doing that was to attempt a commentary along the lines of those famously done by the likes of Hudson and Tom Fleming. I have no idea what the reaction was to my efforts at Bush House but I subsequently did something similar at the start of the State visit of President Ceauçescu of Romania, this time from the roof of a building opposite Victoria Station as the subsequently disgraced dictator was met by the Queen after his arrival by train. There were police snipers beside me on the roof, my first close experience of the realities of security for political figures.

I enjoyed these experiences because in both cases the Royal press officials had armed me with plenty of material for 'waffling'. I would cheerfully have done much more of this sort of broadcasting but the fact was that being cricket correspondent was, by now, a full-time, non-stop job.

It certainly became so from the moment that the 'Packer Revolution' erupted in England the following May. There has never been a cricket story to match it in my lifetime and only the Bodyline controversy of 1932/3 has done so in the game's history as an international sport.

Greig was, from the outset, a central figure. I had arranged to meet him in his room at the Hilton hotel during the rest day of that Centenary Test. Before we discussed the relatively mundane matter of the game itself – although it was, happily, a wonderful game of cricket and a great, efficiently organised occasion – he told me of his meeting with 'a guy called Kerry Packer' and advised me that his interest in the game could lead to something 'very big'.

He could not tell me more but I should have followed up his friendly hint more assiduously than I did. It came to light only two months later that Tony had played a central role as a go-between between Packer and many of the world's best players, signing them on for matches that Packer had hoped might run simultaneously with 'established' international cricket.

That was never going to happen and the reaction amongst most cricket followers when the news broke at Hove in May 1977 was largely hostile. Greig was seen as the betrayer of a system that had elevated him to the highest honour in the English game. Although John Woodcock was vilified by some for suggesting that he was not an Englishman 'through and through', the observation was spot on in that Greig did not feel that deep loyalty to the established order of English cricket that would have prevented him from – in essence – following Mammon rather than honour.

The great majority of people in his position, presented with the same set of circumstances, would have done the same thing as he did in dancing to Packer's tune, but others, with a different background and upbringing, might have felt compelled to say 'thanks but no thanks'. I know that I would have been in the latter category, which is not to say that I do not entirely understand why he acted as he did.

In Sussex Greig is remembered as someone who had bigger fish to fry and who ultimately failed to deliver as a captain. He was incapable of giving less than 100 per cent to any game of cricket because of his competitive nature but once he had become an important England player he was not one of those who, like Mike Brearley or Graham Gooch, could give county cricket his undivided attention at the appropriate time

The Centenary match, and various receptions and dinners, were attended by practically every surviving cricketer of each country, which was a joy and fascination in itself. The Queen was famously asked for her autograph by the mischievous iconoclast Dennis Lillee as she met the players at tea-time on the final day. That she saw some cricket − and, by an extraordinary coincidence, an Australian victory by precisely the forty-five runs that had separated the sides in the original match at Melbourne in 1877, was due largely to an innings of marvellous style, character and elan by Derek Randall.

I was on the air when Alan Knott was lbw to Lillee to complete a victory that had looked far from certain while England were chasing their 463 to win. *Wisden*'s report of the game, by Reg Hayter, records that it was not until 'after some time' the match was over that someone spotted the identical result. In fact I had told my listeners in both countries at the time thanks to the sharpness of my bubbly friend Graham Dawson, then a rising star with ABC Radio, who whispered the fact in my ear.

Graham and his wife, Shelagh, kindly saved me some hard-earned tour money more than once when I stayed with them in Melbourne and Judy's cousins, Ian and Susan Hayman, often did the same for me in Sydney, allowing a welcome break from the routines of hotel life. Ian had been the youngest brigadier in the Australian army when he suffered a stroke in his forties but Susan, from the well-known MaCarthur-Onslow family, showed as much stoicism as her husband in nursing him for the rest of his life.

For the players there has never been an easy tour of Australia. In both 1978/9 and 1986/7 there were reasons why the home country was not at its strongest, although that, of course, is no excuse because England at home are seldom able to field their best possible side. Usually it is a simple matter of key players being injured but in 1978/9 several of the best Australians were otherwise engaged in Kerry Packer's World Series Cricket. When Mike Brearley reluctantly returned with his team the following winter to play the full Australian side – and the West Indies too – in matches that were not for the Ashes but were played with just the same intensity, Australia won easily. It was an indication, however, of the soundness of their cricketing system that some very good players had filled the breach, men who, like others since, might otherwise have languished in State cricket without getting the chance to wear the 'baggy green'. They included Rodney Hogg, Bruce Yardley and Allan Border.

It was the two three-month stints in Australian winters in successive years that pushed me into my career switch in the 1980s. Judy had given birth to our third child, Lucy, in 1979 and had no wish to spend another few weeks in hotels. As usual I was split between the fun of the job and the desire to be with my family.

Eight years later I was BBC cricket correspondent again and back on the road – or, more accurately, back in the air and on it. This time it was unofficial rebel tours to South Africa that, to a limited extent at least, diluted the strength of Australia's attempt to regain the Ashes. It did not make the 1986/7 series any the less enjoyable to report. Not only did England successfully retain the Ashes but they swept the board in two separate one-day tournaments as well. They started the tour ingloriously (remember Martin Johnson's 'can't bat, can't bowl and can't field) and lost the last Test to leave a deceptively close-looking final score of two matches to one, but in between they had a ball, on and off the field. So much so that their Henry VIII of a captain, Mike Gatting, never short of things to do after dark, got away with oversleeping one day and missing the team bus so that someone else had to call heads or tails at the toss. On some tours that would have been a major incident. On this one it was an amusing sideline.

There was an element of complacency about England's performance in the final Test in Sydney, on one of those typical Bulli soil pitches that turn with increasing viciousness as they wear under a hot sun. Would that there were more of them these days. I remember especially the way in which Ian Botham decided to try to conquer the hitherto completely unknown Peter Taylor – 'Peter Who?' as one evening paper dubbed him in a cruel headline when his selection was first announced.

It was typical Botham to be so confident and belligerent , of course, but having been caught behind for sixteen off the red-haired off-spinner in the first innings, he tried to hit him out of the ground immediately he got to the crease in the second. Beaten in the flight, he succeeded only in lofting the ball high towards the Ladies' Stand, in front of which he was caught for a duck. Great was the Aussie rejoicing, both then and when the leg-spinner Peter Sleep shot a ball through John Emburey's defences to win the game by fifty-five runs.

Later in that winter of 1986/7 Australia beat England in the final of the World Cup at Eden Gardens in Calcutta and they did not relinquish their grip on the old country for the better part of twenty years afterwards. It was a dispiriting era for England, with humiliations such as the two defeats by the Australian Academy that Mike Atherton's team suffered in 1994/5 all too sharp a reminder of the gulf that had opened up between the two countries.

In a way it was nothing new. It took some time after the burning of that bail near Melbourne for Australians to establish their mastery – indeed it was not until their fifth home series that they did so – but England captains from Gubby Allen to Andrew Flintoff have generally come home with empty hands and their leonine tails firmly tucked between their legs. Between the earth-shaking series in 1932/3, famous or infamous according to your point of view, and the 2010/11 tour, England played seventeen series for the Ashes in Australia. They lost eleven and won only four of them.

Never has there been a bigger or longer build-up to a Test series than the one in Australia in 2006/7. Never, too, has there been a greater or swifter anti-climax. The Australia side that utterly overwhelmed and virtually humiliated Andrew Flintoff's hapless team, regaining the Ashes after only fifteen days of cricket, undoubtedly ranks with some of the best XIs of all time.

Australia and the Caribbean have been the favoured tours for British supporters, as for the media. Their numbers have grown almost exponentially. In the early 1970s there were very few camp followers. Two of the stalwarts were the late Spen Cama, an Anglo-Indian with a penchant for snuff, and Bernie Coleman, a benign soul who made a small fortune as landlord of the best pub in Wimbledon and has used it with great generosity. So, when he died, did Cama, who left large legacies to Sussex and to his own Sussex club, the Preston Nomads. (Cricket has been lucky to attract many wealthy patrons who adored the game without being any good at playing it. In my time Sir Tim Rice, who charmed his Australian audience when he gave a brilliant

'Bradman Oration' before the Adelaide Test in 2010, has also given extremely generously to many cricketing causes, but Sir John Paul Getty II, a shy recluse by the time that I knew him, was probably the greatest philanthropist. He contributed a big sum towards the building of the new Mound Stand at Lord's and created his own beautiful ground at Wormsley, where he was also responsible for enabling the reintroduction of the majestic Red Kite.

As far as I know, Getty never watched Test cricket abroad, but there was a sudden surge in the number of travelling supporters cheering on Mike Gatting's team to rare success in Australia in 1986/7. They paved the way for the first recruits to the Barmy Army, who started giving such vocal support to Mike Atherton's various touring sides. The 'Army' have generally been popular with the locals wherever they have been and, of course, they provide pubs, hotels and restaurants abroad with good business, as do the more upmarket touring groups, invariably including parties from MCC.

The 'barmies' are undoubtedly much appreciated by the players. In Barbados in particular it has probably made the difference between success and failure in a couple of Test matches. I greatly admire their loyalty to England through thick and thin, and their sense of humour. I don't mind their songs in moderation but I do resent their monotonous chanting. It is both self-regarding and inconsiderate. Undoubtedly a lot of listeners to *Test Match Special* dislike it too.

The noise level at international matches everywhere now is vastly greater than it was everywhere except India and in some islands of the Caribbean. Personally I miss the hush of suspense and the bursts of applause that followed an outstanding piece of cricket. But cricket mirrors society. Peace and decorum are harder to find than they once were.

If I had to pick just one of the various individual clashes of titans I have witnessed during forty years of Anglo/Australian rivalry, it would be Botham versus Lillee; muscle versus menace; valour versus venom. Their duels, between Ian Botham's third series against Australia in 1979/80 and Dennis Lillee's retirement a year after a final Ashes fling in 1982/3, were relatively few given the long and distinguished careers they both enjoyed, but they were also microcosms of the stirring tradition of Anglo/Australian rivalry.

It was not just that these two proud warriors were amongst the greatest cricketers ever to represent their countries. It was the fact that they recognised in one another key figures in the opposing camp, on whose individual battles the outcome of the war itself might depend, a little like those individual contests between Andrew Flintoff and Ricky Ponting, or Kevin Pietersen and Shane Warne, in more recent Ashes series.

It was the electricity that invariably accompanied their duels, whether Lillee was bowling to Botham or Botham to Lillee, that heightened the fascination. They were similar characters, with a trace of the larrikin in their approach to cricket and life. Like poles repel, so there were sparks when they met, invariably eye-balling one another like rutting stags before the first clash of antlers. Once the battle was lost or won, they enjoyed many a glass in each other's company, first of beer, then, in sophisticated retirement, of wine.

I have liked Lillee a lot in occasional meetings since – he is president of the WACA now; full of fun and a willing raconteur – but I saw his less attractive side at close quarters immediately after his contretemps with Mike Brearley in the 1979/80 series, when the England captain, a bit testy himself during that tour, objected to his experimental use of an aluminium bat during the Perth Test. He had faced four balls from Ian Botham before Brearley objected to the umpires on the grounds that it was damaging the ball. Lillee was told to change his bat but argued the issue for ten minutes, for which flagrant disregard for authority I had given him unequivocal verbal stick. Clearly he had not got over his annoyance when, after play on a later day in that game, I went into the dressing-room to interview Ian Botham about the state of play. Lillee was sharing a beer with his rival and greeted me with: 'Here comes Christopher Wankin-Jenkins.'

Ian laughed, but with me not at me. To me his generosity of spirit has always been his greatest feature and if he has sometimes given his wonderfully loyal wife Kathy a few causes for regret (or worse) he absolutely deserves his iconic status and his knighthood. This is not only the national hero of, in particular, 1981, but the man who, until recently, still made large advertising money by eating what look like small bales of hay for breakfast, who has periodically walked vast distances to raise huge sums of money in aid of leukaemia research, who drives a Bentley and a Jaguar because they are 'British' cars (and perhaps because he receives some other benefits for the privilege) and who hits a golf ball, sometimes, like a professional (he probably plays as often as the average pro!).

It was always a question of close debate whether Ian or one of his three outstanding contemporaries, Imran Khan, Kapil Dev and Richard Hadlee, was the best all-rounder. Gary Sobers was ahead of them all but Ian's status is written in figures: he scored 5200 runs in Test cricket alone, hit 80 sixes in the season of 1985 and was the first all-rounder to take both 300 Test wickets and score more than 5000 runs. As a catcher at second slip there has been no one better.

1981 immortalised him, as everyone knows. That year is to English cricket as 1415, and Agincourt, to English history. The all Western Australian partnership of Lillee and Terry Alderman started the first chapter by dismissing the tender England captain (Botham was the youngest since Monty Bowden in 1888/9) for one and thirty-three at Trent Bridge, where England lost a tense, close match. A crestfallen Botham lost the leadership to Brearley after his pair in the drawn game at Lord's.

I was in the BBC television, rather than radio, box when he scored 50 out of 174 in response to Australia's 401 (Botham six for 95), then went out to bat in England's follow-on innings at 105 for five. The situation was beyond desperate, but Botham's audacious century off 87 balls, enabling England to set Australia 130 to win in the fourth innings, would have been part of a glorious failure but for Bob Willis's ferocious fast bowling in the final act of the match. Commentators should be neutral and the hardest thing to do as that bouleversement unfolded was to keep the emotion out of my voice.

I was on TV again, still 'subbing' for Jim Laker, when the titans had their last great confrontation at Manchester. Lillee hurled himself into the duel when Botham came out to bat, this time at 104 for five. Both he and Alderman, swinging the ball off a length, had their tails up. The series itself depended, almost certainly, on an England recovery, now or never. Botham responded with an exhilarating display of attacking batting, highly skilled and, more than just bold, physically courageous. Time and again he hooked Lillee's bouncers from in front of his temple, unguarded by a cap, let alone a helmet. In two hours he scored another hundred, this time off eighty-six balls, smiting six sixes. Twenty-four years would pass before English crowds saw such a spectacle again in an Ashes series.

No wonder we celebrated the astonishing series of 2005. Every match was wonderful and each of the five unforgettable, unpredictable contests, at Lord's, Edgbaston, Old Trafford,

Trent Bridge and The Oval, could so easily have produced a different result. For England the eventual two-one margin was a blessed redemption and even Australians appreciated that it was good for the game. Many of those who took part, like Warne, Gilchrist and Brett Lee, say that they enjoyed it as much as any of their victorious campaigns.

Their attitude was typical of Australian sportsmen. They hate losing and will sacrifice much to win, but if they are bettered they are gracious. I wish I could say the same about their prime ministers. John Howard, whom I had first met at a dinner party with Colin Cowdrey, given by the Australian manager of Barclays Bank in a beautiful apartment overlooking Sydney Harbour, badly let himself down when he presented World Cup winning medals to England's rugby team in 2003 with all the grace of a gaoler handing meals through prison bars to criminals he despised.

An equally poor example had been set, albeit less publicly, by Bob Hawke when England won the Ashes at Melbourne in 1986/7. I had been asked to a make a brief appearance at lunch in a large function room in the great Southern Stand (so great that it holds more spectators in one area than the whole of Lord's) at a time when it had become obvious that England were about to win the fourth Test and, with it, the series. Speaking to the 3000 or so people in the room, Hawke actually uttered the words: 'If there's anything worse than a whingeing Pom, it's a winning Pom.' He did not appear to be joking.

16

INDIA

*No one forgets his or her first experience of India, even if it comes
in a bowl of mulligatawny. It is smell as much as taste that brings
back my first visit to the subcontinent in 1976. At 4.30 on a dark
November morning there was something in the air of India that has
lingered ever since.*

It was the sharp, damp smell of dew-laden air mixed with the
tang of smoke from dung and wood fires, often experienced on
this and subsequent visits during bus-rides to airports to catch
flights ridiculously scheduled a little after dawn. To me that
early morning smell, repeated in the cool evenings of the Indian
winter, is even more characteristic than the odour of drains or
sewage which, in the cities, often underlies and mingles with
spices and petrol fumes during the hotter hours of sunlight. By
contrast, the sweet scent of jasmine in public or hotel gardens
often beguiles those who are privileged to remain separated
from the incredible rush and bustle of daily life.

Gosh, that bustle! For most Indians I dare say, even now that
the vast nation is bursting forward into one of the two great
economic powers of the 21st century, life is still a frenetic rush

to earn a living. Thirty-five years ago the rickshaw puller in Calcutta, bare-footed on the side of one of those wide, chaotic streets with all manner of faster transport pressing him towards the pavement, had little time for self-pity or to compare his lot with that of anyone else, but to see him was to sense his affinity with peasant life in any city of any country throughout most of human history. The poor are always with us.

On cricket tours one was generally up amongst the middle-classes at least, insulated from this daily struggle for life, but one had to be very insensitive not to notice it, or not to thank one's lucky stars that, whatever the frustrations of a broadcaster or journalist in those days before the internet, there was usually going to be a decent meal and a comfortable bed at the end of the day.

The term 'decent meal' is relative. I discovered many years after that first visit, following an endoscopy to investigate my chronic indigestion, that I have a hiatus hernia. It is both a very minor and a common condition but it could explain why garlic and chilli, two of the staple ingredients of most Indian dishes, simply do not agree with my constitution. So, while others around me tucked into their curries with delight, I picked my way around them, wimpish as a bather reluctant to step into the shallows of a cold sea. No doubt as much because of this reluctance to embrace the local fare as because of any lack of hygiene I have never completed a tour of the subcontinent without getting a serious tummy upset.

Once, on the ill-fated England tour of 1992/3, when Graham Gooch and others fell ill after eating prawns in Madras, I managed to get through more or less unscathed until the last port of call, Bombay. I had been looking forward to staying once again at the country's most famous hotel, the Taj Mahal at Apollo Bunder, opposite the Gateway of India.

The 'Taj', scene of ghastly terrorist murders in 2008, was a haven when first experienced by me in 1976. Judy and I rapidly changed our plans and stayed there later on the tour, having originally accepted the kind invitation of a shipping friend of my father's to stay at his empty beach house in Juhu. That was an unfortunate decision, despite an interesting meeting there with a wise old man who told me that the stars were predicting a sudden fall from grace for Mrs Gandhi at the forthcoming elections. The stars proved much more accurate than the opinion polls, because she lost heavily.

We had arrived at the beach house – in fact a very large, fusty old place with a single elderly servant – with our infant sons, late at night. Poor James, not yet four, was put in a large room by himself and was terrified when a large rat scurried across the floor. That was just the start. Judy and I were just getting to sleep when the house shook and a thunderous sound revealed the fact that, although beautifully placed in one respect beside a sandy beach, the house was also just off the runway of Bombay airport. Our decision to move back to the comfort of the hotel sooner rather than later was made the next morning. I had got out of bed bursting with the anticipated pleasure of breathing in the ozone from the Indian Ocean and having my customary swim before breakfast. There at the water's edge were scores of male figures, all squatting on their haunches. Even from a distance and with their clothes covering their activity as best they could it was all too evident that they were defecating.

So, back to the Taj! Ever since it was built it has been recognised by all the swanky hotel guides as one of the great hotels of the world, although its Marlburian architect threw himself off a balcony to his death when it was first opened because it had been constructed the wrong way round. The top-floor restaurant at the hotel, like the beautiful old building itself, with its high ceilings, lovingly polished wood and abundance of marble, is five-star.

Rewarding myself with a meal there in the company of friends, after several weeks of self-denial, I selected the lobster bisque as my starter. You may or may not believe it, but I promise you that the last mouthful had barely passed my lips before my face whitened, perspiration beaded my forehead and my stomach began to churn. For two days, possibly more, I was a prisoner in the bathroom.

Lightning is not supposed to strike twice, but it did when I returned to Bombay, now Mumbai, at the end of England's tour in 2005/6. The circumstances, alas, illustrate the accident-proneness that has besieged me all my life.

It had been an enjoyable and relatively short tour, starting with a rousing drawn Test in Nagpur after Andrew Flintoff had taken over the England captaincy from the injured Michael Vaughan. England capped three new Test players in that game – Alastair Cook, who started with sixty and a second-innings century, Monty Panesar and Ian Blackwell. By the last match in what was now called Mumbai they had introduced a fourth, Owais Shah, who played a prominent part in a victory that was also memorable for the success of the Hampshire off-spinner Shaun Udal, one of those seasoned journeymen county cricketers who would no doubt have done the same many times over the years if ever they had been given the chance.

On the evening after my last day of reporting I had suggested a particular restaurant, which had been recommended to me, for an end of tour get-together for the BBC commentary team but, as usual, I had more work to do than any of them because of my primary responsibility to *The Times*. This is how the events of that evening unfolded:

20.15: Nearly finished the third (quotes) piece for the paper. Receive text message from Aggers (Jonathan Agnew) – 'See you there' – acknowledge it and assure him of imminent departure, unaware battery is low, despite recent recharge.

20.40: Leave hotel in breezy mood with work done looking forward to some r and r and a very, very fine bottle of Indian red. Tell doorman to make sure that driver understands destination – the Copper Chimney at Worli, as recommended to me by the amiable Indian commentator Harsha Bhogle and passed on to Aggers as the ideal place.

20.41. Enter super-comfortable (old and battered) black and yellow taxi and ring office to check that my copy has safely landed. Speak for fifteen minutes to the ever enthusiastic, professional but sometimes rather loquacious Marcus Williams, not realising that this is further running down the battery to a fatal degree.

21.00: 'Are you sure we are going to Copper Chimney?

'Worli, Sir.'

'Copper Chimney?'

(With frown) 'Copper Chimney, Sir'

'Much further?'

Big frown.

'Are we nearly there?'

'Ten minutes, Sir.

Send message to Aggers asking what's for pudding and suggesting that the driver appeared to be lost.

21.20: Triumphant shout: 'Copper Chimney, Sir.'

Fork out 300 rupees. Driver, looking doubtful, insists on waiting.

21.21. Restaurant manager has no record of a booking by Mr. Agnew. Or by Mr. Jonathan. Or the BBC. They have not seen Mr. Bishen Bedi. Nor Mr. Geoffrey Boycott. Nor do they give the impression that in any case they would distinguish them from Adam.

Quick inspection of entire room reveals no one familiar.

'Jonathan, Sir? Upstairs Johnson and Johnson.'

'Ah. That must be it. Thank you.'

Up the stairs like Basil Fawlty and open door to find I have stepped into the middle of some lecture, or marketing meeting of the aforementioned Johnson and Johnson. All heads turn.

'Sorry.'

Down the stairs, again like Basil.

'I think it must be another Copper Chimney. Can you please ring your other restaurants to find out which has the BBC party? About ten people probably. Bishen Bedi and Geoff Boycott might be there. Old cricketers.'

21.30–22.00: Distracted phone-calls by the manager, whilst customers come in and out.

I text Aggers again. No response. Text anyone else I can think of who would be there.

Phone starts to warn of low battery. Goes blank.

'Have you got a Nokia recharger, please?'

Joy. They have.

'Can you find the restaurant where the BBC party is?'

'No, Sir. Please sit. I will try again.'

'Please ring the Taj Mahal hotel and let me speak to them.'

Long wait for reception to answer. Eventually get message through at third attempt. Which Copper Chimney had they booked the table for Mr. Agnew?

'When was booking made?'

'Yesterday, I think.'

'Sir, it will be different receptionist. I will try to locate and ring you back.'

22.30. Taj return call. Cannot find receptionist. Off duty now. All spirit deflated.

'Can I have the Nokia phone please. I must go.'

Locate driver and begin to return to the Taj. More attempts to text everyone. Finally make contact with Peter Baxter.

23.00. Arrive as everyone is longing to go to bed after a merry party.

Mike Selvey kindly agrees to stay on to share a bottle. Food apparently very good. I would be happy with soup or bread but ask if anything is recommended?

Stephen Fry, a surprising but most witty and welcome addition to the original party, in India making a TV programme, says that the chicken was good. I order 'boneless chicken'. It looks very red and tastes like raw garlic which I know will do me no good but I am too tired to care.

23.45 approx. Arrive back at hotel room. Ah well, only one piece to do tomorrow; some shopping; a chance at last to lie by the pool and read, then a delightful daytime flight home in a Virgin 'Upper Class' seat on Friday afternoon.

23.45 and 30 seconds: Urgent need to go straight to bathroom. Very urgent indeed, in fact.

Five miserable days later, after being given many pills by the hotel doctor and suffering a most uncomfortable journey home, an analysis revealed that I had had E.coli poisoning. By then my normal eleven stone and a bit had become ten and a half stone.

If the food seldom attracted me in India, most other aspects of life there did, not least, naturally, the cricket. There has never been an England tour there to match my first in 1976/7. John Lever, popularly known as J.K., was the star as England swept to an unassailable lead in the first three Tests with a bowling attack of high quality that also included Bob Willis, Chris Old and Derek Underwood.

The impact made by Lever's success in Delhi was reflected in a decision to set up ball-by-ball commentary on the closing stages of the first Test, only the fourth time that this had been attempted. To my delight the experiment was repeated in Madras and the last two Tests. We used a mainly English team but there has never been any shortage of knowledgeable commentators from India, including the plummy voiced Pearson Surita, who sounded like a Maharajah, and 'Jackie' Baroda, who actually was one. He was introduced each morning on Radio Three as 'Fatasingh Gaekwad, the former Maharajah of Baroda', but Bob Hudson's suggestion was that his fellow commentators should call him 'Prince'. I always thought that sounded rather as if one were addressing a dog.

English bowlers were not supposed, according to past England touring teams, to get lbw decisions from Indian umpires but Lever got several in the first Test at Delhi with his late inswingers, a fact that might have had something to do with Greig's statement, at his opening press conference on the morning of the team's arrival, that 'in my view Indian umpires are the best in the world'.

Apart from Richie Benaud no one appreciated the importance and practical value of the media more than Greig. He was always happy to talk, did so with passion and intelligence if not always profound care and, so far as I was concerned anyway, did not change post-Packer.

In India, generally speaking, he charmed both the media and public. He had a real flair for PR and conveyed both his belligerence and his sense of fun. On reflection I dare say that, like many others, he under-estimated the intelligence of many Indians.

Things changed later on that tour when, at Bangalore, it became clear that one of the umpires had been appointed by an embarrassed home Board to make absolutely sure that the home team won. 'That was a very surprising decision', I suggested diplomatically during ball-by-ball commentary as Mohammad Ghouse lifted his finger to send another England batsman back to the pavilion. 'Surprising?' thundered my temporary summariser, the lovably outspoken Robin Marlar: 'it was a ghastly decision, outrageous! That ball wouldn't have hit another set of stumps. You know it and I know it.'

India duly went on to win that game and in the last at Bombay England only just managed a draw, thanks to fine defensive batting against the spinners, but the overall honours had already gone to England. They were helped by internal divisions in the home dressing-room, notably between their two finest players, the fiery captain, Bishen Singh Bedi, the most beautifully balanced spin bowler of them all, and the more calculating Sunil Gavaskar, second only to Sachin Tendulkar among the many marvellous Indian batsmen since Partition in 1947.

No previous BBC cricket correspondent had been to India and I was feeling my way for much of the time, a heavy reporting schedule depending on the quality of telephone lines that frequently failed, to my hair-tearing frustration. For longer broadcasts I would have to travel to studios to confirm line bookings, a long-winded business requiring the drinking of copious amounts of very sweet tea. The amount of paperwork required to get anything done was unbelievable. (Cashing a traveller's cheque was often a day-long experience.)

One Saturday I had to dash to a local studio after play, hoping to give a live report of the day's cricket for *Sports Report*. Unfortunately the studio was being 'modernised'. There were wires everywhere and for several frustrating hours the engineer in the studio tried in vain to get through to London. I could imagine the producers in London wondering where their idle correspondent was. Relaxing in a bar somewhere, probably. At last, at about 10.30 pm in Jullunder and with only some thirty minutes of *Sports Report* left, he made contact on a thin sounding line, with an echo. I dashed into the studio to give my report and play down an interview with one of the players, whereupon the studio door opened again and the engineer came back, accompanied by a very important looking Sikh, dressed in a smartly tailored navy blue safari suit. His black beard was expertly trimmed and the rest of his black hair enveloped by a matching blue patka. 'Desist please, Sir', said the engineer as I prepared to utter my opening words to an expectant audience far away in the studio in London. 'Chief Minister for Punjab has arrived to give party political broadcast.' I knew from the Minister's unyielding countenance that there was absolutely no point in arguing. I could have wept.

There was almost another abortive broadcast just after Christmas when I was persuaded by the producers in London to get Tony Greig to a local studio in Delhi for what was then quite an unusual type of transmission: a live phone-in. As usual, he was co-operative but our taxi drive to the main studios of All India Radio on a dark and foggy night seemed to go on for ever. Eventually the driver drew up in front of some impressive looking wrought-iron gates, firmly closed to all-comers. On the gate was a large notice proclaiming the owners of the premises: 'Oil India'.

Communications, or the lack of them, explained almost everything that went wrong on tours of India, sometimes extending to players arriving at matches without cricket kit that had gone by train and been delayed. The equipment was never lost for ever, however, because it was always, on that and several subsequent tours, guarded personally by a faithful 'minder' called Govind, a powerfully built man with a handsome round face who would sleep on the floor of dressing-rooms at night to look after the property of the teams under his care.

Touring teams and press parties tend to have many happy memories of tours of India, if only because the wholly different culture helps them to stick together and share experiences. On a subsequent tour there was, for example, an interminable coach journey, most of it made in the hours of darkness, en route to a one-day international in Jamshedpur. The tour guide seconded to the press party by the local travel agents was an earnest and well-meaning little man called Ragu, whose local knowledge came to the fore as we approached this sprawling industrial city, home of the vast Tata steel empire, along a narrow road in the Dalma Hills.

The coach suddenly stopped and we were aware of heated words being spoken between the driver of the coach and people outside. After hours of backaching travel this was all we needed. Ragu opened the side door and went out to investigate. There were more loud exchanges before he came back inside and the engine started up.

'What was all that about', one of us asked Ragu.

'They were dacoits', he said. 'Armed bandits bent upon mischief.'

'What did you say to them?' someone asked.

'I told them to bugger off', said Ragu, revelling in the laughter and cheering that followed.

Our hotel, when eventually we arrived, was on the rough side but we were only there for a night so the fact that there were only communal bathrooms and that 'running water' in the chilly, spartan rooms meant a bowl with a jug could be cheerfully borne by those of us with a public school education. Not so Mike Beale, the extremely well fed correspondent of the *Daily Star*. As I was settling into bed I heard his broad Brummie voice wailing down the echoing corridor outside: 'I demand to see the manager! I refuse to be treated like an animal!'

My most indelible memory of events off the field on my various tours to India also involved the *Evening Standard*'s correspondent, John Thicknesse. On one occasion in Calcutta we had played golf, on a rare day off, at the delightfully Raj-reminiscent Tollygunge Club. There was a strike of taxi drivers that day, so we had reached the club by means of the little-known underground train which runs for a few miles below the main thoroughfare of this great but chaotic city. It turned out to be both clean and cheap, and conveyed us much more pleasantly than the London Underground from our very smart hotel, the Grand Oberoi (most comfortable feather pillows in the world!) to a stop close to the Tollygunge.

Following our usual highly competitive game and a drink, the sun had set and John refused (or probably we mutually agreed not) to walk back to the tube in the dark. The return journey was therefore a problem until one of the members at the bar, an obviously inebriated well-to-do Indian female, offered to drive us back. With some trepidation we accepted but her passage down the drive towards the teeming main road ahead was so erratic that another member tapped on the window and said: 'Desist' (a favourite word for Indians of a certain generation). 'You are not fit to drive.'

She ignored him and we decided that the die was cast. There was no other way to get back. John was in front, myself behind. She had gone a few hundred yards into the thick of Calcutta's disordered traffic when she suddenly stopped at an angle of forty-five degrees to the oncoming cars, carts, buses, lorries, etc, felt into her handbag, pulled out a cigarette, turned to John and said, with slurred voice but in her extremely posh Indian accent: 'Give me a light, darling.'

'Thickers' was already highly agitated as only he could be. 'Get out of the seat and move over' he said. 'I'm driving. Come on, get out.' They exchanged places – I forget which of them got out of the car amidst the chaos but probably John – and we proceeded to have the most hair-raising journey, at once hilarious and terrifying, with John gradually warming to his task although neither of us had a clear idea of the right direction and she was by now virtually comitose. John let out yelps of pleasure, like Toad of Toad Hall, as rickshaws, donkey-carts and cyclists scattered into the gutters from the path of the car. Horns blared constantly and there was the occasional emergency stop but eventually and miraculously the Grand Hotel hove into view.

'Are we going to have a drink?' asked the good lady as the door of the passenger seat was opened for her by a commissionaire in a top hat and matching uniform. 'Certainly not', said John firmly. 'I'm afraid that we have work to do', I said, 'but thank you so much for the lift.' Goodness knows how she got home.

John had been at Harrow with the Maharajah of Jaipur, who had accordingly invited him to come to his palace for dinner. I was invited too, an opportunity surely too good to miss, especially as I had already met the Raj Mata, a famous socialite and patron of local causes who, even in her old age, was a woman of striking beauty and charisma. Starting life as Princess Gayatri Devi of Cooch Behar, she had been an MP in her own right before all the princely titles were officially taken away in 1971. Soon after she had spent five months in gaol for alleged tax offences but now she was in elegant retirement.

Alas, her stepson, 'Bubbles', whose father, Man Singh, had been both a famous soldier and an outstanding polo player, turned out to be, at this stage of his life at least, an alcoholic.

Not only was there no sign either of dinner or of the Raj Mata, but John and I were treated to a deeply embarrassing two hours or so during which we toyed with drinks whilst he repeated himself incessantly, occasionally punching his old school friend on the shoulder and over-ruling our polite attempts to leave. When he needed another drink, he yelled at terrified servants who supplied what was demanded before leaving his presence backwards, cowering close to the floor. It was an appalling insight into the worst aspects of the old India, although not, I'm sure, a typical one. Despite the rapidly emerging wealthy middle class, these contrasts of class and wealth have not fully disappeared.

Happily, however, nor have some of the magnificent palaces. Jaipur's City Palace is a huge creation full of beautiful features, including the pink frontage of the Palace of the Winds, the Hawa Mahal, with its mass of small windows designed so that the ladies could remain in purdah but still look out onto the bustling streets below. In 1976 there seemed to be almost as many camels in the streets as vehicles and people. Apart from the Taj Mahal itself, a genuine wonder of the world that fulfilled all expectations, the most memorable of the various forts and palaces I saw on that trip was the Amber Fort, built on the site of an old Hindu temple above the valley leading to Jaipur. Set amongst rugged hills it was memorable for the first and only elephant ride of my life, making the steep climb painless apart from some shaking up of the nether regions; for the beauty of the stone, glass and ivory carvings; for the views from ornate, unglazed windows; the monkeys clambering over the ramparts, already wise to the fact that tourists might mean food; and for two enormous silver urns, which the Maharajah's grandfather used to have filled with water from the Ganges and transported with him on his travels.

Another, rather less exalted, aristocrat from Rajasthan, the generous and popular Raj Singh Dungarpur, was a highly influential cricket administrator, whether or not he was in some official post. A big man with an easy charm, he had been a useful enough fast bowler to play eighty-six first-class games for Rajasthan. For years, at the Cricket Club of India in Bombay, he was the equivalent of Lord Harris or Gubby Allen at Lord's, dominating the scene at the graceful old Brabourne Stadium through his princely bearing, private means, deep knowledge of the game and integrity. He had a flat overlooking Lord's but I shall always think of him sitting in a cane chair on the outfield at the Brabourne, drinking something refreshing from a glass filled with ice and talking cricket. He was as comfortable there as a faithful old Labrador sitting by a stove in the kitchen.

He had devoted his life to the game, managing Indian teams abroad, chairing the national selectors and helping young cricketers, wherever they came from. It was Raj who got the rules changed at the CCI so that Sachin Tendulkar could change in the dressing-rooms at the age of fourteen, and who promoted the youthful, shy (and Muslim) Mohammad Azharuddin into the captaincy of India.

He and I were once staying in the same hotel during an ICC meeting in Australia when a note was passed under my door that showed that he spoke better English (albeit always with a strong Indian accent) than he wrote it. Scrawled in pencil, it read: 'Have had to leave erly for airport but, for the whole times sake, I want to tell you excluzively that we had made brake-through in Indo/Pakistan relations. Soon we will be playing each other again. Ring me any time, Raj.' It was typically generous of him, both to want to give a journalist friend whom he trusted a 'scoop' and also to be working to get cricket between the two rival nations going again after one of the many political aberrations. There are a few men in India who give the impression that they would crawl over anyone to gain a personal advantage but Raj was more typical, certainly of his own generation, when it came to respecting other human beings.

On a later visit to Jaipur for the 1987 World Cup I stayed with press and broadcasting colleagues amidst the (then) fading grandeur of the Rambagh Palace. Its scale was magnificent but such important features as plumbing and food were at that time rather less impressive, to the extent that cynical journalists soon referred to it as the Ratbag. It was on this trip, on the day before a match between England and the West Indies, that I attempted to give moral support to Peter Baxter at the vast Sawai Man Singh Stadium, where an elegant pink and white pavilion, topped by twin cupolas, occupies the whole of one end of a large, open ground. Opposite we sat in a makeshift commentary position under an awning that did not prevent our being roasted for two hours while several bare-footed engineers, having successfully established that there were broadcasting lines from London to Delhi and Delhi to Jaipur, sweated in vain to solve the insurmountable problem of establishing the final communication between the Jaipur Post Office and the cricket ground.

We had a more or less consistent link the following day, enabling my co-commentator, Jack Bannister, to inform his listeners that Gladstone Small had just completed a fiery 'smell' at the Pavilion End. It was quite possibly a correct statement.

It is ironic, and rather marvellous, that India, where communications used to be so unreliable, is now the place where technology is, as Harold Wilson might have said, white hot. All of us have discovered the timings of trains in England by speaking to someone in Bangalore or sought advice on our British Telecom broadband connection from some other technical wizard in the same city. This is the same Bangalore where, two days before the

Test match in 1977, I was concerned to find that my commentary box was an unfinished mish-mash of plywood and wet concrete hanging perilously in space. By the morning of the match, of course, it had been transformed by typical Indian industry into a smart new booth with a commanding view.

On my first tour I had had a particularly bad time during a match in Jullunder, less because the Skylark hotel was memorably spartan than because the young radio technician who had been assigned to help me to get through to London on unreliable lines throughout the three-day game had failed almost every time. On the last day of the game, frustrated once more, I was on the point of telling him how useless I thought he was when he handed me a note thanking me for my 'superb hospitality and warm and sweet friendship'.

Hospitality to visitors is often warmer in the East. Thanks to the BBC World Service I acquired a loyal fan from the pleasant orange-growing city of Nagpur. He used to listen to commentaries in the days when World Service sport, so much more varied and popular than the unimaginative news bulletins which these days is all that our unenlightened Government will pay for, was regularly transmitted to the subcontinent. Amardhin Malik and his wife insisted on travelling all the way to Madras to meet me, shower me with gifts and entertain me to dinner, during a Test match. When, at last, I returned to Nagpur for Alastair Cook's maiden Test match in 2006, my first visit since 1977, I was royally entertained again, this time at their family home, complete with its most prized possession, a vintage Armstrong Siddeley.

I fear that I have never fully applied all that I should have learned from the subcontinent, amongst them two lessons from that 1977 tour, both occurring at Poona during a match between MCC and West Zone. Word had quickly gone round both the players and the media party that Poona (now Pune) was the place for tailors, the Savile Row of India. Accordingly I had a grey tropical suit made for me that was cut to measure and delivered within three days for an incredibly cheap price. The moral was the opposite of 'all that glitters is not gold', namely 'not all bargains are genuine'. The suit never fitted properly and languished in my cupboard for years before going to the Oxfam shop.

At the lunch interval on the first day of that match in Poona there was a more profound illustration of what should be the true priorities of life. John Thicknesse had boiled over when someone beat him to the only telephone in the press box. 'I've only got five minutes until my deadline', he expostulated, with a desperation in his voice that I quite understood. 'John, John', said the calmly unconcerned K.M. Prabhu, correspondent for *The Times of India*. 'What are five minutes against eternity?'

17

PAKISTAN

All Quiet on Frontier: Three Dead.

To me that genuine headline, if memory serves correctly from Pakistan's premier English newspaper, *Dawn*, encapsulates the country. Quiet, like peace, is relative and Pakistan, bloodily born, as Nehru dramatically phrased it, 'at the midnight hour' on 14 August 1947, has ever since been like a land that erupted from an earthquake beneath the sea. The aftershocks have never ceased. It remains politically the pivot of the world, at once an exciting and dangerous place.

For as long as I can remember cricketers (and other sportsmen) have been reluctant to go there. That had something to do with the food, something with the feeling that, in the days before neutral umpires, no one would get a fair deal from local officials, and not a little to do with fear, both of the known and the unknown. Foreign Office advice, even at the most peaceful times, has always been to travel there with caution.

The profoundly depressing and all too convincing allegations of spot-fixing by some of its cricketers in 2010 underlined the fact that, as Imran Khan has always publicly claimed, deep-seated corruption is at the heart of the country's problems, insidiously creeping through cricket as it does through every other part of life in the sixth most populous country in the world. As another senior contemporary politician, Sardar Abdul Qayyum Khan Jatoi, federal minister of the People's Party, expressed it: 'If a thousand people are engaging in corruption, the one who does not is hurting himself.'

The country has been out of bounds to touring cricket teams and their entourages since the grotesque attack by terrorist gunmen on the Sri Lanka team, travelling to a day's play at the Gaddafi Stadium in Lahore on the third morning of a Test match on 3 March 2009. Naïvely, as these atrocities proved, I had always argued until then that the fears of those players who refused to go there were without foundation. Cricketers, I wrongly believed, would never be a target in a land where it was the most popular sporting interest.

I had never hurried to the front of the queue to go to Pakistan, more for family reasons, and the fact that tours there were generally deemed to be lower key than those to Australia, India, South Africa and the West Indies, than because I believed that it was a dangerous place for anyone to go merely as a cricket reporter. Now that the country is for the foreseeable future out of bounds to touring teams, however, it seems more than ever a privilege to have been there, to have watched some of the greatest cricketers ever produced by any country and to have experienced at first hand some of the paradoxes of a poor, beleaguered nation, battered frequently by natural disasters, constantly undermined by corruption and political violence, yet characterised by proud, proficient, devout and in many ways disciplined people.

As in India there is not a little red tape in Pakistan. Even getting a visa from the Pakistan High Commission in London is a day-long experience. The last time that I did it I decided to arrive as soon as the relevant office in Kensington was open, catching an early train to be sure. I need not have bothered. The queues outside were long and, once in the crowded room where the process is started – dingily lit, musty, smelling of sweat: a microcosm of Pakistan bureaucracy in the heart of London – I got into the wrong queue. Journalists had to get a special stamp from a special executive and I was told that it might not be possible to get the visa that day. I used all my powers of persuasion and the relevant official's love of cricket, to get him to bend the rules and was eventually told to come back at four pm, after prayers. Foolishly I had chosen a Friday.

I first went to Pakistan in early October 1987, to cover matches there and in India in the first of the three World Cups held to date on the subcontinent. My pocket diary gives an indication of how my life then (and ever since) has been filled fairly close to the brim. The three days before my departure read: Friday: Office in morning. Leave Redhill 1pm. Filing, prepare dinner party wine, chairs etc, mow lawns. Dinner party 8pm: Bonds, Palmers, Wigans, Lloyds, Watsons. (Judy has never thought it a big deal to cook a three-course meal for twelve without any help). Saturday: prune raspberries, clear grate, collect logs, filing, finish lawns (?). Sunday: Chapel, Radley; golf; Angela party. Monday: To Lahore.

'To Lahore' was not as simple a journey as it sounds. At Kuwait, where the plane stopped either to refuel or to take on new passengers, more bags were counted onto the plane than there should have been. Even then, before 9/11, security staff were aware of the possibility of a bomb being planted in unaccompanied luggage. The holds were emptied and the 400 passengers had to be ushered onto the hot tarmac to identify their own baggage.

The whole process took four hours and the consequence was that I and seven other journalists on our way to cover the tournament missed our onward flight from Karachi to Lahore. We felt safety in numbers but it was frustrating, the more so when we were obliged to take our place with a huge scrum of pushing locals at Karachi airport, all presumably also trying to catch the 8.45 flight. The airport hall was hot, crowded and dimly lit and in all respects that was typical of travel on the subcontinent. Flights from one city to another were often late and always uncomfortable.

By comparison, life was relatively straightforward once I got to Pakistan. Everything there revolved around travel, cricket and serving my two masters at that time, the BBC and *The Cricketer*. The country was going through one of its quieter periods and I remember writing home that Pakistan seemed more efficient than India, not least because all the BBC lines booked actually came up on time.

There was, however, a strange incident on the day after my late arrival in Lahore. As soon as the time difference permitted I tried to ring home to let Judy know that I had made it to my destination. In these days before mobiles the call had to be made through the hotel switchboard.

'No, Sir, that will not be possible, Sir', said the operator. 'There are no lines to England because of the hurricane.'

'Hurricane?' I said, looking out at a still and sunny morning outside my window. 'Don't be ridiculous. Of course there isn't a hurricane.'

'Sir, please listen to me, Sir. There has been a hurricane in England!'

Like Michael Fish, I took some convincing.

If only all the journeys could have been as impressive as the one that I took with press colleagues in two minibuses on my last visit to Pakistan in 2005/6 when we experienced the magnificently constructed motorway that links Lahore to Islamabad. The contrast between the normal bedlam of the streets and this shining example of modern civil engineering was unreal. It was like finding a priceless diamond in a muddy puddle. But it was not for the hoi polloi, because the toll charges no doubt exceeded the monthly wages of the majority. Our journey was therefore unsullied by other cars, except for the odd Mercedes sweeping past at high speed, no doubt chauffeur-driven for either an industralist or a politician.

Even then the journey did not go quite according to plan. We made serene progress until one minibus was stopped for speeding by traffic cops (who probably outnumbered the vehicles) and the other one, mine, was forced to stop by an over-heated radiator. The driver had to leave us on the side of the road for a time while he ran to a local farm for a bucket of water.

On the whole transport by road was preferable in both Pakistan and India to flying. Air travel at the best of times is, to my mind, the least attractive form of transport, with the exception only of driving along any English motorway on a Friday and the M25 specifically at almost any time of day or night. Jammed motorways, after all, involve much the same combination of delay, discomfort and stress as air journeys, with an added ingredient of extra danger. (At least the M25 is not yet as permanently clogged as the airport road to the city from Bangkok where I once broke the long flight back from Australia to have a holiday with Judy in Phuket. Drivers on that route have apparently got used to spending all night on the road and carry a suitable receptacle for natural relief.)

That first airport scrum in 1987 was not the best introduction to Pakistan. First impressions were not improved, either, by the fact that both the porter who beat many rivals to seize my trolley at the airport, and the bureaucrat at the desk, did their best to short-change me. Had this been India the mention of the word 'cricket' might have cut some ice as we argued our case with the senior official to get onto the flight that would allow us to start work in time to satisfy our employers, but it was only when John Woodcock had the bright idea of telling them that I was 'C.M-J, the famous cricket commentator' that at last we made headway. The light of recognition dawned in the receiver's ear and the rest of the journey was relatively plain sailing.

The popularity of ball-by-ball commentary on the BBC World Service thus proved even more potent than the possible handing over of the precious duty-free Scotch that I always carried on the subcontinent on the advice of seasoned travellers like Woodcock. It may not be so necessary these days but it had medicinal qualities, real or imagined, and could always be used in a minor crisis like this to persuade a reluctant ally.

Not that some Pakistanis of influence were short of their own supply of Scotch. The biggest bottle I have ever seen was at a party in Peshawar some years later when my colleagues and I were asked to an outdoor dinner in the elegant house and garden of the local carpet 'king'.

The scent of jasmine filled the night air on that occasion and some very decent French wine seemed to be available in plentiful supply for those who, like me, preferred it to whisky or the sweet soft drinks normally offered at more official functions in Pakistan. Could this gorgeous environment really be set in the midst of the most dangerous city in the country, on the edge of the North West Frontier, where refugees from Afghanistan were obliged to set up any sort of home they could find, gun-making was one of the main industries and anyone with the necessary cash could order a bespoke Kalashnikov? It was surreal but enjoyable. At the end of the evening we were addressed by the carpet magnate himself, shown some fabulous examples of what we could buy at any of his main city emporiums and urged not to miss the chance to go home with a beautiful silk or woollen rug, intricately hand-woven, at prices that were, he claimed, discounted especially for us.

Derek Pringle, once of Cambridge University, Essex and England, by now my successor on the *Daily Telegraph*, had heard the sales pitch before, having toured the country both as player and journalist. He was determined not to be beguiled again by one of these rugs, having bought several in the past from his friend Waqar, son of the carpet king himself; but, a few weeks after the party, he found himself once again in a large store in Lahore, looking at one beautiful rug after another as they were unfurled invitingly before him. Waqar sensed from experience that English resolve was starting to falter as a particularly beautiful piece with a scarlet vegetable dye held his eye for just too long.

'You are an old and deeply valued customer, Mr. Pringle', he said. 'Look at the colour. Look at the quality of the wegetable dye. Please, name your own price.'

'I could not possibly tell you what I'd pay for that, Waqar: it would be a complete insult.'

'Mr. Pringle', was the response. 'It would be a *pleasure* to be insulted by you.'

A deal, naturally, was done.

Most of the things that went wrong on trips to Pakistan were due to a misunderstanding of some sort. It was occasionally necessary to share rooms at the more obscure venues. John Thicknesse was drawn with Peter Baxter before and after one such match. Before breakfast on the second morning, John, virtually an insomniac, said to his room-mate: 'I know people say I'm selfish but I'd like you to know that I was awake at three o' clock this morning and felt like a cigarette so I went outside into the corridor to smoke it. I passed the time of day with a soldier. We must have talked for ten minutes without either of us understanding a single word the other was saying.'

During the later tour of 2000/2001 'Pring', Peter Hayter and I went on a trip by steam train up the legendary Khyber Pass, close to the border with Afghanistan, an area familiar to the British for centuries and to readers of novelists from Kipling to Khaled Hosseini of *Kite Runner* fame. Most days on a tour were working days for journalists so we were extremely lucky to find both a free Saturday to make the journey and a lull in the troubles that allowed the would-be tourist enterprise to organise the trip while we were there.

It was sufficient of a novelty for villagers to gather by the edge of the track cheering as the old British engine chugged its way up the steep passes to rugged hills with bare slopes the colour of a kestrel's breast. The train was powered by two vintage locomotives built in the 1920s and now converted to oil-fired motion, one pulling from the front, the other pushing from behind. The route covered only 31 miles each way but took most of a vivid sunny day, passing through 34 tunnels and over 92 bridges and culverts. The steam safari climbed more than 3900 feet to Landi Kotal, within sight of the Afghan border. It was unforgettable, not least for various parades en route by military bands and lunch at the smart and immaculately maintained barracks of a regiment of the Pakistan army

Pakistan is, naturally, acutely conscious of its other contentious border, with India. In Kashmir, that mountainous and beautiful state that in the case of many of its citizens would rather have its own independence, troops from the two nuclear powers have been firing at each other almost daily for years. Much less seriously, indeed as if they are taking part in a sport, the guards of the rival armies have, until recently, met each other every evening of the year in an extraordinarily choreographed demonstration of military pride at the border post of Wagah.

I am glad to have seen this extraordinary performance at first hand. Deadly serious though it was below the surface, it was a bit like attending a football derby match. Imagine two rival groups of soldiers bristling with aggression at each other like the All Blacks doing their traditional haka at the start of a rugby international and you will have an idea of the spectacle. I found it entertaining and rather funny when I saw it on the Pakistan side of the border, not least because a bas-relief of one of the heroes of the country on an arch close to the border gates – probably the young Jinnah – looked uncommonly like John Le Mesurier in his role as Sergeant Wilson in *Dad's Army*.

Before the national flag of each nation was lowered ceremonially, as it was every evening from the 1960s to 2010, when it was decided to replace the ceremony with something more gentle, the brass-studded border gate was locked at sunset after hand-picked soldiers from each army, all tall, handsome, bearded warriors in super-smart uniforms and head-dresses topped with a fan like peacocks' tails, goose-stepped towards each other, stamping their feet like angry goats. On the Saturday evening that I attended, fiercely partisan citizens of each country lined up on vantage points on each side of the gate, cheering like rival groups of football supporters, half in amusement but half, too, in patriotic fervour, as the soldiers strutted and glared menacingly at one another. As they were about to clash, the Pakistanis in blue-grey salwar kameez, the Indians in khaki, veered slightly and what looked likely to be a blow to their respective opponent's head changed in the last instant to an aggressive salute.

Pakistan and India have fought three full-scale wars since Partition in 1947 and the horrendous terrorist murders in

Mumbai in 2008 interrupted cricketing relations for the umpteenth time. Seen from an objective angle the racial and religious differences seem stupid but, of course, in all human relations old wounds go very deep and there are those in whose interest it is to keep them festering. Blessed, indeed, are the peacemakers.

As in India, so in Pakistan, such contrasts! The best French restaurant at which I have ever eaten, the Café Aylanto, is in Lahore's fashionable Gulberg Three district where, alas, a bomb has exploded since my last visit in 2005, with fatal consequences. Without fuss or inflated prices, its chef served those with a taste for Western food. It was worth the hectic journey after dark, by taxi or motor rickshaw, from the hotel that served much less deliciously simple food, far more expensively.

Other places, naturally, were less satisfying. On that last England tour to Pakistan, when the England team that had triumphed against Australia in the summer quickly began to disintegrate because of injuries to Michael Vaughan, Simon Jones and Ashley Giles, several of the press party were unable to find beds at the prime hotels in Multan and Faisalabad. At the Shiza Inn – soon subtly renamed by Jonathan Agnew off the air – I slept in a hat because the air conditioning was so fiercely cold. The dining room staff were immensely obliging I remember but one evening I disturbed a large rat in the so called 'Business Centre', a room off the small hotel's main foyer, when it emerged curiously from a gaping hole in the wall that it obviously shared with wires of various colours. It jumped over my feet and scuttered through the open door towards the reception desk.

Filing stories from there to London was painfully hit and miss, so I got to know that room well. Later, when I collected my last batch of laundry, two of my shirts began literally to crumble like biscuits as the threads of cotton parted from each other.

Naturally, I complained to the manager, who responded with a classically Billy Bunterish excuse: 'Sir, it was not that the iron was too hot, it was that your shirts were very poor quality.'

In Faisalabad we stayed at the Chenab Club, which had a well-maintained grass tennis court and some old-fashioned charm, albeit a little too old-fashioned. The only things that my sensitive stomach would accept from the unchanging menu were the soup, oily though it was, soggy plain rice and the Cornetto ice-creams that were usually available for pudding like manna from heaven.

One or two of the rooms at the club had bathrooms with the once familiar 'squatter' facilities, with footmarks thoughtfully marked on either side of the hole in the floor to show the user where the feet should be placed. My own had a bathroom shower that produced jets of either stone cold or red-hot water, with no temperatures in between. Still, one could walk to the ground and occasionally spoil oneself with a more expensive meal at the Serena Hotel. Moreover, the Chenab was far superior to the bed and breakfast lodge where my travel agents had deposited me for three nights during the previous tour, with another journalist, Ted Corbett, and his long-time partner, the statistician Jo King, both of whom were more stoical about the modest (but well-maintained) accommodation than I was.

When I arrived my room had so many mosquitoes that I was bound to be a mass of itches the following day; trying to swat them was as difficult as catching the snitch in a game of quidditch, so I asked the landlady, who was eager to please, to fumigate the room whilst I went off to enjoy the tasty open-air barbecue in the sharp evening cold of the garden at the Serena. When I returned, after a watchful walk at full pace through dimly lit streets, the room was so full of chemical spray that it was like walking into one of the old pea-soupers of 1950s London. Not only were mosquitoes certain of death but so, I felt, was I. Happy days.

Four games stand out from all those that I have seen in Pakistan. The first, during the 1987 World Cup in which I later switched to India for a number of the later games, was played on an exhausting day that started with a long journey in a dingy bus to the Municipal Stadium at Gujranwala. We started well before the sun had risen and arrived back at the hotel at around midnight. It was England's first game of that tournament following their long but happy tour of Australia, who were destined to beat them in the final at Calcutta. A two-wicket victory in the opening game against the West Indies was thrillingly achieved with three balls in hand after Allan Lamb had unleashed one of his occasional volleys of balanced, pocket-battleship hitting. Courtney Walsh conceded thirty-one off his last two overs, twenty-two of them scored by Lamb. It seemed exceptional at the time but Twenty20 has made such bursts of scoring look almost pedestrian.

The amazing final day of the Karachi Test in 2000 started unusually for me. At the time a builder from Brighton (an English version of Basil Fawlty's friend O'Reilly as it happened) was creating an outdoor sun-room for us at home and I thought it would be a good idea to import some cane furniture from Pakistan to furnish it. Consequently, before play started I went off with our excellent travel agent, Bilal Ahmed, to a furniture-maker whom he knew. I ordered a full set of tables and chairs, plus two of those wonderfully comfortable looking chairs known as 'steamers' that they used to have on passenger liners, and paid the craftsman up front for the lot. I was delighted with the price and he with the business.

There were two snags, the more serious becoming apparent

many weeks later when Bilal contacted me with the best price he could get for the furniture to be shipped to England. It was about fifty times the cost of the furniture itself, meaning that I might just as well have gone to our local Garden Centre. I told him to find a good home for all those beautifully made items.

They would, undoubtedly, have been superior to anything bought in England, which would probably be imported in containers anyway. Craftsmanship in Pakistan, as in India, is generally superb and they can produce almost anything to a high standard. I have, for example, well-cut cotton shirts, comfortable leather slippers and a leather briefcase, not to mention rugs, that have lasted far longer than their modest price suggested they would.

The other problem with my visit to the furniture-maker was that our negotiations took quite some time, so I got to the ground a bit late, having, like all good judges, confidently predicted yet another of the batsmen-dominated draws that are typical of Tests on the flat pitches of Pakistan. On the contrary, Ashley Giles was in the middle of an outstanding spell of left-arm slow bowling that netted him three for 38, including the crucial wicket of the masterful Inzamam-ul-Haq. Rapid blows followed from Darren Gough and Craig White so England were suddenly presented with a relatively easy target to gain a rare victory. It became, in fact, only the second ever achieved by England in Pakistan where, to date, only six of the twenty-four Tests played between the two have not finished in a draw.

Moin Khan, the home captain, was determined that the status quo should not be disturbed but Mike Atherton and Marcus Trescothick got the touring team off to a rollicking start, chasing 176 to win. In the second worst display of deliberate time-wasting I have seen, excelled for nefariousness only by the West Indies at Port of Spain ten years earlier, Pakistan bowled forty-one overs at a rate of five minutes an over before bold batting by Graham Thorpe and Graeme Hick enabled England to scramble home in virtual darkness in the forty-second. By then the fielders could not see the ball but the batsmen just about could. It was laudable umpiring, notably by the senior official Steve Bucknor, to insist that play should continue.

I should add that many an England captain would have done his best to slow the game down, if rather less blatantly than Moin, when faced with defeat. Still, it was a singular triumph for this particular captain, Nasser Hussain and his close ally, Duncan Fletcher, who were beginning to turn the national team towards better things. Writing the various stories and end of tour verdicts for *The Times* that evening at the Pearl Continental hotel in Karachi, knowing that I would be flying back to a family Christmas at home, was long and hard labour, but wonderful too. There is nothing so uplifting to readers of the cricket pages in the depths of winter as an England victory overseas, especially one so unexpected as this.

The last indelible memories of cricket in Pakistan are of the thrilling fast bowling of Shoaib Akhtar and the classical batting of the inscrutable Inzamam in 2005, and of the frightening moment when a gas canister exploded at the boundary's edge during the Faisalabad Test (the only one of the three that England did not manage to lose). There had been much talk of terrorist activity before the tour and I am sure that when that deafening explosion occurred and the crowd nearby scattered like raindrops in a storm there was no one at the ground who did not immediately think that a bomb must have exploded.

The only man not perturbed, it seems, was the buccaneering all-rounder Shahid Afridi, who took advantage of the temporary mayhem by screwing his studs into the pitch to try to get some purchase for the bowlers. Unfortunately for this gifted but naïve cricketer, he was caught by a television camera, just as he was a few years later when he bit the side of the ball to try to get it to reverse swing. Might one call this singular personality just a soupçon impetuous?

What has happened since to Pakistan is desperate. Terrorism has prevented the staging of international matches at home and in 2010 a *News of the World* sting all too convincingly uncovered alleged corruption on the part of three members of their team, including two of the best fast bowlers in the world. Salman Butt, innocent seeming but as captain the most to blame, Mohammad Asif and Mohammad Aamer, not yet nineteen years old, were all found guilty late in 2011, despite expensive legal representation. After exhaustive hearings they were each banned from all cricket for at least five years by an experienced panel of ICC judges, one of them the widely respected and famously liberal Albie Sachs of South Africa. The three cricketers and the agent who sucked them in all subsequently received gaol sentences after the criminal trial in London. It was necessary *pour encourager les autres*.

I first became aware of the corruption that starts with the complicated network of illegal bookmakers in India when I was working for the *Daily Telegraph* in Sharjah in the 1990s. I was reporting on a tournament that was eventually won by an England team under Adam Hollioake, almost certainly with the help of some contrivance from Pakistan. I had suspected nothing until I went to check a competition rule and found two very famous former Test captains, one from India and one from Pakistan, whose demeanor was so shifty and suspicious that I simply knew that I had stumbled inadvertently on a match-fixing scam.

As most now appreciate, there are two kinds of 'match-fixing'. First, spot-fixing for money, such as deliberately bowling a wide or a no-ball at a prearranged moment in the game, or two batsmen limiting their scoring during a period of overs to an agreed amount of runs. Secondly, and obviously worse, there have been examples of attempts actually to fix a result, requiring the involvement of several corrupt players. The whole business is sordid in the extreme and anathma to all those who love cricket. The lesson of history is that the sooner decisive action is taken against wrongdoers the better.

The scams seem to have started during one-day matches played away from the mainstream in the 1980s and 1990s in countries such as Sharjah. For once the ICC, driven by the ECB chairman at the time, Lord MacLaurin, took decisive, and relatively effective, action by appointing the distinguished policeman Lord Condon as head of the governing body's Anti-Corruption Unit, set up in 2000. Three Test captains, Salim Malik of Pakistan, Mohammad Azharuddin of India and Hansie Cronje of South Africa were banned – and disgraced – for life and a regime of education, investigation and prevention was put in place by a department now headed by another senior British policeman, Sir Ronnie Flanagan. But other leading players known to be involved were sullied without being banned (including the earlier India captain whom I had sensed was fixing things in Sharjah) and the constraints of the law prevented Condon and his team from nailing anyone else.

The education process for young international players, who are all shown warning videos of how they might be sucked into corruption without realising it as soon as they play under-19 representative cricket, has been successful to the point where Condon felt able, when he retired, to describe cricket as a 'very clean sport', one that was setting an example to sports like tennis and athletics in dealing with corruption. But the passionate following for cricket both on the Indian subcontinent and amongst the diaspora, the habit of gambling – by Condon's estimate 'a billion dollars worldwide bet on a single match' – and the sheer complexity of cricket makes the game peculiarly susceptible to criminal deceit.

Partly because of the corruption that appears to be endemic in many forms of life in Pakistan and partly because their players are paid no more than an estimated £3000 a Test, about half the basic fees earned by their English and Australian opponents, the likes of Mohammad Aamer, the most gifted of those found guilty, are more vulnerable to temptation than most. Not that this was an acceptable excuse, unless it was true that the guilty players feared for themselves and their families if they did not co-operate with criminals. Aamer, after all, was rich beyond the dreams of almost all other eighteen-year-olds in his country. He was the most glittering talent to have emerged since Wasim Akram, a cricketer of legendary skill tainted in the report by the Pakistan Judge Qayum, but he was young enough to return to international cricket.

Preventing corruption is the hardest part of the ACSU's responsibilities. They ban mobile phones in the dressing-room, for example, but wealthy young players can have more than one phone, and there is always the lavatory. In England in 2009 three players reported approaches from would-be micro-fixers during the Twenty20 World Cup, won by Pakistan, and a year later a young Essex cricketer was arrested for an offence identical to those alleged to have occurred in the 2010 Lord's Test.

Good men, like the coaches of the Pakistan team in recent years, Bob Woolmer and Geoff Lawson, have worked with honest officials such as the former PCB chief executive Ramiz Raja to make Pakistan team selection fairer and to give the best players proper contracts. Facilities at the cricket stadiums in

Lahore and Karachi, cities not directly affected by recent natural earthquake and flood disasters, are excellent, as they are at Lahore's National Cricket Academy. Brilliant young cricketers continue to emerge, but it seems that cricket generally, Pakistan cricket in particular, and many innocent citizens of this sad and complex nation will never be completely free from the consequences of moral weakness.

18

NEW ZEALAND

The Wellington Test disappeared down the appropriately named Basin in a whoosh of wind and rain from the Antarctic at a time when it was already certain to become the third draw of a dreadfully disappointing series . . .

The pitches, the weather and the lack of star quality on both sides made the whole series desperately mundane. Fortunately the good weather on the first three days at the Basin Reserve ensured good crowds on a ground with a real cricketing atmosphere (the hill here has grown even as Sydney's has shrunk) but generally crowds were small and even if they were to be better for the four one-day internationals the odds were that the New Zealand Cricket Council would not be announcing a profit . . .

The expensive England bowling averages tell how this series was a case of mediocre bowlers being frustrated by the torpidity of the pitches. Dilley, like Chatfield for New Zealand, was the exception, but DeFreitas took four wickets at 43, Capel five at 54, Emburey three at 78, Radford one at 132 and Hemmings none at a cost of 107. Hemmings rolled cheerfully back into the England XI at Wellington but predicted in advance that the pitch would last a fortnight. These old pros know, you know . . .

It is truly hard in my experience not to enjoy any trip to New Zealand but this beautiful, isolated, weather-beaten land was the last of the major cricket-playing nations that I visited and some of the disadvantages of travelling there to watch cricket are contained in that dispatch to *The Cricketer* in 1988. The pitches, and therefore the matches played on them, too often lack life and the national passion for Rugby Union leaves cricket as a poor relation. Add the complications for a newspaper reporter of the time difference between Australasia and Europe and it is easy to explain why the visits of MCC and England sides over the years have tended to be low key.

The ground at Wellington is, in fact, the only one of the country's major cricket grounds on which Rugby Union is not played most of the year. If the pitch for the first match on which I watched Test cricket there was a batsman's paradise, those on subsequent visits have produced some lively games, not least in 2008, on my last tour as *Times* correspondent. Jimmy Anderson and Paul Collingwood, two of England's doughtiest cricketers in recent times, were mainly responsible, but it would have been a very close game but for a spritely and opportunistic century by a stocky little wicket-keeper destined to be forgotten by all but the closest students of the game. The likeable Tim Ambrose proved then that every dog has his day.

For some time the visits of touring teams from England used to be tagged on to the end of the much higher profile series for the Ashes in Australia. Those who could, both players and journalists, went home early, leaving the pleasures of New Zealand to others. As soon as I experienced them, I knew what I had been missing. Here were beautiful and varied scenery, small cities, a high standard of living, good food, many superb wines, glorious and empty golf courses and, above all, Anglophile people (generally speaking) with old-fashioned values.

Even in 1987 black Morris Minor cars like the first one that I had driven in 1962 (number plate 7381 U) were common. In New Plymouth, I recall, the Christmas lights were still illuminated after dark in March. Things happened slowly here and some found it all a bit dull: 'Will the last person in New Zealand please turn out the light' was the familiar insult at one time. Certainly it was not the place for people who come alive at night, although one such, the late 'Crash' Lander, former cricket correspondent of the *Daily Mirror*, once persuaded me to the high-rollers' room at the Christchurch Casino, where I proceeded to lose fifty dollars in a game of blackjack in the time that it takes to blink three times. Only on a visit to the greyhound track at Hove in aid of a charity many years before had I found a way of losing money so quickly.

From a selfish viewpoint the wonderful thing about tours to this country was the relative lack of interest in the cricket. There were more days off than usual, less demand for interviews on my tour as BBC correspondent, or for feature articles when I returned in later years for the *Telegraph* and *Times*. This was touring more as it must have been for my predecessors in more leisurely times. England teams have usually played well in conditions not unlike their own, despite the admirable way in which New Zealand sides have generally punched above their weight. That was especially in the era when Jeremy Coney was their cerebral captain. He had the great advantage, too, of being able to call upon match-winners. Richard Hadlee and Martin Crowe would have been almost the first bowler and batsman picked in any World XI at the time.

It was no coincidence that England's best performance in a World Cup away from home occurred in 1992. Their preparation for a final against Pakistan at Melbourne had consisted of a focused but relatively relaxed tour of New Zealand. The tournament that followed, held jointly in New Zealand and Australia, was the best since the first one in 1975.

In the end England succumbed to Imran Khan's monumental will and the wiles of Wasim Akram and Mushtaq Ahmed but most things had gone right for them until then, especially during the first phase of the trip. Phil Tufnell spun them to victory with only ten minutes left in Christchurch, flighting the ball like a shuttlecock to take seven for 47. At Auckland that enigmatic man and cricketer Chris Lewis later gaoled for drug-smuggling, played a leading role with bat and ball. But it was another Englishman of West Indian origins who unwittingly left the most lasting memory of the Wellington Test.

The giant Gloucestershire fast bowler David Lawrence had begun his tour by dismissing another unfortunate cricketer, Trevor Franklin, with a bouncer that cannoned to the wicket-keeper off the batsman's forearm, breaking it in the process. The umpire wrongly gave poor Franklin out before he went to hospital for his X-ray. Fate had worse in mind for Lawrence on a hot afternoon at the Basin Reserve. As his front foot landed in his delivery stride his left knee buckled and he crashed to the ground like a felled oak tree. The knee-cap had split horizontally into two parts. His scream of agony was appalling.

As on all my tours, it was often the smaller places and lower profile games that I enjoyed most. Since they were not televised one was able to tell listeners or readers about places and players with which few if any would be familiar. Dunedin, for instance, proudly known, by locals mainly descended from Scottish forebears, as the Edinburgh of the south, may have had a rather ugly cricket and rugby ground, Carisbrook Park, but it also possesses a superb golf course almost in the middle of the town, Balmacewen. It wends its way through hills, some bare

273

and green, others covered in fir-trees and all very reminiscent of Perthshire.

Not far from Otago there is the sort of wildness that makes the country so special. There are huge colonies both of gannet and albatross – the only time that I have seen those huge and wandering sea-birds. 'And a good south wind sprung up behind, the Albatross did follow.' Here, too, as in many parts of the coast of both islands, you can see plenty of seals and sometimes also whales. Judy and I had a thrilling time one afternoon off the north of the North Island just before my work began on my last visit, following the swift black and white orcas, as they disappeared, then appeared again with menacing leaps ahead of our speedy little boat, like super-charged submarines.

The most charming and accomplished of the New Zealand cricket commentators with whom I have worked (although not the longest-serving, who must surely now be the loyal and ebullient Bryan Waddle) is Iain Gallaway. A war-time RAF pilot and greatly respected lawyer, he always invited me, and Judy when she was with me, to his comfortable and, by New Zealand standards, very large Victorian house. A traditionalist if ever there was, who always referred to Britain as 'home' although he had been a Kiwi all his life, he showed me proudly around his old grey-stoned school, Christ's College at Christchurch, where he was a governor. The boys, many of them looking big enough for an All Black scrum, still wore shorts all the year round. In 1988 he also took me to the Dunedin Club, which was defiantly old-fashioned and outdid even the Melbourne and Adelaide Clubs – and the Weld in Perth, Western Australia – for stuffiness.

There is no doubt that the Antipodeans can outdo the British sometimes when it comes to being behind the times. By comparison the East India Club in St. James's Square, which I joined when journeys home to Sussex and back up to Lord's or The Oval during London Test matches took so long that I seemed scarcely to be tucked up in bed before it was time to get up again, is far friendlier and also less exclusive. It does not bother me that there are 'smarter' clubs for a pukka chap to belong to!

Gallaway never commentated other than briefly on tours of England – Waddle and his predecessor, the no less genial Alan Richards were the 'staff' men for Radio New Zealand – but he was the first to cover an overseas tour for RNZ, travelling to India and Pakistan in 1955/6 as the sole representative of the entire Kiwi media. He serviced both radio and the NZ Press Association. At one match he claimed to have broadcast from the middle of a tree-trunk in Lahore and he later shared a commentary box with the fabled but not very distinguished India Test batsman the Maharajah of Vizianagram, who averaged eight in his three games for his country. Iain told me that 'Vizzy' fancied himself as a pundit so much that when he was not asked to do the Tests by All India Radio he organised a special game for the touring team against his own XI at Benares so that he could commentate on it, which he solemnly did for all three days.

Two grounds in particular in New Zealand linger in the memory for their sheer beauty, in the same way that Arundel does, and a number of other glorious English grounds. Pukekura Park at New Plymouth, too small, unfortunately, for major matches other than the occasional one-day international, is a sumptuous botanical garden. With its wide variety of trees and large lake it is rather reminiscent of Sheffield Park in East Sussex, where several of the early Australian sides played in the late 19th century. At Pukekura the playing area is like a bowling green, with steep banks on three sides and tiered seats cut into the turf, shaded by trees at the top that positively throb with the whirr of cicadas. From high vantage points you can see both a sea dotted with oil-rigs and, inland, the 8000-foot snow-capped extinct volcano, Taranaki, reminiscent of Mount Teide in Tenerife.

Anybody who has seen any of the films made of J.R.R. Tolkein's *The Lord of the Rings* will be able to imagine the other ground near Queenstown on the South Island. Open to the four winds, it is surrounded on all sides by high, jagged and rocky mountains, themselves straight from fantastical fairy-tales.

I funked the bungy-jump in Queenstown but went white-water rafting. It is for excitements like these, rather more than the cricket, that New Zealand always seems worth the long journey.

19

SRI LANKA

You have read about dark and stormy nights but this one was differ-
ent. There was no howling gale, just a vertical descent of water from
a black sky, as if the plug had just been removed from some giant
lake. Drivers in Sri Lanka often have to contend with tropical storms
like this, but not in a taxi apparently held together by sellotape, nor
in one whose windscreen-wipers had long ago given up the ghost. As
what seemed to be buckets full of water splashed continually against
the front window, conjuring visions of Jack Hawkins on the bridge
in The Cruel Sea, *my thin and anxious looking driver turned his*
steering wheel from side to side, his eyes pressed right up against the
glass like a blind man in a blizzard.

I am not quite sure how I survived that first car journey in Sri
Lanka, nor a few I have made there since. In 1977 I had arrived
from Bombay on a thirty-four-seater Avro Anson. Eventually the
driver and I made it to the most famous building on Colombo's
sea-front, the Galle Face hotel, a handsome old stone building
looking out across its lush front lawn to waves pounding in off the
Indian Ocean.

My room on this first visit was large enough to house a family, with mahogany furniture that looked as though it had been there for at least a century, plumbing that was not exactly state of the art and no shortage of cockroaches for company, especially on that first night when many of them seemed to be seeking shelter from the storm. The hotel has been given a facelift since but what it lacked in modernity then was amply compensated for by the sheer style and colonial grandeur of its public rooms and surroundings.

This visit by the MCC team was no different from any of the others that had been made by English touring teams over the years to the little country that generations of British had known as Ceylon, a prime source, inter alia, of tea, textiles, coconuts and cinnamon. Even in 1977 the lush green tropical island off India's southern coast was not considered to be anything more than a convenient stopping point on the route to Australia. In the days of sea travel it had given sides on their way to their first 'serious' port of call, Freemantle, an opportunity to break the interminable voyage and get some useful cricketing competition from men whose great natural talent had remained unsung. On this trip, for Tony Greig's team a sandwich between a long tour of India and a short one to Australia to take part in the extravagant celebration of the centenary of the first Test in Melbourne, Sri Lankan cricketers were doing more than simply wonder whether it was not time that the rest of the world began to take notice of them. They had begun to play more regular games against Test-class opposition and the lobbying to become a full member of the ICC had started in earnest.

Limited-overs cricket would not transform attitudes and popular taste in India for another six years, when the unexpected victory of Kapil Dev's team in the final against the almost invincible West Indies at Lord's dramatically changed the course of cricket history; but in Sri Lanka the World Cup had already offered a chance to compete with the best and the message was spreading that it would not be long before they were playing Test cricket. I blush now to think that when I was asked by radio commentators and others whether this was a realistic ambition in 1977, I answered that they would first need to start playing more than weekend amateur cricket. The truth was that their school and club cricket was already so strong, their technical methods already so correct, that greater experience of three- and four-day cricket, and of different sorts of pitches overseas, was all that they lacked.

Only five years after that England were back in Colombo to play Sri Lanka's first official Test and by 1996 they were beating Australia in a World Cup final in Lahore after pioneering the idea of all-out attack in the early overs of fifty-over matches. The buccaneering left-hander Sanath Jayasuriya was the first to open the window and throw away with a flourish the conventional caution against the new ball. It was an even more accomplished artist, Aravinda de Silva, who played the match-winning innings in the final that confirmed his country's status as a world power in cricket. The other essential ingredients were the leadership of Arjuna Ranatunga, a tubby little street-fighter with an astute mind and a determination never to be cowed by any opposition; the unique genius of the off-spinner Muttiah Muralitharan; and the skill of the left-arm swing bowler Chaminda Vaas.

Muralitharan is, famously, a Tamil from the hill town of Kandy. His success was threatened by a physical defect, an inability fully to straighten his right elbow which gave the appearance that he was throwing rather than bowling the ball according to the laws of the game, but bio-mechanical scientists and modern technology combined to exonerate him. His bowling enlivened every match in which he ever played during a career of astonishingly prolific wicket-taking. That it made him universally popular in his home country belied the shadow that hung over the island.

Officially the twenty-six-year civil war between the Tamils and the majority Sinhalese, who have formed the Government ever since Sri Lanka was granted independence from Britain, did not start until 1983, but I had become aware of the bitterness of some Tamils in an unusual way many years earlier. At Cambridge I had captained the Fitzwilliam College side, whose star batsman was a highly-bred Sinhalese named Vijaya Malalasekera. He has been a friend ever since and he still remembers the innings he played in the semi-final of the Cuppers competition that year, one that played him back into form and also back into the University team before winning a second Blue. (We managed to win the final without him.)

On the eve of the semi-final there was a knock on my door late at night from another Sri Lankan, one Kumar Ponnambalam, who had been a fringe player in the side. Why, he asked me, had Malalasekera been picked for the game but not himself? I gave him, as tactfully as I could, the obvious reason, namely the latter's superiority as a player. 'I think it is because I am a Tamil', he replied, unimpressed. I did my best to convince him that I was quite unaware of any such ethnic difference between himself and Vijaya and that my reasons were 100 per cent cricketing. Thirty-three years later, in 2000, Kumar, who had become a leading defence lawyer and an active, although not apparently militant, leader of the Tamil Congress party, was shot dead by an unknown assassin almost immediately after a Tamil Tiger suicide bomber had tried unsuccessfully to blow up the then president, Chandrika Kumeratunga.

Vijaya has wisely steered clear of his country's volatile politics but is also a lawyer by academic training, called to the English bar. He lives in a street named after his distinguished father, G.P. Malalasekera, who was a revered scholar and teacher, specialising in Buddhism, and later a diplomat who was Sri Lanka's first ambassador to the Soviet Union and also High Commissioner to Britain.

The kindness shown to me by Vijaya, who still recalls my broadcasting from his garden in 1977 clad only in a towel because of the heat and the fact that I had just emerged from a shower when the BBC rang, is typical of that displayed by many Sri Lankans. Whether they are successful businessmen like another even more outstanding cricketer, Sidath Wettimuny, or lowly waiters at hotels, the willingness to look after their guests reveals a generosity and humility that is increasingly uncommon in a selfish world.

It is no wonder that so many involved with cricket in England hastened to help when the tsunami wreaked its appalling destruction after the earthquake under the Indian Ocean on Boxing Day in 2004. Prominent among them, happily, were MCC, who raised a large sum towards the building of a medical centre and cricket ground at Seenigama on the south-western coast of the island on the site where a murderous wave had washed away homes, livelihoods and lives themselves. I made a moving visit there when Mike Brearley was President of MCC in 2007 and again four years later when, as President myself, I was able to see the progress made under the resolute leadership of Muralitharan's friend and manager, Kushil Gunasekera. He is one of those rare people who exudes genuine goodness.

Kushil's home village of Seenigama was more or less swept away close to the point where 1500 were killed in a train. It has been completely rebuilt with investment from various sources, including MCC and Surrey, who staged matches that paid for two beautifully maintained cricket fields and an indoor school. Upal Tharanga, a hero against England in the quarter-final, comes from a neighbouring village but the number of outstanding young cricketers from the area is multiplying.

Kushil gave his ancestral home, 250 metres inland from the beach and structurally intact despite being hit by the second wave to ceiling height on the ground floor, as the base for what is now the MCC Centre of Excellence, a complex servicing twenty-eight local villages. It is staffed by a mixture of professionals and volunteers. I met a gap-year student and a retired teacher, both from Australia, and an English couple spending two weeks helping at the diving centre that is providing 100 per cent employment for its graduates. Coral-mining has been banned since the tsunami, partly because the waves struck hardest where the coral had disappeared, but trained divers now get guaranteed employment working on harbours in Colombo and the Middle East.

The centre is now much more than a medical facility, with a dental clinic, a maternity clinic and pyscho-social support, all unheard of outside Colombo not long ago. Another large room and a shaded courtyard provide space for a large pre-school for children from a widening area, with four teachers. When Judy and I visited they were all seated on the ground surrounded by a huge selection of fruit and vegetables, each priced at a little below market value, which their parents would later buy and take home.

Other rooms in the spotlessly clean complex offer carefully organised and scheduled classes in business development, computer training, English learning, and a wide range of skills. Amongst them are cookery (it was 'how to make a pineapple gateau' on the day we visited) dress-making, candle-making, patchwork, lace-making and 'beauty culture', all aimed at increasing the productivity and self-esteem of women and girls. For the men there are classes in electrical and home wiring, plumbing and photography. Both sexes get a chance to learn business skills and IT. Quite recently they have started an outsourcing business (BPO) which is bringing in income from other than charitable sources. The plan is that the whole community project will eventually finance itself.

The emphasis is on empowering people to find decent employment and on lifting their standards of hygiene and of living generally. Graduates of the educational schemes now teach there themselves and, unlike many other post-tsunami schemes, this one is run without any corruption by highly committed people.

It is a curious fact of life that calamity brings out the best in most human nature, at least from the moment that the dust settles. While England's cricketers were making their weary return home after their ten-wicket mauling by Sri Lanka in the World Cup quarter-final, I was travelling north in a Russian MI 17 helicopter chartered from the Sri Lankan air force by the Laureus Sport for Good Foundation. Sir Ian Botham and Michael Vaughan were there too. They are two of many famous sports stars who give their time to support sport-related community initiatives in poor areas as a tool for social change.

Below us the bustle and skyscrapers of Colombo quickly gave way to paddy fields, farmland, coconut palms, rivers, lakes overflown by flocks of white egrets, isolated villages and miles of thick forest. The journey to Mankulam would have taken at least seven hours by car along the A9. From the RAF's sports ground in the capital to a rough school field in the war-ravaged north it took us an hour and twenty minutes.

Surrounded and escorted by armed soldiers, we moved to a large area of brown earth which only two years previously had been a jungle battlefield in the thirty-year civil war between the Tamil Tigers and the Sri Lankan army. A few majestic tamarind trees had been left by the military after the mines had been cleared and four giant yellow JCBs had almost finished flattening the area. A small podium, with awning to provide shade, allowed Major General Udawatta, the area commander, to explain that this would be the educational and recreational fulcrum of an urban development scheme at Mankulam, 56 miles from Jaffna, 200 from Colombo.

The Government, happy to lend support to two sparkling new cricket stadiums for the World Cup but still not doing enough in the opinion of many to rehouse some 200,000-odd civilians displaced by the time of the brutal end to the war in May 2009, was doing the right thing here. President Rajapaksa had granted the national icon Muttiah Muralitharan fifty acres for a project close to his heart. Kushil's mission now was to do for the battered Tamils of the north what he has already achieved for tsunami victims in the south. I was able to recommend to MCC that we should again become involved with fund-raising towards the cricket facilities.

It was typical of Botham to want to be involved. Later that day, however, I was embarrassed when, at a press conference in Colombo, he was asked what he had seen in the inaccessible north and gave an over dramatic account of a wilderness scarred by mortar shells, bullet holes and burnt-out trees, most of this from his imagination rather than from what we had actually seen. The truth was that a boy with one leg, the other presumably blown off by a mine, was the only actual evidence of previous horrors.

With Botham and Vaughan I watched a cricket match between local schools and later made presentations of vital provisions (double-bed mosquito nets, kerosene lamps, water containers and a torch) to extremely poor villagers. Despite their naturally beautiful surroundings they looked downtrodden and under-fed, but the Foundation had now embarked on a succession of monthly gifts like this. Already they had received 300 essential school packs and 125 bicycles. Meanwhile President Rajapaksa, not a politician to be crossed and certainly one in need of greater scrutiny from a compliant media, was pressing ahead with plans, financed by China, for an airport in his own heartland in the south-east of the island. Enhanced tourism in the east, where many of the island's best beaches lie, and the Yala Game Park offers sightings of leopards, should follow. Albeit too slowly, life seems to be getting better for the minority Tamil and Muslim populations.

I may have arrived in Sri Lanka in a ferocious rain storm, and it does seem to rain a great deal, hence the quite extraordinary lushness of the vegetation in every part of the country, but its inviting beaches, its working elephants, its innumerable swaying palm trees and religious sites that extend back 3000 years make it an attractive place even to those without any interest in cricket.

Nowhere, however, is perfect. Every time one goes there there is talk of a new road somewhere but it never seems to be completed. Journeys to Colombo from more exciting venues like Galle and Kandy are tortuous in the extreme. Much as they do throughout the subcontinent, intrepid drivers of motor three-wheelers dash for the nearest gap in competition with swaying lorries and a variety of cars, motor bikes and scooters, while dogs wander about the road in every village and occasionally get run over.

Most visitors are supplied with a personal driver and mine have varied in quality over the years. The most charming was an elderly Anglophile who called himself Cyril. Always smartly dressed in a chauffeur's uniform, his large, circular horn-rimmed spectacles perched under a peaked black and white cap, he was an erratic driver even by day, moving in sudden spurts followed by unaccountable periods in which it seemed that the speed limit had suddenly become five mph. Perhaps he occasionally nodded off. When it came to nightfall it was clear that he could see almost nothing. His method was to line up oncoming headlights with the white line in the middle of the road, then to sway inwards at the last moment, hoping that there was no one coming up on the blind side. He relied, I am convinced, primarily on the deities in whom he believed, an impression reinforced by his insistence at stopping at various temples en route to pray for a safe journey. But, like almost all Sri Lankans he was always eager to please. How could one criticise anyone whose opening questions each morning were always: 'Have you had your morning dip, Sir? And your bacon and eggs?'

20

SOUTH AFRICA

There is only one way to arrive in Cape Town if you are lucky enough
to have the chance and it is not by landing on a strip of concrete
in an aeroplane. The first sight of the great slab of Table Mountain
approached from the sea one early morning forty years ago is fresh
in the mind still. The country has drawn me back time and again
since but that first visit early in 1964 was both the most exciting
and the most disturbing.

Only one first experience of a foreign country has matched
it since, another arrival by sea, this time to New York after
a voyage made free in return for some talks about cricket to
a largely uninterested audience of American passengers. So
stormy was the crossing in April weather much like that experienced by the fated passengers on the maiden Atlantic crossing
of the SS *Titanic* that the open decks had been out of bounds
for most of the trip, but that was forgotten as Judy and I had
our first glimpse of New York from the boat deck of Cunard's
most famous post-war liner, the *QE2*. We slid past the Statue of
Liberty at eye level as the Manhatten skyline approached and the
ship's hooter blasted out a throaty greeting to the Staten Island

ferry, chugging busily past us like a child's bath toy. So early in the morning was it, and so freezing the dawn, that my jaws were paralysed by cold and unable to form coherent speech.

Everything was less familiar as Cape Town approached on a much warmer morning in 1964. Officially I had been 'working my passage' on the twin-screw motor vessel *City of York*, a beautiful ship that combined the conveyance of cargo with accommodation for 200 passengers. I slept either in the green-painted infirmary, or in a spare cabin that suffered little by comparison with the luxurious ones for which passengers had paid as much or a little bit more than they would have done for the bigger ships of the Union Castle line that plied the same seas from Tilbury to Cape Town.

From the outset that voyage was bliss. I was given virtually no work to do other than acting in an unofficial public relations role for the distinguished old firm now directed from his office in Camomile Street in the City by my father. I fell in love, or thought I did, with the blonde and beautiful young nurse/nanny but it was only an affair of my dreams, like one of Roy Orbison's. She already had an *amour* on board, a worldly wise young officer from South Africa who both talked a better game and looked considerably hunkier than the recently retired schoolboy whose knowledge of girls had been confined to some kissing and cuddling towards the end of holiday dances.

Only a few months later, inspired by the romantic nature of a voyage at sea, not to mention freedom from the care of exams and the rules of school life, I felt grown up enough to take a much more genuine interest in the opposite sex from which public schoolboys of the time were sheltered. Having made no progress with the sweet and beautiful children's nurse, however, the best I managed was a comment from an elegant lady on the ballroom floor one evening: 'You dance like Fred Astaire.'

This from the charming wife of a former Scottish rugby international, Eric Loudon-Shand, who had lost an arm in the war. She and her genial husband must both have been in their seventies.

On the voyage home two months or more later I did form my first mildly serious liaison with a girl of my own age, a young South African who was no great beauty but extremely fit. Her parents had separated and she had little time for the younger stepmother travelling to Britain with her father, so she was happy to escape their attentions. Once the fortnight at sea had ended, however, we met only to establish that the attraction was purely physical. One evening in my room at Cambridge she said in relation to something that one of her parents' black servants had done: 'He was only a kaffir anyway so what would he know?'

She was probably only aping the views of her parents but the scales fell at once from my eyes and that was the end of our liaison. Naïve as I was I had nevertheless been appalled by the whole experience of apartheid in practice. It was the cruel pettiness of it all that brought home what I had read in Alan Paton's moving novel *Cry, The Beloved Country*. During a few weeks in Cape Town, living in digs and playing some cricket for Western Province's midweek side, including a few games at the gorgeous and then undeveloped ground at Newlands, I travelled from suburb to suburb by train. To buy a ticket I had to go through an entrance marked 'Whites Only'. The trains themselves had to be separated, of course. So did every entrance to every building.

It was both absurd and degrading, whatever colour you were, but, of course, especially if you were not white. One day I went instead by bus. Surprised to discover that all races were for once allowed on board, I offered my seat to a large and elderly Bantu lady, who accepted my gesture with exaggerated gratitude.

Seeing this act of simple courtesy, the bus conductor practically spat at me and told me to leave his vehicle at the next stop.

This was one of two occasions when I found myself walking back to my digs. The second involved a longer journey, in a much chastened mood. I had been to a horse-racing meeting one Saturday afternoon at Kenilworth, starting with a wallet full enough to allow modest bets on several races but finishing completely empty. That afternoon I was almost a lone white man amongst a seething crowd of mixed races, for most of whom an afternoon of bad luck was much more serious than it was for me. I learned a lesson about never gambling more than you are prepared to lose.

South Africa was still a long way then from the proud establishment of a 'Rainbow Nation', but cricket was soon to feel the first tremors of the earthquake that would give birth to a fairer society. One of the earliest stories of my journalistic career concerned the hullabaloo after the Oval Test of 1968 when the England selectors named their touring party for South Africa and decided to leave out the man who had just made a commanding century against Australia, Basil D'Oliveira. I got on well with Basil in later years when we occasionally spoke at the same dinner, although I could never keep up with his thirst for alcohol when the dinner was over and the guests had gone. It was truly formidable and eventually, I fear, caught up with him. He was, however, an impressive cricketer and man.

There are many who believe that the Cricket Council (in which, on such matters, MCC still had as strong a voice as the Test and County Cricket Board) left him out of that touring party because they knew that picking 'Dolly' would not be acceptable to South Africa's Government and their intransigent president, Dr. John Vorster.

Having talked since to many people involved, including the captain of England at the time, Colin Cowdrey, and the chairman of selectors, Doug Insole, I believe their version that both the original tour party, which had preferred Tom Cartwright to D'Oliveira, and the subsequent decision to replace Cartwright with D'Oliveira when the former had to withdraw because of injury, were decisions made for cricketing, not political, reasons. The consequence of the eventual selection, of course, was that Dr. Vorster called Dolly a 'political cricket ball' in a speech in Bloemfontein, an Afrikaans stronghold, and called the tour off.

The further consequence was that South Africa's subsequent scheduled tour to England in 1970 was also cancelled, this time by Harold Wilson's Labour Government, for reasons of security, and that from 1970 until 1992 South Africa played no official international cricket. Brian Johnston and I shared the reporting of the dramatic announcement of the 1970 cancellation, following lobbying from Peter Hain's 'Stop the 70 tour' pressure group, whose threats had led to barbed wire being placed round the square at Lord's. I loved my involvement with an issue as great as this and saw at first hand the profound effect that major political stories could have on sensitive souls such as Billy Griffith, the secretary of MCC.

It was, strictly from a cricketing point of view, the greatest shame that South Africa was ostracised just at the time that the country had produced the best side in its years as an all-white cricket team. An astute captain, Dr. Ali Bacher, had marshalled a team including Graeme and Peter Pollock, Barry Richards, Mike Procter and Eddie Barlow so effectively that in the early months of 1970 they gave a strong Australia team the biggest hiding it had ever had in almost 100 years of playing Test cricket. South Africa won the first Test by 170 runs, the second by an innings and 129 runs and the last two by more than 300.

Eventually the combination of sporting isolation, economic boycotts and the sheer power of world opinion, condemning the Nationalist party's stubborn racial segregation policy as utterly unjust and indefensible, forced the political changes that led to the release of Nelson Mandela and the birth of the 'Rainbow Nation'. Brilliant cricketers such as Clive Rice and Vincent van der Bijl therefore missed the international careers their talent would have ensured, but so, as recent historians of non-white cricket have faithfully documented, did many unsung cricketers of darker hue. Almost immediately the sheer competitiveness of South Africa's sporting culture enabled the national team to hold its own once their status as pariahs ceased.

For a while I was of the opinion, mistakenly, that a blanket ban, preventing even teams of mixed colour from touring, would merely set back South African cricket while leaving the politicians unmoved, but I came to see the logic behind Hassan Howa's opposition to compromise. There could, indeed, be 'no normal sport in an abnormal society', the effective mantra of SANROC, the South African Non-Racial Olympic Committee. Once the ICC had expelled South Africa it was clear that the isolation would have to continue until that society changed radically.

In the intervening years I went back to the country twice to monitor the attempts by the remarkable Dr. Bacher in particular to keep cricket's flame burning. A man of immense personal drive, he pursued the goal of non-racial cricket by any means he could. He insisted on multi-racial sides in the domestic competitions and made energetic attempts, often with the help of English coaches from county cricket, to build bridges with coloured teachers in the townships in order to initiate, or regenerate, cricket in underprivileged schools.

Bacher would no more let go of his dream of a genuinely multi-racial cricket administration than a dog would relinquish his bone. But he never undersold his case, once reporting to the press after an ICC meeting that he and his loyal associate, Joe Pamensky, had received a standing ovation for the presentation they had just given on the progress being made. 'That's not quite correct', said the more realistic Pamensky. 'We were standing, they were sitting.'

The little doctor from Johannesburg, like the bearded one from Downend in Gloucestershire in the previous century, was not a man to be deflected from his vision. Harnessing business contacts, he began offering enticing sums of money to cricketers from overseas to play in what became known as 'rebel' tours. Reporting for both the BBC and *The Cricketer* I witnessed two unofficial Tests in the series between South Africa and the West Indies which had much the same intensity as the real thing. Painfully struck on the ear by Sylvester Clarke in one of these games after ducking into a bouncer, an ageing Graeme Pollock was given a taste of what it was like playing against the even fiercer fast bowlers of that period.

Most of the West Indians came to regret their involvement, because it meant burning their boats at home in return for earning money of the sort that would not become available to mercenary cricketers until the dawn of the Indian Premier League. Purely as a cricketing exercise, however, these games made fascinating watching and it was obvious that Bacher's attempts to encourage non-white cricket from the grass roots up were starting to bear fruit.

When, at last, Mandela was released he set a glorious example that has enabled all South African sport to flourish. Forgiveness, and the policy of peace and reconciliation applied by other men of goodwill like Archbishop Desmond Tutu, made possible the rebuilding of a nation that might so easily have been torn apart by vengeance. The dreadful injustice of the past had damaged many things as well as millions of people. One effect of the period of isolation in cricket was that a generation of South Africans had grown up without Test cricket.

They have never supported it well since, despite the consistent success of the national team, but there are players to spare these days. Kevin Pietersen and Jonathan Trott, both South African-born and bred but each with a British parent, enabled Andrew Strauss, English-bred and educated but born in Johannesburg and the son of South African parents, to lead England to successive victories in series against Australia.

South Africa have been the stronger side, if not by much, in each of their three home meetings with England since they returned to the fold. They have been enjoyable visits for me, enhanced by exciting visits to big game parks and, in 2010, to the site of the battles between the Zulus and the British Army at Isandlwana and Rorke's Drift close to the Buffalo river in Natal. Nor does one necessarily have to go to the well-run, well-trodden haunts of tourists to get a taste of African adventure. During the World Cup in South Africa and Zimbabwe in 2003 I was driving a hired car from East London in the Eastern Province to Port Elizabeth further west. Just as dusk was descending I was overtaken by a battered looking truck with a number of local workers crowded into the open back of the vehicle. It had accelerated past me to a distance of around twenty yards when something flew towards my car from the truck too quickly for me to swerve.

It turned out to be the silencer which had sheared off and, as I very quickly realised, flown straight at my nearside front wheel, bursting the tyre instantly. By the time that I pulled up a few yards further ahead, on the edge of a township called Alexandra, the truck had disappeared. Never a handyman, I did not relish in any way the prospect of trying to fit a spare tyre in the rapidly enveloping darkness. Everything outside was quiet now. I decided first to ring my landlady at the bed and breakfast house where I was staying in Port Elizabeth, to tell her that I would be delayed.

'Lock all your doors and windows at once', she advised, with a note of panic in her voice. 'Ring the police immediately – and the car hire firm.' I did both, finding it difficult not to be apprehensive in view of the country's reputation for crime. It was very hot in the car, however, and, while waiting for the police to come to my rescue I opened the two front windows to get some air. Immediately I was aware of several fingers creeping over the glass on either side, belonging to hitherto unseen figures outside. To my relief I quickly realised that they belonged to children from the nearby township. 'Why have you stopped here?' they asked, very politely. I told them why. 'Our father has sent us to see if you need help', they said.

They could not have been friendlier, although I judged it wiser to refuse their request to get inside the car. Before long two policemen arrived on motor bikes, told them to go home and changed my tyre with minimum fuss and maximum efficiency. 'You might not have been so lucky in some places', they said, but I cannot believe that a burst tyre suffered on any road in Britain would, in the end, have resulted in so little trauma.

Crime figures do not, I suppose, lie, but it is a question to some extent of looking after yourself. On my first trip to South Africa as a nineteen-year-old my two most exciting journeys were those made to the Kruger National Park in days when not everyone had experienced African wild life at first hand as seems almost to be the case now (there was nothing more amazing, to my eyes, than the sheer incredible tallness of the giraffes); and another from Cape Town to Johannesburg on the famous Blue Train. I was sharing a compartment in the sleeper with three others and found myself in the bottom bunk as darkness fell and everyone decided that it was time to turn in. Above me was a solidly built Afrikaner who had been friendly over a drink earlier in the evening. As I was beginning to doze I was suddenly aware of a revolver hovering beside my head. I froze. An instant later it was followed by the top of his head: 'Don't worry', he said. 'If anything threatens us, I've got this.'

In Zimbabwe, which I visited for the first time before the country was elevated to Test status, I dare say that burst tyres or the sight of a gun seem like the smallest of inconveniences to the great majority. The long misery for the majority under Robert Mugabe's authoritarian rule has overshadowed cricket as it has every activity in what once seemed a blessed country. Its natural attractions are obvious. Judy and I had an exciting visit to a camp beside the Zambezi, where a herd of elephants padded through the individual sleeping huts one evening and we came very close to being upended by a hippopotamus as it rose with what seemed like the force of a whale a few feet from the canoe that we were jointly paddling. Since the talk in the camp was all about a recent visitor who had died in hospital after his leg had been severed in two by a hippo in the same area, this was altogether too close for comfort.

I could not visit Zimbabwe without writing something about their steady superiority at the time amongst the second rank of cricketing nations.

Graeme Hick had made his name in England by then but after seeing the facilities in the main ground in Harare and talking about the development of the game in schools to the national captain, David Houghton, and to various administrators, including the personable but, by association, tainted, Peter Chingoka (who has somehow survived the rises and falls of Zimbabwe cricket ever since), I had no hesitation in recommending that the country should be given Test status and full ICC member-ship. Such an argument in an influential newspaper was a small feather in their cap but it would probably have been better for all if Zimbabwe had attained one-day international rather than Test status. More often than not, unfortunately, they have been, like most of their citizens, whipping-boys.

For some time, blessed with cricketers of world class like Houghton, John Traicos and later Heath Streak and Andy Flower, they justified their elevation. Alas, cricket disintegra-tion followed social disintegration, as it always must. Fortunes, as I write, seem to have begun their long turn but everyone has been waiting for Mugabe's death.

2 1

THE TIMES

'You can do the job on your own terms. You needn't go on every tour
if you don't want to. We will pay you well. We want to cover cricket
really well. We know you can use your influence to strengthen our list
of writers and make The Times *cricket pages the best.'*

These, or words to this effect, represented the beguiling prospect laid before me by Keith Blackmore, a far-sighted journalist
with a shrewd idea of what makes people tick, as we sat in my
study at home early in 1999. Then one of the two senior figures
on the sports desk, but destined to become the paper's Deputy
Editor, he had taken the trouble to come to see me, knowing
that, like most of my counterparts on other newspapers, I was
exhausted after an especially demanding tour of Australia. This
was the start of his attempt to persuade me to leave the *Telegraph*
to take on one more challenge.

The wearying nature of the long tour of Australia had induced
Alan Lee, the gifted and industrious successor to the revered
John Woodcock as cricket correspondent, to turn instead to a
sport he loved even more, horse racing. But I was tempted, more
so when I met Keith again with his colleague, David Chappell,

during a pub meal at Warnham. They both lived in Brighton and had gone out of their way to join me at a convivial and convenient place, tired though they must also have been after breaking their journey back from Wapping.

The gentle wooing process was completed by the Editor himself, Peter Stothard. An intellectual with long, dark, curly hair who cares about the writing of good English, he now edits the *Times Literary Supplement*. He also travelled from London to Sussex to talk to me at home and it was when his chauffeur-driven car came sweeping down the drive that I knew that, flatteringly, they really wanted me.

It was still a desperately difficult decision to make. The *Telegraph* had for so long been *the* cricket paper and they had looked after me well on the whole, even if, in my desire to do the job well, I had driven myself a bit too hard. Looking in the mirror revealed someone thinner and greyer than when I had started the business of being a daily cricket writer nine years before. Knowing that I was suddenly in a position to improve my financial status significantly, an opportunity that, at the age of fifty-four, would not come again, I still prevaricated. I did not want to be disloyal, nor to let down Jeremy Deedes, still the managing editor, who had 'signed' me in the first place.

I spoke first, of course, to the sports editor, David Welch, who was pragmatic and understanding. Then I was rung – but not visited – by the *Telegraph*'s own lofty intellectual editor, Charles Moore. Since it was foolish to look gift-horses in the mouth, I plucked up the courage to ask for a substantial rise. He said that he wanted to keep me and duly offered me a decent upgrade but *The Times* were offering a fair bit more. I took the chance to air my unhappiness about my occasional niggles over grammatical style, and also about recent petty complaints about expenses from one of the watchdogs who did not appreciate how expensive hotel life in Australia had become. Charles was reassuring and I found myself agreeing to stay.

I did so mainly because I felt that it would be disloyal to move to the arch rival, but the moment that I put the phone down I regretted it, and I did so even more when I conveyed my decision to Stothard, whose verdict I can hear now: 'All you are saying is that gentlemen don't change clubs.' That was the truth of it. I knew, and Judy knew from my anguish over the next twenty-four hours, that I would regret it bitterly if I did not change my mind.

I did so, to Moore's annoyance. 'You've behaved badly', he told me on the telephone. I had not: I had behaved indecisively, which was all too characteristic. He and I both knew that journalists, including high-profile ones, switch papers quite often, and that the workplace generally is far more mobile than it was in the days when a man stuck to one job or one firm all his working days. Some weeks later, indeed, I spoke at the same *Wisden* dinner as the revered Bill Deedes, Jeremy's father, and, with due respect to Charles Moore's authority and integrity, a journalist of greater value to the *Telegraph* than himself. Bill could not have been more understanding.

I cannot think why, but I am told that there was a stunned silence in the Sports Room in Canary Wharf when it was announced over the PA one evening that I was going to make the move. There was much speculation about who would take over and I was on good enough terms with Welch to discuss who it should be. They plumped for Michael Henderson, a quite brilliant polemical writer with a great love of music who had it in him to become, in a quite different style, a second Neville Cardus. Tall and bespectacled, his neck often swathed in a scarf and his head usually covered on sunny days by the sort of hat that might have been chosen by Oscar Wilde on his way to meet

Lord Alfred Douglas, 'Hendo' was excellent company, trench-
ant in his views on cricket, football, politics and the declining
values of the British nation, especially if there was a pint of
bitter to hand.

He lacked only staying power to last the by now gruelling role
of a globe-trotting cricket correspondent. He could be highly
personal and sometimes cruel in his assessment of players, which
did not make him every reader's cup of tea. Quite a few of them
followed me to *The Times*, appreciating the improved county
coverage and my attempts to be balanced on all the issues. Others,
I'm sure, found Henderson a livelier read. It took some courage
on his part, for example, to describe Kevin Pietersen's walk as
'camper than a row of tents'. In fact I think he used the phrase
in a later piece for *The Times*, but it was certainly not untypical.

The fact is that his work is always readable, rich as it is in
strong and genuinely heartfelt opinion, and lucidly expressed
by a writer far cleverer and better read than I am. But he was
irascible and easily bored, not least on the England tour of
South Africa in 1995/6 when the phone in his room was failing
to work properly in a hotel that was second-rate at best. His
solution was to open the window and to chuck the telephone
receiver into the swimming-pool below. Later that winter there
were no less severe tests of his patience during the World Cup
on the subcontinent.

Michael had had enough and returned to the peripatetic
life of a free-lance, less secure but, perhaps, happier. He was
succeeded by the more prosaic Derek Pringle, who for several
reasons was a sound choice: industrious, intelligent, steeped in
cricket, with the added cachet of having played for England with
distinction; also personable and a bachelor who was prepared to
take on the same load without family distractions.

I worked as hard as ever for my old employers until the day

before I joined *The Times* at the start of the 1999 World Cup. I was sorry to leave many of my old colleagues, not least the gentle and competent Keith Perry, who succeeded Welch as sports editor, but I liked everyone who worked on my new paper's much more intimate sports desk. Blackmore, with his keen eye for a popular human story and Chappell, with his balanced approach, were an excellent team. Marcus Williams, an old-school professional journalist, looked after the organisation of the cricket (and rugby) pages. He was devoted to his job, loved and understood his two favourite sports, had time to talk to everyone and believed in excellence. He was the last journalist I saw to wear an anti-glare eye-shade, like those once worn by tennis players and by newspaper reporters in films such as *Citizen Kane*. Whenever the phone rang on his desk he would answer 'Sporting' with the relish of a man eager for the next good story. It was a sign of much changed times when he was suddenly made redundant late in the summer of 2010.

Amongst his responsibilities had been to decide which writer went to which match, a burden that I had always borne at the *Telegraph*, so this was another bonus from the change of employer. On the promise that every County Championship match would be fully reported, I persuaded one or two of the best *Telegraph* county cricket reporters to move with me, notably the willing enthusiast Geoffrey Dean and the assiduous Neville Scott, a reporter who always makes the most of the space he is granted. Neither seemed to me to have been fully appreciated before and it meant that there would be more chances for the plentiful supply of worthy writers available to the *Telegraph*.

We were joined by Pat Gibson, one of the ablest, most diligent and balanced of all the cricket writers of my time.

The Times already had some good and reliable writers, not least Richard Hobson, a quietly spoken journalist from Nottingham with an independent mind, genuine love of the game, good judgement and, essential for anyone working for newspapers these days, a capacity for hard work. Now deputy to my celebrated successor, Mike Atherton, Richard has grown impressively in authority since I suggested that he should be given the chief responsibility for our coverage of one-day cricket.

Until the demands of the job began to wear me down again, I greatly enjoyed my years on *The Times*. I cannot believe there has ever been a calmer or more charming sports editor than Chappell, although there was an iron fist beneath his velvet glove when it was necessary to clench it in the interest of his pages.

I recall two examples, the first at Old Trafford in 2001 when, for the only time, he very politely and tactfully suggested to me that, after a dramatic final day's play and the late, unexpected seizure of the second Test match by Pakistan, my copy needed a little revision. Lesser men and lesser newspapers might simply have used a senior sub-editor to wield a large blue pencil.

David knew me to be a little sensitive about the merest change of a semi-colon so, once the inadequate piece for the first edition had been rushed into print, he rang me on the mobile and convinced me, weary as I was after five days of hard work in Manchester, to stop at the nearest motorway café and rejig the story. Looking at my first effort as I sipped one of Sam Costa's finest froffy coffees, I was appalled by, amongst other things, my failure to give due weight to the big television story that five of England's dismissals in one of their customary collapses had come from no balls that the umpires had failed to spot. Fond as I was of the embarrassed official, the late and much lamented David Shepherd, I had underplayed the significance of his uncharacteristic laxity. Chappell's judgement was sounder.

The other occasion was during a tour of Sri Lanka, where the time difference works in the reporter's favour, generally speaking. I had taken sufficient care over my day's report, filed from a hotel where the communications were sometimes uncertain – and duly had been on this particular evening – for it to be well past midnight when I got to bed. Three hours later, in that state of profound sleep from which no one wishes to be stirred, the telephone beside my bed began ringing insistently. At the other end was David, informing me apologetically that Sir Donald Bradman had died and that 1000 words were required within half an hour. The combination of Bradman and Chappell brooked no argument. It is amazing how the brain stirs into action when confronted with a deadline like that and a story of that magnitude.

On the whole I think it was generally accepted that for the majority of my relatively short period of nine years as *Times* correspondent the cricket pages were the best in the business, despite strong competition from the *Guardian*, the *Telegraph* and, sometimes, the *Independent* and the *Mail*. There were readers who simply refused to support any publication owned by Rupert Murdoch, so not everyone appreciated the improvements. Towards the end of my time, as space became more variable and unpredictable and Premier League football dominated sports coverage to the exclusion of too much else, the *Telegraph* had probably regained pole position, although these assessments are always subjective. Recently the sports pages of *The Times*, given more space and shrewdly edited by Tim Hallissey, have been second to none, not least in the overall coverage of cricket.

It was, I suppose, my bad luck that there were some painful years for the paper following the apparently hasty decision under Robert Thompson's editorship to start producing a tabloid, or, as he called it, 'compact' version, in 2004. There were several traumatic months for all involved when hard-pressed staff inside were producing both a broadsheet and a tabloid newspaper every night. The more conscientious writers in the field were sending pieces of different lengths to suit the relevant formats, but we all knew that the blueprint for the future was, as Eric Morecambe might have said, the short, fat and hairy version.

Murdoch took another bold decision when he started charging online readers for the privilege of reading *The Times* in 2010, a calculation that seems to be paying off handsomely as the sale of iPads has enabled newspaper reading on the move in a flexible and very compact format indeed. No more bashing your neighbour in the face accidentally on the 7.42 to Waterloo as you struggle to turn the page of your elegant old broadsheet.

The newspaper itself has improved immeasurably from an aesthetic point of view under James Harding's editorial control since its clumsy first venture into the tabloid market but I cannot help raising my eyebrows when the first words on a front page of what was once 'the Top People's Newspaper' are 'What Men don't want for Valentines'.

22

SPARKLING TEAMS AND CHAMPAGNE MOMENTS

England's rise to the top of the tree in Test cricket in 2012 inevitably invited comparison with other outstanding teams. Since Don Bradman's 1948 'Invincibles', whose prowess escaped my attention at the age of three, they have been, in chronological order, England under Len Hutton and Peter May in the mid 1950s; Ali Bacher's South Africa team in the late 1960s just before their long isolation; Australia in the era of the Chappells; the West Indies sides under Clive Lloyd and Viv Richards, their panoply of hounding fast bowlers generally too hot, calculating and accurate for everyone for some fifteen years from the late 1970s; and the Australian combinations led first by Steve Waugh and then by Ricky Ponting in their years of world domination from 1999 to 2008.

I doubt if there was ever a better balanced combination than these relatively recent Australian sides. Bradman's 1948 team was invincible in its time, but bottom heavy with seamers when it bowled England out for 52 and 188 to complete a summer of triumphs at The Oval. Any team with the most prolific batsman of all time was hard to beat, as Australia were from Bradman's second Test match on (in his first they lost to England by 665 runs). By the time his own post-war team reached a peak in 1948 there was a formidable bowling attack in Lindwall, Miller, Bill Johnston and the nagging Ernie Toshack to support a batting line-up of Morris, Barnes, Bradman, Harvey, Miller and Loxton. Don Tallon was no doubt a more reliable keeper than Gilchrist but neither Ian Johnson nor Doug Ring was much of a spinner judged by the highest standards.

England in the middle 1950s, by contrast, had as talented a pool of resources as at any time before or since and, as with Ponting's side, there never seemed to be any weak links. There may not have been the same ruthlessness, quite, but that is merely because it was a different era. Consider the XI that played the first Test against South Africa at Trent Bridge in 1955: Kenyon, Graveney, May, Compton, Barrington, Bailey, Evans, Wardle, Tyson, Statham and Appleyard. It included none of the three recently discarded or retired titans, Bedser, Edrich and Hutton; but there was no need either for Trueman, Loader, Laker, Lock or Cowdrey, to name but five.

As every keen South African knows, the best side in their long era of white-only cricketers was never able to flaunt its talent except in the series in which they thrashed Australia at home by four matches to nil in a four-match rubber in 1969/70. That team contained sufficient world-class players to have been a match for anyone: Barry Richards, Graeme Pollock and Mike Procter were great cricketers, men like Trevor Goddard, Eddie Barlow, Ali Bacher, Lee Irvine, Dennis Lindsay, Peter Pollock and John Traicos very good ones.

Ian Chappell's Australia side in 1974/5 would certainly have been a match for Ponting's, always remembering, however, that they would have had to overcome Warne. The two Chappells and the dashing Doug Walters would have tested Warne, if not mastered him, and while Dennis Lillee and Jeff Thomson were operating together, with Max Walker and Ashley Mallett in support, they were another fearsome combination.

Barely half so fearsome, however, as the the West Indies teams who, under Clive Lloyd and Viv Richards from the late seventies to the early 1990s, dominated all opponents. Their best XI in 1980 would have been: Greenidge, Haynes, Richards, Kallicharran, Lloyd, Gomes, Deryck Murray, Marshall, Roberts, Garner and Holding. The near invincibility came, of course, from the fast bowling. Never in the history of the game has there been a combination to match that quartet. Yet in the same period there were ferocious fast bowlers of the highest quality who would have been given the new ball by every other country: Colin Croft, Wayne Daniel, Sylvester Clarke, Winston Davis, Norbert Philip and so on. Still to come were the likes of Winston and Keith Benjamin, Ezra Moseley and the mighty duo of Curtly Ambrose and Courtney Walsh.

It was depressing at the time for purists and lovers of the game's variety that, despite slow bowling all-rounders as useful as Roger Harper and Carl Hooper, the West Indies seldom had any need of spinners. But such was the formidable strength of the fast bowling for so long that in most conditions they would have steam-rollered most teams at any point in history.

Students of Australian success after 1989, unbroken except briefly in India, Sri Lanka and England, will have some difficulty in deciding whether Ponting's team was better than those commanded by Mark Taylor and Steve Waugh. The XI, for example, that beat West Indies at Brisbane in 2000/2001, during the record run of sixteen Test wins in a row, was Slater, Hayden, Langer, Mark Waugh, Steve Waugh, Ponting, Gilchrist, Bichel, Lee, MacGill and McGrath. No Warne but MacGill, his reserve, took 208 wickets in 48 Tests. He was a brilliant little bowler, lacking only Warne's extraordinary accuracy, temperament and consistency.

If you were to draw Ricky Ponting's 2006 XI to play for your money in a trial of strength against any but the 1980 West Indies you would consider yourself to be in with a good chance of a sudden improvement to your bank balance. First and foremost you would have in Shane Warne the greatest of all leg-spinners bowling for you, not just with incomparable accuracy and power of spin but with seldom equalled zeal and will to win. In temperament he was like a spiritual son of one of Bradman's trump cards, 'Tiger' Bill O'Reilly. In Ponting you would have a captain who, despite his eventual failures, revealed rare depths of determination and in whom leadership brought even more from a quick-eyed, quick-footed batting talent that had made him Australia's greatest match-winner since Keith Miller. Unlike most of the outstanding Australian batsmen he has gone on too long, but, at his best, only Greg Chappell has equalled him amongst the Australian batsmen I have seen.

By 2006 Glenn McGrath was past his peak but still an utterly reliable performer, guaranteed to hit the seam on a length and off-stump line time and time again, the basis of all good fast bowling. If he had not trodden on a ball just before the start of the 2005 Edgbaston Test I dare say Australia would have won that series. That they did not had much to do with Andrew Flintoff's surging strength and the way in which he undermined the two bullying left-handers, Matthew Hayden and Adam Gilchrist. A year later, Gilchrist's totally uninhibited hundred from fifty-seven balls at Perth was a reminder that great cricketers will usually have their revenge.

Warne and McGrath retired together after the Sydney Test, as did Justin Langer, not a great player, quite, but an immeasurably determined one and an assiduous worker on his technique with a fine record of 7650 runs from his 104 Tests at an average of 45. The mighty Hayden, who, with Gilchrist, followed these three into retirement soon afterwards, shared first wicket partnerships with Langer that averaged 51. Only Bobby Simpson and Bill Lawry averaged better as a partnership – 59 for their 3596 runs. In all countries only Desmond Haynes and Gordon Greenidge, with 6482, exceeded their output in runs.

From the opening batsmen to the new ball bowling attack of McGrath and Brett Lee this was a perfectly balanced XI without a weak link. England may have been weaker than they had been in 2005 but Australia were stronger in four individual respects: at that stage Michael Hussey was averaging 82 after fifteen Tests; Stuart Clark had taken 42 wickets in eight games, played mainly on good batting pitches, at the extraordinary average of 17; Michael Clarke had returned to the side to sharpen the fielding with loose-limbed brilliance and to make the most of another rare batting talent after a period of repentance and hard work. He scored 378 runs at 94.5 in the series with two centuries. Finally Andrew Symonds had at last made the most of his long-recognised gifts, balancing the team as the number six batsman, a sensational fielder, and – like Brian Close or Bob Appleyard – a swing bowler one moment, an off-spinner the next.

Ponting's team lost only one of its first 21 series, losing by a single game to England in 2005 but winning 19 and drawing the other. Warne and McGrath took 1271 Test wickets in all between them.

The best teams become clearer with time and the same is true of the 'champagne moments', even if the earliest of mine were witnessed only at second hand:

1953 (two young for champers!): England regained the Ashes at The Oval after (just on) nineteen years. Hutton, Edrich, May, Compton, Graveney, Bailey, Evans, Laker, Lock, Trueman, Bedser. If ever a side deserved MBEs to a man it was that one. Happily, most of them eventually got medals of one kind or another. The captain and master batsman, and his leading bowler, were knighted. I got to know all these heroes and in my year as MCC president dedicated a mature oak tree to the toughest of them all at Sir Alec Bedser's other sporting haunt, West Hill Golf Club, near his lifelong home at Woking.

1954/5, Sydney: This was the game that sparked that rarity, a comprehensive England win in a series in Australia. Christmas was approaching, it was cold at home and I remember my father in his dressing-gown coming in to tell me that Tyson, Statham, Bailey and Appleyard – but especially the ferociously fast Frank Tyson – had bowled Australia out.

1956: Jim Laker's incredible nineteen wickets at Old Trafford. I have clear memories of every phase of that extraordinary match, and of going outside to play cricket in the garden as soon as Len Maddocks had been lbw to complete the rout. Off went Jim to his immortality with his sweater over his left shoulder, and everyone's ecstasy carefully suppressed.

1958: Surrey's seventh Championship title in a row. All the usual suspects: Peter May, the smiling amateur with a professional's ruthlessness; Kenny Barrington on the rise; Bedser and Loader, Laker and Lock. Micky Stewart brilliant at short-leg. Arthur McIntyre neat as a pin behind the stumps. An efficient, confident team with all the necessary talent and self-belief to keep on winning.

1960: The tied Test in Brisbane. Three wickets in the last over, Wes Hall with his shirt hanging out and mayhem. Frank Worrell, the personification of dignity. Joey Solomon the unlikely hero at the denouement. I saw him in the clubhouse of the golf course in Georgetown, Guyana, a few years ago, now just a local hero.

1963: The never-to-be-forgotten draw at Lord's. Ted Dexter in his pomp. Hall and Worrell again; Brian Close in his finest hour. A radio experience this time: I was listening in the pavilion in my last year at school. John Arlott, Robert Hudson and, at the death, Alan Gibson, calmly and extremely clearly taking us through that last, pulsating over by Hall. The run out of Derek Shackleton, the appearance of Colin Cowdrey with his arm in plaster, the mild anti-climax of the final ball, blocked by David Allen. Yet the satisfying appropriateness of the result, honours even, all passion spent.

1966: Hove and Lord's. The West Indies again and two matches to savour: Sussex beating them by nine wickets when John Snow took seven for 29; then Gary Sobers in supreme form when it mattered most, baling his team out with his cousin, David Holford, when they were 95 for five in the second Test at Lord's, after Colin Milburn had made 126 not out.

1968: Derek Underwood's ruthless hounding of Australia after the rain. Nine fieldsmen round the bat and sawdust everywhere. No Ashes but a drawn series, and justice at last, one felt, after a succession of series in which England were as good as their rivals but could not finish them off.

1973: Trent Bridge, the friendliest ground of all. Bevan Congden scores the first of two successive Test innings of 170 odd to delay an England victory under Ray Illingworth. I have to dash down the M1 to be in time for our first child to be delivered. Brian Johnston announces the birth and an astrologist writes to say the stars portend that he will become a cricket commentator. Close: James became a barrister.

1974: Sabina Park. Dennis Amiss saves England with a noble innings of 262 not out on my first tour for the BBC. There is a romance about breaking such news and telling how it happened. Radio had the broadcasting of overseas Tests to itself then.

1975: Lord's on a glorious summer's day. The first World Cup final. Clive Lloyd in his pomp, Viv Richards brilliant in the covers, the West Indies triumphant but Australia tough to beat as always. A long and happy exhibition of the limited-over game at its captivating best, in the days before it became tired and overdone.

1981: Headingley. This has to be the Dom Perignon 2000. Ian Botham's wonderfully free-spirited innings and Bob Willis's sensational fast bowling on a horribly tricky pitch on the last day. There is nothing in cricket so exciting as a close fourth innings run chase and in all the circumstances, after Australia's customary victory at Lord's and Botham's pair, this was simply amazing. As in 2005 the games that followed, at Edgbaston and Old Trafford, were scarcely less inspiring and Botham, as bowler and batsman, was no less inspired.

1985: Edgbaston in glorious weather and more Aussie bashing! David Gower easing into the ball like a sailing boat on the breeze, ten wickets in the match for Richard Ellison, and Edmonds and Emburey in happy harness.

1986/7: The MCG. The last series victory in Australia. I am on the air when Gladstone Small takes the catch off Phil Edmonds that wins the Ashes.

1994: In my time winning in the West Indies has been as hard as in India or Australia. They had been invincible for a decade so the Barbados Test, when Alec Stewart scores a hundred in each innings and Angus Fraser takes eight for 75, is Michael Atherton's finest hour as captain.

1994: Antigua. Brian Lara breaks the Sobers Test record score, for the first time. No batsman gave me more pleasure.

1995/6: Atherton again: the famous rearguard at the Wanderers. Ten hours and forty-five minutes of unyielding concentration

2001: A day when reporting required exquisite objectivity. Robin Martin-Jenkins, down breeze (for once) from the Denne Hill End, takes seven for 51 against Leicestershire at Horsham in a season when he also scores a double hundred against Somerset at Taunton. His captain, Chris Adams, calls him 'a complete cricketer now who could play for England'. Somebody more influential disagrees.

2003: Sussex's long-awaited first County Championship title. Murray Goodwin scores the winning runs early on a sunlit final afternoon at Eaton Road. Inveigled away for a rare lunchtime pint, I almost miss it. A few more go down the hatch when the words have been written. The ultimate team performance.

2004: Kensington Oval. Matthew Hoggard takes a hat-trick and soon the work started by Steve Harmison at Sabina

Park is completed. Winning the Ashes has started in the Caribbean.

2005: Australia win the Lord's Test as usual but only after being shocked by the ferocious Harmison at the start of an exalted series. Edgbaston, Old Trafford and Trent Bridge follow; three of the best Tests of all packed into a few heady weeks followed by Kevin Pietersen's clinching *tour de force* at The Oval. Edgbaston has to be the pick: that desperate finish and the intense relief when Geraint Jones clings onto the final catch to enable victory by two runs. Had a review system been in place, the catch might not have been allowed.

2006: Bombay. An England victory against the odds, always the most exciting. It all goes wrong for Andrew Flintoff, the captain and all-rounder, soon after but this is a great team effort, with Andrew Strauss, Monty Panesar and Shaun Udal also to the fore.

2006: Sussex, again. James Kirtley's sensational burst of bowling to win the C&G Final at Lord's.

2009: The two Andys, Flower and Strauss, begin their alliance in the Caribbean with defeat in Jamaica – all out fifty-one – but Strauss unveils to those who do not know him the high quality of his character and talent with a dominating hundred in the first innings of the next Test, played on the old Recreation ground in Antigua after a false start on the new one. Simultaneous signs of a deep and lamentable West Indian decline, but also of far better things to come for England.

2010: The revival confirmed. Victory for the old country against Australia in Adelaide as Graeme Swann, the best English finger-spinner since Derek Underwood and a sunny character who loves life and cricket, seizes his chance to take five wickets on a wearing pitch. At Melbourne the Ashes are regained after a typical Australian comeback at Perth; at Sydney the series is concluded by a third innings victory and a third big hundred for Alastair Cook, the captain in waiting. Not a bad time to be visiting Australia as BBC commentator and MCC President!

23

CHANGE – BUT NOT ALL DECAY

Cream-flannelled cricketers on green-grassed grounds unsullied by garish sponsors' logos. No chanting from the crowd, just a gentle murmur and polite applause as a clean-bladed bat flows through the oncoming line of a crimson cricket ball and a fielder bends nimbly in the covers, eschewing any dive if he can, to avoid a cleaning bill. In the commentary box the description is restrained, dispassionate; in the press box there is total concentration on the game. There has to be, because there are no television monitors. No laptops either; nor bloggers and twitterers. It is a simpler, less hurried world.

'Evolution' in cricket actually came closer to revolution at the end of the 1970s, due largely to the ambitions of a television mogul.

It is arguable at least that nothing, not even computers and the internet, changed life in the 20th century more fundamentally than television. Its influence has dictated every development in cricket since Kerry Packer, the inheritor from his pioneering father Frank of Australia's Channel Nine, decided that he wanted Australia's Test cricket on his own channel, at any price.

Superficially cricket and its professional players benefited hugely from the ramifications but the other side of the equation is that administrators everywhere are dependent on income from television. It is, of course, no different for any of the other professional sports. How do they all expand awareness, attract the young and generate publicity? It can only be done through wide television coverage. How do they finance the grass roots? Through television income. But television tends to want more and more for its contracts, especially more of the big names and the most famous or fashionable countries and clubs.

How the media game has changed since I first gained a foot-hold on its outer rim. For a whole generation after the war the news got to Ghent, from press boxes round the cricket world, by means of typewriter and dictation to a copy-taker at the newspaper office.

Much patience was required on both sides, and there were frequent misunderstandings, such as the occasion when the back page of the *Brighton Evening Argus* reported all the bats-men at Hove having difficulty with the ball moving around off a lamp-post on a length. The second edition changed the lamp-post to 'damp spot'.

Crackly lines were as bad as the often disinterested, but usually highly professional, copy-takers. An unfortunate eques-trian correspondent by the name of Horsley-Porter, with a suit-ably plummy voice, once had to repeat the 'Horsley-Porter' three times down a bad line from Badminton or Burleigh, with increasing exasperation, before the bored cockney voice at the other end came back: 'I know you're a flippin 'orse reporter, mate, but what's your bleedin' name?'

Technology has altered the process of cricket writing, and to a lesser extent broadcasting, as it has changed so many other aspects of life. The facility to communicate instantly has plenty of advantages but it does not necessarily make for an easier life than the one enjoyed by correspondents on the first tours after the war, when typewriter and telex were the means by which an account of the day's play would be conveyed home, after a delay that was unavoidable. For a start many more words are demanded of all correspondents these days, especially since online newspapers became almost as important as their newsprint versions. The faster the words appear, the happier everyone is, but life for the journalists is much more hectic at both ends of the operation. There is, alas, less laughter.

I have torn out more of what remains of my hair since laptop computers became essential equipment for the journalist than ever I did when accompanied by my Olympia 'Traveller De Luxe'. I have a better ability than most to lose words that I have sweated pints to assemble, by pressing the wrong key at the wrong time, but there is no other way now.

One became as wedded to and dependent on a laptop as to a treasured spouse. One of the most traumatic days of my life was the one early in 2004 when a pair of professional thieves stole mine (the computer, not the spouse) at Gatwick Airport on my way to cover England's tour of the West Indies. One gentleman with an East Mediterranean accent and appearance distracted my attention with an unfathomable question whilst another, quite unseen by this polite Englishman trying to understand what he was saying, whisked away, in one black bag, my traveller's cheques, my camera, my binoculars, my driving licence, a generous supply of American dollars just collected at the Bureau de Change, and, worst by far, the little machine that held all my cricket writing in the previous three years or so and a small library of emails and email addresses.

I alerted an airport official as quickly as I could and over a telephone gave a member of the airport police a description of the man I had seen. 'Sallow-skinned, East Mediterranean perhaps' I told him. 'Wearing a dark blue overcoat; thick- set; about forty-five to fifty I'd say.' I knew I had no hope of seeing my possessions again when an officer appeared at least twenty minutes later and began his inquiries with: 'So it was a couple of black fellows, was it?'

The only consolation that I had was the sympathetic reaction from people at *The Times*. David Chappell, the sports editor and later managing editor, quickly made sure that essentials such as money were shipped out to me. Traveller's cheques were stopped and a replacement laptop was sent out with my colleague, Pat Gibson, who, happily, was following me to Jamaica a day or two later. The Sports Room secretary immediately began the process of getting a new driving licence. She improved my morale, too, by assuring me that journalists were quite often parted from their laptops through misfortune or carelessness.

Much the worst experience of my professional life, however, occurred on the day of a totally unprecedented event in Test cricket. I refer to the previous England tour of the West Indies, the first day of the first Test in Kingston, abandoned after 61 balls and 56 minutes because of a dangerous pitch. This was obviously a front-page as well as back-page story. Getting the balance right was important. With all information gathered and all press conferences concluded, I sweated a few pints through the hot, humid late morning and afternoon, seated a trifle uncomfortably in the unsophisticated, but perfectly adequate and excellently positioned, old press box at Sabina Park. One by one I wrote carefully crafted pieces for both the news and cricket sections of the *Daily Telegraph*.

My crisis came out of the blue. To this day I have only an uncertain theory about what I did but one touch of the wrong button, as I was in the process of transmitting my copy electronically to

London, proved fatal. I had highlighted both stories and suspect that I simply hit the 'X' button rather than the 'C' next door to it. Instead of copying the words, I therefore obliterated the lot. No doubt the subsequent touch of the correct button would have saved me from the agony that followed and I would know what to do now, but then I still had to learn the lesson. All the words that I had so painstakingly put together disappeared in an instant and my increasingly panicky attempts to retrieve them proved fruitless.

By now I was melting from a combination of the heat and stress, the latter made much worse by the terrifying truth that, given a time difference of some six hours, the deadline for the first edition was imminent. Well-meaning colleagues and an expert in the Systems department at the *Telegraph* made various suggestions as to how the stories might be summoned back from the computer's hard disk but the fact was that they could not.

There was nothing for it but to dictate my copy from scratch, some 3000 words in all, down a by no means perfectly clear line. This had to be done against the clock, approaching the hot topic from different angles for the two stories. Any hope that I had of retrieving at least some of what I had written with a clear mind, of delivering some sort of balance of fact and opinion in lucid sentences, disappeared when someone suddenly turned on reggae music and blasted it forth at an unbelievably high level of decibels over the PA system.

There was a loudspeaker next door to the open press box and the din thundered around the virtually deserted ground, roaring into my ears and drowning what remained in my head. Thank goodness I had an intelligent and helpful copy-taker in London who sensed my desperation, but there was no real coherence to what I offered him and my unfortunate readers next morning. This for one of the most dramatic cricket stories ever!

If I had known from the start that I was going to dictate my copy, as would have been the case in typewriter days, I would have planned accordingly and it would have been, relatively speaking, no problem, always provided that phone communications had been working. There were countries where, once upon a time, they seldom did. As I have mentioned, the subcontinent and Guyana used to be particularly unreliable, ironically in the former case given India's pre-eminence in technology these days.

Any disadvantages of using laptops, especially now that wireless links have become so common and simple, are at least balanced, probably outweighed by the help that modern communications offer to any member of the media. To give but one example, there are now statistical packages covering almost any aspect of Test cricket that can be updated after every game and called up more or less instantly. They are extremely useful and they save carrying more than the latest *Wisden* around in bags that already seem heavy enough.

The changes have been less marked in radio cricket commentary. The pattern was laid down long ago, especially by Howard Marshall in the years before the Second World War. He was a model and remains so but he might not have appreciated the encroaching presence of the 'expert summariser'. Gradually the former player has, with the best intentions, taken some of the commentator's ground. I have never found anyone unsympathetic to work alongside, although some have a better idea than others of when to resist talking and let the commentator dictate the rhythm of the dramatic events that may be unfolding. Even on radio there is room for a pause occasionally.

Whatever the medium, everyone is more 'news conscious' these days. When Brian Johnston was in his pomp, controversy could be avoided if he thought it was bad for the game. It is no

322

longer possible to ignore such issues as patently incorrect umpir-ing decisions, bowlers with suspect actions, or, since the dreadful revelations of recent years, the outside possibility that, unless everyone is on guard, aspects of some international matches might still be fixed in various ways by cricketers prepared to take the money of unscrupulous punters or bookmakers.

Generally speaking, nothing much gets past the television cameras. Their coverage has become marvellously sophisti-cated, usually but not by any means exclusively for the game's good. Even with large electronic screens to show instant replays of wickets and boundaries, spectators on the ground do not get the intimate service available to them on their screens at home but, in England at least, the effect of televising the increasing number of Tests and internationals has actually inflated the size of crowds. Perhaps they go to escape the commentators.

The warts and all coverage has, superficially at least, brought everyone closer to the middle. The players are paid enormously more than they used to be if they reach the top but it is at the cost of having their every gesture caught in close-up and every aspect of their game analysed. Modern counterparts of the distant heroes of the pre-war age have become familiar faces, as liable to public ridicule as they are to adulation.

The game has always reflected changes in other aspects of life and always will. From a media perspective I regret only the fact that it is no longer easy to get to know cricketers well, even on a tour when one is travelling round a country with them. There is less time for friendly games of golf or for informal socialis-ing because of crowded itineraries. Conversations with players are sometimes confined to those orchestrated by the travelling team press officer, who would massage the news, if he could, as effectively as Alastair Campbell once controlled information from Downing Street.

Happily, a little independence is still possible in the way that one interprets cricket, either as commentator or writer. Since I started cricket has become more a business, less a game. The Twenty20 version and the advent of multi-million pound franchises in India threaten the long-established patterns of the international game but chronicling it all remains for the lucky few an extremely agreeable way to make a living.

24

SUSSEX AND ENGLAND

Nick keeps his ancient tractor in a barn on the edge of the fields that abut the Victorian cottage where my wife and I live in West Sussex. In July he comes along with Valerie to collect any hay left on our own little field after the rabbits have finished munching. The tractor saves them time but otherwise they are, like Sussex's cricketers, continuing a tradition that goes back centuries. Hay time and harvest; hard work and, given health, food and shelter, happiness.

We have been in the parish since 1978, more than thirty years, in three different dwellings, but in that time I have left the country for at least a part of almost every winter in pursuance of cricket, hopping from one continent to another with, it sometimes seems, barely a moment to catch breath. Nick's life has been a bit more static: he once went to the Isle of Wight for a holiday; but he soon got homesick. His father, he remembers, had the same problem once when he went to Kent. Neither of them really saw much point in leaving their own county.

These days Sussex is part of the busy South East where fields like those on which Nick and his farming father grew up are always in danger of being developed to create a few more homes for 'executives'. But there is an ancient pull every bit as magnetic as the modern one and I feel it every time I drive down our lane: if I go right I am heading for London, for the excitements of a magnificent city but also the noise and the traffic and the endless miles of brick, glass and concrete. If I turn left my spirit always lifts, for that way leads to the Downs and the sea.

There are far more beautiful stretches of coastline around Britain than the chalky strip between Kent and Hampshire and there are hills and mountains altogether more rugged and awesome than the South Downs (which should, of course, be the 'Ups') but for all the sad connotations of Beachy Head I defy any stable soul not to be stirred by the sudden glimpse of vivid blue from the bare and rounded top of the Downs. No sight is more likely to bring to mind those rousing lines from *Richard II*: 'this precious stone set in the silver sea . . . this blessed plot, this earth, this realm, this England.'

Anyone who has read Bill Bryson's brilliant *Notes From a Small Island* will be unlikely to forget its marvellously funny beginning in which he recalls the mean and tyrannical landlady who confounded his expectations of England when first he landed in Dover. Compare my experience on the day before a Test match in Nottingham, just after retiring from the main cricket job on *The Times*.

I had chosen to drive north late the evening before the game and, not uncharacteristically, I could not find the bed and breakfast that I had booked, on the recommendation of a local pub which had been unable to provide a room. Down a telephone line a kindly voice, in an accent unmistakably from the Nottinghamshire/Lincolnshire area, guided me to the right place, like an air traffic controller. The route on this rapidly darkening summer's evening took me off the A52 down a series of tiny lanes, close to Belvoir Castle (pronounced Beaver, naturally) and eventually to a cosy little house beside a narrow road beyond a humpback bridge over a canal that cannot have more than a dozen vehicles crossing it daily.

A tawny owl hooted as the moon started to appear above sheep-nibbled fields. I was greeted like the prodigal son by strangers to whom I would be paying £50 a night for a bed in a room so well equipped and so comfortable that it would put any hotel to shame, however many stars it might boast. Did I want coffee, tea, hot chocolate, Horlicks or perhaps a whisky? Or just a comforting bath?

In the morning I awoke to the fluted tune of a blackbird, rising above a varied chorus: thrush, chaffinch, robin, great tit and others I am too inexpert to discern. The little garden was full of flowers. There was no sound of cars or planes or trains. The room had a shelf full of books, all of which I would have liked to read. The decoration was immaculate, the pictures tasteful and interesting, the bathroom full of smart shampoos and soaps. The fridge had a jug of fresh milk and bottled water, although the ice-cold water from the tap was, a notice said, drinking water. There was a variety of teas and coffees and a tin of biscuits.

The breakfast table was laden with good things: half a dozen different fruits, perfectly presented; four different flavours of local honey; two fresh loaves of bread, white and brown; and a menu offering every imaginable combination of bacon, eggs, sausages, tomatoes, mushrooms and the like. Soon my choice was presented, grilled to perfection by a skilled, friendly and unpretentious cook. Sue is also a professional florist, her husband, Norman, a skilled electrician. They are quietly house proud but this is only a sideline to help ends meet.

They and their environment prove that there is still an England to be proud of for all the things that make me angry, like litter, the obsession with soccer and celebrity, traffic jams and tower blocks, not to mention all the rip-off hotels that are such a contrast to this little English heaven in the Lincolnshire Wolds. I loved that advertisement in which a guest checking out of just such a hotel is asked by the receptionist if he has had anything from the minibar. Has he enjoyed his stay, she asks further, and perhaps the view of the sunset from the swimming pool? 'Yes', he replies, like any polite Englishman. 'That'll be another £15 then', she says (or words to that effect).

A privilege to have travelled so much it may be, but Britain is still for all sorts of reasons – Radio Four would be one – the place to live. Were I starting again I might settle for a quiet life in Rutland but Sussex has not been a bad alternative, over-populated though it is.

Until the coming of the turnpikes the chalky downlands may have been a very remote part of England, but they were also the scene of relatively sophisticated farming activity for the ancestors of my friend Nick. Close by, in the wooded valleys of the Weald where cricket spread so rapidly in the 18th century, there was much of what passed in England then for 'industry'. The historian William Camden wrote of Sussex in the 1580s being 'full of iron mines, all over it, for the casting of which there are furnaces up and down the country, and abundance of wood is yearly spent'.

It is a varied as well as an ancient shire, therefore, that the cricketers of Sussex represent these days in their fastness at Hove, cheek by jowl with Brighton. In the days of Fry and Ranji it was a fashionable resort for swells and commoners alike. Today it is 'London on Sea', as full of different nationalities as London – or, for that matter, county cricket.

There are at least nine different written references to cricket matches in Sussex villages before 1700. Out of the county where village cricket blossomed between the deeply shadowed woods of the Weald and the bare green sweep of the Downs has sprung a tough modern team drawn from many places, none more productive than Pakistan. It is extremely unlikely that Sussex County Cricket Club would have achieved what it did during the Chris Adams era of the late nineties and early 2000s without the happy but fortuitous recruitment of the inspirational Mushtaq Ahmed but there were enough locally produced players still in the team for genuine links with the county's long history.

Traditionally this has been the county for families. From Edwin and William Napper in the mid-19th century, to George and Joseph Bean, through the Doggarts, the Gilligans, the Langridges, the Oakes, the Parks, the Wells and the Newells I believe that forty pairs of brothers have played cricket for Sussex. I have probably missed some but they all tell something about the soul of the county. If there is little sentiment in the modern game, wise captains and coaches still tap into this sense of history and community. It is no coincidence that after every victory the current team still gets together for a hearty rendition of 'Sussex by the Sea'.

I naturally felt more of an affinity with all this when Robin, our second son, began to make his way as first a junior but then a pivotal member of the Sussex team. They won the County Championship for the first time in 2003 and went on to win every other county trophy during his career from 1996 to 2010.

25

R.M-J

*Robin Martin-Jenkins, whose captain, Chris Adams, had said over-
night that he now regarded him as a 'complete cricketer who could
still play for England', claimed Joe Denly and Martin van Jaarsveld
leg before with successive balls in his first over, both men playing
back to length balls.*

Cricketing fathers are notorious bores and, like flies on a sandwich, often a damned nuisance. That is true whether they know
next to nothing about the game or a fair bit. I know I was no
exception to that rule, hard as I tried to be dispassionate in my
unusual position of sometimes having to write about my son.
Twice, I even had to commentate on his performance 'ball by
ball'. It was not easy, but it was a great privilege.

On the first occasion, in a semi-final against Surrey at Hove,
he got Alec Stewart out with the first ball of the match. On the
second he was given out caught behind off his pad off Glenn
Chapple in the final of the Cheltenham & Gloucester just when
he was starting to rescue his team from a dreadful start against
Lancashire. It is as well I was not on the air myself at either
moment, especially because I knew he had been the recipient

of a poor decision at that apparently vital moment at Lord's. Professionalism would have triumphed no doubt, but at the expense of natural honesty about my feelings. I'm told that I kicked the waste-paper basket very hard at the back of the commentary box.

If one cannot brag a bit in an autobiography I don't know when else it can be done so I cannot resist some wallowing in the pleasure that Robin's efforts gave Judy and me, along, of course, with moments of agonised disappointment. Every parent will recognise the feelings.

He was a relatively heavy baby and, showing an early inclination to emulate his father, he arrived late. As I recall it required a brisk and purposeful walk by his mother around Winkworth Arboretum near Godalming before the sleeping giant started moving at all. But whenever he showed signs of being a big baby in another sense in the months that followed, it was never a problem to divert Robin's attention. Just produce a ball and roll it towards him and his natural good humour would be restored. It did not seem long before he was propelling it back to the top of the stumps.

The early characteristics never changed. When he was a day boy at Cranleigh prep school on the Surrey/Sussex border, the only way to get him to do his prep on long summer evenings was to promise a game of cricket when, and only when, the sums had been done, the essay had been written, the dates had been learned or the verbs conjugated.

As time passed he managed to keep a reasonable balance between the necessary work and the longed-for play, but in those days, whilst playing the stern parent, I felt for him and recalled my own yearning for the playing field as a long academic labour began. It was obvious from an early age that he was an outstanding talent amongst his peers, as all who become first-class players always were and will be. I used to have to bite my tongue as other parents boasted about their talented children, invariably exaggerating their brilliance: 'Charlie's a fantastic little cricketer. He's in the second XI and I'm told he's bound to be in the firsts next year.'

There was some satisfaction in replying, with a proper English reserve, that one's own sons played a bit too; forbearing to mention that they had been in the firsts for ages.

James, two years in the Radley side, was a gifted batsman and useful bowler who improved technically under Les Lenham's coaching at Oxford, before turning his chief attention to golf. His younger brother did not, like James, make ninety-six at the age of ten in a school match but by the same age he was already a demon bowler and relatively heavy scorer. The former Sussex cricketer John Spencer, the outstanding coach of Brighton College who used to take Easter classes at Horsham, told me one day with conviction: 'He could go all the way.' At about the same time Robin scored two centuries in one day in the Sussex Junior Cricket Festival.

I treasure, too, the memory of some of the rare occasions when I got the chance to watch him playing as a schoolboy cricketer, knowing from garden cricket that the talent was there. My wife saw much more of him playing in matches than I was able to do, doing all the hard work of ferrying him about in the car for holiday matches for Horsham and Sussex; and, of course, making chocolate cakes for innumerable teas.

I just did the easy bit, watching when I could, which, unfortunately, was seldom. At one prep school match when he was the captain I arrived when the opposition team were hopelessly placed at something like 30 for eight, RM-J having taken seven of them. I prayed that he would take himself off so that I could see him play an innings of reasonable length. The Lord obliged, as he generally does when you need a boost. To give another bowler a chance, Robin took himself off and the opposing school's last two wickets duly more than doubled the total. The captain, who in those days opened the batting as well as the bowling, proceeded serenely to a not-out fifty and the game was swiftly won.

At Radley he made a century in his first match as a junior colt and was immediately promoted to a higher age group by Alan Dowding, the former Oxford captain, who ran his junior sides at Radley with great sympathy and sagacity. In the first match that I saw him play for the first XI Robin took an exceptional catch down by his bootlaces at third-man from a scything cut hit with great power by a batsman later destined to play for Gloucestershire, a moment that possibly turned the game and proved that there was courage and commitment in him as well as the essential hand-to-eye co-ordination.

He had joined his elder brother in the Radley first team at the start of his second summer term. When Guy Waller, the master-in-charge and future Cranleigh headmaster, asked me if he should regularly play in the XI so young I said that I thought that a year's wait would do him no harm. I had in mind the fact that in my own school days Mike Griffith, now the highly accomplished chairman of MCC's cricket committee, seemed to have become an introverted personality for a time, partly because he was promoted to play with (and outshine) older boys when he was young. I was also aware of the strong opinion of the England coach Micky Stewart that English school cricketers do not get pushed hard enough early enough if they show great promise but my other strong reason for persuading Guy to be patient was paternal. This was James's chance to be a relative star in the first XI. He duly contributed effectively as both a batsman and medium-pacer to a very successful side.

A year or two later Robin's bowling potential became apparent to me when, in a match against Wellington, he unleashed a Harmison-like delivery that flew through to the wicket-keeper at head height. This off a good length on a slow and sleepy pitch. Robin Dyer, the former Surrey batsman, now Wellington's master-in-charge, immediately recommended that he should play for England Schools and he duly did.

The only problem in those years was that he bowled too much for all sorts of representative sides. Perhaps as a consequence such whippy pace only appeared occasionally in later years. When it did he was as dangerous as many who were preferred for England teams. In particular I watched with pleasure as he gave that gifted Australian Michael Bevan one of the most torrid examinations of his career when he returned to play against his old county for Leicestershire. In the *Telegraph* Simon Briggs compared his bowling that day to that of Curtly Ambrose. Such fire was the exception not the rule, unfortunately, but it was some recompense for the times when RM-J had been run out for nought or one, unselfishly trying to give the esteemed Bevan the strike late in a Sunday League innings.

He can probably blame me for encouraging an ambition to play cricket for a living in the first place, but in truth the seed did not need much planting; indeed, it was never deliberately planted at all. When he was given a mock job interview in his later days at school by an adviser on suitable careers, he replied to the woman who had asked him what he wanted to do that he wished to play cricket. She smiled and said: 'Yes; but what do you want to do *for a living*?'

Robin got both Alec Stewart and Graham Thorpe out when Sussex played him in the first team for the first time in a Sunday League match at Horsham in 1995 after a series of good performances with both bat and ball for the second XI.

Parents of any performer who makes it to the public eye, however obliquely, will understand the suppressed excitement we used to get simply from seeing his name in brackets in the small print of the daily paper. 'Kent 246 (R.S.C. Martin-Jenkins 5 for 62)' added an extra dimension to one's day and it continued to do so whenever we switched on Ceefax to follow the course of a match on television, ball by agonising ball. We were elated when a new entry in white on the screen told us that 'Martin-J' had got a wicket, or reached a fifty and accordingly deflated when it was a case of 'Martin-J lbw Anderson 8'.

There were many ups and downs and once or twice he was left out of the team but for the last ten years of his fifteen at the club he was more or less an automatic choice in any form of the game, despite a growing challenge to his place from the vibrant young all-rounder Luke Wright, whose spectacular hitting in Twenty20 cricket soon caught the eye of the national selectors. Robin was less dramatic but, generally, more consistent. All that he earned as a professional was the product of Sussex's belief in his ability and character; and his own dedication. He worked hard to build his fitness and physique and to overcome his early proneness to injury.

Throughout his career he could still be talked out by overtly aggressive opponents like Dominic Cork and he did not always have sufficient faith in himself. I believe, and so do many others, that he could have played for England but I remain proud of the way that he learned how to build an innings; overcame glandular fever and all sorts of injuries that restricted his elasticity as a bowler; controlled a youthful fallibility against fast bowling; widened his range of shots in the one-day game; and maintained his reliability as a bowler and fielder. I am sure that he did sometimes, but I never saw him drop a catch.

He would have played a bit for England, I am sure, if he had been able to convince the selectors that this was what he wanted above all else. I know that they felt – wrongly – that he was not quite as 'hungry' as the likes of Matt Prior or Luke Wright, who was only once preferred to him as Sussex's first-choice all-rounder until eventually they played regularly together. Selectors take much account of the sort of overt keenness shown by Prior and Wright, and of their admirable willingness to work ceaselessly to improve, but Robin's ambition and capacity for hard work were never openly displayed.

Selectors also like young players who, if not picked for representative teams, go abroad in the winter in search of more experience, but that was not possible for Robin once he got married. Flora had been the only girl for him since they met in their first year at Durham University's Hild Bede College. She became a foreign languages' teacher despite suffering two serious illnesses, one of them prolonged, in the ten years before, to their great joy, she gave birth to Isabella Mary, alias 'Missy', on Boxing Day 2009.

Flora frankly admitted in a magazine article that for years she hated the game so much she could not even say the word 'cricket'. The lot of a professional cricketer's wife can be tough, as it can be for a cricket journalist's wife. They have to find a way to plough their own furrow, which is rather easier if you are earning the sort of high salaries now commanded by international players.

'R.M-J' proved himself a true all-rounder, finishing with a first-class average of 31 both as a batsman and as a bowler and taking his wickets at an economy rate of 2.96 runs an over, a figure that indicated how well he had played the role as foil to the match-winning Mushtaq Ahmed in Sussex's Championship-winning seasons. Overall his haul was more than 9000 runs and

500 wickets and even in limited-overs cricket his economy rate was 4.31, unusually 'mean'.

As in politics, there are always regrets in cricket. He did not score all the runs that his gift of timing suggested he might have done; nor was he often a lucky bowler like some. His best balls seemed always just to miss the outside edge and if, as they do, a slip catch went down it seemed to my subjective eyes that it was often off a ball from Robin. But his team-mates know him as a good man to have in the side when the pressure was on. He always tried might and main for the team; usually entertained; and always played the game with generosity of spirit. To a man, the umpires, a group who really see the game from the inside, spoke well of his competitive but honourable approach.

When he became a father he resolved to seek a job in teaching, agreeing with Sussex that he would leave in July to prepare for a new life at Hurstpierpoint, who had chosen him to teach Geography, Religious Studies and Sport. They must have been increasingly pleased at the prospect as their new recruit produced a series of exceptional performances with both bat and ball, in his last season, including match-winning centuries on 'sporty' green pitches at Bristol and Derby. He was given a rousing send-off in his last game at Hove, a televised forty-over match in which he smote a couple of sixes to underline my one regret about his career, namely that he did not bat high enough in one-day games to build any lengthy innings. It was a happy evening, supported by some 2000 of his loyal supporters at Hove. Sussex won comfortably against a weak Worcestershire XI.

After the game Judy, Flora and I were invited into the dressing-room by Mark Robinson, the coach who had built outstandingly well on the foundations laid by his predecessor, Peter Moores. The departing all-rounder was presented with a huge frame containing his favourite pair of green corduroy trousers, hitherto worn at all end-of-season parties, now signed by all his mates. He gave an impromptu speech expressing his thanks and telling the youngsters to follow the code that had guided the club since their days of disunity and failure fifteen years earlier: in a nutshell the message was 'all for one and one for all'.

The chairman, Jim May, who with Tony Pigott, Robin Marlar and one or two others had been a largely unsung architect of the revolution that overturned the well-meaning but complacent old Sussex committee before the 1998 season, issued a generously worded tribute to Robin, calling him 'a fantastic servant to the club over fifteen years' who had played a vital role in their success and was also 'one of the genuinely nicest guys in the game'.

That was pleasant to read and so were the national averages at the end of the season. Robin was second in the batting, with six Test batsmen immediately below him, having scored 629 runs in 13 innings, mainly on lively green pitches; and 17th in the bowling, having taken 30 first-class wickets at 19 runs each in his nine games. Sussex were top of the second division when he left and they duly finished as champions of that division, thus bouncing back at once to the top grade that they had left the previous year mainly because of weariness while contending for all the one-day titles simultaneously.

26

PLAYING THE GAME

*I am batting against Guildford on the ground where Surrey play
each season. Their county second XI fast bowler Eric Neller is thun-
dering in again with heavy tread and angled run, like John Price of
Middlesex. It is a half-volley, swinging away towards the slips. He
usually curves it like a banana from his hand, sometimes to catch the
edge but on this day, for once, always the middle of my bat. It is one
of those rare occasions when it seems the simplest thing in the world
to stroke the ball sweetly through extra cover for another four because
my feet are moving into the right place without thinking. I have
made a hundred against the Old Cheltonians for the Marlborough
Blues earlier in the week and I have seldom been in form like this
before. Never will be again, in fact, for I shall never have so much
time to play as I did in these carefree summer vacations.*

I remember that week so well, I think, because usually I lacked
confidence in my batting. I saw demons in opposing fast bowlers
that I was quite capable of dealing with, but it is fatal to go into
bat thinking about them. It was the biggest reason for not making
the most of what I had been given, and also the main reason for
my pride in the way that Robin overcame the same doubts. It is a

cliché but I strong mind is crucial in sport. Mine has usually been weak, even now when I think too much about a three-foot putt.

I once lost a three-set tennis singles at school when I had been six-love, five-love in front. The Australian cricket captain Steve Waugh used to speak of applying mental disintegration on his opponents: mine was usually self-inflicted.

I have been more or less as thin as a palm tree since I was about sixteen. Until then I might almost have been described as well-built. For a few happy years I was incapable, it seemed, of bowling a ball anywhere other than straight at the middle stump and therefore returned analyses such as eight for 16 for my prep school. The *St.Bede's Chronicle* records that I took 55 wickets from 173 overs at an average of 5.5 in first XI games in 1958 and scored 352 runs at 39.1. According to the report M-J 'captained the side very well. His knowledge of the game and his keenness were an inspiration to the rest of the team.' That sort of thing tends to go to your head.

The trouble was that my head got further away from my body when belated puberty arrived and I never again enjoyed the same natural accuracy with my bowling.

If I have a serious regret it is that following the game professionally has left too little time to play it myself. Most of us, whatever our age, go out to play cricket in the hope of winning, scoring a hundred and taking a large handful of wickets. Ironically for those who regularly experience all these joys, the challenge of the game is rather different. Peter May, still generally regarded as the finest English batsman to have started his career after the Second World War, once told me that he finally stopped playing the game because it was too much of a strain to be expected to score a hundred every time.

Peter did his bit after retiring early from the first-class game with a glittering average of 51 and 85 centuries, 13 of them for England. He played some club cricket and various charity matches after that but, essentially a shy and modest man, he found it hard work being a celebrity and the centre of attention.

He was not, of course, in any way typical. The majority of us want to go on playing as long as possible, fondly imagining, perhaps, that we are still improving. Alas, age cannot be denied. There are examples of remarkable cricketers who have somehow kept themselves fit and supple enough to play regular cricket at an advanced age – the former Bedfordshire wicket-keeper David Money, for example, played regularly until he died in his eighties and so too did another amateur keeper, the renowned cricketing scholar Gerald Howat – but for most of us the flesh becomes weaker (or fleshier) no matter how willing the spirit.

Cricket is often used as a metaphor for life and there is no doubt that in both the ideal combination is one of youthful virility and the wisdom that can only come from experience. Ah, that supple movement that once came so easily! It was W.G. himself who said that he gave the game up finally because the ground began to seem too far away. I remember thinking as a young bowler that I would stop playing when I even threatened to become one of those stiff-backed mid-offs who would feebly fail to get down quickly enough to cut off a firm drive from one's bowling that ought to have been gathered up effortlessly in two swift-swooping hands.

What a joy it was to feel on top of the job in the field, threatening destruction to any batsman who contemplated risking a run! Or to bowl with barely a hint of stiffness or pain. Or to go out to bat in one of those occasional patches of form when it all seemed easy.

Memory does not erase – but does tend to push to the back of the mind – the days of dreadful self-doubt, when opposing fast bowlers seemed much fiercer than they were; or when the stiff arm would keep dropping the ball short, with inevitable consequences; or when that steepling catch seemed eminently missable; or when that fast-travelling slip catch did nothing but sting the outside of a tentative hand as it moved too late to the blood-red bullet hurtling in a blur somewhere to right or left.

All that Robin achieved, of course, I should love to have done myself. I enjoyed my brief, belated flirtation with county cricket but most of the games I played after leaving school were for local club sides – Cranleigh before I married, Albury and Horsham later – and for wandering sides, including MCC, Free Foresters, the Arabs, I Zingari and the Marlborough Blues.

There was always an enjoyable OM cricket week at the school in July, comprising two-day matches and a boozy night or two after which the phenomenon of 'pillow spin' was too often experienced when one finally got to bed. My purple patch occurred, I think, in the summer after I had left Marlborough, 1964. A Blue was predicted for me but the debilitating failure of confidence returned as an undergraduate, notably one day in the freshman nets at Fenner's in April when I knew I was being watched from behind the nets by the captain, Ray White (Cambridge, Transvaal and Gloucestershire) and George Cox, the wise old Sussex professional who coached Cambridge at the start of the summer term.

For some inexplicable reason my feet would not move and I failed to get into line against an unexceptional quick bowler, a failing more likely to occur to me personally in the constricted space of a net than in the middle. No doubt they made up their mind then that I was not made of the right stuff, an opinion probably enhanced when I suffered a migraine shortly after receiving a painful blow on the knee during one of the trials.

I do mean migraine, not headache. Since adolescence I have suffered occasionally from the classical form, partially losing my sight before the onset first of flashing lights, then of the 'blinding' headache. For many years I used also to be physically sick, several times, before the attack would begin to go away but the discovery of the drug imogran put a stop to that and helped towards swifter recovery. I discovered far too late that dehydration made an attack much more likely, especially on the cricket field or golf course.

It was, naturally, much easier to excel at cricket when the mind was as free of care as it was as a student on vacation and, of course, when pitches were as good as they usually were at Marlborough in July. But I shall never forget the extraordinary sight of the black and yellow bruises that covered a line down the left side of Jake Seamer's torso when he changed in the dressing room after playing for the Marlborough Blues against the Eton Ramblers. The pitch had become damp after rain and then begun to dry under a hot sun, the classic formula for bowlers of all types. Eton had the Wiltshire captain Ian Lomax, a brawny local farmer, who had 'run off' with Henry Blofeld's first wife, Joanna. (Henry's first two wives were both called Joanna, which, given his tendency to muddle names, was convenient for him.) He was too hostile and physically dangerous in these conditions for most of the Blues but Jake, by then well past fifty, bravely held the fort.

The fastest bowlers I personally encountered were C.S. Smith of Cambridge and Lancashire and the young Bob Willis. Smith, knighted for his services to architecture, had a Fred Trueman-like action with a long final drag and several witnesses reckoned him to be as quick as Trueman. He played against Cranleigh CC every year, either for MCC or for Peter Wreford's XI.

One or other was a fixture in alternate years in Cranleigh's own very enjoyable cricket week, played on the vast flat

'Common' that staged a widely popular tennis tournament every August.

I had my successes against Smith, scoring a hundred against him and some less exalted bowlers in one of these games, but on another occasion he greeted me with a bouncer which I managed to hook for six over square-leg, only for my cap to fall onto the stumps and dislodge a bail. I walked reluctantly as everyone said 'bad luck' but the square-leg umpire, Harry Hodges, later told me that he would have given me not out on the grounds that my stroke had been completed when the cap came off.

Against Willis my fall was rather less noble. I hung around for a while as this deceptively awkward looking young beanpole, mop-haired, silent and mean, ran through Cranleigh playing for the Cobham club, Avorians. At the time he was starting to make his first appearances for Surrey and either that winter or the next one he was called out to reinforce Ray Illingworth's side in Australia, starting his often under-rated international career with immediate aplomb. My streaky innings against him ended with a top-edged cut to fly-slip. Two of my team-mates, John Vallins, later headmaster of Chetham's, the renowned music school in Manchester, and Eddie Harper, a noted musician himself, got behind the high bounce of Willis's short balls more stoutly than I had.

It was strange I found, when facing fast bowling, how sometimes one could summon the necessary will and sometimes not. That was true of batting generally. The best innings I ever played, I think, was in a Foresters match at Vincent Square in Westminster when, opening the batting, I rattled to fifty in the first few overs of the match before, all too characteristically, offering a catch to extra-cover and departing with the knowledge that I could have scored many more with a little more application. That day, however, I had played by instinct and certainly above myself, one reason, perhaps, why I suffered a paralysing migraine almost as soon as I got back to the pavilion.

I had another miserable attack soon after another of my better innings, in a final of the Surrey twenty-over competition, the competitively fought evening knockout tournament started after the war and named after the wives of the founders. The 'Flora Dora', like any knockout sporting competition, always gave scope for giant-killing and I was on a winning side in the final twice, first for Cranleigh, then for Albury, both smaller clubs than the like of, for example, Guildford and Farnham.

Our Cranleigh side, circa 1963 to 1973, had some very good cricketers, including (apart from Peter May's rare appearances) the genial Cliff Eede; a brilliant stocky little wicket-keeper in Peter Adams; the Surrey second XI all-rounder Rod Turrell, who could have succeeded as a professional; and John Bushen, a left-handed batsman of rare talent who would undoubtedly have starred for Surrey had he wanted to do so. The club could call on staff from the adjacent public school and often did so. John Holdstock was a regular, a stuffy opening bat who seldom failed. Peter Carroll, on his way from Sydney to get a double Blue at Oxford before becoming, amongst other achievements, an extrovert captain of Royal St. George's Golf Club, played for a season before getting a strong taste for socially less eclectic clubs like IZ and the Arabs. The village team had also been strengthened from time to time by the imposing hitter Nigel Paul, briefly of Warwickshire, and Ian Campbell, who as a schoolboy at Canford in the mid-1940s had scored more than 1000 runs in successive seasons.

Only one of our occasional players more or less guaranteed a victory, however: Andrew Corran, a genuinely fast bowler of great craft who had taken the new ball for Oxford and Nottinghamshire. Andrew was master-in-charge of cricket at the school in most of the years when I managed (captained) the MCC side there, as I later did at Charterhouse and Marlborough. He was a genial man of civilised tastes whose wife, Gay, mixed beauty and wealth with great talent as an artist. His first concern at one of those MCC games was to make sure that a barrel of King and Barnes Sussex bitter was available to the opposition at all times. No doubt there was more than one motive, but the ample supply of ale seldom prevented one of my regular players, John MacDonald, from luring the schoolboys to destruction with highly flighted leg-breaks. John was a British Airways pilot who had retired early to play and watch as much cricket as he could. He died of a heart attack at Lord's shortly before the start of the first Test of the famous series against Australia in 2005, having queued from early in the morning to get his favourite place in the pavilion.

Leg-spinners of any quality always flourished in the club cricket that I played. A clever little bowler from Middlesex, Stuart Feldman, took shoals of wickets for the Old Paulines and so, for the Old Alleynians and Wimbledon, did Simon Dyson, who, unlike the other two, did not rely on flight but on quick, fizzing leg-breaks and googlies. He so impressed Trevor Bailey when he played with him in the Cricketer Cup that Trevor said immediately that England should take him on tour.

Generally club cricket was a batsman's game, however, none the worse played as it is still in 'jazz hat' cricket when the norm is for the side batting first to declare at around half-way in the match with somewhere between 250 and 275 on the board, then to set the opposition the challenge of getting the runs. There was seldom a bad game when played in this positive, as opposed to aggressive, spirit and spinners always played their part. I lost count of games that culminated in the side batting second hanging on for a tense draw with nine wickets down, although another leg-spinner, the Cambridge Blue Mike Kirkman, has never forgotten my bowling him with the final ball of a match between Albury and the Old Alleynians. He and his last wicket partner had held on for half an hour. To my final flighted off-break he played a forward defensive of exaggerated care, only for the ball to trickle back under his bat and gently to remove a single bail. From the fielding side's perspective at least, it was richly comical.

Of course pitches could be too good. Playing for the Arabs against the Bradfield Waifs at Bradfield one day I chased leather in the field all morning and early afternoon while the home side scored 221 for one in 62 overs. The Arabs, with their Etonian openers Rupert Daniels and Clive Williams both scoring centuries, knocked off the runs for the loss of one late wicket in thirty-six overs.

Many a wandering club, like the Arabs, was started by a group of cricketing friends, among them the oldest extant club of them all, I Zingari; but none, so far as I know, set out, as the Willow Warblers did, in 1991, with the intention of playing a maximum of 100 matches. That was the plan when Tom Bristowe and his brother, Mike, the youngest of four cricketing brothers at Charterhouse of whom Will, an Oxford Blue in 1984 and 1985, was best known, decided to start a team to play occasional matches with and against cricketers they liked.

Along the way they had immense fun, playing against long-established clubs such as IZ, Free Foresters, Arabs, Butterflies and Sussex Martlets, and on some of the most beautiful grounds in southern England. In all the Warblers played 81 games, involving just 57 members, including five who were still playing in county cricket when the experiment ended exactly as intended. Tom, the club's driving force except during the two years that he spent with an American merchant bank in New

York, decided to draw stumps, true to the original intention, as soon as it became harder to find teams of the right strength for what had rapidly became rather an impressive fixture list. Busy working lives, marriage and the responsibilities, in some cases, of fatherhood had begun to get in the way of playing.

The Warblers were always a genial bunch of cricketers, attempting to be true to their 'cardinal' virtues of prudence, courage, temperance and justice, but they were always competitive. Their greatest success on the field occurred in glorious surroundings at Wormsley, where as strong a team as could be mustered, including several former Oxbridge and Durham players, overcame a Paul Getty XI replete with current and former first-class cricketers. Great philanthropist as he was, the late Sir Paul, and those who handpicked his teams, preferred to win: it was the only time the Warblers were not asked to renew a fixture.

I was lucky enough not only to play in the first game at Wormsley, but also to be the first man to make a fifty there. Opening the batting for Sir Paul's team against an MCC side with some notable cricketers, including the Indian Test spinner Dilip Doshi, I was sufficiently inspired by the truly perfect surroundings and the considerable crowd to play a decent innings. This was one of several occasions in similar matches – the others usually for charity – that I have deliberately given my wicket away, although in this case the sacrifice had something to do with the attraction of being able to linger with Judy and other guests over the lunch of salmon, Chablis, strawberries and cream.

My later home-based club cricket was played at Horsham in the sylvan surroundings of Cricket Field Road and on pitches that, season in, season out, have always been amongst the best in the country. Not only was the company of fellow Horsham cricketers congenial – if, occasionally, a bit rough – but the benign batting conditions were ideal for someone like me whose job meant only occasional games, many of them for the mid-week 'Thursday XI'.

Sussex have played in most seasons at Horsham for more than a hundred years and one knew there would be a hard, well-prepared pitch. Opponents always wanted to put out as strong a side as possible here, especially in those days before cricket leagues came south. Sunday matches were often more important than Saturday ones and in one such game, playing for Cranleigh in the 1960s, a beautiful high summer's day, I managed to get to ninety-six before I was caught and bowled to the genuine dismay of the wicket-keeper. All the way through my innings he had kept up a complimentary running commentary from behind the stumps. He was John Dew, the local doctor.

Wicket-keepers, as all cricketers know, are a devious lot, generally speaking. There are those who reckon that John's constant banter – he would stand up to everyone except the quickest bowlers – was designed to aid the Horsham cause. Actually, it was just his natural enthusiasm, which is not to say that he wasn't a very competitive cricketer, a brilliant wicket-keeper and a useful batsman, especially when the chips were down, who had played for Sussex second XI and for the full County team, against Worcestershire and Warwickshire, in 1947.

Very few men have spread such joy on and off a cricket field anywhere. It was his happy destiny (and his choice) to live virtually all his life in Horsham, most of it spent in his surgery, singing in the church choir, or on that lovely ground. Cricket was not his only passion. He had captained his school, Tonbridge, at rugby, and he gave as much time to his Christian faith, his family and to developing a deep appreciation for music and nature. When he died of cancer in 2008 the large and beautiful parish church of St. Mary's that separates the ground from the prettiest street in the town was literally over-brimming with those who had come to say goodbye to their beloved GP.

He had been president of the cricket club for forty-four years. He had irrepressible enthusiasm and instant, utterly genuine charm, emphasised by a hearty laugh. I can see and hear him now beside the pavilion at Cricket Field Road, or on the adjoining greensward leading up towards Denne Hill, aptly known now as the John Dew Ground. His rasping voice would offer encouragements and admonitions to all the young cricketers under his wing at any of the thousands of matches or weekday practice sessions that he organised with a small army of helpers:

Good shot, Michael!

Well done, Christine!

What happened to that bat of yours, Harry? You're supposed to hit the ball with it, not drop it. Well done, though. What a good innings!

Five wickets, Angela. Really? Gosh, they must have been useless batsmen!

He knew exactly when to build young cricketers up, when gently to make fun of them, when to give them wise advice, how to make them feel involved: above all, magically, who they all were, not just their own names and characters but also the names of their mothers and fathers, even of their brothers and sisters. He loved cricket but he also loved and respected people of all types and ages.

The same was true of Sandy Ross, another Sussex man with whom I played a lot of cricket, not least for MCC because, despite an active family life and his employment as an effective manager of a chain of roadside catering establishments (and later as a school bursar and cricket coach), he was always available for any of the matches that I managed. His open, freckled face was regularly lit by the warmest smile of anyone I have known. He seemed either to play or watch cricket every day of every English summer.

Built not unlike Alec Bedser and blessed with huge hands with which he could cut and swing the ball even when he got heavier in his middle age, Sandy took shoals of wickets for all the many clubs that he represented, including all ten for only twenty-six in a Sussex League match for East Grinstead. He was only sixty-one when he collapsed and died instantly of a heart attack when he was fielding in a match for the Sussex Martlets. Again an unusually large parish church, East Grinstead, was full to the brim to say farewell.

Apart from a holiday appearance when I was still a schoolboy, for Oporto against Lisbon in Portugal's annual expatriate 'Test' match, the first cricket that I ever played overseas was in South Africa during my gap year. I was largely unsuccessful, frequently getting stumped, but I had my successes for media teams in later years, including one at the Cable & Wireless ground in Barbados against a team captained by the former Test batsman Peter Lashley. For some reason I forgot my youthful inhibitions about hitting the ball in the air and repeatedly enjoyed the satisfaction of smiting a medium pacer back over his head for six, greatly helped by a strong wind behind me. There was also a small triumph in Sydney when I was presented with a genuine bronze medal of the type issued to men of the match in events sponsored by Benson and Hedges. I had taken some wickets and made the top score as our motley crew regained the 'Ash'. This made a pleasant contrast to a humiliating experience at a Birmingham League ground on the rest day of a Test at Edgbaston when I broke a bone in my hand missing a caught and bowled chance, then foolishly batted before going to hospital for an X-ray. In agony I soon missed a straight ball from the Aussie media's opening bowler, Martin Blake. An Australian news team was filing the game in the hope of a bit of fun at Pommie expense and duly found the ideal clip for the closing item of their evening news bulletin: 'The Pommie media did no better than their Test team when they lost to the Aussies in "Birming-ham", helped by this beauty from Martin Blake which sent famous commenator Chris Martin-Jenkins back to the pavilion for a sorry duck.' No mention of the agonising broken bone, naturally.

These were games of no importance, of course, to anyone except those involved, which is true of almost all amateur cricket, but they matter at the time. I enjoyed scoring runs in benefit matches because it gave me the chance to show the professionals that I could play a bit too. Over the years I enjoyed myself in Malta, Corfu and Dubai – in all these cases relishing the even bounce provided by smooth concrete pitches – not to mention India, Pakistan, Australia, New Zealand, South Africa and the West Indies.

All this was not a bad consolation for not playing the game professionally. Like Lord Cobham, who preferred batting against his own bowling to 'eating pâté de fois gras to the sound of trumpets' as his definition of heaven, I was a better batsman than bowler. It therefore came as a pleasant surprise to discover, when I was asked recently if I had ever got a Test batsman out, that over the years I can remember dismissing nine of them, excluding Enid Bakewell, star of an England ladies' tour of Australia. Some of the men were better batsmen than others: Paul Hibbert and Bobby Simpson (Australia); Tony Greig,

Graham Roope, Richard Hutton and Angus Fraser (England); John Morrison (New Zealand); and Alvin Kallicharran and Ranjie Nanan (West Indies).

I was not, of course, fit to tie the bootlaces of any of them but it is amazing what anyone can achieve by being in the right place at the right time!

27

FROM CRICKET TO GOLF

Old cricketers turn to golf. Very few of them become any good at it, including me, but many of us grow to love it almost as much. Except in foursomes, the best form of the game, it lacks the element of team involvement provided by cricket, but it offers most of the other challenges, especially the mental ones. Cricket requires a batsman to strike a moving ball, golf only a stationary one, but both games reward strategic thinking, presence of mind, concentration and, perhaps above all, confidence.

Having shamelessly bragged about all those soft Test victims, I can now reveal with no less pride that not long ago I finally did a hole in one, at the age of sixty-five (an eighteen-hole score that I can only dream about). Naturally, I exclude the 'aces' that I achieved quite often on my self-made garden 'course' at home, when I regularly used to plop them in on the sixth, the famous pond hole, sometimes even first bounce out of the pond itself. When it came to doing the real thing, however, no one was looking.

I was playing all by myself shortly before sunset on a fine Sunday evening at Kooyonga, a course of high quality at Adelaide where Don Bradman used to play and with which my own home club, West Sussex, has reciprocal rights.

Approaching the 167-metre (183-yard) seventh in a relaxed frame of mind, but with no great expectation following my customary mixture of poor and decent strikes on earlier holes, I knew that I had hit a four iron as well as I could. The ball, a Precept 'Laddie' bought from the Pro an hour earlier in case I should lose a few, disappeared over a rise at the front of the green, heading for the flag. It was, however, an unprecedented pleasure to find it lodged between the bottom of the pin and the inside of the hole. There was only one other person on the course, a local with whom I shared the startling news in case he should feel like a free drink afterwards. 'Well done', he said. 'Unfortunately I don't think it counts.'

It was less satisfactory than it must have been for Ronnie Aird, one-time secretary and later president of MCC, at the other course where I am lucky enough to be a member, Royal St. George's at Sandwich. Having, like Tony Jacklin on a different occasion, holed in one at the 16th, he turned to his opponent, who was just preparing himself to try to follow him in by some miracle, and said: 'I'm sorry, but I think that's my hole.' He had been in receipt of a stroke.

Jacklin's ace at the Dunlop Masters is much better known, naturally. It more or less guaranteed his tournament victory and set him on the course for the glorious double of the Open and the US Open in the same year. He was regaled in the bar afterwards by a rather superior member of Royal St. George's. 'You're Jacklin, aren't you', the man of the moment was asked.

'Yes, Sir.'

'Did a hole in one at the 16th I hear.'

'Yes, Sir.'

'Well done. What club did you use?'

'Six iron, Sir.'

'Six iron? Wrong club.'

Would that I had such confidence in my golfing opinion. I have always been prone to self-doubt about my swing, no doubt extremely well founded. Time is running out if I am to get much lower than my present handicap of fourteen, twice that of my younger brother's and ten more than my elder son's. Both of them played much more than I did as young men and there is no doubt that the earlier you learn the mechanics of the golf swing the better.

Golf was always the best means of getting away from the grind of a cricket tour. I had some tense battles over the years with, amongst others, John Thicknesse and Vic Marks, with whom I once got stuck on New Year's Eve after a titanic battle at Royal Cape Town Golf Club. The staff had gone home early and had locked the clubhouse, leaving us with no option but to climb onto a flat roof and clamber down the other side into the car park. Knowing South Africa's obsession with crime and security it is a wonder that we did not set off alarms loud enough to waken the dead.

Foursomes contests were even better. My partner was often Jack Bannister, the former Warwickshire seam bowler, a successful bookmaker and incisive journalist in later life and one of the most versatile men I have ever met, blessed as he was with a brain like a computer. We enjoyed many a close match against John Thicknesse and John Woodcock, although Jack and I invariably had to pay for the drinks.

Like his friend Richie Benaud, Jack was a loyal member of the media golfing teams that for many years I have assembled during Birmingham Test matches to play against Edgbaston Golf Club before breakfast, usually on the third morning of the Test. Despite the support of heavyweights such as Paul

Allott, Ian Botham and Mark Nicholas, all low-handicap golfers – even sometimes of the redoubtable Ted Dexter – most of us usually end up on the losing side, and therefore paying for our breakfasts. In one of these games I plonked my nine iron from the tee into a bunker in front of the green at the shortest hole on the course. The four of us looked on in amazement as a fox emerged from trees, trotted across to the bunker, plucked the ball into his mouth and set off into more trees on the other side.

A no less unusual incident occurred in a foursomes match against Headingley Golf Club when, at another short hole and at a critical point of an even match, I hit a decent tee-shot to the edge of the green, about a yard beyond another bunker. Thereupon my opposing driver hooked his shot from the tee deep into a wood on the left. The hole was as good as ours. I was going through the motions of helping our opponents to find their ball – clearly an impossible task but these were two Yorkshiremen – when my partner, Jack Bannister again, strolled across and said to me a little sheepishly: 'You're not going to believe this, Christopher, but our ball is now in the bunker and we have still played only one shot.'

Moving his trolley towards the ball he had inadvertently touched a rake with the wheels and the rake in turn had glanced the ball neatly into the sand. Time was pressing and I am ashamed to admit that when one of our opponents suggested that we should move on and call the hole a half (with a cunning and opportunism of which only a Tyke could have been capable) we meekly complied. Experts on the rules told me later that we should simply have replaced our ball in its original position with a penalty of one stroke.

Every autumn, at the end of the cricket season, I go to Norfolk to play with a collection of cricket writers for the 'coveted' green jacket and the Irish shillelagh awarded every year to the champion golfer of the Gibbons Golf Society. The name derives from the little-remembered Worcestershire stalwart H.H.I.H. 'Doc' Gibbons, who happened to be the first name alighted upon in a copy of *Wisden* when the honourable company who founded the Society were deciding what to call themselves.

Their first informal gathering for some end-of-season golf in Ireland soon developed into a regular annual tournament for a core of eight journalists, based in recent years at Hunstanton and Brancaster, two of the best links in England. Martin Johnson, Mike Selvey, Vic Marks, Derek Pringle and myself have been what football programmes used to refer to as the 'ever presents' of the last fifteen years or so. David 'Toff' Lloyd, former cricket correspondent of the Press Association and the *Evening Standard*, and Graham Otway, a cricket and golf writer of long experience, were two of the founding fathers, with Johnson, Selvey and the latter's long-time friend David Norman, a Londoner who settled in East Anglia and ran a successful engineering business. He has been a tireless local organiser and, in our more impecunious days, a generous host.

No one has since worn the jacket more often than Johnson, the iconoclastic writer on (mainly) cricket, rugby and golf whose articles have delighted readers of the *Independent*, the *Daily Telegraph* and the *Sunday Times*, amongst others. He never writes a piece without raising a smile, and usually a laugh, from some astute observation of the human frailities of the sportsmen he is writing about. He started his journalistic life on the *South Wales Echo* and graduated to the *Leicester Mercury*, where he persuaded the sports editor to give him a trial as the paper's cricket writer. No one has insulted so many professional sportsmen in print yet retained their affection and respect. It was he who observed of Mike Gatting's 1986/7 team, shortly before they stormed to victory in the first Test in Brisbane, that the touring team had only three problems. They couldn't bat, they couldn't bowl and they couldn't field.

That was his passport to wider fame and greater fortune, but Johnson, who plays in Gibbons tournaments under the guise of the ice-cool Swede Martin Johansson, spends much of his time these days working on the Society's website (gibbonsgolf. com) and would cheerfully spend every day of his life on a golf course somewhere. Indeed, when the former *Times* Editor Peter Stothard was interviewing him for the cricket correspondent's job on the paper, he was asked, rather earnestly, what his ambitions were. 'To retire as soon as possible and spend all my time on the golf course' was his disarmingly honest response.

I would get bored, I fear, if I were to retire completely and to play golf every day, superficially attractive though it may seem, but I am almost as keen on the game now as I was on cricket as a schoolboy. Now, as then, I do not practise enough, despite splashing out on a small artificial green at home: mainly for the benefit of my grandchildren I told my wife. When their time comes I shall tell them the truth: it is a simple game. The best advice for any golfer is to consider nothing other than watching the back of the ball and hitting through it towards the target, with the head kept firmly down until the ball has left the club.

I should leave more sophisticated thoughts about the art of the golf swing to others such as the late Walker Cup player and captain of the R and A, Michael Lunt. 'What do you think about on your back swing?' he once asked his predecessor as captain of Walton Heath, the circuit Judge John Bishop. 'I just try to watch the back of the ball', replied his Honour. Michael walked on a few yards before asking again, with a slight chuckle as if John had been joking. 'Very good. But seriously, what *do* you think about?'

There are a few golfers who operate on a higher plane than the rest of us. I am content to strive only for a bit more consistency. As the cricket-besotted Canon Lyttelton could not go down the nave of his own cathedral at Lichfield without wondering if it would take spin, so I cannot spend much time in a hotel room without getting a coat-hanger out of the cupboard and playing shots with an imaginary ball to an imaginary green. The game hooks you like that. A pity I hook the ball so often when a real fairway confronts me.

I have to be content with glory reflected from my son James, who played for two years in what must be amongst the best golf teams that Oxford University has ever produced. They overwhelmed Cambridge by thirteen points to two, a record margin, in his first match at Rye in 1994 and his team-mates in that and the following year included no fewer than six different winners of the renowned President's Putter, with ten wins between them.

Charlie Rotheroe has won the Putter three times, Tom Etridge and Richard Marrett twice, Steve Seman, Neil Pabari and Mark Benka once each. James himself reached the semi-final in 2001. I managed to see the last few holes of his quarter-final win over Marrett and, the following morning, a tense semi-final defeat against the subsequent winner from Sunningdale, Bruce Streather.

Having watched his second match as an undergraduate, at Royal Lytham & St. Annes, I already knew that watching one's offspring drive, chip or putt was as nerve-racking as seeing him bat. Anxious not to get too close and possibly thereby put him off, I was watching his very tense singles match (eventually lost by a single hole, the only point that he dropped in his four matches against Cambridge) from some way distant, trying, by standing on tiptoe, to get a view of what was happening on the green. By walking backwards a few yards towards higher ground, my eyes still locked on the middle distance, I thought that I would be able to see a bit more through a gap in the small gallery of spectators but unfortunately I over-balanced and fell backwards into a bunker. Charlie Chaplin or Norman Wisdom could not have done it better. So intent was everyone else in the drama that no one noticed my loss of dignity. Meanwhile, James missed his putt.

The golfing achievement of which he is proudest came the year after he came down from Oxford when Radley won the Halford Hewitt, the hotly contested Old Boys Championship held each April on the links of Deal and Sandwich, for the first and only time. He and Tom Etridge played as the top pair and won all but the first of their six matches.

Most of my still limited amount of golf is played on the heathery heath of the West Sussex course at Pulborough. It is a lovely piece of natural golfing country, blessed by sandy soil that keeps it open in the wettest weather. In winter especially it is one of the finest inland courses, not long but shrewdly laid out and tougher than it looks, with lovely open views to the Downs. At any time of year it is a haven of peace with none of the air or road traffic that can spoil the pleasure on other courses.

St George's at Sandwich, it is a two-ball course, so rounds take only about three hours rather than the four or so that are common at four-ball clubs. To be able to play occasionally at Royal St George's is, of course, a privilege, and usually a joy too, no matter how strongly the wind is blowing over those wild links. Soon after I had joined the club, barely knowing a course where each hole is a little world in itself amongst the dunes, I got back from reporting a match at Canterbury in time for a few evening holes. No one else was about. Even the larks had gone to bed as the dusk became deeper. I allowed myself one more hole, firing a drive into the gloaming, before setting off for the clubhouse. Two problems followed. I never found the ball and, looking in all four directions from the top of a mound, I could not for the life of me remember where the clubhouse was.

28

FAITH

A hotel room in Brisbane. Another Test starts in two days. The room is restful, decorated in soft shades of grey; and comfortable, even luxurious, but, like all hotel rooms occupied only by one person, soulless. Lying here, awake when I should be sleeping but jet-lagged and woken by a sun that has risen at 4.45 am, I take up less than a third of the huge bed.

The air conditioning hums and I wish that I could open the big, straight plate-glass window that would give to this stale room, smelling very slightly of other guests' perspiration, some fresh early morning air off the broad river below. If only it was not locked 'for reasons of health and safety'.

I am not going to throw myself out, for heaven's sake, even though I know that I should be more excited than I am by the forthcoming match, the privilege of describing it, the extreme good fortune that someone else is paying most of the bill for me while I wonder what time to descend in the lift to the warm swimming pool below to get the exercise to justify indulging in a cooked breakfast, sitting by the river.

Distance lends enchantment, certainly; and familiarity breeds, not contempt so much as a relative apathy. Thirty-six years ago, in a nasty yellow-brick motel, there were none of these luxuries but it was all a bright new adventure.

Am I wearied by too much of the same? Is it jet-lag or have I lost my focus?

·I look at the Bible notes I brought with me because gradually it seems to be getting rarer for hotels to put Bibles supplied by the Gideons in the drawer beneath the bedside lamp. 'You must constantly monitor the level of your commitment to Christ, the growth of your faith, your home life, your relationships, your integrity, your work ethic, your thoughts and your habits.' I read, and consider.

Terrible things have been done by men throughout history in the name of religion. Every time there is a tragedy – another slaughter of innocents, another heart-rending famine, another earthquake, or another person we know suddenly inflicted by some cruel and random disease – it is extremely hard to accept the conventional religious response that God is a mystery whose ways we can never understand in this existence.

'God' may not be the description that suits everyone but I feel that I have been in many ways blessed and protected on my own journey through this teeming, unjust, tragedy-strewn world. More than that, I feel that we all have an instinct to thank a great creator for the incredible beauty of nature, the astounding variety of living things and the unfathomable vastness of space.

Every time I start to doubt, I think of Blake's 'To see a world in a grain of sand, and a heaven in a wild flower, hold Infinity in the palm of your hand and Eternity in an hour'. There is no proof of a divine creation but it is extraordinary how every child of every nationality, born to a religious environment or not, smarts when he tells his first lie. We are born with a knowledge of good and evil, even if it is the way that we are brought up that shapes what we do with it.

It is much easier for those who have been blessed with a good education and time to spare to wrestle with the meaning of life, but everyone should try. I have struggled harder than some, if only to prove the truth of St. Augustine's aphorism: *Our hearts are restless until we find our rest in You.* I envy those who can simply accept that God is God and take the further step to belief in the infallibility of biblical revelation.

I used to write essays about 16th-century reformers such as Thomas Cranmer, Hugh Latimer and Nicholas Ridley. They believed that, ever since Adam, Eve and their defiance, humanity has been corrupted, and therefore that human reason can play no part in our understanding of God. Their conviction was that revelation in the Scriptures is how God has revealed himself. But the Tudor reformers represented a lacuna in the life of the Church. Most Anglicans these days would agree that the Bible, reflecting many cultures and circumstances over a long period, can be contradictory.

Much of the history that I learned at school and university, not least the Tudor period, revolved around the Church. Cruel deeds committed in the name of religious bigotry ought, perhaps, to have put me off for ever but from the moment that I felt the distinct warmth of the Holy Spirit through the touch of the Bishop of Sherborne's hands at my Confirmation in 1961 I have tried to cling to the Christian faith against a powerful urge to doubt.

It was relatively easy to aspire to a genuine faith at school, with a beautiful chapel and glorious choral music to inspire, preachers such as Father Trevor Huddleston and Antony Bridge (the once atheist Dean of Guildford) to thunder about Good and Evil from the pulpit, and the cerebral Canon Perceval Hayman, Judy's godfather, thoughtfully leading communal worship. There was, especially, something truly magical about evening prayers beneath the imposing gold reredos, especially on a warm summer's evening. Familiar words from the Book of Common Prayer have, for me, never lost their power:

'O God, from whom all holy desires, all good counsels and all just works do proceed; Give unto thy servants that peace that the world cannot give; that both our hearts may be set to obey thy commandments, and also that we, being defended from the fear of our enemies, may pass our time in rest and quietness; through the merits of Jesus Christ our Saviour. *Amen.*'

All the warm assurances of Evensong can swiftly be lost in the rush and challenge of what many would call the realities of life, but we are no different from animals if we do not make time for serious thought about the delusion, or reality, of religious faith. I know that there is no logic, let alone proof, when it comes to matters of faith. Christians, for example, pity the tragic naïvety of young men brainwashed into becoming terrorists in the name of Islam, men prepared to murder innocent people in the belief that when they, too, are blown up it will take them instantly to bed with an unlimited supply of beautiful maidens; but the same Christians profess to believe in resurrection, heaven and eternal life. There is, nonetheless, an instinct so powerful that it should not be denied. Deep down I do believe, albeit sometimes too faintly, that God exists, that there is an ultimate, unfathomable plan (now we see through a glass darkly) and that Jesus Christ led the life that everyone should try to follow.

I know that this is not the same as saying that he was and is the Son of God but the extraordinary spread of Christianity is surely proof that those who knew him and spread the word after his death were convinced of his divinity. The very improbability of Christianity may be proof of its veracity. How could a vast and enduring faith survive more than two thousand years on the very unlikely premise that the humble son of a carpenter was also the son of God, sent to redeem a lost world? The Jews, living in an occupied state, were looking for an avenging king. They were challenged instead by an obscure, humble, passive leader who preached forgiveness.

When it comes to the assertion that 'all scripture is God-breathed', it was surely impossible for reasonable minds to believe in the literal truth of the Bible even before the publication of *On the Origin of Species*. And yet, and yet. Look at a thousand natural wonders, let's say a buzzard soaring with astonishing speed beneath a high blue sky, borne by thermals like a bubble on a river. Try to deny that the sight does not stir a sense of awe that seems utterly instinctive.

Faith cannot be faith if it is discovered *only* through reason, so it has to be a matter of trust. In the words of the hymn, beloved of both weddings and funerals for its lovely tune and its beautiful words, 'In simple trust like those who heard, beside the Syrian Sea, the gracious calling of the Lord, let us like them, without a word, rise up and follow thee'.

I come back to faith again and again, even after some less than tragic setbacks of my own in recent years, including, in 2008/9, the contraction first of pneumonia, then, a year later, of acute hepatitis. I greatly admire those who can cling tenaciously to their faith when they are ill. I found it hard not to become depressed and obsessed with my temporary misfortune.

At such times, however, I recall the advice that sharing one's troubles with Christ is like throwing him a gentle catch with an orange. 'My burden is easy and my yoke light.'

The questions that arise in any reasoning mind are as old as Christian faith itself and millions of words have been written around them. In his profound but difficult book *Dynamics of Faith* Paul Tillich argued that reason, far from being inimical to faith, is the precondition of faith. 'Faith is the act in which reason reaches ecstatically beyond itself.'

The voice of doubt within me asks whether the idea that man is made in the image of God could itself be man made and whether the same might apply to the supreme claim of the Gospels that Jesus Christ is the way, the truth and the life and that no one can come to the Father by any other means. But this is the essence of the Christian faith: that you can do it only, like plunging into unknown water, by relinquishing your own puny and fallible power and trusting that the divine infallible omnipotence will hold you up. More than that: that it will give you life in greater abundance than you have ever imagined.

I can and by instinct do accept the idea of a great creator of all the utterly amazing life on earth, confusing as it may be that, so far as we know, this is the only planet with the right scientific ingredients for life in one vast universe which is itself only one of an unimaginable number of other universes, ever expanding. It boggles the mind, does it not? With many others, I'm sure, I have to say *Lord, I believe; help thou my unbelief*. But I try to say it the other way round.

29

CONFESSIONS

I have been having occasional senior moments since I was about seven.
At times my progress through life has been a struggle to keep one step
ahead of complete chaos. It might be summed up by the invoice that
I received one day in 1974 from Messrs Brady and Renaud, a long-
established firm of electrical contractors in Cranleigh, which read:
   Call to Old Harry's Cottage, East Clandon, to investigate faulty
dishwasher.
   Trace to switch in 'Off' position   £10.00

I have always been prone to aberrations like this, one reason
why punctuality has always been a struggle. That John Cleese
film *Clockwork*, in which his normal punctuality was foiled by
a number of little time-wasting setbacks leading to personal
calamity, spoke eloquently for me. As a friend once said, 'Things
do tend to happen to you, Christopher.'

Only on my last tour of New Zealand in 2008, for example
(by which time I ought to have been beyond repeating mistakes
on my laptop, my journalistic lifeline), I managed, by the erro-
neous push of a single key, somehow to erase forever the lengthy
Test preview article on which I had been working all day. It was

late at night by this time and I am afraid it was too much for me, one-eighth Portuguese as I am. Cleese in his Basil Fawlty mode could not have bettered the cries of anguish that rent the hotel corridor, nor torn so many hairs from his head.

As I have found from a few previous examples of this particular personal debacle, the worst thing about it is that it happens when you are very tired. For at least half an anguished hour afterwards, the brain is frozen by the awful realisation that the words have gone and cannot be recovered, ever, by any means, even by recourse to the best technical computer brains. You can therefore not remember how you started your piece, let alone how it went on. At least, on this occasion, unlike the one in Jamaica, I was not up against a deadline.

The point is, though, that I am often lucky as well. To give only one of many examples, on one occasion I dropped the keys of my hired car through the railing of a bridge besides which the car was parked. It is debatable whether it would have been better to drop the mobile phone, the notebook, the sunglasses or the hot cup of coffee, all of which I was also carrying at the time, but it happened that the keys fell towards a local professional cricketer passing below the bridge, who caught and returned them and in the proceeding conversation gave me some very interesting information that I would never otherwise have acquired.

It led to one of my rare journalistic 'scoops', most of them acquired more by luck than by industry and because cricketers and cricket people have trusted me with information. If my reputation for absent-mindedness has been exaggerated, I cannot deny that I have muddled my way to some sort of prominence in my field despite the truth that some days of my life can be a little like a sit-com starring Michael Crawford.

Long ago I learned to plan ahead and to rely on a well-filled diary, but as the Scottish bard observed, the best-laid schemes . . . I generally hit my head on a low beam, or forget where I put my glasses, or arrive a minute late for whatever I'm doing next because, despite the best intention of leaving a reasonable amount of time to get to the next assignment, I have received a phone-call just as I depart, then got behind a tractor, then missed the first train and finally got on one that sits outside Victoria for ten minutes because of a signal failure.

It really is not always my fault. During an October holiday in Corfu a few years ago Judy and I were taken by our hosts, Robin and Rosemary Gourlay, on a day-trip to Albania to see the outstanding Greek and Roman remains at Butrint. There is a ferry that takes passengers across to the south-western Albanian port of Saranda, which was still full of run-down, bullet-strewn buildings. Once driven in a smart Range Rover, by Robin's impressive local contact, through the countryside and across a gentle river on an old-fashioned chain-ferry, the country's natural charm outweighed the terrible legacy of Communist rule. We spent a happy late morning and early afternoon inspecting the World Heritage site, aware that we needed to be back in good time for the return ferry to Corfu at half past four.

Up swept our vehicle onto the quayside some fifteen minutes before the carefully checked time of departure. But there was consternation as the passports were inspected. The ferry had just departed. There it was, a blob halfway to the horizon, gradually receding into a speck. Now Robin Gourlay, a sometime director of BP, spoke excellent Greek and immediately assumed command of the crisis. He demanded to be put in immediate touch with the captain of the ferry. It happened that another Greek ferry had hit a quayside a few days before, with disastrous results, allegedly because of an inebriated skipper. Making use of the fact that he was accompanied by 'a very well-known writer on *The Times*', he thundered down the line that there would be more abysmal publicity for Greek merchant shipping unless he immediately turned the boat round and came back to fetch us.

The ferry had undoubtedly left early, having seen no one waiting on the quay, but it was still a remarkable, and gratifying, sight to see the captain obeying orders and steaming back towards us. The other passengers, including the former chief sports sub on the *Telegraph*, Brian Stater and his wife, were not exactly pleased to have to return to Albania and start their journey afresh. But we were given free cups of tea for our inconvenience.

I bumped into Brian and his wife again a few days later when I emerged from the ocean on a beach where they were strolling in isolation. I must have looked like a drowned rat, having plucked up courage to swim in the calm waters from one bay to another, albeit careful to keep within my depth in case my stamina failed me. 'You remember that James Bond scene, where Daniel Craig comes out of the water?' Brian later related: 'Well, it was nothing like that.'

Those who have heard me commentate on cricket in calm and reflective mode may think that I was exaggerating when I said that my life is really a well-concealed comedy. But it is true. It has, for example, been well documented (and grossly embroidered) by my writing and golfing friend Mike Selvey and others, that I once came down to the foyer of a hotel on the north coast of Jamaica with my suitcases in hand and my bill paid, ready to drive across the island to Kingston. As Mike and I were about to leave in the same hired car I decided to make a call to my office. To my irritation, none of the numbers that I pressed seemed to respond in the normal way. I had pulled out of my pocket not the said mobile, which was sitting upstairs on a table, but the television remote control from my just vacated room.

A few years ago I started a hue and cry at home because my mobile was missing again. My wife and daughter were enlisted to search the house from top to bottom. No good, so I rang my office at *The Times* and asked them to cancel the sim card forthwith. Another phone was posted to me and when it arrived three days later I had one more search before donning my golf shoes to play some practice shots in the garden. Something hard under the sock in my left shoe turned out, of course, to be the missing article.

30

CRISES – AND CONSOLATIONS

We all have a mixture of good and bad luck, but one of the arts of life is not to take them too deeply to heart. I find it hard. Unlike the insurance company in the advertisement of a few years ago, I fear that I do tend to make a drama out of a crisis.

There have been a few, too. I have told of the terrifying day in Jamaica when I lost my front- and back-page stories with one touch of a single letter on the keyboard of my laptop, and of the theft of my briefcase at Gatwick Airport as I was leaving for a tour of the Caribbean. But these were not completely isolated examples. I had twice had other laptops stolen in my time as *Daily Telegraph* correspondent, once from the back of my locked car, parked near Hammersmith Bridge in London, the second time from the Media Centre at Lord's on the very day that the sparkling new press box was being used by journalists for the first time

There was, eventually a happier outcome – up to a point – when another of my briefcases was stolen overnight from my car, which had been parked overnight in the drive of Brian Johnston's house in Boundary Road on the eve of the 1982 Nat West Cup final at Lord's. This was a particularly smart case, made of leather and sable skin, which had been presented to me and to all the other members of a cricket tour to Dubai, including the former England cricketers Mike Denness and John Snow. On this occasion there was, as I recall, nothing of great value inside other than my driving licence, my glasses and some other personal items, plus pages of proofs for the next edition of *The Cricketer* and other articles of great professional importance to me.

I informed the local police, naturally, who gave me leave to mention my loss during my radio commentary on the final later that day. I asked on the air for the case to be returned to me if possible, especially as there were things inside of much significance to me but little to anyone else. The following afternoon I was commentating for BBC television on a John Player League game at Chelmsford when my wife answered the phone to a man who wanted to speak to me. Judy said that I would be back later in the evening and asked who was speaking. He was, he said, ringing on behalf of a 'friend' who had found the briefcase. She expressed her relief and asked if he could take it to a police station, since its loss had been reported. His friend could not do that, he replied. He wasn't very nice and he might smash the glasses and throw the driving licence and the papers away. He thought that he might want some kind of reward for their safe return, too.

He rang off then but when I got home Judy told me about the call and I rang Paddington Green Police Station for advice. They told me that if he rang back I should try to arrange to meet him in a public place and to tell him that I would be prepared to pay money for the safe return of the case and its contents. Sure enough, he did ring back late that night and we arranged to meet at Victoria railway station the following afternoon. We agreed a specific train from Redhill, and a meeting just beyond the ticket barrier of the relevant platform. I gave him a description of what I would be wearing and we agreed a sum of money, I forget now precisely what.

With some trepidation on the next day I duly cashed a cheque for the money – £100 I think, worth rather more then – and caught something like the 3.36 from Redhill. Not untypically, I very nearly missed the train and had to make a dash along the platform to catch it. Once inside it was as if I were in an Agatha Christie film. To me the detectives, three of them as I recall, were fairly obvious by their macintoshes and newspapers; somehow not your typical afternoon travellers from Surrey to London. But the train was on time and, with butterflies churning inside, I allowed most of the other passengers to precede me before making my way to the barrier, discreetly accompanied by the men in macs. On the other side of the barrier a tall, pale-faced, youngish man was waiting with some papers in a polythene bag. There was no sign of the briefcase, alas. 'I thought you had the case', I said to him. 'The papers are here', he said. (Some were, some weren't, and my glasses and driving licence had gone.) 'OK', I said: 'Here is the money.' The moment that he took the envelope and exchanged the polythene bag, a uniformed policeman seemed to appear from nowhere in support of the detectives and the arrest was made.

It was all quite dramatic and so, in a no less nerve-racking way, was the subsequent trial at the Old Bailey when the oddest thing was that the thief and I had to wait to give evidence in the same room. I could not help wondering if he would want revenge, whatever the verdict. He was found guilty of demanding money with menaces and sentenced, with other crimes taken into account, to a jail sentence of, if I remember correctly, three years. Like many of his kind, he seemed more a sad than a vicious character.

Cars were less secure then and perhaps all of us are more security conscious. Some of these accidents of life are avoidable, some not. My unfortunate bout of E. coli poisoning in Mumbai was a case of the wrong sort. If only I had been able to leave at the planned time. But, then, as so often, I seemed to have a little bit more work to do than most other people. Rightly or wrongly, I had put doing a good job before having a good time.

It was William Haley, the renowned *Times* Editor, who said: 'hard writing, easy reading'. I don't know whether the thousands of articles about cricket that I have churned out over the years, many hundreds of cricket reports in my BBC days and more than a handful of books on cricket have been easy to read but it is certain that an awful lot of sweat was shed in preparing them.

Conscientiousness, the assiduous approach, has been for me both a reason for achieving, but also a bar to fun and relaxation. My poor wife has despaired of my constant failures to hold good to my intention to leave five minutes earlier or to get to the table in good time for a lovingly cooked hot meal. I have always seemed to have something to finish.

One form of happiness for me is a clear desk, one I have seldom enjoyed. I suspect, however, that the alternative is almost as bad. Relaxation is for habitual relaxers but to the workaholic it can seem like boredom. I have had some wonderful days sitting by the sea with a good book in places such as Barbados, but I can never sit still for long before plunging in for a swim.

At home, although energy levels are not what they were, the urge soon comes to hit a ball or to go for a walk with the dog, especially the latter since Pepper, a gentle Border Collie bitch who has been a paragon since puppyhood, came into our lives when we moved back to Tismans Common in 2005.

The real truth, I think, is not that I have been an exceptionally hard worker but rather a slow one, a bit of a perfectionist and someone determined to fit sixty seconds into a minute.

When we were paying for our children's education financial worries were perennial, as they are for most people. Somehow, however, they did not have the debilitating effect that they did for more than a year after our decision, in 2004, to downsize our living quarters as a means of supplying a capital sum to put towards my pension when I retired as cricket correspondent of *The Times*.

We found what we believed to be the ideal solution in the same parish, Rudgwick, that we had lived in for twenty-five years. Arun Cottage, once owned by the gifted actress Julie Walters and her husband, is pretty and practical, a Victorian cottage that was less secluded and had much smaller rooms than Naldrett, but which still has a rural aspect, enough room for a tennis court and a full-pitch shot and the capacity to cater for at least some of an expanding family at such times as Christmas and Easter.

Our old house, with its handsome Georgian frontage, lovely position and forty-two acres, albeit most of them rather poor fields, should have sold well, but timing is everything in the buying and selling of houses, as it is in most things. The market was just at the start of its downturn for houses in that sort of price bracket and a quick sale was ruled out by the fact that we had not been able to afford to modernise it as we should have done to attract well-heeled Londoners looking to move to the country. I was badly advised about its realistic value.

The sale of Naldrett House took more than a year. The consequence was a combined mortgage and bridging loan that rapidly dwindled our savings and gnawed away at the minds of Judy and me like the sea at a piece of flimsy coastline. General doubt about the economy had taken hold and no one seemed prepared to take the plunge that we had.

It was hard to relax and have faith that it would all come right. Several times a sale seemed tantalisingly close, especially when a Rudgwick family we greatly liked seemed genuinely tempted. Eventually I gave our original agents a deadline beyond which we would switch to another firm. Within two days two originally interested parties were bidding against each other again, albeit at a level some way below even the latest estimates of the house's value. Judy and I knew that the engaging Scottish family who eventually bought the house were the ones who really wanted it, because we had personally kept in touch with them. The relief was intense when Judy rang me in May 2005 whilst I was working at The Oval to say that contracts had finally been exchanged. It all worked out well in the end. We have been extremely happy at Arun Cottage.

Followers of English cricket will remember well that strange tour early in 2009 when everything seemed to go wrong for England. The captain and coach, Kevin Pietersen and Peter Moores, were sacked a week or so before the tour; England were bowled out for fifty-one in Kingston; the second Test on the new white elephant of a ground in Antigua was called off after ten balls because the bowlers could not run in on an outfield comprised entirely of soggy sand; and the West Indies twice held out for tense draws on the last day of Test matches that England had looked like winning. Judy and I had a wonderful time, spending the first two weeks of that trip on a beautiful cruise ship, the *Silver Shadow*, but even then things went wrong personally.

We were due to leave London on the day that it snowed more heavily in the south than it had for nineteen years. Heathrow was closed, the unfortunate travel company, ITC, which had carefully planned a comfortable journey to Miami for 200 or so British passengers going to the Caribbean to see the first two Tests, had to rearrange flights the next day. We were amongst the last group to arrive on the ship, at six in the morning about thirty hours late. We had eventually got onto a Virgin flight to New York where it was also snowing heavily. At least JFK Airport continued to function. Needless to say, unfortunately, the Americans seemed to deal with the extreme weather far more efficiently than our people in London. They had a large fleet of snowploughs working up and down the runways; and de-icing the wings of aircraft taking off is simply normal routine for them in winter.

On such occasions I definitely have a guardian angel but I have paid for this tendency to keep others waiting occasionally, which is, of course, nothing more than selfishness. It preys on my conscience. On the last morning in Barbados I woke in a pool of sweat after dreaming, with more than usual vividness, that I had left a Test match at lunchtime to go to re-park my car. I cannot think why or where – this was a dream. A whole series of calamities followed, including my way being barred by a high iron gate, unhelpful gatemen saying that there were no more places in the car park, and a mad rush down an endless staircase, three steps at a time, only to find another door closed. All the time I was aware that I was due to commentate immediately after lunch but my mobile would not work to inform the producer. And people kept holding me up by recognising me and asking for the latest score.

I awoke with relief to the sound of birds singing on a warm tropical morning with a blue sky overhead made more interesting by small, white cumulus clouds. The sea beckoned for a swim before breakfast and, having shed the burden of daily writing, I had no work to do before catching another flight to Trinidad.

So why such a harrowing little dream? The answer, no doubt, is that worriers like myself will always find something to be anxious about and that the unpunctual get their just deserts.

Health and high self-esteem are the two keys to happiness, the elusive target of all of us. I continue to be, like most men, a confirmed hypochondriac. Something is usually aching, often my neck, which is only slightly shorter than that of a giraffe. When I consulted a renowned muscular-skeletal specialist, the former Cambridge cricket Blue Dr. Ian Thwaites, he tried everything: a jab or two of cortisone, a few attempts at acupuncture and some educated manhandling. He concluded by putting me on a tiny dose of pills once used as anti-depressants.

It was an odd cure for a stiff neck but he knew exactly what he was doing. There was, in fact, nothing wrong with my head and plenty wrong with my mind. When it comes to a mood of depression, though, I have, thank goodness, always found it quite hard to sustain it for long. Damon Runyan observed that that most of life is six to five against. I believe that, most of the time, it is actually five to four on.

On the whole I have found that the unbearable lightness of being is actually quite tolerable. I tend to see wild flowers rather than weeds. In other words there is a touch of the Micawber in me, not least, I'm afraid, when England are 94 for six against Australia, needing a mere 320 to win. They seldom do, naturally, but to have spent more than half my life pretending to be an authority on the reasons why, and still to be reasonably fit, thank God, in my middle sixties, makes me appreciate that I have been extraordinarily fortunate, whatever may lie ahead.

31

FRUSTRATIONS

Wonderful thing, technology; truly wonderful. Yet computers and new generations of mobile telephones provide the great paradox of our time. In one way these ever smaller, more versatile and sophisticated machines 'save' time to a miraculous degree. Wikipedia may not be infallible but it makes the old Encyclopaedia Britannica *look like an elephant racing a whippet. In another way instant communications work and hound the user until he or she becomes no freer than a slave. Twenty-first century peace is a screen cleared of all emails and a mobile switched firmly to 'off'.*

There is too much of the irascible Victor Meldrew in me. All my life I have been prone to quick bursts of temper, generally concealed in public but frequently released in private, to my shame. I come to the boil less because of my own little mistakes, like pushing the toaster handle down a second time for a quick browning but forgetting until I smell burning, than because of the abundant frustrations of modern life. Notable amongst them are the sometimes infuriating habits of computers, especially when you have got nine-tenths of the way through some online transaction before being told that you should have given your date of birth *before* your mobile number and your mother's maiden name; the knowledge that you will never switch one on without having lots of emails that you do not need; and the hair-tearingly relentless inhumanity of mechanised telephone responses.

It is extremely difficult to remain entirely calm when first you hear a voice telling you how important your call is, but that there is an unusually high 'volume' of calls that day, so you are being held in a queue; then when all suddenly goes silent before you hear a high-pitched hum; then when, having tried again and managed this time to get past the same first two steps, you are asked: 'If your inquiry is about X please press A, if you want Y please press B.' That hazard safely negotiated, you are requested to produce a security password that you have forgotten.

I could go on at some length about the frustrations of a contemporary life in which standards often seem to get lower. Why, to give but one small example, do all sandwiches and baguettes produced for people on the move in Britain now have to have a sour-tasting mayonnaise to keep them apparently fresh, rather than good, natural butter? I don't want the ubiquitous 'mayo', thank you. Such changes are always, it seems, for the convenience of the producer and packager rather than for the consumer.

I shall confine myself here, however, to something that I am supposed to know something about, the standards set by our newspapers and broadcasting authorities. Aiming to the mass market for obvious reasons, instead of keeping a proper balance between the original BBC mantra, to 'inform, educate and entertain' they seem to be obsessed with soccer and celebrities. When it comes to 'news' the emphasis is too often on what somebody has said rather than on something that has happened.

Nor is just what they say that can be frustrating. As with jokes, it is also the way that they say it.

Scriptwriters, talented though they are, must take some of the blame for failing to provide actors with English as it is actually spoken, or at least should be spoken. Perhaps statements in plays such as 'I think I'll go and *lay* down or 'I was *sat* there minding my own business' may be excused if they are conveying common English usage, but the more grammatical errors creep in and become fashionable, the less structure to the language there will be. When such errors are repeated in broadcasts or newspapers it is more a case of laziness or ignorance. Rather pompously and pedantically, I suppose, I bridle when I see a headline asking 'Who did what to *who?*' or a sentence such as 'The future depends on him being able to deliver the goods'. So 'him' is going to deliver the goods is him?

If we abandon the simple essential of every English sentence, the subject, verb and object, we abandon all pretence of any structure. 'Whom' seems in the process of being almost deliberately abandoned by newspapers and scriptwriters, as if by some kind of inverse snobbery that considers it passé to write or speak proper English.

I wince when I hear contributors to programmes on radio or television (especially politicians) saying that they will 'try *and* do something', instead of 'try *to* do something'. Or, worse, when in what are presumably carefully written bulletins, newsreaders or reporters say, every day of the week, such things as: 'A group of scientists *have* written a critical report; or 'the board of directors *have* resigned, or 'one in five children *have* played truant', rather than the grammatically correct *has*; or '*if he had not dropped the ball he would have scored a try and the eventual result may have been different*' rather than *might* have been different. Will the vast majority of journalists, especially those in Australia now aped by British ones, not appreciate that 'may' is the present tense, 'might' the past; and that while 'may' expresses a definite possibility, 'might, expresses the idea that it is just possible but unlikely? The collective noun debate, I should add in fairness to all sports editors, is confused by the long-established habit in Britain of referring to representative sports teams as if they are a plural entity. We say 'England *have* scored 208 for six' when strictly it should be 'England *has*'. The Australians get this right: we don't.

These are subtleties that good communicators should cherish and preserve, not arrogantly and ignorantly ignore. They reflect poor education too. Even enlightened newspaper editors seem to have abandoned a proper distinction between any subject and object.

I know that the counter-argument is that if something can be understood it is acceptable English. New vogue words sometimes add usefully to the language. I accept, too, that lazy linguistic fashions imported so willingly and uncritically from America (*showcased, immortalisation, outside of* etc) are more a matter of taste than things that are right or wrong. The same is true of pronunciations (*tempor-ary, skedule* etc) But poor basic grammar simply demeans the language.

32

CRICKET'S FUTURE

Twenty20 cricket is the often exciting fashion of the moment. Some believe that it is the game's only future but they are wrong. For all its popular appeal, it has essentially demeaned a multi-faceted game.

At its professional level cricket, like champagne, is more often than not in a state of ferment. Despite the sudden passion for franchises involving vast sums of money and what we had better now call the 'Twenty20 Revolution', the instant version will not supersede Test cricket.

'Cricket is the new football' we were told, curiously not in reference to Twenty20 but in 2005 when an exalted Ashes series was gripping a wider than usual proportion of the British public. Only two years later came the first 'global' Twenty20 tournament in South Africa. India happened to win it (better still, beating Pakistan in the final) so much of India's vast population was captivated, much as the explosive fast bowling of Lillee and Thomson enthused Australians, amongst them Kerry Packer, in 1974/5.

Cricket's popularity ebbs and flows, like the game itself, but it keeps flowing. Not because it is the new football, but because it is the old cricket, a series of duels between a batsman and a bowler in a team context, a game demanding greater discipline, technique and intelligence than any other.

In 1900 cricket was 'in the very direst peril of degenerating from the finest of all summer games into an exhibition of dullness and weariness' according to the great Victorian all-rounder A.G. Steel, following two hot seasons in which batsmen had had things too much their own way and there were too many draws. Historians now call the era to which he was referring the 'Golden Age'.

It is not dullness and weariness that everyone is worried about now, but glitz and superficial razzmatazz: a boiled-down version of a profound game that is hauling in television advertisers, not to mention easily pleased spectators, in India, the land where passion for the game knows no bounds. The consequences are that more than just a few leading players are becoming millionaires, that the bash, dash and dazzle game is getting wider exposure, but that at the same time the game is in danger of losing its balance.

Cricket cannot live by Twenty20 alone. The game's skills and tactics have to be learned in a harder school. That is not to say, of course, that the advent of the Twenty20 leagues is not a historic landmark for professional cricket nor a great opportunity for the game's further expansion so long as the leading administrators – and players more powerful than ever before – show some restraint. But the broader view will not be taken by business folk keen to cash in on the fashion for quickfire cricket. There is obvious danger to the international game when Twenty20 franchises offer players greater riches for less work

Hindsight suggests that the brilliant original concept of the Indian Premier League had serious flaws. First, by choosing the eye-catching means of a public auction for players who had already been promised a generous enough base rate by the BCCI for their six weeks of cricket, the IPL created salaries inflated to the point at which they threatened to unbalance all other forms of cricket, especially Tests and one-day internationals.

If Andrew Symonds could have his initial US$250,000 salary, guaranteed by the BCCI for joining the league, inflated to $1.35 million by his franchise, why would he bother to play all the year round for Australia? He had come late to international cricket for one so talented and he had enjoyed his prominent role in winning back the Ashes in 2006/7 but the self-discipline and dedication required to keep his place seemed less important when such easy wealth came his way. Very soon, he and his Australian employers parted.

The total income of the India captain, Mahendra Singh Dhoni, was estimated at around US$25 million in 2010, of which only $200,000 was his central contract for India. Dhoni had originally found his fame and fortune as an international cricketer but there is clearly a danger, if the IPL continues to thrive, that younger ambitious cricketers will see the Indian league and Twenty20 cricket in other countries as a much easier way of making a fine living from the game without having to suffer the rigours of Test cricket. Ravi Bopara, for example, temporarily rejected by England's selectors after a promising start, did well in the 2010 IPL but in the auction the following year he was not selected for another contract, partly because the timing of the season in England prevented him from committing to the full tournament.

Lesser cricketers from India, Australia and other countries got lucrative contracts instead, in some cases, ironically, because they had failed to make it to their national squads and could therefore give the 'bash and dash' game their full attention. A little-known Australian named Dan Christian was taken on for three years at a salary of $900,000 for three years. It is surely the duty of administrators planning the game's future to ensure that the prime purpose of every ambitious young cricketer should be to play for his country. Rewards for doing so have to be commensurate with the honour, and fixtures have to be planned to keep a proper balance between international contests and the cricket played by franchises.

A second strategic error was made by the BCCI and Lalit Modi, the dynamic businessman who drove the IPL into existence with the help of the International Management Group. IMG is the company with tentacles profitably entwined in most televised international sport. The BCCI chose not to reward the other international boards for allowing their own contracted players to participate. The sop, instead, was to create yet another spurious international tournament, the 'Champions League', contested by the finalists in the various domestic Twenty20 competitions in other countries. In England this has forced the ECB to change the pattern of the county season for the worse. Yet the money promised to national boards participating in the 2010 Champions League had still not been paid six months after it had been promised.

For the BCCI it has been no great problem since they were taking the profits from selling the franchises but in other countries it has meant administrators having to renegotiate contracts, a process requiring heavy legal fees. The unity of national squads has been threatened in consequence and the arrangement of fixtures in an already crowded programme has been further complicated.

The IPL could not have taken off as spectacularly as it did without the energy, initiative and drive of Modi but he evidently became carried away by becoming a media star. His downfall started in April 2010, after he had added two more franchises to the original eight, none of which could expect any profit from their investments for a number of years. The BCCI relieved him of all responsibility for the IPL and, a few months later, lodged a complaint against him with the Chennai police alleging misappropriation of Board funds of around US$105 million relating mainly to the allotment of media and commercial rights.

Modi was also accused of a conflict of interests because of family involvements in franchises but he was not alone in that. One of his accusers, the BCCI secretary N. Srinivasan, was on the board of India Cements, owners of the Chennai Super Kings. Accused of just such a conflict, he defended himself by saying that he had received clearance from the senior figure in Indian cricket, the Cabinet Minister and now ICC chairman, Sharad Pawar.

When I started writing and talking about cricket the game was run, albeit with too little regard for the financial well being of the top players, by administrators whose main concern was the maintenance of the long tradition of Test cricket. England and Australia usually held sway in the ICC. Now the power has passed to India and the game's future will depend on how responsibly they use it.

The advent of Twenty20 is just the latest shift in a game that has always mirrored social trends. Packer's cricket in coloured clothes was innovative, it seemed, but they played in coloured kit, albeit rather more tasteful, in the 18th century. Twenty-overs-a-side cricket matches themselves are not new. Like many amateurs, as I have mentioned, I played them on summer evenings in the 1960s. It was just as much fun then, because matches were always vital and competitive.

Nor is slickly marketed cricket anything unusual. William Clarke of Nottingham was every bit as much an entrepreneur with his touring England XIs in the 1840s as Modi in the first decade of the 21st century. Almost a century before Clarke, moreover, one of the driving forces behind the very first professional cricketers was the fact that aristocrats with too much time and money wanted to bet on matches and, much like the aficionados of Bollywood and the captains of Indian industry, they rather fancied owning their own teams.

So, gambling on cricket is not new either. Inderjit Singh Bindra, the wily Indian administrator from Chandigarh who did most to bring the fifty-over World Cup to India for the first time, estimated that around £90 billion had been wagered on the IPL when it had reached the end of its long and fevered first round in 2008. That was astonishing, but so is the fact that in 1743, when Richard Newland of Slindon (Sussex) led 'Three of England' against 'Three of Kent' on the Artillery Field in London (where cricket is still played), the crowd was 10,000 and the purse £500. At twopence per entry that would still have made a tidy sum for the promoters. A contemporary report said that 'near £20,000 is depending' on bets associated with the Earl of Sandwich's matches at Newmarket in 1751 between 'Old Etonians' and 'England'. The prize money was £1500. Today that is worth £225,000. *Plus ça change.*

Provided there is no corruption – and history tells that there has to be unstinting education and supervision to prevent it – the sudden fresh injection of money into the game will be good, not just for the lucky few players in the right place at the right time, but for its expansion into new areas of the world, particularly the largely untapped 'markets' of China and the USA.

It is all a question of balance. 'Take but degree away', the Bard warned, 'and hark what discord follows.' In India the launch of the IPL was novel because of the city franchise concept and the huge sums being paid to the players. Other countries have hastened to exploit the trend but, as with all sport (all entertainment indeed) created for television, it will be over-done. Some games will be exciting, some boring. People will truly need to care who wins if the concept is to succeed in the long term.

Assuredly the IPL made a dramatic initial impact. Its very wealth and exposure demanded that it would. But one of the virtues of the World Twenty2o tournaments that are now a regular feature on the ICC's agenda is their brevity: two weeks. By contrast the first franchised league tournament in India consisted of fifty-nine games in six weeks and by 2011 it had grown to seventy-four. Advertising on Indian television, measured in billions, was expected to raise even more revenue than in the six-week ICC World Cup on the subcontinent that preceded it, but soon even Indians may feel that the pudding has been over-egged.

That, of course, has been true of professional cricket in England and Wales for too long. ECB officials encouraged the ambitions of the owners of extra grounds as international venues and challenged them to bid against each other for the right to stage games, with the consequence that by 2011 many of them had got into serious financial trouble. Worthy as the modern developments at Durham, Southampton and Cardiff have been, they have merely obliged the board to accept more and more international fixtures. It is easy to be wise in hindsight but the same officials made terrible fools of themselves when they got into bed with a Texan called Allen Stanford who turned out to be an international fraudster. Not one of them resigned and none, alas, seemed capable of putting principle before the pursuit of more and more cash.

It would be a surprise if, despite these grave misjudge-ments, a City-based franchised competition is not attempted in Britain soon, either by the ECB or by a commercial group.

With some courage and foresight, however, and a less obsessive belief that more income necessarily means a better game, it should be possible in the long term to preserve eighteen, or at least sixteen, first-class counties as the best bridge between the amateur and professional game in England. County cricket evolved and has proved flexible, despite seldom making sense as a business at any stage of its history. In a country where most of the population now lives in cities it is not the system that would best serve the game in Britain if you started with a clean sheet but with salary caps, still greater incentives for fielding a higher proportion of England qualified players, and profits from international cricket shared only on condition that significant money is spent on local clubs and schools, the county system can adapt to the latest seismic shifts in the game.

The columnists who run down domestic cricket without watching it themselves are in most cases simply ignorant. They fail to recognise the work done by counties for young cricketers in their areas, or the fact that standards are high, especially in the intensely competitive four-day championship. They ignore the fact that players such as Alastair Cook, Ryan Sidebottom and the South African-bred Jonathan Trott have in recent years moved seamlessly into Test cricket because they are better prepared for the step up than they once were. They forget that the Championship is comfortably the best-watched domestic competition in the world, even allowing for the fact that most of it is played when the great majority are unable to watch it. Millions still follow it voraciously online, witness page hits for county cricket on Cricinfo and other specialist websites such as Thecricketer.com that exceed twenty-five million season after season.

There are those who think Test cricket to be doomed as well as county cricket. But the two-innings version of cricket will always have more possibilities than a limited single innings; and games played for their country will always mean more to professionals, deep down, than those for cobbled-together franchise clubs, no matter how great the rewards.

Crucial decisions by captains or umpires; changing pitch or weather conditions; sudden shifts of fortune; moments of individual inspiration: these are the things that decide Test matches and give them their fascinating complexity.

One has to accept, of course, that professional players think deep into their pockets as well as to their hearts. They recognise that Test cricket is the supreme form of the game and the shop window that makes them famous and attractive but for these reasons it has to be the form of the game that pays them best. By the same token, if administrators say, as they all do, that Tests are what matter most, they have to market them better.

It could only encourage the sometimes silent majority who follow the Test scene, without necessarily having the time or money to go to watch matches themselves, that India, economically the most powerful cricket nation, overtook Australia and South Africa in 2009 as, officially, the best at the five-day game. That was a profound consolation, surely, for their 'failure' to win the Twenty20 World Cup in England in that year. (Not many will remember who actually *did* win it.)

In a restless world that thrives on change and novelty it may well be that the rolling World Test Championship to which the ICC is gradually feeling its way will give impetus and focus to some of those series that currently attract only local interest. A championship every third year, with fifty- and twenty-over World Cups in between, would have a symmetry that the international game currently lacks.

When the ICC decided to experiment with a system that allowed players to refer umpiring decisions made on the field to a third umpire equipped with television replays and other gadgetry, they over-ruled a principle that applies to every cricketer in non-televised matches, namely that he or she should accept an umpire's verdict without demur.

I thought that Hawk-Eye, which goes by other names elsewhere, would shorten Test matches but although it has helped spinners it is often one of the batsman's many friends. In cases where the fielding captain asks for a review of an umpire's 'not out' lbw decision, for instance, bowlers are not even allowed the full nine inches' width of the wicket if balls are predicted to be hitting only the side of the stumps; or the full height of the wicket if the prediction shows less than half of the ball touching the bails.

Test cricket needs pitches that give the bowlers some help. That is not to say that it needs surfaces that make life impossible for batsmen but the fall of a wicket is the most dramatic moment in the game. The old convention that the benefit of doubt should go to the batsman was never part of the law. It reflected a time when umpiring was much more prone to error than it is now. The mantra of the ICC's cricket director, David Richardson, was that his 'Decision Review System' would prevent umpir[...]. Patently that is desirabl[...]ut if technology is to be [...] principle sh[...] be to see that justice is

33

MCC PRESIDENT

England v. India at Lord's: the final day of the 100th Test between
the two countries, by chance also the 200th Test since it all became
official in 1877. The sun is out, the air is warm and people have
been queuing since three in the morning to get a prime place to
watch a day's cricket pregnant with possibilities. England's players
run round the outfield an hour before play starts. Ringing cheers
echo round the stands as they pass each one: Allen, Tavern, Mound,
Edrich, Compton, Grandstand, Warner. The trees at the Nursery
End, shining like pearls in their mid-summer splendour, wave gently
as if in supporting acclamation.
When two Indian batsmen emerge from the

a third umpire equipped with television replays and other gadgetry, they over-ruled a principle that applies to every cricketer in non-televised matches, namely that he or she should accept an umpire's verdict without demur.

I thought that Hawk-Eye, which goes by other names elsewhere, would shorten Test matches but although it has helped spinners it is often one of the batsman's many friends. In cases where the fielding captain asks for a review of an umpire's 'not out' lbw decision, for instance, bowlers are not even allowed the full nine inches' width of the wicket if balls are predicted to be hitting only the side of the stumps; or the full height of the wicket if the prediction shows less than half of the ball touching the bails.

Test cricket needs pitches that give the bowlers some help. That is not to say that it needs surfaces that make life impossible for batsmen but the fall of a wicket is the most dramatic moment in the game. The old convention that the benefit of doubt should go to the batsman was never part of the law. It reflected a time when umpiring was much more prone to error than it is now. The mantra of the ICC's cricket director, David Richardson, was that his 'Decision Review System' would prevent umpiring howlers. Patently that is desirable but if technology is to be so widely used the first principle should be to see that justice is done.

These are big problems but passing problems too. In the literal sense it could, indeed, be argued that cricket has entered another golden age. Only if it is viewed solely as a means of making gold will it cease to captivate the young. Enthusing the next generation is the prime responsibility of players and administrators alike and whether or not they are succeeding is the true test of the game's health.

33

MCC PRESIDENT

England v. India at Lord's: the final day of the 100th Test between the two countries, by chance also the 2000th Test since it all became official in 1877. The sun is out, the air is warm and people have been queuing since three in the morning to get a prime place to watch a day's cricket pregnant with possibilities. England's players run round the outfield an hour before play starts. Ringing cheers echo round the stands as they pass each one: Allen, Tavern, Mound, Edrich, Compton, Grandstand, Warner. The trees at the Nursery End, shining like pearls in their mid-summer splendour, wave gently as if in supporting acclamation.

When two Indian batsmen emerge from the nets at the Nursery End to cross the velvety turf towards the stately old pavilion, still more excited cheers arise. Anglo-Indians are here in force and the Tebbit test has never worried them. There is Rahul Dravid and there . . . is it Sachin himself? Will he score his 100th international hundred today to save his country once again?

My hope, like that of many, is that England will win but only after the phenomenal Tendulkar has reached his landmark. I watch, entranced, from the President's box, preparing myself for a day entertaining no less expectant guests.

Jim Swanton, who loved MCC, served on various committees and would love to have been asked to be the club's President, used to instil in me that the announcement of the new incumbent every May was a matter of national significance and should be an important news story. These days it might attract a line or two in some daily newspapers but even to the majority of MCC's 18,000 members, let alone the man on the Clapham omnibus, the presidency is not something that much concerns them. Because of the importance of Lord's to English cricket, however, it is still a role with some influence.

That I was in the Grandstand rather than the Media Centre in July 2011 stemmed from a telephone call soon after my retirement as *The Times* cricket correspondent, from Sir Michael Jenkins. I had only briefly met this charming and erudite fellow, a distinguished diplomat who had also written a beautifully crafted memoir of his childhood experiences in France long before he turned to a successful career in business. He became the first chairman of MCC, having been the chief architect of the subtle modernisation of the club's governance towards the end of the 20th century. The spirit of sensible modernisation that the changes introduced encouraged many more commercial activities and led in 2006 to the appointment of the avant-garde Australian Keith Bradshaw as Secretary and Chief Executive of MCC. He succeeded my Cambridge contemporary, the respected, more conservative Roger Knight.

MCC's main committee is, and always has been, high-powered so I was flattered to be asked if I would consider putting myself forward for election. I requested a year to sort out my altered circumstances but said that I would stand in 2009. It is an illustration of the popularity of what I have done for a living that more members should have voted for me than for anyone else, including the man in second place, Sir John Major!

I had only been on the MCC committee since the previous October when John Barclay, the 2009/10 President, rang me at home one March evening as I sat in my office contemplating the imminence of spring. At the time I was feeling my way, impressed by the wide range of the club's business and the quality of the members around me, not least the recently departed chairman, Charles Fry and the shrewd, quietly efficient new one, Oliver Stocken.

John himself was proving a popular and conscientious president, greatly helped by his no less ebullient wife, the artist Renira. I had shared a hundred partnership with him for MCC at Brighton years ago and we had got to know one another better in recent years, especially since I had become a trustee of the Arundel Foundation that he directs. I thought that he was probably calling on Arundel matters that evening. This being one Englishman talking to another he began by discussing the weather, before moving on to the recent cricket in Bangladesh. Then the bombshell. 'I've got something much more important to ask you. How would you feel about becoming the next president?'

I was dumbfounded and said so. I asked for a night to think about it and to discuss the implications with Judy. Whether or not I accepted, no one else on earth was to know about this, including my children. The name of the next president is always a tightly guarded secret until the club's AGM in May.

John encouraged me before I put the phone down. 'You know everyone in the game' (well, a lot of them). 'You know everything there is to know about cricket' (hardly). 'You make brilliant speeches' (a matter of opinion). 'You'll be brilliant, I know you will' (typical Barclay: a prince of hyperbole). 'And Judy will be brilliant too' (true).

So many others had given much more time to the affairs of the 'Premier Club' than I had, not least, of course, because being a daily cricket correspondent had precluded any closer involve-ment on my part. I had 'match-managed' (captained and raised teams) in various MCC matches against schools throughout the 1970s, served for three years on the Bi-Centenary committee under the chairmanship of the dynamic Hubert Doggart, in the mid-1980s; and in 2007 I had been surprised and honoured to be asked to give the Cowdrey Lecture at Lord's, the first time that it had been made by anyone other than a famous Test player.

The lecture was a great opportunity to pontificate in a differ-ent forum and it was generously received. This was a recog-nition, perhaps, that journalists and broadcasters might have a useful overview of affairs in world cricket, but the presidency was a different kettle of fish. I felt just like Vic Marks, whose comment when he heard the news a few weeks later was a rather bemused 'bloody hell', followed by his usual chuckle.

I knew when I took on the purple that it would be a very busy year. I was aware that bouts first of pneumonia then, from nowhere, of hepatitis, had aged me a bit over the previous twelve months. But this was an honour and I owed some return to the game that had paid my bills for so long. I would not welcome the extra travel and all the nights in London; I would miss the opportunities to play more golf as I had planned; and endless committee meetings are not really my cup of tea. Nor did I want to give up altogether writing and talking about the game. Weighed against the opportunity to represent the largest, most famous and influential cricket club in the world, however, these were small sacrifices. I accepted John's offer the following day and sat on the secret with Judy for a month or more before my appointment was announced at the AGM in May.

Within weeks I realised what a tremendous privilege it was. MCC, the 'private club with the public function', has been a club for more than 220 years. By 2014 it will have been based on the present ground at Lord's for 200 years. It is both the conscience of the recreational game and, through its world cricket committee, the independent voice of the international one.

It guards the laws of the game and reviews them when necessary.

It has a fixture list against schools and clubs numbering more than 450 a year. During my year one of the most pleasant duties was to present mementos during tea intervals in the first of the two Tests at Lord's to the schoolboys who had scored hundreds or taken five wickets in the previous season against MCC. Each of them had spent a memorable day being entertained by club officials and many of them will become new playing members before long.

MCC also runs and pays for several overseas tours a year, encouraging the game in faraway places as it always has. In 2011/12 there were tours to Namibia, Greece, Hong Kong and China, and Bermuda.

The club has 18,000 full members, 5000 associate members, a long waiting list that it currently takes about twenty-one years to climb unless anyone joins as a player; and a loyal staff of around 200 people. Some of them have the responsibility of maintaining a big and still beautiful ground in the middle of London. The estate costs about £2 million a year just to maintain. At my first appearance at one of the quarterly meetings of the Estates committee, to give one inkling of what this involves, it was reported that there had been 1402 work orders on the lifts alone, 1172 of them routine checks by staff, the remaining 230 carried out by subcontractors every month.

The Lord's ground staff, under Mick Hunt, seem to be ceaselessly at work, even in the winter. Their base, a group of low, single-storey sheds beside the Nursery Ground, is a little empire in itself, filled with mowers and rollers and smelling of oil and grass. Men and machines produce what are regularly rated amongst the best pitches in the country, catering at different times for Test players, Middlesex home matches, military cricketers (not all of them medium), University players, schoolboys, club and village cricketers. I presided over examples of all of them during my year and only left disappointed after one of them, when the semi-finals and final of the Schools Twenty20 tournament in July, scheduled for the Nursery Ground, were ruined by wet weather. This is a fast-growing competition, however, and I hope that in future the semi-finals may be followed by a final on the main ground to be played before one of Middlesex's floodlit T20 matches, thus ensuring a larger crowd and an even greater buzz for the teams that reach Lord's.

Playing there, after all, is the dream of every keen cricketer from every country in the world, which is one reason why so much of my year was spent debating whether the ECB's original intention of denying the West Indies a chance to play there on their tour of 2012 made any sense from anyone's point of view. By a mixture of gentle diplomacy and hard bargaining we got there in the end, thus guaranteeing a far bigger crowd than the first Test of 2012, originally scheduled to be played at Cardiff, would otherwise have attracted. That, of course, also ensured that there would be a much greater profit for the ECB to distribute.

I must beware romantic allusions to the sun never setting on cricket at Lord's but the fact is that, thanks to a superb indoor school, the game is being played in some way virtually every day of the year, whatever the weather. The Club spends more on cricket than on anything else, naturally. The lion's share of the budget, £600,000 a year at present, goes towards the sponsoring of cricket at Oxford, Cambridge, Cardiff, Durham, Leeds/Bradford and Loughborough, all universities with the requisite coaching, facilities and strong fixture lists to allow bright young students the chance to carry on both with their higher education and their hopes of a career in the professional game. In 2011 just on 20 per cent of the 397 England-qualified county cricketers had played for the six MCC Universities.

Everything about MCC and Lord's is lovingly preserved. The whole place is presented on Test match days like a bride on her wedding day. The Long Room, with its lofty ceilings, beautifully lit pictures and elegant decorations, is as lovely a stage for a public lunch or dinner as almost any palace or stately home. The members, and English cricket itself, can feel pride on such occasions. Visitors pay substantial amounts for their tickets but they know that they are somewhere special.

It goes without saying that the players feel the same. Year after year the famous sloping ground inspires exceptional performances, especially from cricketers from overseas. Australians love the place so much that they lost to England only once in the 20th century, when Hedley Verity bowled them out, with fourteen wickets in one day, in 1934.

Individual feats of a hundred or five wickets are enshrined on the honours boards in the dressing-rooms. Above the visitors' changing-room players in all matches are treated to the best cooked, most delicious and wholesome food. Until 2010 it was prepared by a brilliant English cook, Linda Le Ker. Her French husband was the best 'front of house' man in the business before their joint retirement. It looked as though my presidency might coincide with rather less exalted cooking and service at the various members' dinners in my year in the chair but I need not have worried: the standards have been maintained by their successors.

Presiding over a club and ground that together have formed a national institution for more than 200 years is no sincecure:

when he was President the former Prime Minister Sir Alec Douglas-Home, who, as Lord Dunglass, had played on the ground as an Eton schoolboy, famously observed that there was more paperwork to deal with than there is in Whitehall. It is not just the main committee but the abundant sub-committees which produce all this reading matter. They cover:

Cricket (that is all cricket played at Lord's and by the Club all over Britain and on overseas tours; the Laws, and MCC's sponsorship of the main cricketing universities and various grass-roots initiatives);

World Cricket (the quietly influential pressure group mainly comprising famous former players of various nationalities who meet twice a year to debate and advise on issues facing the game);

Finance (everything to do with the income and expenditure of a business with a turnover of some £35 million);

The Lord's Estate (maintaining the ground and its assets);

Membership (everything to do with the rules and rights of members and the associated clubs, including Real tennis, golf, squash, chess and bridge); and

Arts and Library.

MCC has a highly accomplished curator in Adam Chadwick, who supervises the Library and Museum not just from the basis of great knowledge but also with tact and pragmatism. The collection of archives, pictures, books and cricketana, including, of course, the Ashes urn, is both vast and valuable. Duplicates were sold at the auctioneers Christie's in 2010 for a profit of £536,000, all of which was immediately ploughed back into the judicious acquisition of further cricket archives at the appropriate time. On Chadwick's advice we decided to invest in a beautiful painting by Henry Walton of cricketers at Harrow School, playing around the time of Hambledon's high noon, just before curved bats gave way to straight ones, wickets acquired a middle stump and bowlers began to lob the ball to a length rather than roll it along the ground.

I had never been to one of these big auction house sales before. It was quietly dramatic with some well-known cricketana collectors gathered in the warm, brightly lit room at Christie's, making almost imperceptible bids, often against a row of agents on telephones who were seated just above the floor and who swallowed up the majority of the items for anonymous bidders. The auction raised £536,000 including a world record for an individual cricket book £151,255 (against a top estimate of £70,000) for William Epps' *A Collection of All the Grand Matches Played in England from 1771 to 1791*. Published in 1799, it is extremely rare – there is not even a copy in the British Library – and it seemed unnecessary for MCC to possess two of the handful of copies still extant.

Half a million pounds seems a decent return on old books that had often been left to the Club in wills but it demanded enormous preparatory work on the part of the small library staff to make sure that permission was granted. The bottom line is placed into perspective by the fact that it cost more than that recently to buy a single picture to add to MCC's collection of originals, the painting by Lewis Cage of *The Young Cricketer* which now hangs in the Long Room.

The President is encouraged to attend meetings of all these committees and I tried to do so in all cases except finance. I know my limitations: I am to finance as Lady Gaga to the recruitment of mercenaries in the defence of Malta against the Turk in the 16th century. Despite this it was essential to be on top of the general principles of what contributed to the profits and losses of the Club and, for the purposes of grasping the main issues confronting the main Committee (which meets eight times a year), to know what was going on in all the other committees.

I was surprised by the commitment required but tried to abide by the adage that a job worth doing is worth doing properly. I started my year with a visit to one MCC – a speech after dinner on 2 October at Malmesbury Cricket Club in Wiltshire (unfortunately a more painful event than anticipated because I had just had two teeth removed and the stitching of the wound had caused an ulcer on my tongue that got worse with every painful word that I uttered) – and ten months later cut the ribbon on a pavilion extension at another MCC, Mistley CC in Suffolk. This followed a terrific match between Mistley and Marylebone that ended with a six into the boundary hedge to give the local club victory with two balls of the match left: no wonder the community spirit was so joyful at a splendid marquee dinner afterwards.

The majority of the journeys during the year, excepting the longer ones to Australia, Sri Lanka and India, were to Lord's and back. During the year I presided and spoke at 48 dinners; attended 26 committee or sub-committee meetings and five private meetings on MCC matters (plus a couple of conference calls, both of which saved a lot of petrol). I joined eleven additional events for MCC members plus five days of the club's Golf Society and went to eighteen other events or matches in my capacity as President.

By comparison the twenty-four match days I attended at Lord's seems a rather small amount, but seven of these were followed by receptions for players and at all of the games Judy and I were as hospitable as we possibly could be to our guests in the President's box. We wanted everyone to feel truly welcome and at ease and Judy was so good at achieving that, having taken infinite pains to seat people at lunch next to someone with whom they would have something more than cricket in common.

We were allowed four guests of our own choice each day. The remaining twenty were friends or associates of the club: influential folk such as the High Commissioner for India, the immaculately bearded Maharana of Udaipur, Sir Mervyn King (one of English cricket's greatest supporters anyway) or the attractive and vivacious Lord Mayor of Westminster, Susie Burbage. I wish we could have entertained even more people in that perfectly positioned box, where the food, drink and personal service are all worthy of a six-star cruise liner. These occasions, from the Test matches to the final of the Village Championship, were, to me, the icing on the cake. They were also exhausting: I felt every bit as tired when the last guests had meandered (in some cases) towards the lift as I do at the end of a day's commentary.

By the end of September I totted up 136 days of what might be called physical commitment to the presidency but there were emails, phone calls or letters relating to club affairs of one kind or another that occupied some part of virtually every day. For most of the year the club, with all its pleasures and problems, seemed much like a family, to the extent that I would worry about them at night as often as not.

For a short time, before the introduction of a club chairman to maintain consistency, presidents served for two years. I would undoubtedly have found the role easier in a second year because I would have known what was important and would probably have felt more relaxed generally, but, of course, it would have extended the considerable commitment.

I was loyally supported throughout my year not just by other members of the committee but also by the executives. No one revered the traditions of Lord's more than MCC's secretary between 2006 and 2011, Keith Bradshaw from Tasmania, whose resignation towards the end of my year in office came as a great disappointment. In my explanatory letter to members I tried to get the right balance, saying why Keith was leaving, detailing the means of choosing his successor and firmly scotching the inevitable rumours (and would-be press stories) that he had been sacked.

A friendly fellow by nature with a lovely smile, Keith had recovered with great fortitude and a wonderfully positive attitude from bone cancer. He had had other problems in his personal life but they had not impaired his devotion to a job that he loved doing. Sadly, however, his mother had died suddenly on the opening day of the Test match between England and Sri Lanka at Lord's in June, which set off a chain of events that made it essential for him to return to his home country for good at the end of the summer.

At least the last Test adminstered by him, against India, was a resounding success, culminating in a win for England late on the last day before a ground filled to capacity, mainly by last-minute spectators attracted by the free entry offered to children and a modest entry price of £20 for adults. It was typical of Keith to get the balance just right. The eventual profits were a record for any Test in England, making over £4 million for the ECB to plough back into the game, and a further £2 million to help finance MCC's multi-faceted cricketing activities.

From the moment that he arrived at Lord's Keith, helped by the affable David Batts, the former hotelier who had transformed the Club's catering, had made a positive impression on members and the wider public by his friendliness and his ready acceptance of new ideas. His decision-making, in common with his predecessors', was limited to a degree: as the government is run by the cabinet with loyal and unbiased support from the Civil Service, so MCC is run as much by its General Committee as by its executives.

They have the final say on whether to recommend such major developments as the Vision for Lord's, the lavish plan to expand the ground over the next decade or more, before putting it to the full members for the final verdict. This had become by far the most contentious issue by the time that I became President. There had been discussion about the 'Vision' for years and expenditure on various plans amounting to more than £3 million, spent mainly on fees to professional advisers. The debate perhaps went deeper than the question of how the ground should be developed, touching on the central issue of MCC's very purpose: is it about maximising profit from Lord's for the greater good of cricket, or about preserving the ground's uniqueness? I think that even the most ardent would-be developers would agree that it would be a sin to turn Lord's into another concrete bowl.

The man who had been chairing the development committee, the able Welsh QC Robert Griffiths, had put heart and soul into his role but had lost support from some in his attempt to hasten the acceptance of the grand vision for the future of the ground, involving property development at either end.

The master plan by the architects, Herzog & de Meuron, was exciting and imaginative, but it also involved, in its original version, vast expenditure to move facilities at the Nursery End below ground and a property deal that would involve the creation of up to five huge blocks of apartments between the Nursery and the gardens of St. John's Wood Church, a 'vision' that many opposed.

Robert could not see this, nor that the vast expenditure envisaged on the development would be a gamble. There was no guarantee that the new facilities, even if they received approval from both members and the planning authorities, would be profitable in future. To his mind, as he said both in public and in private, the whole plan had been widely praised. As an example of far-sighted architectural imagination it had, but a shuttered eye was being turned to the environmental cost of the Grand Design, quite apart from the financial risk of going ahead.

I had serious personal doubts, and I knew that they were shared by many members who had been given a rather partial view of the future in various unofficial leaks to the press. Those huge new buildings would tower over the northern end of the ground, where the trees of St. John's Wood churchyard still give Lord's the feel of a cricket ground rather than a stadium. I felt that this need not be 'the inevitable price of progress'. There was also a question mark over the long-term sustainability of a ground with greater capacity.

Matters came to a head in late January. Robert was frustrated at the lack of progress, especially in securing agreement with the property developers, Almacantar, whom his high-powered committee had identified as the partners most likely to deliver a deal with MCC that would enable work to begin at the Nursery End. Unwisely he suggested to the Chairman and Treasurer that they should consider their positions.

They did. One Saturday morning in January I opened my emails and discovered that the issue had reached crisis point. Either these two key members of the main committee would stand aside, or the development committee would have to be wound up.

I decided to call on the Club's three trustees, Sir Tim Rice, Mike Brearley and Anthony Wreford, to take an independent look at the reasons for Robert's frustration and whether or not there had been unreasonable delays on the part of the executives and senior committee members in their dealings with Michael Hussey (no relation), the boss of Almacantar.

In the period before the next crucial committee meeting in mid-February, the trustees spoke to all concerned and came to the conclusion, as I expected, that Oliver Stocken and Justin Dowley had acted with no more than reasonable caution. Neither was against the idea of entering into negotiations with Almacantar but neither could go forward with someone whom they believed to be pursuing his own agenda.

Knowing how one journalist in particular, my *Times* colleague Ivo Tennant, had been given confidential information from previous committee meetings by a source never definitely identified, I was concerned that there might be a further damaging leak before the committee met. I persuaded the trustees that the proposed way forward should be kept a total secret between ourselves until the meeting started.

Although Oliver was to chair the meeting we had to tell him nothing about the main item on the agenda. I cannot divulge details of confidential committee deliberations other than those that have already been made public but it would be true to say that the meeting on 16 February was as full of passion and human drama as most Shakespearean plays. I was quickly obliged to take the chair and reluctantly to cross swords with one of the sharpest barristers in the land, who had given a lot of his time and expertise to the Vision for Lord's, completely unpaid, of course.

Robert was understandably crestfallen but he had misjudged the mood by challenging the senior officials. Eventually the committee, helped by the balanced views of a former Prime Minister who had seen more momentous conflict than this in Downing Street, was unanimous that the development committee should be disbanded and that a smaller negotiating group, led by Justin Dowley and Keith Bradshaw, should be appointed to begin negotiations with Almacantar that did not prejudice other means of developing new stands. This was, at least arguably, a natural end to the development committee's work, although its chairman emphatically did not agree.

MCC's press officer issued a statement that evening that made no mention of any offers to resign, but that side of the story nevertheless appeared under Ivo Tennant's name the next morning.

Robert made it clear that he had not changed his mind, but he is a resilient character. He remained chairman of the important Laws sub-committee and stood for election to rejoin the main committee in October 2012, backed by John Major and another QC, Lord Grabiner. This brought forth new stories, one of them, in *Private Eye*, seriously ill-informed.

It suggested, utterly falsely, that the departure of Keith and David Batts was a consequence of their disaffection with the decision taken to reconsider the 'Vision'.

The article further suggested that Oliver and Justin had pulled off a 'coup'. This was absurd: they were chairman and treasurer, so no 'coup' was required. The worst calumny was the strong suggestion that Phillip Hodson had effectively been appointed my successor because he was in cahoots with Oliver.

The decision to ask Phillip to be president was entirely my own, made once I had decided that it was time to appoint someone from north of Watford, preferably a Yorkshireman in view of their poor recent representation in the role. Only three Yorkshire-bred men had been president in the 20th century, hardly a fair representation of their influence on the history of English cricket. I sounded out in strict confidence two of my former press box colleagues, John Woodcock and Robin Marlar, both with a long experience of MCC affairs but both no longer involved. Both gave my selection top marks.

My successor will have one duty which I presume to be unique for an MCC president, namely the presentation of an Olympic medal after the archery tournament at Lord's during the London Games. Just after I left office in 2011 I had the intriguing experience of doing the same after the men's individual competition in the 'London Prepares' competition. I handed over a medal and a cricket bat as a memento to the winner, Brady Ellison of the USA, and another to the second placed Korean, Im Dong Hyun, who had broken his own seventy-two-arrow points record earlier in the tournament. Both had shot brilliantly in a high wind, firing their arrows over the square from the Pavilion End towards the Media Centre. I was struck not just by their accuracy but the speed with which they drew the bow, a lesson to any golfer, incidentally, that setting up and executing a shot need not take as long as it usually does.

I am lucky that I have now returned to the main committee as an elected member and that I remained a member of the Arts and Library committee and two working parties, one charged with deciding on Bradshaw's successor, the other working on incorporating MCC under Royal Charter to protect both the members from public liability and the Club's assets. I did not therefore feel bereft, suddenly cut off as yesterday's man, as Tom Graveney told me he did from the day that he ceased to be President in 2005.

So many occasions will live in the memory, not least the lunch to celebrate the Duke of Edinburgh's ninetieth birthday celebrations and his many sporting patronages. It was planned and executed with meticulous precision, but it was also relaxed and enjoyable. This had much, naturally, to do with the character and experience of the Duke himself but food, wine and the presentation of the Long Room, complete with carefully thought-out table plans and suitable trophies on display, were all, like everything at Lord's, from the highest drawer. HRH arrived at the appointed minute in his green Land Rover, hopping out at the door of the Museum to be introduced by me and senior members of the committee to small groups representing about forty other sporting clubs of which he was patron. Over lunch in the Long Room, while the two teams prepared for the England v. India Test starting the following day, I talked to the Duke about a range of subjects, mainly equine, before making a short speech and presenting him with a unique maquette of a fielder by the sculptor Antony Dufort. The Duke gave every impression of enjoying himself, despite drinking no more than half a glass of pale ale.

The Cowdrey 'Spirit of Cricket' Lecture went well again, too. In the year after my own effort in 2008 the Club had delved even further into what the Aussies call 'left field' when Archbishop Desmond Tutu, the twinkling former Archbishop of Cape Town, came willingly to sprinkle his peculiar charm on Lord's. Our choice in 2011, Kumar Sangakkara, could not have gone down better. He was eloquent, revealing and charming about the game and its social background in Sri Lanka. Predictably his carefully worded criticism of political interference in cricket in Sri Lanka caused a stir back home in Colombo.

Sangakkara's lecture was seen as yet another example of MCC's recent enlightenment, but one or two members are never entirely happy with what goes on behind the imposing wood and glass doors of the committee room, despite the changes of recent years. It is some time since, according to J.J.Warr, one member said in amazement to a colleague as they passed beneath the windows in front of the pavilion during the afternoon of a Test match: 'I've just seen something absolutely extraordinary. A woman talking to E.W. Swanton in the committee room.'

The woman in question was the Queen. Since then, thanks to the enlightened views of, amongst others, Colin Ingleby-Mackenzie and Tim Rice, both past presidents, women have become members and have an active playing section. The girl I first met as Rachael Heyhoe, humorous publiciser of women's cricket and a talented batsman of classical style, was the first female member on the committee and is now the first female trustee. I was delighted to be President when the portrait of her that the Club had commissioned was unveiled in the Long Room. Whether or not she considers that almost as great an honour as being appointed to the House of Lords with the title Baroness Heyhoe Flint of Wolverhampton is not for me to say. She may yet become the Club's first woman president.

Through regular website communications and the release of summarised committee minutes, the members who want to keep in touch with Club affairs – a minority when it comes to most of what is discussed – are kept much better informed than they used to be. Amongst the occasions I most enjoyed were the monthly dinners in the winter in the lovely room beside the players' dining room at the top of the pavilion. These occasions enable members, mainly local ones for obvious reasons, to enjoy good food in like-minded company and to hear a single informal speech from a guest chosen by the President. Mine were Angus Fraser, Lord Brooke of Stoke Mandeville – alias Peter Brooke, a deeply knowledgable cricket-lover, Jeremey Coney, Dennis Amiss, Claire Taylor and the campaigning journalist Christopher Booker, who plays cricket still for his Somerset village although well into his seventies.

These occasions, and the more formal ones in the Long Room at which I believe I must have presided more than any previous president, run like clockwork, as do most of the club's affairs, thanks to the efficiency and experience of several largely unsung stalwarts, including the pavilion manager, Grant Halstead, and the deputy chief executive, Colin Maynard. Colin is the Sir Humphrey of Lord's, a dapper, courteous man who, after some thirty years of service, possesses knowledge of all precedent.

His high standards and meticulous attention to detail are evident in almost every activity undertaken by MCC. There is, too, a dedicated group of secretaries, linked by a love of the game.

Between them the Secretariat guided me through my year with a sure and sympathetic hand. During a busy winter in 2010/11 I spent six weeks in Australia and two on the subcontinent for the ICC World Cup. I made nine speeches in ten days in my MCC role in Melbourne, where Judy and I, along with other members of the committee, were generously entertained in the pavilion by our counterparts at the other MCC. We were even asked to lunch in their spacious and elegant dining room on Christmas Day, on the eve of a momentous Test match. John Lill, a popular and successful past Secretary of Australia's MCC, welcomed us with his successor Stephen Gough and did his best to convince his British guests that the very green looking pitch would be a beauty to bat upon. Andrew Strauss begged to differ the following morning, put Australia into bat and his fast bowlers routed Australia for ninety-eight.

Home or away, there was seldom a dull week. In only my third week in office, for example, having broken my duck in the first few days with speeches at the annual dinners of Malmsbury CC in the west and North Runcorn in Norfolk, I had a members' meeting and supper on the Monday, a cricket committee meeting on Tuesday, a main committee meeting on Wednesday and the annual dinner of the Brian Johnston Memorial Trust on Thursday. All these events required the allowance of two and a half hours' journey time because of the uncertainties of travel from Sussex to London.

I have to admit that so much responsibility and activity in a single year was exhausting at times. I came home from Australia with a cough that lingered for at least a month, but did my best at a series of dinners and a Special General Meeting, held in the Long Room at the end of January. This was to ask members to ratify a proposed increase in the number of associate members by 1000 to a total of 5000 in 2011 and, if that presented no problems, by a further 1000 a year later. Thereby we would be able to reduce by a little the (then) twenty-one-year waiting list for would-be full members of which, at the time, there were 10,000. The resolution was passed, if not without some well-meaning protest.

The really busy part of my year – the AGM, choosing the next president and a summer of entertaining at most of the games at Lord's throughout the summer – still lay ahead when I left England again on a two-week trip to Sri Lanka and India for the closing stages of the World Cup. Again combining MCC and BBC duties, I was encouraged, not to say inspired, by the way in which our post-tsunami project in Sri Lanka has developed. The MCC Centre of Excellence at Seenigama in the south-west of the island now caters, free of charge, for the needs of more than twenty-five local villages and 20,000 people a year.

After the Test match in June, MCC held a dinner at Lord's in tribute to Muttiah Muralitharan which rasied about £50,000.

Every year the President approaches the AGM in May with some trepidation because of a small, articulate but somewhat obsessive band of MCC members who seem to have a permanent mission to embarrass and criticise the committee. Most of them no doubt mean well. I was determined to let them have their say without indulging them too far. Generally I was deemed to have done so in the long meeting in the Banqueting Suite at Lord's that coincided with the national vote on the Alternative Voting System.

I was able to begin with a joke about this. The committee, I said, had taken a vote on whether we should change all the

MCC voting procedures to AVS. Sticking to the usual system came second, so we were sticking to the usual system. It went down well because it was topical but my address to members at the start of the meeting was a bit more serious, starting on a positive note by quoting a letter from a member in his nineties who 'sits in those marvellous reserved seats for old codgers that Fiona Bean organises so wonderfully'.

Fiona Bean is one of many generally unsung heroes and heroines on the MCC staff who together present to members and public alike an extremely friendly face at Lord's these days, a fact that reflects very well on the senior staff and in particular on the secretary and deputy secretary.

The old image of fortress Lord's, guarded by retired prison warders and run by men with white moustaches beneath their panamas who like to go to bed in their egg and tomato tie – always a caricature – has long gone. There may be a very occasional exception when it is revived because it suits an argument being peddled by one of my colleagues from that bastion of virtue, the national press, but the popular and admirably well conducted Lord's tours, the opening of the outfield to spectators during the lunch interval on two occasions during Tests in 2010 and 2011 and the use of the Long Room for several very popular gala dinners during the winter months had all demonstrated what an accessible place Lord's has become, without losing its magic as far as the members are concerned.

Those dinners were eagerly and gratefully attended by non-members, who were circulated because they often buy tickets for matches. It showed the affection and almost the reverence in which Lord's is held.

There were many days, of course, when the President's 'duty' would better be described purely as 'fun'. They included five days during the season spent with the MCC Golf Society. For some reason I played rather above par (although never below it) on a couple of these days, thus giving myself the happy experience of presenting myself with a prize.

Two of the best occasions had nothing to do with cricket but instead with the long tradition at Lord's of tennis – Real or Royal, as opposed to 'lawn'. All the camaraderie of amateur sport was evident at a dinner in the Long Room for all ages after the men's and women's University matches between Oxford and Cambridge. There was a harder edge to the match in which the brilliant Australian player Rob Fahey retained his European title but the Long Room dinner that followed was equally relaxed.

Relations with both the ECB and the ICC were, for me, perhaps the most interesting aspect of the 'job'. Having sounded off about domestic and world affairs in print or on the air for so long, it was interesting to discuss problems from the inside for a while, especially by sitting in on the twice-yearly deliberations of the MCC's World Cricket Committee. Chaired by A.R. (Tony) Lewis until he passed the baton to Mike Brearley after a final meeting in July 2011, this group lent credence to the Club's role as an independent voice in the game, helped by the willing participation of outstanding cricketers such as Geoff Boycott, Martin Crowe, Tony Dodemaide, Rahul Dravid, Majid Khan, Shaun Pollock, Mike Gatting, Anil Kumble, Barry Richards, Alec Stewart, Michael Tissera, Courtney Walsh and Steve Waugh. Steve Bucknor provides umpiring expertise and Dave Richardson, the former South Africa wicket-keeper, a valuable link with the ICC.

We had a lively meeting over two days in Perth just before the Test match in December when Waugh, as quiet and rapid of speech as Boycott is loud and deliberate, suggested that cricketers under suspicion of corruption in future should be subjected to lie-detector tests. Not long afterwards he took one himself and passed it convincingly in the view of an expert in polygraphy. To Waugh it was proof that such tests might at least guide people towards a fair verdict in any future cases of match fixing.

This was just one of many riveting discussions on more familiar issues of the day, including the governance of the world game; regulations for one-day internationals; the unbalancing effect of the Indian Premier League and its largely unwanted offshoot, the Champions League; the umpires Decision Review System; over rates; world championships; floodlit Test cricket and the possible use of pink balls. MCC's cricket secretary John Stephenson, the former Essex, Hampshire and England all-rounder, has overseen extensive research on pink (and other coloured) balls at Imperial College in London and is convinced that it is the best bet for the staging of Test cricket under floodlights in countries were crowds have fallen away seriously in recent years.

Dravid played for MCC in Abu Dhabi in the game between the Club and the champion county in March 2011 (typically he scored a century) and agreed with most of those who played that it was a highly visible ball both by day and night. Twilight (a brief period in most parts of the *southern* hemisphere) was the one time when he thought that it might be trickier than normal when batting against a super-fast (90 mph plus) bowler, but that problem could be overcome by arranging an interval at sunset.

'There have not been many presidents who have underestimated their importance in the world of cricket', wrote Jonathan Rice in his book on the Presidents of MCC. I dare say I was no exception. I enjoyed the splendour of the surroundings, got thoroughly involved in every aspect of the Club's activities, probably took it all a little too seriously and at times thought about little other than Lord's and MCC. For a year it was highly flattering and pleasant to be addressed by everyone as 'President' and to realise that one was briefly the figurehead of a great and valuable institution.

34

A BEND IN THE RIVER

Shortly before the start of my year as MCC President I had had two experiences that persuaded me that this should be something of a crossroad in my life.

I had intended to walk the length of the South Downs Way with my brother David. Alas, I got a septic toe from an ingrowing toenail shortly before we left on the demandingly up and down 100-mile hike from Eastbourne to Winchester. Antibiotics had helped clear away most of the poison but it was still festering and, no doubt as a result of favouring my other foot, I tweaked a muscle somewhere in my left thigh on our short first afternoon leg to the beautiful and sleepy downland village of Alfriston.

Two days further along, or up and down, the track, my brother, who had risked wearing new trainers rather than his mountaineering boots, had huge blisters on both feet and I had been reduced to a painful shuffle, like an old man trying to walk with his legs tied together. We had done about fifty-nine of the hundred miles when I decided that it would be stupid to go any further.

Having previously walked longer distances, albeit only for a day at a time, during two of Ian Botham's fund-raising walks for leukaemia research, I had expected better of myself. The ailments were simply badly timed but I loved the views, learned from David the names of a few of the wild flowers along the way and, as always, relished the pub meals and homely bed and breakfast houses that he had selected en route, no matter how long seemed the final mile downhill from a track once trodden by neolithic man. I managed to walk the remaining miles by myself the following spring, this time in the company of my dog, who wondered why the walk was so short and so slow.

A fortnight after the original failed attempt to walk in five days a track that my daughter had comfortably traversed in two and a half, with my toe and muscle back in working order, I had left home at six am to beat the M25 traffic and driven north to Manchester to cover Lancashire's final match of the season against the prospective new county champions, Nottinghamshire. It was mid-September and, to no one's great surprise, it was raining by the time that Judy rang me halfway up the M40 to inquire whether I had meant to leave my overnight bag in the kitchen.

Fortunately I had taken precautions against the probability of just this absent-mindedness by retaining in the car one of those smart little bags that airlines hand out on long-haul journeys. Shaving gear, toothbrush, toothpaste, folding brush and comb, paper hankies, even moisturisers: they were all there.

Few setbacks are quite as bad as they first seem, I reflected the following day as, with rain pouring down and no prospect of play at Old Trafford, I utilised my golf kit to go for another walk, this time along the Dane Valley Way, close to the farmhouse that was offering me a comfortable bed and an excellent breakfast for £50 a night.

Walking beside the rushing brown water of the Dane,

expecting to see dippers at every bend in the river, made me think afresh that the time had come to slow down a bit: as Walter Hagen put it, to smell the flowers. But most of what I still do feels immensely worthwhile. Given luck with my health, I hope that there will be no need to pull up stumps on my various commitments for a while yet. I shall try to be content with whatever is round the corner. Some things do come to those who wait, especially if they wait in the right places.

INDEX

(CMJ and RMJ in subentries refer to Christopher Martin-Jenkins and Robin Martin-Jenkins)

Aamer, Mohammad, 266, 268
ABC, 86, 109, 143, 165, 220
Abrahams, Harold, 99
Adams, Chris, 314, 329, 330
Adams, Peter, 345
Adamson, Steve, 196
Afridi, Shahid, 265–6
Agnew, Jonathan, 2, 121, 124, 130, 138–9, 140, 142, 202, 238–9, 261
Ahmed, Bilal, 263–4
Ahmed, Mushtaq, 273, 329, 336
Aigburth, 207
Aird, Ronnie, 355
Akhtar, Shoaib, 265
Akram, Wasim, 268, 273
Albury CC, 342, 345, 347
Alderman, Terry, 232
Allen, Capt. Burls Lynn, 23–4
Allen, David, 312
Allen, Gubby, 147, 228
Allen, Lily, 139, 140
Allen, Richard, 59
Allerton, Jeremy, 102
Allott, Paul, 356
Alston, Rex, 117–18, 129
Ambrose, Curtley, 308, 334
Ambrose, Tim, 271
Amiss, Dennis, 119, 164, 186, 219, 313, 414
Anderson, Alva, 167
Anderson, Jimmy, 271
Andrews, Eamonn, 96, 99
Appleyard, Bob, 165, 307, 310, 311
Arabs, 342, 345, 347

Archer, Jeffrey, 61
Arlidge, Jack, 209
Arlott, Dawn, 127
Arlott, James, 126, 127
Arlott, John, 119, 121–3, 125–6, 127–31, 215, 312
Arlott, Timothy, 127
Arlott, Valerie, 125
Armfield, Jimmy, 140
Arnold, Geoff, 15, 164
Ashes, England win/retain, 2, 148, 213, 227, 233, 311
Ashton, Malcolm, 154
Ashton, Mrs, 39
Asif, Mohammad, 266
Atherton, Izzy, 171
Atherton, Mike, 146–7, 171, 228, 264, 303, 314
Atkins, Robert, 120
Austin, Michael, 199
Australia, 212–33
   Gabba in, 218, 221–2
   multicultural nature of, 217
   opening of Parliament in, 222–3
   wines of, 215
Australia national side:
   and England 1948, 306–7
   and England 1953, 311
   and England 1954–5, 311
   and England 1960, 312
   and England 1962–3, 150
   and England 1968, 312
   and England 1972, 119
   and England 1974–5, 219–20, 222, 307–8

425

and England 1977, 222, 225
and England 1978–9, 226
and England 1979, 3
and England 1979–80, 230–1
and England 1981, 231–2, 313
and England 1982–3, 230
and England 1985, 3–4, 313
and England 1986–7, 226–7, 229, 233, 314
and England 1994–5, 228
and England 2005, 146, 232–3, 309, 315
and England 2006–7, 228, 309
and England 2009, 1–2
and England 2010–11, 4, 154, 213, 218–19,
    315–16, 415
and England 2011, 119
first official Test in England of, 131
in rebel SA tours, 226
and South Africa 1969–70, 307
and South Africa 1970, 291
and South Africa 2006, 11
and Sri Lanka 1996, 279
and West Indies 2000–1, 308–9
Australian, 119
Avorians CC, 344
Azharuddin, Mohammad, 248, 267

Bacher, Ali, 291, 292–3, 306, 307
Bailey, Greta, 149
Bailey, Rob, 172, 173
Bailey, Trevor, 9, 121, 144, 146, 147–50, 307,
    311, 346
Bakewell, Enid, 352
Balding, Ian, 51, 107
Baldry, Long John, 77
Bannister, Alex, 158
Bannister, Jack, 249, 356, 357
Barclay, John, 398
Barclay, Renira, 398
Bardot, Brigitte, 13
Barker, Lloyd, 172, 174
Bark-Jones, Raymond, 28
Barlow, Eddie, 291, 307
Barmy Army, 218, 229
Barnard, Miss, 41
Barnes, Sid, 307
Baroda, 'Jackie' 241
Barrett, Ted, 199
Barrington, Ken, 1, 307, 311
Bascombe, Chris, 72
Bash, Showkhat, 124
Basingstoke, 207
Bath Journal, 47
Baxter, Peter, 119, 137–8, 140, 141, 240, 249,
    258–9
Baxter, Raymond, 106, 116

Bazalgette, Christopher, 93
BBC:
    Beyond the Boundary, 119, 140
    CMJ becomes cricket correspondent of, 3, 89
    CMJ joins, 95–6
    Five Live, 99, 110, 120, 160, 200–1
    Late Night Extra, 113
    Radio Four, 121, 328
    Radio Three, 120, 137, 165
    Radio Two, 113
    Sport on Two, 118
    Sports Parade, 98
    Sports Report, 96–100 passim, 102, 103, 106,
        118, 242
    Sports Session, 102
    Test Match Special, see Test Match Special
    Today, 109, 111–14, 160, 172
    World Service, 102, 117, 173, 250, 257
BCCI, 388, 389–90
Beale, Mike, 244–5
Bean, Fiona, 417
Beddow, Mike, 210
Bedi, Bishen, 238–9, 242
Bedser, Alec, 9, 307, 311, 311
Bedside Cricket (Martin-Jenkins), 197
Beecham, Sir Thomas, 140–1
Beer, Ian, 47, 53
Bell, Peter, 28
Bemmant, 'Sarge', 69
Benaud, Richie, 85–6, 133, 241, 356
Benjamin, Keith, 308
Benjamin, Winston, 308
Benka, Mark, 360
Bennett, Alan, 158
Betjeman, John, 32, 48, 127
Bevan, Bob, 195
Bevan, Michael, 334
Bhogle, Harsha, 238
Bichel, Andy, 308
Biddlecombe, Terry, 108
Bindra, Indira Singh, 391
Bird, Dickie, 123, 138
Birkenshaw, Jack, 164
Birmingham, Roy, 86
Blackmore, Keith, 298–9, 302
Blackwell, Ian, 237
Blair, Tony, 51
Blake, Martin, 352
Blofeld, Henry, 121, 134–6
Blofeld, Joanna, 343
Blunden, Edmund, 16
Blunt, Sir Anthony, 51
Bodyline, 120, 224
Bonetti, Peter, 138
Bonnet, Rob, 114

INDEX

Booker, Christopher, 414
Bopara, Ravi, 388
Border, Allan, 226
Botham, Ian, 11, 89, 148, 174, 227, 230–2, 283, 284, 357, 422
Botham, Kathy, 231
Boumphrey, David, 38
A Bowl of Cherries (Melford), 199
Boycott, Geoffrey, 121, 144, 147, 162, 163, 164, 219, 238–9, 418
Boyle, Sir Dermot, 100
Boyle, Lady, 27
Bradfield Waifs CC, 347
Bradman, Don, 154, 221, 303, 306–7, 355
Bradshaw, Keith, 397, 406–7, 410
Brearley, Mike, 226, 230–1, 281, 409, 418
Bridge, Anthony, 365
Briggs, Simon, 334
Brighton Evening Argus, 318
Bristowe, Mike, 347
Bristowe, Tom, 347–8
Bristowe, Will, 347
Broad, Stuart, 123
Brocklehurst, Belinda, 88–9
Brocklehurst, Ben, 88–9, 90, 91, 92, 93–4
Brooke, Lord (Peter), 140, 414
Brooke, Paul, 52
Brown, Alan, 205
Brown, Freddie, 121, 144
Bruce, Robert the, 25
Bucknor, Steve, 265, 418
Burbage, Susie, 406
Burnet, Jock, 72
Burnet, Pauline, 72
Burns, Michael, 150
Burrows, Bob, 96, 98, 100–1, 118, 165
Bushell, John, 345
Butler, Bryon, 106
Butt, Salman, 266
Butterflies CC, 347

Callaghan, John, 210
Cama, Spen, 227
Cambridge University, 42–3, 62–77
    Fitzwilliam College, 62–3, 66–7
    Footlights, 73–4
    playing fields at, 68–9
Camden, William, 328
Campbell, Donald, 159
Campbell, Ian, 345
Canada national side, 124
Candlin, Gladys, 40
Candlin, Hugh, 40
Cape Summer, 150
Capel, 270

Cardus, Sir Neville, 9, 85, 208, 210
Carey, Michael, 199, 220
Carpenter, Humphrey, 53
Carr, Donald, 162
Carroll, Peter, 345
Carter, Peter, 55
Cartwright, Tom, 84, 291
Cavenagh, Matt, 179
Ceauşescu, Nicolae, 223
Chadwick, Adam, 403
Chamberlain, Neville, 18
Champions League, 389, 419
Chandler, Diana, 189
Channel Nine, 84, 86
Chapman, Percy, 55
Chappell, David, 298–9, 302, 303–4, 320
Chappell, Greg, 220, 306, 309
Chappell, Ian, 220, 306, 307
Chappell, Trevor, 306
Chapple, Glenn, 330
Chatfield, Ewen, 270
Cheltenham, 207
Chichester, Sir Francis, 50
Chingoka, Peter, 296
Christian, Dan, 388–9
Clark, Stuart, 310
Clarke, Michael, 310
Clarke, Nolan, 175
Clarke, Sylvester, 293, 308
Clarke, William, 390–1
Cleese, John, 369
Close, Brian, 310, 312
Coker, John, 42
Coldham, Jim, 197
Coleman, Bernie, 227
Collard, Miss, 40
Collingwood, Charles, 140
Collingwood, Paul, 271
The Complete Who's Who of Test Cricketers (Martin-Jenkins), 197
Compton, Denis, 9, 150, 307, 311
Condon, Lord (Paul), 267–8
Coney, Jeremy, 124
Coney, Jeremy, 125, 272, 414
Congdon, Bev, 178
Constantine, Harry, 92
Cook, Alastair, 2, 237, 250, 316, 393
Cook, Peter, 43
Cooper, Henry, 100
Coote, Adrian, 59
Corbett, Ted, 262
Corfu, 187
Cork, Dominic, 335
Corran, Andrew, 345–6
Corran, Gay, 346

County Championship, 202, 203, 204, 207
Cowdrey, Chris, 135, 186
Cowdrey, Colin, 91, 150, 168, 219, 233, 291, 307, 312
Cox, George, 69, 342
Cox, Mark, 70
Cozier, Tony, 165, 169
Cranleigh CC, 342, 343–4, 345, 349
Cricket Characters (Martin-Jenkins, Ireland), 197
Cricketer, The, 10, 79–95, 199, 271
    CMJ interviewed for post at, 79
    CMJ returns as editor of, 89, 106, 111, 185
    Wisden Cricket Monthly amalgamates with, 94
Croft, Colin, 308
Crole-Rees, Tony, 163
Cromwell, Thomas, 65
Cronje, Hansie, 188, 267
Crowe, Martin, 272, 418
Crowson (chauffeur), 27
Cuudeford, Norman, 109–10
Cumbes, Jim, 96
Cummings, Peter, 72
Cuppers, 70, 71
Curtis, Alan, 131
Cyril (driver), 285–6

Daily Express, 5
Daily Mail, 304
Daily Telegraph, 4, 5, 79, 83, 84, 120, 193, 258, 272, 304, 334, 358
    CMJ moves to, 92, 200
    CMJ writes for, 198–212, 320
    and CMJ's *Times* move, 298–302
Dalby, W. Barrington, 99
Dancy, John, 14, 48, 60
Daniel, Wayne, 308
Daniels, Rupert, 347
Davies, Emrys, 206–7
Davies, Dr Tony, 178
Davies, Tony 'Dabber', 186
Davis, Winston, 308
Dawn, 252
Dawson, Graham, 225
Dawson, Shelagh, 225
Day, Sir Robin, 112, 140
de Burgh, Chris, 52
De Caires, Dorothy, 171
De Caires, F.C., 171
De Jong, Nicholas, 44
de Lisle, Charles, 197
de Lisle, Tim, 197
de Lotbinière, Seymour, 132
de Manio, Jack, 111
de Rohan, Maurice, 141
de Silva, Aravinda, 279

de Torre, Ken, 41–2
De Vries, Jacob, 106
Dean, Geoffrey, 302
Dee, Jack, 139
Deedes, Anna, 200
Deedes, Bill, 200, 300
Deedes, Jeremy, 200, 299
Deeley, Peter, 199, 200
DeFreitas, Phillip, 270
Denison (fellow pupil), 42
Denly, Joe, 330
Denness, Mike, 161–2, 163–4, 165, 219, 220, 375
Dev, Kapil, 231, 278
Dew, Dr John, 349–50
Dexter, Ted, 150, 312, 357
Dhoni, Mahendra Singh, 388
Diana, Princess of Wales, 73
Dilley, Graham, 270
Dixey, Godfrey, 100, 101–3
Dodemaide, Tony, 143, 418
Doggart, Hubert, 60, 399
D'Oliveira, Basil, 81–2, 290–1
Doshi, Dilip, 348
Dowding, Alan, 333
Dowley, Justin, 410–11
Downing, Brian, 152
Downton, Ali, 174
Downton, Paul, 174
Drake, Nick, 52
Dravid, Rahul, 396, 418, 419
Drummond-Hay, Anneli, 100
Drury, Peter, 10
Dufort, Antony, 413
Duggleby, Vincent, 100
Duncan, Susanna, 76
Dungarpur, Raj Singh, 248–9
Dunn, Angus, 50
Dunn, John, 113
Dyer, Robin, 334
Dyson, Simon, 346

Ebbw Vale, 206–7
Ede, Cliff, 345
Edgbaston ground, 205
Edgbaston Golf Club, 356
Edinburgh, Duke of, 412–13
Edith (great-aunt), 25
Edmonds, Phil, 4, 313–14
Edrich, John, 15, 219, 220, 307, 311
Edwards, Laurence, 64
Elizabeth II, 222–3, 225, 413
Ellerman Lines, 19
Ellison, Brady, 412
Ellison, Richard, 313
Elton, Ben, 65

Elton, Geoffrey, 65
Elwyn, Michael, 52
Emburey, John, 227, 313
England and Wales Cricket Board (ECB), 204,
    211, 389, 392, 418
England national side:
    Ashes won/retained by, 2, 148, 213, 227, 233,
        311
    and Australia 1948, 306–7
    and Australia 1953, 311
    and Australia 1954–5, 311
    and Australia 1960, 312
    and Australia 1962–3, 150
    and Australia 1968, 312
    and Australia 1972, 119
    and Australia 1972–3, 230
    and Australia 1974–5, 219–20, 222, 307–8
    and Australia 1977, 222, 225
    and Australia 1978–9, 226
    and Australia 1979, 3
    and Australia 1979–80, 230–1
    and Australia 1981, 231–22, 313
    and Australia 1985, 3–4, 313
    and Australia 1986–7, 226–7, 229, 233, 314
    and Australia 1994–5, 228
    and Australia 2005, 146, 232–3, 309, 315
    and Australia 2006–7, 228, 309
    and Australia 2009, 1–2
    and Australia 2010–11, 4, 154, 213, 218–19,
        315–16, 415
    and Australia 2011, 119
    and India 1976–7, 240–3
    and India 1977, 150–1
    and India 1992–3, 160, 236
    and India 2005–6, 237
    and India 2006, 315
    and New Zealand 1973, 178
    and New Zealand 1973, 178
    and New Zealand 1992, 272–3
    and Pakistan 2000, 263–5
    and Pakistan 2005, 265
    and South Africa 1948–9, 129–30
    and South Africa 1968, 81–2, 290
    and South Africa 1970, 291
    and Sri Lanka 1977, 278–9
    and Sri Lanka 2011, 407
    and West Indies 1959–60, 150
    and West Indies 1966, 312
    and West Indies 1974, 3, 156–66, 313
    and West Indies 1976, 137
    and West Indies 1990–1, 172–4
    and West Indies 1994, 314
    and West Indies 2004, 191, 314–15
    and West Indies 2009, 315, 379–80
    and West Indies 2012, 401

Englefield, David, 30
Essenhigh, David, 57–8
Etheridge, John, 152
Eton Ramblers CC, 343
Etridge, Tom, 360, 361
Evans, Bert, 23
Evans, Godfrey, 150, 307, 311
An Evening with Johnners, 133–4
Evening Standard, 124, 159

Fagg, Arthur, 162
Fahey Rob, 418
Farnham CC, 345
Fawlty Towers, 43
Feeny, Paddy, 117
Feldman, Stuart, 346
Field, Lindy, 174
Fingleton, Jack, 119, 144
Firmin, Julie, 80
Flanagan, Sir Ronnie, 267
Fleming, Tom, 223
Fletcher, Duncan, 265
Fletcher, Keith, 220
Flintoff, Andrew, 148, 213, 228, 230, 237, 309,
    315
Flower, Andy, 297, 315
Fonteyn, Margot, 40
Foot, David, 211
Forbes, Henry (son-in-law), 180
Forbes (née Martin-Jenkins), Lucy (daughter), 89,
    126, 422
    birth of, 180, 226
    in London Marathon, 180
Fordham, Michael, 154
Fowler-Wright, Roger, 84
Fox, Edward, 140
Franklin, Trevor, 273
Fraser, Angus, 314, 352, 414
Fredericks, Roy, 164
Free Foresters CC, 342, 344
Frindall, Bill, 119, 121, 152–4
Frindall, Debbie, 153
Frith, David, 87–8, 90, 94
Fry, Charles, 398
Fry, Stephen, 65, 240

Gallaway, Iain, 274, 275
Gandhi, Indira, 135, 159–60, 236
Garner, Joel, 308
Garnett, Tommy, 14, 45, 49, 51, 53
Garry (dog), 47
Gatting, Mike, 227, 229, 358, 418
Gavaskar, Sunil, 11, 242
Georgetown Golf Club, 171–2
Getty, Sir John Paul II, 92, 229, 348

Ghouse, Mohammad, 242
Gibbons, 177
Gibbons Golf Society, 358, 359
Gibbons, H.H.I.H., 358
Gibson, Alan, 90, 113, 145, 208, 312
Gibson, Mike, 70
Gibson, Pat, 190, 302, 320
Gilchrist, Adam, 233, 307, 308, 309–10
Giles, Ashley, 261, 264
Gillard, Julia, 217
Goddard, Trevor, 307
Gomes, Larry, 308
Gomez, Gerry, 161
Gooch, Graham, 222, 225, 235
Goodlad, Alastair, 51
Goodwin, Murray, 314
Gordon, James Alexander, 105
Gough, Darren, 264
Gough, Stephen, 415
Gourlay, Robin, 371–2
Gourlay, Rosemary, 371
Gower, David, 102, 313
Grabiner, Lord, 411
Grace, W.G., 9, 341
Graveney, Tom, 9, 13, 186, 307, 311, 412
Gray, Bill, 89–90
Green, Alan, 110
Green, David, 57, 210
Green, Geoffrey, 99
Greenidge, Gordon, 308, 310
Greer, Germaine, 74, 75
Greig, Tony, 86–7, 148, 161, 162–3, 164–5, 219,
    220, 222, 224–5, 241, 243, 278, 352
  and Packer, 86, 224
Griffith, Billy, 291
Griffith, Mike, 50, 57, 58, 88, 333
Griffiths, Robert, 408–11 passim
Grigson, Geoffrey, 128
Guardian, 127, 130, 210, 304
Gubbay, Raymond, 134
Guyana, 169, 170–1
Guildford CC, 15, 88, 339, 345
Gunasekera, Kushil, 281–2

Hadlee, Richard, 149, 231, 272
Hadman, Bill, 51
Hain, Peter, 291
Haley, William, 377
Halfyard, Dave, 205
Hall, Wes, 13, 312
Hallissey, Tim, 304
Halstead, Grant, 414
Hamilton, Bill, 106
Hamilton, David, 113
Hamilton, Sir H.P., 28

Hammond, Walter, 140, 193, 194
Hampshire CCC, 56
Hampshire Hogs, 93
Harding, James, 304
Harmison, Steve, 3, 315
Harper, Eddie, 344
Harper, Roger, 308
Harris, Anita, 77
Harris, Les, 10
Harris, Rolf, 215
Harvey, Jonathan, 50, 70
Harvey, Neil, 9, 307
Haslewood, John, 91
Hassett, Lindsay, 9, 144
Hastings, Max, 202
Hawke, Bob, 233
Hayden, Matt, 191, 308, 309–10
Hayes, Frank, 164
Hayman, C.H. Telford, 77
Hayman, Ian, 225–6
Hayman, Judy, see Martin-Jenkins
Hayman, Muriel (mother-in-law), 77, 179
Hayman, Canon Percival, 365
Hayman, Susan, 225–6
Haynes, Desmond, 308, 310
Hayter, Peter, 172, 259
Hayter, Reg, 90, 225
Headingley Golf Club, 357
Hemmings, Eddie, 270
Hemsley, Ted, 96
Henderson, Jon, 158
Henderson, Michael, 300–1
Hendrick, Mike, 2, 164
Henson, Leslie, 43
Henson, Nicky, 43
Herman, Lofty, 56
Heyhoe, Rachel, 414
Hibbert, Paul, 352
Hick, Graeme, 265, 296
Hickson, Peter, 71
Hilary-Smith, Magnolia, 64
Hilary-Smith, Mr, 64
Hilda (great-aunt), 26
Hill, Eric, 209
Hirst, Chris, 72
Hitler, Adolf, 23
HMS Belfast, 10
Hoad, Bill, 10
Hoad, Phil, 10
Hobbs, Jack, 127
Hobjoy, Miss, 38, 39
Hobson, Richard, 302–3
Hodges, Harry, 344
Hodgson, Larry, 201
Hodson, Phillip, 411

Hogg, Rodney, 226
Hoggard, Matthew, 314
Holding, Michael, 308
Holford, David, 312
Holland, Noel, 80
Hollioake, Adam, 266
Holness, Bob, 113
Holroyd, John, 345
Holt, Bimby, 80
Home, Sir Alec Douglas, 403
Hooper, Carl, 308
Hopper, 'Jack', 51
Hopps, David, 210
Horsey (fellow pupil), 54
Horsham CC, 342, 348–9
Houghton, David, 296, 297
Hourmouzious, Christopher, 37
Howa, Hassan, 292
Howard, John, 233
Howat, Gerald, 341
Howell, Kevin, 110
Howerd, Frankie, 77
Huddleston, Father Trevor, 365
Hudson, Robert, 105, 109, 118, 131–2, 133, 223, 241, 312
Hughes, Merv, 4
Hughes, Simon, 142
Humphrys, John, 111, 112
Hunt, Mick, 400
Hurst, Alan, 3
Huson, A.C., 126
Hussain, Nasser, 3, 265
Hussey, Marmarduke, 223
Hussey, Michael (businessman), 409
Hussey, Michael (cricketer), 2, 3, 310
Hussey, Susan, 223
Hutton, Charmaine, 92
Hutton, Len, 9, 150, 165, 306, 307, 311
Hutton, Richard, 92, 186, 352

I Zingari CC, 342, 345, 347
Ibbotson, Doug, 207–8
ICC, 248, 266, 267, 292, 390, 392, 394–5, 418
Idle, Eric, 74, 75
Illingworth, Ray, 146–7, 186, 187, 344
Im Dong Hyun, 412
I'm Sorry I Haven't a Clue, 139
Imran Khan, 199, 231, 252–3, 273
Independent, 358
India, 234–51, 266
India national side, 128, 386
    and England 1976–7, 240–3
    and England 1977, 250–1
    and England 1992–3, 160, 235
    and England 2005–6, 237

    and England 2006, 315
Indian Premier League (IPL), 293, 387–94 passim, 419
Ingham, Mike, 110
Ingleby-Mackenzie, Colin, 81, 413
Insole, Doug, 291
International Management Group (IMG), 389
Inzamam-ul-Haq, 264, 265
Ireland, John, 197
Irvine, Lee, 307
Izzard, Eddie, 43

Jacklin, Tony, 99, 355–6
Jacklin, Vivien, 99
Jacobs, David, 113
Jaipur, Maharajah of, 246
James, Clive, 64, 65, 74, 75, 215
James. C.L.R., 7
Jameson, John, 164
Janvrin, Robin, 51
Jardine, Douglas, 221
Jatoi, Sardar Abdul Qayyum Khan, 253
Jayasuriya, Sanath, 279
Jemma, Sister, 26
Jenkins, Sir Michael, 397
Jenkins, Vivien, 194
John, Elton, 5
Johns, W.E., 12
Johnson, Ian, 307
Johnson, Martin, 172, 227, 358–9
Johnson, Richard, 78, 90
Johnston, Barry, 124
Johnston, Bill, 307
Johnston, Brian, 3, 89, 106, 116–17, 119, 121–5, 126–7, 130–4, 139, 160, 186, 195–6, 291, 322, 374
    CMJ writes to, 116
Johnston, Denis, 52
Johnston, Pauline, 123, 125
Jones, Clem, 222
Jones, Geraint, 315
Jones, Peter (actor), 192–3
Jones, Peter (broadcaster), 96–7
Jones, Peter (cricketer), 204
Jones, Simon, 261
Julien, Bernard, 161
Junior (fisherman), 171

Kallicharran, Alvin, 15, 160–2, 164, 308, 353
Kanhai, Rohan, 162, 164
Keeling, Jack, 37–9
Keeling, Valerie, 40
Kennedy, Alex, 56
Kent CCC, 14, 204
Kenyon, Don, 307

Khan, Majid, 418
King, Collis, 175
King, Jo, 262
King, Sir Mervyn, 406
Kirkman, Mike, 347
Kirtley, James, 315
Knight, Roger, 107, 397
Knight, Syd, 10
Knott, Alan, 79, 161, 164, 219, 225
Knowles, Raffie, 161
Kortright, Charles, 84–5
Kumble, Anil, 418
Kumeratunga, Chandrika, 280

Laker, Connie, 159
Laker, Jim, 9, 90, 150, 152, 232, 307, 311
Laker, Peter, 159
Lamb, Allan, 222, 263
Lambie, Beryl, known as Bix, nee Walker, formerly
    Lynn Allen, Matyasek
Lambie, James (formerly Jiri Matyasek) (cousin),
    24
Lander, 'Crash', 272
Langer, Justin, 308, 309–10
Lara, Brian, 191
Larwood, Harold, 220–1
Larwood, Lois, 221
Lasdun, Denys, 66
Lashley, Peter, 351
Lawrence, David, 273
Lawrence, Roy, 167–8
Lawry, Bill, 86, 310
Lawson, Geoff, 268
Le Ker, Linda, 401
Lee, Alan, 298
Lee, Brett, 233, 308, 310
Leeds, 210
Leicester Mercury, 358
Leicestershire CCC, 314
Lever, John, 240–1
Lever, Peter, 220
Lewington, Peter, 16
Lewis, A. R., 418
Lewis, Chris, 273
Lewis, Frank, 49
Lewis, Roy, 15
Lewis, Tony, 163
Lill, John, 415
Lillee, Dennis, 164, 214, 219–20, 222, 225, 230,
    231, 232, 308, 386
Lindsay, Dennis, 307
Lindwall, Ray, 9, 13, 307
Llewellyn, David, 210–11
Lloyd, Christopher, 51, 55
Lloyd, Clive, 123, 164, 306, 308, 313

Lloyd, David 'Bumble', 147, 151
Lloyd, David 'Toff', 358
Loader, 307, 311
Lock, Tony, 307, 311
Lomax, Ian, 343
Longmore, Andrew, 91, 92
Lord, David, 40
Lord, Mrs, 40
Lord, Rex, 35, 37
Lord's, 214, 229, 233, 291, 397, 400–2, 405–15,
    416–18
    Long Room at, 402, 404, 412, 414, 417, 418
    media centre, 141, 374
    Mound Stand, 229
    tennis at, 418
Loudon-Shand, Eric, 289
Loxton, Sam, 307
Lund, David, 75
Lunt, Michael, 359
Lynam, Desmond, 96, 97, 101, 111
Lyttelton, Edward, 72, 360
Lyttelton, Humphrey, 139

MacAdam, David, 58
MacDonald, John, 346
Macdonald, Roger, 104
MacDonald-Smith, Iain, 51
MacGill, Stuart, 308
McGilvray, Alan, 2, 220
McGrath, Glenn, 308, 309, 310
MacGregor, Sue, 111
McGuigan, Rupert, 58
McIntyre, Arthur, 14, 15, 311
Mackay, Angus, 96, 97–9, 101, 102, 105, 118
Mackenzie, Kelvin, 105–6
MacLaurin, Lord, 267
McLean, Miss, 40–1
MacNeice, Louis, 49
MacPherson, Stewart, 132
Maddocks, Len, 311
Major, Sir John, 119–20, 139, 397, 410, 411
Makin, Peter, 51
Malaga, 187
Malalasekera, Vijaya, 71, 280–1
Malik, Amardhin, 250
Malik, Salim, 267
Mallett, Ashley, 220, 308
Malmesbury CC, 405
Malta Maniacs, 153
Mandela, Nelson, 292, 293
Mann, Simon, 142
Manning, J.L., 98
Marks, Alan, 220
Marks, Vic, 91, 121, 150–1, 356, 358, 399
Marlar, Robin, 37, 100, 242, 338, 411

Marlborough Blues CC, 339, 342, 343
Marlborough College, 45–60 passim, 343
Marlburian, 49
Marrett, Richard, 360
Marsden, Thomas, 15
Marsh, Rod, 2, 220
Marshall, Malcolm, 308
Marshall, Howard, 121, 322
Martin, Chris, 68
Martin, David, 68, 76
Martin-Jenkins, Alan (uncle), 20
Martin-Jenkins, Christopher:
  acting by, 43, 52
  in Australia, 212–16, 218–23, 226
  at Australian State Opening of Parliament, 223
  at BBC, see BBC: Sports Report; BBC: Test Match
      Special; BBC: Today
  becomes BBC cricket correspondent, 3, 89, 109
  becomes Cricketer editor, 89, 106, 111
  Benaud article ghosted by, 86
  Birkenhead move by, 27
  birth of, 18
  book projects of, 186, 196–7
  boxing taken up by, 42
  briefcase stolen from, 374–6
  at Cambridge, 20, 42–3, 62–77, 342
  club cricket played by, 342–53
  in Corfu, 371–2
  Cowdrey Lecture given by, 399
  at Cricketer, 81–95, 106, 111
  defamation writ against, 173–4
  E. coli poisoning suffered by, 240, 377
  early life of, 25, 26–61
  family life of, 176–84
  first 'book' of, 13
  first commentary audition of, 117
  first overseas cricket played by, 351
  first school of, 28
  gap year of, 60
  golf played by, 31, 32, 171, 177, 245, 354–62
      passim, 418
  hiatus hernia suffered by, 235
  illnesses of, 367, 399
  in India, 234–51
  at Johnston tribute, 134
  Judy meets, 16–17, 63, 75–7
  laptops stolen from, 319, 374
  at Marlborough College, 45–60 passim, 343
  marriage of, 78
  as MCC President, 4, 213, 281, 316, 399, 402,
      404–11, 414–20
  migraines suffered by, 342–3, 345
  in New Zealand, 271–5
  novels written by, 60–1
  in Pakistan, 253–66

and P&O cruises, 186–90
  at prep school, 4, 10, 33–44, 340
  and religion, 364–8
  in revues, 66, 73–4
  in school concerts, 53
  schoolboy bowling accuracy of, 58
  in Scotland, 27
  soccer reporting by, 84
  South Holmwood move by, 9, 28
  in South Africa, 287–90, 292, 294–6
  speaking engagements of, 186, 188–96
  in Sri Lanka, 277–9, 280–1, 282, 283–5
  with Surrey, 14–16, 339–40
  Telegraph post taken by, 92, 200
  Times approaches, 298–9
  Times post taken by, 302
  touring loved by, 158
  verse of, 183–4
  walking by, 421–3
  in West Indies, 156–75
  Wisden editor's role offered to, 90
  in Zimbabwe, 296
Martin-Jenkins, David (brother), 9, 27, 28, 30–1,
      34, 35, 49, 421–2
Martin-Jenkins, Dennis (father), 10, 18–21, 311
  death of, 20
  marriage of, 19
  overdose taken by, 20
  promotion for, 28
  retirement of, 20
  in shipping industry, 19–20
  Territorial Decoration for, 19
Martin-Jenkins, Diana (still-born sister), 21
Martin-Jenkins, Flora (daughter-in-law), 336, 337
Martin-Jenkins (formerly Jenkins), Frederick
      (paternal grandfather), 26
Martin-Jenkins, Freddie (grandson), 180
Martin-Jenkins, Isabella Mary (granddaughter),
      336
Martin-Jenkins, James (son), 10, 31, 89, 156,
      177–8, 181, 196, 332, 333
  birth of, 17, 26, 178–9, 236, 313
  called to bar, 177
  golf played by, 356, 360–1
Martin-Jenkins (née Hayman), Judy (wife), 75–8,
      145, 156, 160, 176–7, 178, 181, 183,
      196, 264, 332, 337, 375, 378–9
  in Australia, 213, 415
  on Canberra cruise, 186
  CMJ meets, 16–17, 63, 75–7
  and CMJ's Presidency, 398, 399, 405–6
  as host, 182
  in India, 236
  marriage of, 78
  in New Zealand, 274

in Sri Lanka, 282
in West Indies, 160, 174, 175
in Zimbabwe, 296
see also Martin-Jenkins, Christopher: family life of
Martin-Jenkins, Lucy (daughter), *see* Forbes
Martin-Jenkins, Molly (granddaughter), 180
Martin-Jenkins, Najwa (sister-in-law), 31
Martin-Jenkins, Nicola (daughter-in-law), 179–80
Martin-Jenkins, Pat (paternal grandmother), 26
Martin-Jenkins, Robin (son), 10, 89, 181, 196, 329–38, 342
   birth of, 179
   last Sussex game of, 337–8
   in Sussex team, 314, 329–30, 334–8
   in West Indies, 174
Martin-Jenkins (née Walker), Rosemary (mother), 18, 20–3, 26
   death of, 22
   marriage of, 19
   medicine studied by, 20–1
Martin-Jenkins, Timothy (brother), 9, 12–13, 27, 31–2, 35, 73–4, 356
Martin-Jenkins, William (grandson), 180
Martineau, Lindy, 102
Mata, Raj, 246–7
Matthew, Brian, 113
Matyasek, Karel (uncle), 23
Maxwell, Jim, 2
Maxwell, Michael, 54–5
Maxwell, Robert, 54
May, Jim, 338
May, Peter, 150, 306, 307, 311, 340–1
Maynard, Colin, 414–15
Mbanefo, Charles, 51
Mbanefo, Louis, 51
MCC, 135, 229, 250, 271, 278, 281, 284, 290, 342, 346, 348, 397–420 *passim*
   Centre of Excellence of, 282
   CMJ as President of, 4, 213, 281, 316, 398, 404–11
   and D'Oliveira, 81
DVD produced by, 150
   voting system within, 416–17
   World Cricket Committee of, 400, 418–10
Medawar, Peter, 50
Melford, Lorna, 198–9
Melford, Michael, 119, 198
Michaelson, Ben, 107
Milburn, Colin, 186, 312
Milford, David, 58
Miller, Geoff, 196
Miller, Keith, 307, 309
Mills, Robert, 210
Mistley CC, 405

Mitchell, Alison, 110
Mitchell-Innes, 'Mandy', 57
Modi, Lalit, 389–90
Moin Khan, 264, 265
Money, David, 341
Montgomery, Field Marshall Bernard, 72–3
Monty Python's Flying Circus, 75
Moore, Charles, 299, 300
Moore, Dudley, 209–10
Moores, Peter, 337, 379
Morgan, Cliff, 105, 109–10, 145
Morris, 307
Morrison, John, 352–3
Mortimer, Gerald, 209
Mortimer, John, 209
Moseley, Ezra, 308
Mosey, Don, 134
Motson, John, 106
Mountford, Adam, 139, 142, 145
Mugabe, Robert, 296, 297
Muralitharan, Muttiah, 279–80, 284, 416
Murdoch, Rupert, 304, 305
Murray, Deryck, 70–1, 308
Murray, John, 110
Mynn, Alfred, 15

Nanan, Ranjie, 353
Naughtie, James, 111, 112
Navratilova, Martina, 190
Neale (née Walker), May (aunt), 22–3
Neale, Phil, 96
Neller, Eric, 339
New Zealand, 270–6
New Zealand national side:
   and England 1973, 178
   and England 1992, 272–3
News of the World, 266
Nicholas, Mark, 357
Nick (farmer), 325, 328
Nolan, Joseph, 218
Nolan, Liam, 96
Norman, David, 358
Northamptonshire CCC, 11
Northumberland, Duke of, 46
Nott, Peter, 72–3

Old Aleynians, 347
Old Cheltonians CC, 339
Old Paulines CC, 346
Old, Chris, 117, 164, 241
O'Neill, Norman, 143
Onslow, Earl of, 194–5
Orange Free State Cricket Union, 188
O'Reilly, Bill, 309
Orr-Ewing, Ian, 133

Orwell, George, 128
Osborne, John, 52
Osborn-Jones, Timothy, 55
Otway, Graham, 358
Oval, 79, 205
  in 1950s, 1
  in 2009, 1–2

Pabari, Neil, 360
Packer, Kerry, 86, 129, 222, 223–4, 226, 317, 386
Pakeman, Mrs, 89
Pakistan, 252–69
  attack on Sri Lanka team in, 253
  and Partition, 242, 260
Pakistan national side:
  corruption among, 252–3, 266–8
  and England 2000, 263–5
  and England 2005, 265–6
Pamensky, Joe, 293
Panesar, Monty, 237, 315
Parfitt, Peter, 188–9
Parkhouse, Gilbert, 206–7
Parkinson, Nick, 59–60
Parks, Jim, 37
Parsons, Richard, 44
Patel, Shilpa, 139–40, 149
Patterson, Rodney, 51
Paul Getty XI CC, 348
Paul, Nigel, 345
Pawar, Sharad, 390
Paxman, Jeremy, 36
Payne, Ivo, 42
Peebles, Ian, 85
Pegley, Colin, 93
Pennington, Michael, 52
Pepper (dog), 377
Perchard, Peter, 92
Perry, Fred, 99
Perry, Keith, 302
Pethick-Lawrence, Emmeline, 29
Philip, Norbert, 308
Pierce, Stan, 10
Pietersen, Kevin, 230, 294, 301, 308, 315, 379
Pigott, Tony, 338
Pimlott, Ben, 51
Playfair Cricket Monthly, 87, 93
Pocock, Pat, 164
Pollard, Vic, 178
Pollock, Graeme, 291, 293, 307
Pollock, Peter, 291, 307
Pollock, Shaun, 418
Ponnambalam, Kumar, 280
Ponting, Ricky, 4, 230, 306, 307, 308–9
Pontypridd, 206
Port of Spain national side, and West Indies 1974, 3

Pougatch, Mark, 117, 142
Prabhu, K.M., 251
Prain, Graham, 78
Price, John, 339
Pringle, Derek, 258, 259, 301, 358
Prior, Matt, 336
Private Eye, 192, 411
Procter, Mike, 291, 307
Purves, Libby, 112
Pyemont, James, 43

Radcliffe, Daniel, 139, 140
Radd, Andrew, 209
Radford, Neal, 270
Rae, Alan, 168
Ragu (tour guide), 244
Raja, Ramiz, 268
Ranatunga, Arjuna, 279
Randall, Derek, 2, 225
Rauf, Asad, 2
Rayner, Ollie, 43
Rea, Chris, 106–7, 109–10
Read, Dennis, 120–1
Redgrave, Steve, 180
Redhead, Brian, 112
Reynolds, Gillian, 120
Rice, Clive, 292
Rice, Jonathan, 419
Rice, Sir Tim, 5, 227–8, 409, 413
Richards, Alan, 275
Richards, Barry, 291, 307, 418
Richards, Viv, 166, 168, 172–3, 306, 308, 313
Richardson, David, 395, 418
Richardson, Gary, 114
Richardson, Peter, 37, 151–2
Ring, Doug, 307
Ripley, Mandy, 91
Roberts, Andy, 166, 308
Robertson, Ian, 106–7
Robertson-Glasgow, Raymond, 9
Robina Woods, 32
Robinson, Mark, 337
Robinson, Mrs, 68
Robinson, Robert, 111
Rooney, Wayne, 9
Roope, Graham, 14, 352
Rosenwater, Irving, 83–4, 87
Ross, Bill, 103–4
Ross, Sandy, 350–1
Rotheroe, Charlie, 360
Rousseau, Pat, 190
Rowe, Lawrence, 164
Royal Cape Town Golf Club, 356
Royal St George's Golf Club, 345, 355, 361–2
Rush, John, 42

Rutherford, George, 82, 153
Rutnagur, 'Dicky', 210
Ryder, Steve, 108
Rymer, Carol, 145

Sachs, Albie, 266
Saggers, mark, 110
St Bede's school, 33–44, 340
Sampson, Andrew, 154–5
Sandy (dog), 182
Sang Hue, Douglas, 161, 162
Sangakkara, Kumar, 412
Sassoon, Siegfried, 9, 49
Saunders, Johnny, 110
Scarborough, 207
Scotsman, 185
Scott, Neville, 302
Seamer, Jake, 55–7, 343
Selvey, Mike, 121, 150–1, 172, 240, 358, 372
Seman, Steve, 360
Shackleton, Derek, 312
Shah, Owais, 237
Sheahan, Paul, 86
Shepherd, David, 303
Shepherd, John, 218
Shepherd, Joy, 218
Sheppard, David, 150
Sidebottom, Ryan, 393
Silk, Dennis, 4–5, 53–4
Simpson, Bobby, 310, 352
Singer, Aubrey, 101
Singh, Anurag, 208
Singh, 'Bubbles', 246
Singh, Man, 246
Skinner, Robin, 60
Sky, 135, 147, 151, 173
Slater, Michael, 308
Sleep, Peter, 227
Small, Gladstone, 4, 249, 314
Smith, C.S., 343–4
Smith, Don, 28
Smith, George, 46
Smith, Kay, 28
Smith, M.J.K., 83
Smith, Mike, 150
Snagge, John, 133
Snow, John, 219, 312, 375
Sobers, Gary, 3, 164, 190, 231, 312
Sokell, Jack, 191
Solomon, Joey, 312
Somerset CCC, 56, 57, 314
Sorley, Charles, 49
South Africa, 287–96

    and apartheid, 129, 226, 289–94
South Africa national side, 120, 129

and Australia 1969–70, 307
and Australia 1970, 291
and Australia 2006, 11
and D'Oliveira, 81–2, 290–1
and England 1948–9, 129–30
and England 1955, 307
and England 1968, 81–2, 290
and England 1970, 291
rebel tours concerning, see South Africa: and
    apartheid
and West Indies' rebel tour, 293
South Wales Echo, 358
Spencer, John, 332
The Spirit of Cricket (Martin-Jenkins), 197
Sporting Life, 24
Spray, Bill, 55
Sri Lanka, 277–86
Sri Lanka national side, 3
    and Asian tsunami, 281–2
    and Australia 1996, 279
    and England 1977, 278–9
    and England 2011, 407
    first official Test by, 279
Srinivasan, N., 390
Stanford, Allen, 392
Stansfield, Capt., 42
Starboek News, 171
Starkey, David, 65–6
Starmer-Smith, Nigel, 108
Starmer-Smith, Ros, 108
Stater, Brian, 372
Statham, Brian, 13, 150, 307, 311
Steel, A.G., 386
Steele-Perkins, Crispian, 51–2
Stephenson, Adrian, 197
Stephenson, Franklyn, 189
Stephenson, Col. John, 192
Stephenson, John, 419
Stern, John, 94
Stewart, Alec, 314, 330, 334, 418
Stewart, Jim, 37
Stewart, Micky, 311, 333
Stocken, Oliver, 398, 410–11
Stollmeyer, Geoff, 162, 168
Storey, Stuart, 117
The Story of Your Life (Lambie), 24Stothard, Peter,
    299, 300, 359
Stourton, Ed, 112
Strauss, Andrew, 2–3, 213, 294, 315, 415
Streak, Heath, 297
Streather, Bruce, 360
Subba Row, Raman, 150
Sunday Telegraph, 24, 84
Sunday Times, 81, 194, 358
Surita, Pearson, 241

Surrey CCC, 117, 281, 311, 330
    CMJ plays for, see under Martin-Jenkins,
        Christopher
Sussex, 325–6, 328–9
Sussex CCC, 163, 203, 314, 315, 349
    RMJ plays for, see under Martin-Jenkins, Robin
Sussex Martlets CC, 347, 351
Swann, Graeme, 2, 86, 315–16
Swanton, Ann, 81, 200
Swanton, E.W. 'Jim', 79–86 passim, 91, 129, 133,
        158, 186, 187, 196, 198, 207, 397, 413
Symonds, Andrew, 310, 388

talkSPORT, 105–6, 135
Tallon, Don, 307
Tambling, Bobby, 138
Taylor, Bob, 164
Taylor, Claire, 414
Taylor, Clive, 158
Taylor, Les, 174
Taylor, Mark, 308
Taylor, Peter, 227
Taylor, Stan, 82
Tendulkar, Sachin, 11, 242, 248, 396
Tennant, Ivo, 410, 411
Test Match Special (TMS), 119–75 passim, 229
    concerns over future of, 119–21
    corpsing during, 124–5, 139
    Day on, 112
    flood of emails to, after England Ashes win, 3
    summarisers on, 121, 125, 144, 145–51
Tharanga, Upul, 281
Thicknesse, John, 159–60, 245–7, 251, 258–9,
        356
Thompson, Derek, 106
Thompson, John, 57–8
Thompson, Robert, 304
Thomson, Jeff, 164, 219–20, 222, 308, 386
Thorpe, Graham, 265, 334
Thwaites, Dr Ian, 380
Tiarchs, Robert, 59
Tilling, Humphrey, 195
Times, The, 4, 5, 100, 118, 120–1, 265, 272,
        298–305
    CMJ approached by, 298–300
    CMJ joins, 302
Timpson, John, 111
Tipper, Tina, 75–6
Tissera, Michael, 418
Toshack, Ernie, 307
Traicos, John, 297, 307
Trescothick, Marcus, 264
Trethowan, Ian, 123
Trott, Jonathan, 294, 393
Trueman, Fred, 121, 130, 131, 144, 146, 147,
        148, 150, 307, 311
Tufnell, Phil, 145–6, 273
Tuke-Hastings, Michael, 119
Turrell, Rod, 345
Tutu, Archbishop Desmond, 293, 413
Tweedie, James, 42
Twenty20, 11–12, 58, 263, 268, 335, 386–94
        passim
    Schools, 401
Twickenham (horse), 107–8
Tyson, Frank, 150, 215, 307, 311

Udaipur, Maharana of, 406
Udal, Shaun, 237, 315
Underwood, Derek, 3, 119, 160–1, 164, 219, 241
University Challenge, 34

Vaas, Chaminda, 279
Vallins, John, 344
van der Bijl, Vincent, 292
van Jaarsveld, Martin, 330
Vaughan, Michael, 145–6, 237, 261, 283
Vaughan-Thomas, Wynford, 132
Verity, Hedley, 402
Vettori, Daniel, 123
Vizianagram, Maharajah of, 275
Vorster, John, 82, 290, 291
Votes for Women, 29

Waddle, Bryan, 274, 275
Walcott, Clyde, 168
Walford, Mrs, 39
Walker, Alec Russell (maternal grandfather), 24–5,
        26–7
Walker, Anne (aunt), 22
Walker, Beryl (aunt), see Matyasek
Walker, Bob (uncle), 22–3
Walker, Ettie (maternal grandmother), 25, 26–7
Walker, Graeme, 58
Walker, Max, 220, 308
Walker, May (aunt), see Neale
Walker, Murray, 192
Walker, Rosemary, see Martin-Jenkins
Waller, Guy, 333
Walsh, Courtney, 263, 308, 418
Walters, Doug, 86, 220, 307
Walters, Julie, 378
Walters, Norman, 66
Warburton, Nick, 140
Wardle, Johnny, 307
Waring, Eddie, 100
Warne, Shane, 230, 233, 307–8, 309
Warner, David, 210
Warner, Pelham, 80, 88
Warr, J.J., 81, 413

Warwickshire CCC, 14, 15
Watson, Willie, 148
Waugh, Mark, 308
Waugh, Steve, 306, 308, 340, 418–19
Way Out in Piccadilly, 77
Webb, Justin, 112
Webster, John, 103
Weekes, Sir Everton De Courcy, 168–9, 190
Welch, David, 202, 299, 300
Wells, Alan, 43
Wells, Luke, 43
Wells, Mr, 38–9
West Indies, 156–75
West Indies national side, 213
    and Australia 2000–1, 308–9
    and England 1959–60, 150
    and England 1966, 312
    and England 1974, 3, 156–66, 313
    and England 1976, 137
    and England 1990–1, 172–4
    and England 1994, 314
    314–15
    and England 2009, 315, 379–80
    and England 2012, 401
    in rebel SA tour, 293
West, Peter, 133, 199
West Sussex Golf Club, 31, 361
Wettimuny, Sidath, 281
White, Arlo, 110, 142
White, Craig, 264
White, Crawford, 158
White, Raymond, 69, 70, 342
Whiting, George, 159
Wicks, Jim, 100
Williams, Clive, 347
Williams, Dorian, 100
Williams, Gerald, 106
Williams, Marcus, 302
Willis, Bob, 3, 164, 219, 232, 241, 343, 344
Willow Warblers CC, 347–8
Willson, Ken, 82

Wilson-Hall, Dr, 39
Winbolt-Lewis, Martin, 51
Wintour, Charles, 159
Wisden, 89–90, 92, 225, 358
Wisden Cricket Monthly (WCM), 87, 90, 91–2
    Cricketer amalgamates with, 94
Wisden Cricketer, 94
    see also Cricketer
Wolsey, Thomas, 65
Women's Political and Social Union, 29
Woodcock, John, 90, 91, 118, 119, 158, 199,
    224, 257, 298, 356, 411
Woodhouse, Charles, 15
Woodhouse, George, 57
Woodrooffe, Lt Cdr Tommy, 112
Woods, Peter, 112
Woolmer, Bob, 164, 167, 268
Worcester CCC, 204, 337
World Cup, 1975, 123, 124, 167, 169, 171, 227,
    233, 249, 254, 263, 272, 278, 279, 294,
    302, 313, 392, 416
Twenty20, 268
World Series, *see* Packer, Kerry
World Test Championship, 394
The World of Cricket, 196
Worrell, Sir Frank, 168, 312
Wreford, Anthony, 409
Wright, Arnold Ronald Donald, 54–5
Wright, Graeme, 90
Wright, Luke, 335, 336
Writing Home (Bennett), 158

Yardley, Bruce, 226
Yardley, Norman, 121, 144
Yarwood, Mike, 192–3
Yorkshire CCC, 117
Young, Andrew, 127

Zimbabwe, 296–7
Zimbabwe national side, 120

ACKNOWLEDGEMENTS

My thanks to everyone who has helped me with this book and in so many ways during my career, including my 'literary' agent, Michael Sissons. (He's the literary one.) Still more grateful thanks to those who taught me and those with whom I have worked on newspapers and at the BBC – not forgetting the sub-editors, studio managers and engineers.

Further thanks to all I have remembered (with affection in almost all cases) in these pages and the many I have, all too characteristically, forgotten. Above all, thanks to Judy for her patience, understanding and support, and to my family of all generations.